The Catalogue of the Suzannet
Charles Dickens Collection

Comte Alain de Suzannet

The Catalogue of the Suzannet Charles Dickens Collection

Edited and with an introduction by
MICHAEL SLATER

Ex Libris
Alain de Suzannet

SOTHEBY PARKE BERNET PUBLICATIONS
LONDON & NEW YORK
in association with
THE TRUSTEES OF THE DICKENS HOUSE

Produced and published by Sotheby Parke Bernet Publications Limited
36 Dover Street, London W1X 3RB
in association with the Trustees of the Dickens House
48 Doughty Street, London WC1N 2LF

Edition for the United States of America
distributed by Sotheby Parke Bernet Publications Limited
81 Adams Drive, Totowa, New Jersey 07512

Set in Baskerville by Jolly & Barber Limited, Rugby
Printed and bound in Great Britain by
The Scolar Press Limited, Yorkshire

Designed by Peter Ling

ISBN 0 85667 017 0

Contents

List of Illustrations

NOTE

Unless otherwise specified, all illustrations that are not of items actually in the Suzannet Collection have been drawn from the T. W. Tyrrell Collection at the Dickens House.

Acknowledgements

I wish to record my heartfelt thanks to the Comtesse de Suzannet for all the help and encouragement she has given me since I first became involved with the Suzannet Collection in 1969, for her gracious hospitality to me at La Petite Chardière, and for many personal kindnesses. I thank her particularly for allowing me to quote in my Introduction and notes from her husband's letters and from the manuscript catalogue of his Dickens library compiled in the late 1940's. I am grateful to my predecessor as Editor of *The Dickensian*, Mr. Leslie C. Staples, for loaning to me his collection of letters from the Comte de Suzannet, and for much general advice. Professor Philip Collins of Leicester University and Miss Sue Lambert of the Prints and Drawings Department at the Victoria and Albert Museum kindly gave me the benefit of their special knowledge in compiling Sections B and G of this Catalogue, Lord John Kerr and Mr. P. J. Croft patiently tutored me in the correct way to present my material, and my friend, Mr. John Grigg, gave me invaluable assistance and much-needed encouragement at every stage of the work. I am also very grateful to Mr. Howell J. Heaney, of the Free Library of Philadelphia, Mrs. Madeline House, Dr. Peer Hultberg and Professor Kathleen Tillotson for answering particular queries, to Miss Marjorie Pillers, Curator of The Dickens House, and to Miss Christine Wattleworth for her impeccable typing of a very complicated manuscript.

M.S.

Introduction

Given his lifelong love of France and the French, we may feel sure that Dickens (who once signed himself in a letter to Forster as "Francais naturalisé et citizen de Paris") would have been gratified that one of the three finest private collections of Dickensiana assembled in this century should have been created by a Frenchman. And he would surely have been still more delighted that so substantial a part of this great collection has now, thanks to the munificent generosity of the collector, Comte Alain de Suzannet, and of his widow, the Comtesse, found a permanent home in the Dickens House Museum, London, where it is seen and enjoyed by the tens of thousands of visitors of all nationalities who come to the house in Doughty Street every year.

Alain de Suzannet was born on 22 July, 1882, at Reichenau in Austria. His father, the grandson of General Constant de Suzannet who had played a leading part in the Royalist risings in La Vendée, 1793-1815, was at that time Secretary to the French Ambassador in Vienna; his mother came from an old-established New York family. It may well have been she who first encouraged the young Alain to take an interest in Dickens; a copy of *The Old Curiosity Shop* that had originally belonged to her father is in her son's collection (see A.10) and it may indicate a tradition of Dickens reading in her family.

Whatever the sources of his enthusiasm, it was in 1912 that the young Vicomte laid the foundation stone of his great collection with the acquisition of a first edition of *Pickwick Papers* bound from the parts. To this he had added before the outbreak of the First World War first editions of *David Copperfield* and *Bleak House*, and sets of the monthly parts of *Nicholas Nickleby, Master Humphrey's Clock, Martin Chuzzlewit, Little Dorrit* and *Our Mutual Friend*. After a distinguished military career he returned home to Biarritz and soon resumed his collecting activities. He was to form notable collections of other English and French authors, in particular of Prosper Mérimée, but his principal affection and enthusiasm was reserved for Dickens. In 1921 he added to his Dickens first editions (notably a copy of the first issue of the first edition of *A Christmas Carol*) and monthly parts (notably the rare *Sketches by Boz* in this form) and bought his first two Dickens letters. The following year saw the acquisition of thirty-nine more choice-letters, to such correspondents as Leigh Hunt, Thackeray, Cruikshank and Mrs. Gaskell, and of the first fragment of Dickens manuscript – part of the chapter in *The Uncommercial Traveller* entitled "A Little Dinner in an Hour". In 1922 also, Suzannet obtained his first set of *Pickwick* in parts (for £400) and certain Dickens "association items". The high standard of quality and interest that he set himself for this latter category may be judged from the fact that the first two such items he acquired were a letter from Dr. Johnson to Mrs. Thrale about the Gordon Riots, of great interest to readers of *Barnaby Rudge*, and some correspondence relative to William Shaw's Academy at Bowes, the real-life original of Dotheboys Hall (see Lot 324 of the Sale Catalogue). During the next three years the Comte de Suzannet, as he had by now become, was mainly concerned with completing his collection of first editions by acquiring such minor works as *Sunday Under Three Heads* and *Sketches of Young Couples* but he purchased also a set of proofs of Cruikshank's illustrations for *Sketches by Boz* and two numbers of the *Gad's Hill Gazette* (see Lots 7 and 147 in the Sale Catalogue). In 1926 he inaugurated what was to become one of the richest sections of the collection by acquiring two presentation copies, a *Nicholas Nickleby*, inscribed by Dickens to Sir David Wilkie and a *Battle of Life*, inscribed to Madame de Cerjat. Books of this kind evidently had a particular attraction for the Comte for he added over twenty more examples to his collection during the next few years; among his Dickensian papers are several documents concerned with tracing and listing these uniquely interesting volumes (see L.16). In 1929 he obtained his first complete Dickens manuscript ("The Schoolboy's Story" – see I.7), thirty more Dickens letters, and three early French translations of Dickens's work (these translations, into French or German, became, naturally enough, a special interest of the Comte's, as a glance through the Sale Catalogue will show). By this time he had for some years been settled in his beautiful home, La Petite Chardière (La Chardière was the name of his ancestral home), in Lausanne and had married a daughter of Admiral Doubassov, formerly *aide de camp général* to Tsar Nicholas II.

The year 1930 was a turning-point in the history of the Suzannet Collection for it was in that year that the Comte bought a truly remarkable series of 184 unpublished letters written by Dickens between 1832 and 1870 to his intimate friend, Thomas Beard. Beard had become acquainted with Dickens when they were both young reporters working on *The Morning Chronicle* and a firm friendship developed which lasted until Dickens's death. Beard was best man at Dickens's wedding and godfather to his eldest son and Dickens's great affection for his old friend and delight in his companionship are amply shown by the many letters warmly inviting Beard to join the Dickenses on holiday at Broadstairs or Boulogne, or to visit them at Gad's Hill. Thomas's brother, Francis, became Dickens's doctor in 1859 and the collection purchased by Suzannet included 24 letters from Dickens to this brother as well as many letters from other members of the Dickens family to both Beards, nine presentation copies to Thomas of Dickens's books, an album of Beard's sister, Ellen, containing a long poem by Dickens (see Lot 304 of the Sale Catalogue), and two Dickens relics (an inkstand and a cigar-case) presented to Thomas and Francis Beard as mementos by Georgina Hogarth. All this material was now offered for sale by a Mr. Cass, nephew of the Beard brothers, and was acquired by the Comte through the agency of Maggs Brothers who, not without reason, described the Beard letters as "most wonderful and fascinating . . . probably the most interesting series that can come into the market".

The Comte was not the man to hoard such treasures, despite the fact that publication of documents like the Beard letters greatly depreciates the market value of the original manuscripts: one of his main motives in collecting was the exceptionally generous and selfless one of making available to all students and lovers of Dickens whatever material concerning the man and his works might come to light. As soon as the Beard letters came into his possession he wrote to Walter Dexter, Editor of *The Dickensian*, to invite his help and suggestions in the matter of publication. The Comte was anxious that the Beard letters should first be published in *The Dickensian* but, because of their bulk, it was eventually decided that initial publication in volume form would be more appropriate and *Dickens to his Oldest Friend*, edited by Dexter, duly appeared in 1932, to be hailed by J. W. T. Ley as "from the biographical point of view, the most important Dickens book that has been published in this country since Forster's 'Life' appeared".

From this time onwards the Comte was always in close, almost daily, touch with Mr. Dexter and every manuscript, letter or group of letters that he purchased was immediately made available for publication in *The Dickensian*. Nor was it usual for a year to pass without The Dickens House being enriched by the gift of some notable item from the rapidly growing collection at La Petite Chardière. The precious page of *Pickwick* manuscript (see I.3) acquired in 1931, for example, was presented to the House just five years later.

In 1931, Suzannet acquired his first original drawing for one of the novels, and it was a particularly choice example, Seymour's sketch for "The Dying Clown" in *Pickwick* (see G.18). He also continued to build up the already established special sections of the collection with a presentation copy of *The Chimes* to Hans Christian Andersen (A.15) and the earliest German translation of *Nickleby* (Sale Catalogue, Lot No. 48). Besides further presentation copies, many splendid and important letters, such as eight to Harrison Ainsworth or the Finlay album (Sale Catalogue, Lot 289), and a copy of the very rare Great International Walking Match placard (A.29), in 1932 the Comte also purchased three items of unique interest: the miniature of Dickens at the age of 18 painted by his aunt, Janet Barrow (G.3); the manuscript of Chapter 9 of *Nickleby* (I.4); and the reading-copy of *Mrs. Gamp* used by Dickens in America (Sale Catalogue, Lot 72). His accessions list for the next four years reflects an increasing interest in original drawings for the novels and many sketches by Phiz for *Pickwick, Nickelby, Chuzzlewit,* and *Dombey* come into the collection as well as Stanfield's charming drawing of "The Carrier's Cart" for *The Cricket on the Hearth* (G.19). One very interesting group of drawings offered to him in 1935 he did not buy, however; these were Thackeray's sketches for a title-page or illustrated cover for *Sketches by Boz* which had been rejected by Dickens as unsuitable. During this time Suzannet was also acquiring very large numbers of letters, such as a series of 22 to Mark Lemon in 1934, another of 32 to Edmund Yates in 1935, and another of 37 to Georgina Hogarth in 1936 (in this last year the Comte's accessions list records a total of over 150 letters). The purchase of Dickens's reading-copy of *The Haunted Man* (B.1) in 1934 indicates a growing interest in this aspect of Dickens's career – three more reading-copies, *Bardell v.*

Pickwick, Nicholas Nickleby at the Yorkshire School, and *Sikes and Nancy* (B.3, B.5, B.6) were acquired in 1937 – and a number of playbills bought in 1935, together with the acting copies of *Not so Bad As We Seem* (H.198) bought the previous year, show that Suzannet was also keen to develop that part of the collection dealing with Dickens's amateur theatricals. Perhaps the single most important accession of this period was Maria Beadnell's sumptuous album (I.1), with its several contributions by Dickens, which came into the collection in 1935 and was described by Suzannet in a *Dickensian* article that year with the same blend of scholarly precision and responsiveness to the intense human interest of the material that characterises his splendid three-volume Catalogue of the Dickens Library at La Petite Chardière that he had had privately printed in Lausanne in 1934.

In 1934 the Dickens Fellowship recognised the Comte's signal services to the cause of Dickens studies by electing him to be one of its Vice-Presidents. With typical self-effacement he wrote to the Hon. Secretary:

> I feel that . . . the members at the Southend Conference in conferring such an honour on a French member of the Fellowship, have had in view the millions of Dickens lovers throughout the world who are not included in the great English-speaking communities, and to whom in my modest person they have extended the hand of sympathy and friendship.

"As for myself," he added, "my interest in all that concerns the Dickens Fellowship and the Dickens House is so heartfelt that I rejoice in any tie which binds me more closely to their welfare and to their present and future activities."

In April 1937 Ernest Maggs wrote to the Comte about the manuscript of Dickens's *Life of Our Lord,* for the serial rights of which the *Daily Mail* had paid £40,000 in 1934. The manuscript was now on offer at £5,000. Evidently, Suzannet was not interested and he must have been startled to receive a year later an approach from another London bookseller offering him the manuscript for £10,000. It was eventually purchased at Sotheby's in July 1939, by the Rosenbach Company for £1,400, passed into private ownership and was finally presented, in 1964, to the Free Library of Philadelphia.

Rather than concerning himself with this spectacular but not very interesting document Suzannet was in 1937 following with the deepest interest and enthusiasm Dexter's preparation of a three-volume edition of Dicken's letters for the Nonesuch Press. For this work he made his entire collection available (in striking contrast to one notable American collector who not only refused to let Dexter have copies of the letters he owned but was not even willing to supply a list of them). Indeed, it seems likely that the Comte's heavy buying of letters between 1935 and 1937 was partly motivated by a desire to make as many of them as possible available for the forthcoming edition; for example, he acquired a series of 83 to John Leech in 1937 just in time for their inclusion in Nonesuch and they were also serialised in *The Dickensian.* Nor did his interest stop short at merely making the letters available. He answered innumerable queries, checked the proofs and saved Dexter, who was working under intense pressure of time and with virtually no assistance, from countless errors: "The excellent work you did for me," Dexter wrote to him on 28 January 1938, ". . . is really amazing and shows remarkable energy and concentration under adverse circumstances" (the Comte had suffered a family bereavement at the beginning of the year). Despite all this effort the resulting edition was inevitably much less complete than it should have been and contained numerous errors of transcription and dating. It was a severe disappointment to the Comte. Believing, however, that it was unlikely any publisher would undertake a new and better edition of Dickens's letters in the foreseeable future, he decided that he could best serve Dickens studies at that juncture by releasing on to the market the bulk of the letters he had been accumulating. He, therefore, arranged for over 900 letters, the Beadnell album and certain other items, to be sold at Sotheby's in July 1938, retaining, as he explained later to Mr. Leslie C. Staples (letter of 19 January 1949) "only those letters that had *important* references to Dickens's literary work". At the same time he resolved to present to The Dickens House all his Dickens manuscripts. Dexter persuaded him to retain in his personal possession the twelve pages of *Pickwick* that he by then owned but the House Trustees gratefully accepted the chapter of *Nickleby* and two other manuscripts, "The Schoolboy's Story" and "Our Commission" (the latter acquired in 1934). These were publicly presented to Lady Dickens, acting for the Trustees, by the French Ambassador, acting for the Comte, at a Mansion House ceremony on 8 July, 1938.

On 29 June Dexter had written to Suzannet "Both Sotheby's and Maggs appear to be very concerned at the possible results of the sale, as they think it an inopportune moment for the disposal of such a great collection, especially as there have been several other important sales (not Dickens) which have taken up the money of the dealers and collectors." These fears proved to be only too justified. The sale, on 11 July, was what is called in the trade "a slaughter" and many splendid series of letters sold for very little – a group of 39 letters to Cruikshank, for example, went for a mere £66, finding their way eventually across the Atlantic and into the collection of Colonel Richard Gimbel. Most of the big items, such as the Beard letters and the Beadnell album failed to reach their reserve and were bought in. It was typical of the Comte's generosity that he at once made a personal gift of the great bulk of the Beard letters to Dexter (they were subsequently presented to the House by Mrs. Dexter after her husband's death) and gave to the House 45 Dickens letters to Georgina Hogarth, the Barrow miniature and the manuscript of "The Bill of Fare" (I.2), all of which had been bought in at the sale. It was also typical that, in the same month that he was disposing of all these now published letters, he was bidding up to £850 for a long and important series of Dickens's letters to one of his early publishers, Richard Bentley, that had just come on to the market in order that they might be published in *The Dickensian*. Unfortunately, he failed to secure them and they passed into the Berg Collection in the New York Public Library and Dickens students had to wait for their publication until the appearance of the first volume of the Pilgrim Edition of Dickens's letters in 1965.

Although he did not succeed in obtaining the Bentley letters, the Comte did acquire some very remarkable items during 1938, Dickens's reading-copies of

Little Dombey and *The Bastille Prisoner* (B.2, B.4), and a copy of the very rare trial issue of *The Daily News* (A.16). The following year he inaugurated a new section of the collection with two pamphlets containing printed versions of speeches by Dickens and also made a very striking addition to his drawings with the complete set of Phiz's drawings for *Little Dorrit* (Sale Catalogue, Lot No. 186). Henceforward he bought few letters restricting his purchases in this field to items of outstanding personal interest, such as the letter to Mary-Anne Leigh (H.1), or else of great interest from the point of view of Dickens's work such as the 1838 letter to Mrs. S. C. Hall about *Nickleby* and the Yorkshire schools (H.59). He continued to buy choice presentation copies such as the *Pickwick* given to Maclise (A.5), acquired in 1940, and in 1945 for the first time added some contemporary dramatisations of Dickens's novels to the collection. Adaptations or plagiarisms of Dickens's works (now much sought after by collectors) seem never to have much interested him, however. His passionate appreciation of Dickens's art could hardly bear such things and it was apparently all he could do to stay in his seat once at a Lausanne cinema, when he had been reluctantly persuaded to go and see the MGM film version of *David Copperfield* (1935).

During the difficult days of the Second World War and in the immediate post-war period the Comte continued to be a staunch friend and munificent patron of the Dickens Fellowship and of The Dickens House. He made several substantial donations to the Fellowship's funds and, soon after the re-opening of the House in 1945, made himself responsible for the purchase of a good strong safe in which particularly valuable manuscripts could be kept. When the manuscript of *Our Mutual Friend* came up for sale in New York in 1944 he sought to buy it with a view to presenting it to the House and, failing in that attempt, entered into similarly-motivated negotiations two years later to purchase the manuscript of *Great Expectations* from the Wisbech Museum. The Charity Commissioners ruled, however, that the manuscript could not be sold and it remains to this day in Wisbech.

In 1947 the Comte acquired a highly interesting item, Dickens's marriage-licence, and this he promptly presented to the House. "This document 20 years ago," he wrote to Mr. Staples, whom he associated with the gift, "would not have evoked great interest in England, but since all that concerns Dickens's private and personal existence has become almost as important as his writings, the Licence should belong to The Dickens House".

During the last three years of his life Suzannet continued to add material of outstanding interest to his collection: the Dickens/Kolle letters (Sale Catalogue, Lot 193); the prompt-books for Dickens's amateur theatricals (H. 194); the Regulations for the Amateur Players (H.160); a page of the manuscript of *Little Dombey* (I.6); and further portions of the precious *Nickleby* manuscript (Sale Catalogue, Lot 308). He was delighted to hear that a new edition of Dickens's letters was being contemplated and wrote to Mr. Staples on 14 October 1948:

> The publisher . . . may achieve a work of the first importance if he is not content to re-issue the Nonesuch text but revises it carefully and incorporates

new matter. But a publication of this kind would be of small value if carried out in a hurry and *only* undertaken with the object of profit. I shall, therefore, make somewhat exacting and binding conditions before patronising it.

He was soon reassured by his contacts with Humphry House, the editor of the proposed new edition, and House's assistant, K. J. Fielding, and, just as he had earlier bought letters so that they should be available for Dexter's None-such Edition, so he now showed himself willing to act in the same way for the new project. When he learned in December 1949 that a London bookseller was unwilling to allow House to copy upwards of one hundred unpublished letters that existed in his stock Suzannet at once bought the letters and presented them to The Dickens House so that they should be available. This was almost his last act as a collector and it was one wholly in keeping with all that had gone before.

I have tended to concentrate, so far in this account, on Suzannet's extraordinary generosity towards the Dickens Fellowship and its officers, and towards The Dickens House. But his learning and his collection were at the service of all scholars once he had convinced himself of their *bona fides*. In 1935 he was visited by a young American, J. Lee Harlan, who was proposing to write a life of John Forster (a task unhappily never accomplished). Not only did the Comte receive this young man very graciously, he even gave him large numbers of Forster's letters from the collection, an act such as research students hardly dare to dream of. Whatever work seemed likely to advance our knowledge of Dickens's life, character and works was certain to receive Suzannet's warm encouragement and practical help. Nor did he shrink from the emergence of a Dickens with a (for some) disconcertingly human face. For all his worship of, and passionate admiration of, Dickens's towering genius as an artist ("He would delight," wrote Mr. Staples "to take down a large London atlas and trace the movements of Dickens's characters through the streets") he was no mindless idolater of the man. He wrote to Mr. Staples on 14 June 1949:

My view is that a *fair* biography of Dickens the Man still requires to be written. All previous appreciations have been either too laudatory or biased in the opposite direction. As regards Kate Perugini, to *my* ears Miss Storey's account [in *Dickens and Daughter*] rings true and (personally) I find that it is impossible to excuse and unwise to palliate Dickens's treatment of his wife (at any time since 1837!) by any reflecting on her own deficiencies. But any writer criticising the man should be bound to search for and proclaim the good as well as the bad: the greater the contradictions in the nature of such a gifted genius, the more human and close does he become.

It is sad that the writer of these eminently sane and fair-minded words did not live to see the publication in 1952 of Edgar Johnson's fine biography of Dickens, a work in which he had had great faith and in the preparation of which he had materially assisted.

The Comte de Suzannet died in December 1950 and his great collection remained at La Petite Chardière in the care of his widow. The Comtesse followed her husband's practice of making the Collection available to scholars, especially to the Editors of the Pilgrim Edition of Dickens's letters who acknowledged in their first volume "her help and many kindnesses". She also continued the Comte's tradition of munificent patronage of The Dickens Fellowship (of which she is a Vice-President) and of the Dickens House, to which she presented in 1966 its first copy of *Pickwick Papers* in monthly parts (A.2). In 1970, the Dickens Centenary Year, the Comtesse generously allowed a large selection from the collection to be exhibited at The Dickens House. Then, in 1971, she set the seal on the long association of the name of Suzannet with the House by presenting to it a very substantial part of the collection, the most magnificent donation the museum has ever received. The remainder of the collection was auctioned at Sotheby's on 22 and 23 November 1971 and is now widely scattered.

In her selection of what to include in the gift to The Dickens House the Comtesse was guided by a desire to present particularly such items as would be immediately attractive and meaningful to all visitors – for example, the Beadnell album, the D'Orsay portraits of Dickens, the Great International Walking Match placard, Dickens's marked reading copies and the drawings by Seymour, Phiz and other illustrators of Dickens. As far as Dickens's letters were concerned – over 90 of these were included in the gift – the Comtesse arranged that all those in the collection actually dated from Doughty Street and all those concerning novels written or partly written there should form part of the gift, as well as many others belonging to every period of Dickens's life which are all of great personal interest, such as the early letter to Mary-Anne Leigh (H.1) or the long chatty letter written to Maclise from America in 1842 with a charming postscript in Catherine Dickens's hand (H.90).

The Trustees of The Dickens House resolved that the rooms in which these treasures are exhibited should be named the Suzannet Rooms and they now form a permanent and fitting memorial to a man who was without doubt one of the most scholarly, discriminating and generous of literary collectors that the world has ever seen.

MICHAEL SLATER

The Dickens House, August 1974

CATALOGUE OF THE SUZANNET COLLECTION
AT DICKENS HOUSE

NOTE

In this Catalogue of the Suzannet Collection at the Dickens House I have included all items once owned by the Comte de Suzannet that are now at the House even when some of these, such as Dickens's marriage-licence, were presented to the House by the Comte as soon as he had acquired them. Unless a different provenance is indicated any given item should be understood as having come into the Dickens House as part of the Comtesse de Suzannet's gift in 1971. "1938 Gift" or "1950 Gift" at the end of an item means that it was presented by the Comte as part of his substantial donations to the House in those years – the background to these is explained in the Introduction. "Dexter Gift" means that the item was part of the large group of letters given by Suzannet to Walter Dexter in 1938 and presented by Dexter's widow to the House in 1946.

In describing the letters in Section H I have noted envelopes as being black-bordered only when the accompanying letter is not written on mourning paper and I have recorded postmarks only on unstamped letters.

The 1971 Sale Catalogue, compiled by P. J. Croft, Roy Davids and John Pashby, is here reprinted as issued, with a few minor corrections.

M.S.

SECTION A

First and Early Editions

A.1 Collection of songs from THE VILLAGE COQUETTES: *Love is not a feeling to pass away*, Ballad, sung by Miss Rainforth; *There's a charm in Spring*, Ballad, sung by Mr. Braham; *My Fair Home*, Air, sung by Mr. John Parry; *No light bound of Stag or timid Hare*, Quintett, sung by Miss Rainforth, Miss Julia Smith, Mr. Braham, Mr. Bennett & Mr. Parry. In the Opera The Village Coquettes, performed at the St. James's Theatre, the Words by Charles Dickens, The Music by John Hullah, *four engraved title-pages 18 pages, folio*   Cramer, Addison & Beale [1836]

Also present are: *Autumn Leaves*, Ballad, sung by Mr. Bennett (*5 pages, folio, Cramer & Comp.*) and *In rich and lofty Station shine*, Duet (*5 pages, folio, Cramer, Beale & Chappell*).

A.2 THE POSTHUMOUS PAPERS OF THE PICKWICK CLUB *in the original 20 monthly parts in 19, first edition, plates by R. Seymour, R. W. Buss and Phiz. Original green wrappers.*   *8vo. Chapman and Hall* [1836-37]

In his unpublished catalogue the Comte de Suzannet has the following notes about this copy (which was presented to the Dickens House by the Comtesse de Suzannet in 1966):

> Dans cet exemplaire, le texte des livraisons II, IV, VII, VIII, IX, X et XII est du second tirage.
>
> Les planches des livraisons I, II et XII sont de la première gravure mais en secondes épreuves. Le fascicule I renferme en outre la deuxième suite de quatre eaux-fortes gravées par Seymour pour ce numéro. Les fascicules X, XI, XIII, XV et XVIII renferment des épreuves des deux suites gravées par Phiz.
>
> Les couvertures des livraisons II, III, V et VIII ne sont pas du premier tirage. La couverture du fascicule II porte *With Illustrations*. Le premier plat de la couverture du fascicule III porte *With Illustrations by R. W. Buss*, mais elle est numérotée I au lieu de III.
>
> L'exemplaire renferme tous les *Avis* de l'auteur et des éditeurs.
>
> Le *Pickwick Advertiser* manque dans les livraisons V, VI, VII, VIII et IX. Les fascicules I, III, V, VI, VII, VIII, IX, XIII et XVII sont incomplets de certaines feuilles d'annonces.

A.3 THE POSTHUMOUS PAPERS OF THE PICKWICK CLUB. With forty-three illustrations, by R. Seymour and Phiz, *engraved vignette title ("Veller"), plates before letters, elaborately bound in fawn calf gilt*   *8vo. Chapman and Hall* [1837]

Original parts bound up with front wrapper of Number XIII preserved. The Comte notes in his unpublished catalogue that the text "renferme plusieurs remarques du premier tirage". Bound up with this copy are the two illustrations by Buss, the two illustrations by Phiz designed to replace these and the sequence of 32 extra illustrations by "Mr. Samuel Weller", of which the Comte notes: "19 de ces compositions sont de T. Onwhyn et 11 sont l'oeuvre d'un graveur inconnu".

A.4 THE POSTHUMOUS PAPERS OF THE PICKWICK CLUB. With forty-three illustrations, by R. Seymour and Phiz, *engraved vignette title ("Veller"), plates before letters, contemporary half-roan binding.*   *8vo. Chapman and Hall* [1837]

Pasted into the front is a letter from Dickens to Chapman and Hall (see H.49). With the volume is an A.L.s. dated 26 November 1948 from Ifan Kyrle Fletcher to the Comte de Suzannet concerning Suzannet's purchase of this item from Fletcher. (". . . I remember that, . . . some work was done to discover what *fracas* was referred to in the letter and I also remember that we did not get very far in the matter. . . .")

A.5 THE POSTHUMOUS PAPERS OF THE PICKWICK CLUB. With forty-three illustrations, by R. Seymour and Phiz. *Contemporary full green morocco, gilt. In a full crimson morocco slip-case, gilt.*   *8vo. Chapman and Hall* [1837]

Presentation copy with inscription on half-title: "Daniel Maclise / From his sincere friend and admirer / Charles Dickens." A roman numeral I and a full stop have been added to the date on the title-page, making it read "MDCCCXXXVIII."

Book-plates of W. H. Arnold and John Gribbel.

A.6 SKETCHES OF YOUNG GENTLEMEN. Dedicated to the Young Ladies. With six illustrations by "Phiz". *Original boards, in red half-morocco slip-case*
   16mo. Chapman and Hall [1838]

Inserted into this copy (from the library of Ogden Goelet) are Phiz's original drawings for the illustrations (see G.5).

A.7 OLIVER TWIST, *3 vol., First Edition, "Charles Dickens" issue, original brown cloth*
   8vo. Richard Bentley [1838]

Presentation copy with inscription on title-page: "Thomas Beard Esquire / From his sincere friend / Charles Dickens."

A.8 THE LIFE AND ADVENTURES OF NICHOLAS NICKLEBY. With illustrations by Phiz. *Contemporary full crimson morocco elaborately gilt, in full crimson morocco slip-case*
   8vo. Chapman and Hall [1839]

The Dedication Copy specially bound for Macready to whom Dickens sent it on 25 October 1839 with a letter now in the Widener Collection, Harvard (". . . The Book, the whole book, and nothing but the book (except the binding which is an important item) has arrived at last, and is forwarded herewith. The red represents my blushes at its gorgeous dress; the gilding all those bright professions which I do *not* make to you; and the book itself my whole heart for twenty months, which should be yours for so short a term, as you have it always . . .").

Inscribed on the dedication page: "W. C. Macready Esquire / From his faithful friend / Charles Dickens."

The letter quoted above has been inserted into another copy of *Nickleby* (rebound, and with Kenny Meadows's "Heads of Nicholas Nickleby" inserted) which was bought by Harry Elkins Widener in 1907 under the impression that it was the actual Dedication Copy and is thus now in the Widener Library. The Comte de Suzannet has placed in the Dedication Copy a letter to Walter Dexter from Flora V. Livingston of the Widener Library, dated 14 July 1942, agreeing that the Widener volume copy is not the Dedication Copy and remarking, "It is too bad that the letter and the real dedication copy cannot be together. But our letter cannot be separated from the Widener collection, so the book will have to come to the letter." (In his unpublished catalogue the Comte observes, "Cette prophétie, ou ce souhait, ne se réalisera jamais avec le consentement du possesseur actuel de l'exemplaire de dédicace de Nicholas Nickleby.")

After Macready's death in 1873 the Dedication Copy, which bears his book-plate, was bought at Christie's by H. W. Bruton and was later acquired by the actor J. L. Toole, whose signature appears on the verso of the frontispiece. On 12 July 1892 Toole presented the volume to E. Y. Lowne, a collector of Macreadiana (inscription to Lowne by Toole on end-papers) and it remained in the Lowne family until May 1942 when it was bought at Sotheby's by Edwards from whom it was then acquired by the Comte de Suzannet.

A.9   THE LIFE AND ADVENTURES OF NICHOLAS NICKLEBY. With illustrations by Phiz. *Contemporary green morocco, gilt, in full olive-green morocco slip-case, gilt.*
8vo. Chapman and Hall [1839]

Presentation copy with inscription on half-title: "Letitia Austin / from her brother / Charles Dickens".

A.10   THE OLD CURIOSITY SHOP, AND OTHER TALES. With numerous illustrations by Cattermole, Browne, and Sibson. *Original brown cloth*
8vo. Philadelphia: Lea and Blanchard [1841]

First American edition of the first volume of *Master Humphrey's Clock*, including *The Old Curiosity Shop* complete. Sibson's extra illustrations etched by Yeager, Cattermole and Browne's designs engraved on wood by Gilbert. The Comte de Suzannet notes of this item in his unpublished catalogue: "Exemplaire provenant de la bibliothèque de mon grand-père Abel French, dont la signature (*A. French Jr.*) est apposée sur la page de garde et sur le titre."

A.11   AMERICAN NOTES FOR GENERAL CIRCULATION. *2 vols., original brown cloth, gilt lettering on spine, in olive-green half-morocco slip-case, gilt*
8vo. Chapman and Hall [1842]

Presentation copy with inscription on half-title: "Charles Dickens / To his faithful friend and / fellow-traveller. G. W. Putnam. / Nineteenth October 1842."

With these volumes is a letter from Putnam to Benjamin Cheney (see J.57).

A.12   A CHRISTMAS CAROL. In Prose. Being a Ghost Story of Christmas. With illustrations by John Leech, *trial issue (title in red and green, "Stave I", green end-papers), original brown cloth gilt, in maroon full morocco case. sm. 8vo. Chapman & Hall* [1844]

Book-plate of William Forbes Morgan.

A.13   A CHRISTMAS CAROL. In Prose. Being a Ghost Story of Christmas. With illustrations by John Leech *trial issue (title in red and green, "Stave I", yellow end-papers), original brown cloth gilt*   *sm. 8vo. Chapman & Hall* [1844]

Purchased from Maggs Bros. by the Comte de Suzannet at an unknown date. Maggs's description of the volume enclosed.

A.14   A CHRISTMAS CAROL. In Prose. Being a Ghost Story of Christmas. With illustrations by John Leech, *First Edition, second issue (title in red and blue, "Stave I", yellow endpapers, original brown cloth gilt*   *8vo. Chapman & Hall* [1843]

A.10

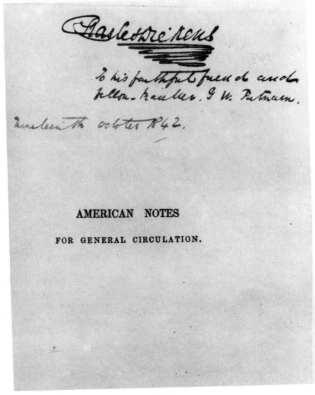

A.11

A.15   THE CHIMES: a Goblin Story of some Bells that rang an Old Year out and a New Year in. Twelfth edition, *original red cloth gilt, in olive-green half-morocco slip-case*
sm. 8vo. Chapman and Hall [1845]

Presentation copy with inscription on title-page: "Hans Christian Andersen / From his friend and admirer / Charles Dickens / London July 1847."

A.16   THE DAILY NEWS *trial issue dated 19 January 1846 bound up with a copy of the first issue (21 January) maroon half-morocco covers*
16 folio pages Daily News Office [1846]

The trial issue is mainly made up of debates, news and messages taken from other newspapers but the two leading articles, dated 26 January, appear to be by Dickens. The first describes the execution of the murderer, James Tapping, at Newgate ("... This was a grand gala day, and beginning the diversions with a judicial murder was a pleasant inauguration of Easter Monday ...") in tone very similar to Dickens's letter to *The Times* (see A.19). The second is a burlesque account of an imaginary trial at the Old Bailey of "A person named *Jones*" for "wilfully and maliciously" causing the deaths of "five bricklayers, seven carpenters, two furniture-warehouse porters, three painters, and a plasterer". A typed note bound in with the issue states that this was written "for the amusement of the author's colleagues and coadjutors who were aware

7

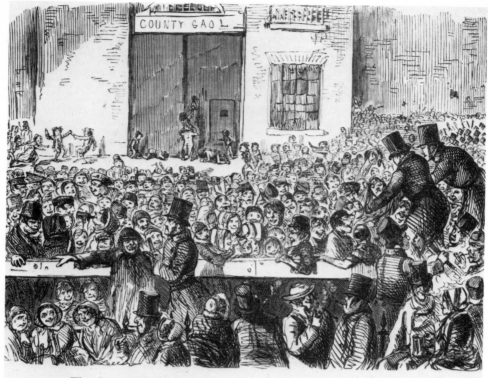

The Great Moral Lesson at Horsemonger Lane Gaol, Nov. 13.

Cartoon by Leech commenting on the Mannings' execution, published in *Punch*, 1 December 1849
(See A.19)

of the haste and pressure under which Mr. Jones, who was the master printer, had been induced at short notice to undertake the work of preparing the rooms and offices in Bouverie Street for the reception of the editor and his staff".

The trial issue also includes a first version of the first chapter of *Pictures from Italy* entitled "Foreign Letters. No. 1. Written on the Road". In the first issue of the *News* the title is altered to "Travelling Letters. Written on the Road". The text in the trial issue also differs substantially from that in the first issue.

With these two issues of the *News* is an extract from Hodgson & Co.'s catalogue of 14 August 1923 in which they are offered for sale.

Another copy of the trial issue is preserved at the offices of The Daily News Ltd., Queen Victoria Street, London. This copy was acquired from Sawyer's by Suzannet in July 1938.

A.17 THE ADVENTURES OF OLIVER TWIST. Illustrated by George Cruikshank. A New Edition. Revised and corrected. To be completed in Ten Numbers. *10 monthly parts, original green wrappers, in red cloth case*   *8vo. Bradbury and Evans* [1846]

In his unpublished catalogue the Comte de Suzannet notes: "Exemplaire entièrement de premier tirage. Texte, planche, couvertures et annonces sont en tous points conformes au collationnement donné par Hatton et Cleaver."

To Bobo. With the affectionate regard of his friend
Gabblewig.)
Twenty Third December 1851. A

CHILD'S HISTORY OF ENGLAND.

BY

CHARLES DICKENS.

With a Frontispiece by F. W. Topham.

VOLUME I.

ENGLAND FROM THE ANCIENT TIMES, TO THE DEATH OF
KING JOHN.

LONDON:
BRADBURY & EVANS, 11, BOUVERIE STREET.
1852.

A.20

A.18   THE CRICKET ON THE HEARTH. A Fairy Tale of Home. *Original*
red cloth gilt   *sm. 8vo. Bradbury and Evans* [1846]

First edition, with illustrations by Maclise, Richard Doyle, Clarkson Stanfield,
Leech and Landseer.

A.19   CHARLES DICKENS, ESQ., ON THE LATE EXECUTION *one 8vo.*
leaf mounted on card, in maroon half-morocco slip-case   [November 1849]

Reprint of Dickens's letter to the Editor of *The Times*, dated 13 November 1849,
describing the shocking scenes at the Mannings' execution at Horsemonger-lane and
strongly urging the Government to put an end to public executions.

"... I believe that a sight so inconceivably awful as the wickedness and levity of the
immense crowd collected at that execution this morning could be imagined by no man, and
could be presented in no heathen land under the sun. ..."

A.20   A CHILD'S HISTORY OF ENGLAND. Volume I England from
Ancient Times, to the death of King John. With a Frontispiece by F. W. Topham.
Original brown cloth blocked in gilt, crimson cloth slip-case.   16mo. Bradbury & Evans [1852]

Presentation copy with inscription on title page: "To Bobo. With the affectionate
regard of his friend / Gabblewig. / Twenty Third December 1851." "Bobo" was the

9

nickname of Frederick Pollock (born 1845) son of Sir William Frederick Pollock, an eminent barrister with whom Dickens became acquainted in Broadstairs in 1850. "Gabblewig" was the name of the part played by Dickens in the farce *Mr. Nightingale's Diary*, performed several times in 1851 as an after-piece to Lytton's *Not So Bad As We Seem*.

On the fly-leaf is a pencilled note by Sir W. F. Pollock explaining the dedication. Another pencilled note appears on the guard-leaf of the frontispiece: "Sold at Mr. Herman's Sale (Sotheby & Co.) May 1883 for £4.17.6".

Tipped into the volume is a fragment of a letter from an unknown correspondent to the Comte de Suzannet quoting relevant passages from Frederick Pollock's *Personal Remembrances* (about Dickens's "Gabblewig" performances, etc.).

Purchased at auction by the Comte de Suzannet in May 1937.

A.21   THE CASE OF THE REFORMERS IN THE LITERARY FUND; stated by Charles W. Dilke, Charles Dickens and John Forster, *in red cloth case*
16 pages 8vo. Bradbury and Evans, Printers [March 1858]

With this pamphlet is a second one (36 pages, 8vo.) entitled *Royal Literary Fund. A Summary of Facts . . . issued by the Committee in answer to allegations contained in a pamphlet entitled "The case of the Reformers . . ."* together with a Report of the Proceedings at the last Annual Meeting March 1858 . . .

A.22   A CHRISTMAS CAROL. THE CHIMES. THE STORY OF LITTLE DOMBEY. THE POOR TRAVELLER. BOOTS AT THE HOLLY-TREE INN AND MRS. GAMP. *4 vols. original green paper covers, in crimson half-morocco slip-case.*
sm. 8vo. Bradbury and Evans [1858]

Copies issued for the Public Readings (*The Cricket on the Hearth* was also published in this form). With the four little books is an A.L.s. from Dickens to Bradbury and Evans dated 7 September 1858 (see H.304).

A.23   THE CHIMES. A Goblin Story of some Bells that rang an Old Year out and a New Year in. *Crimson full morocco gilt, original green paper covers preserved, in olive-green morocco slip-case*
sm. 8vo. Bradbury and Evans [1858]

Presentation copy with inscription on half-title: "Charles Dickens Junior / From his affectionate father / Charles Dickens / Seventh September 1858."

Book-plate of A. Edward Newton. The Comte de Suzannet notes in his unpublished catalogue that this copy of the Reading Edition of *The Chimes* was successively in the libraries of W. Allis, Edwin W. Coggeshall and A. Edward Newton.

A.24   A MESSAGE FROM THE SEA. The Extra Christmas Number of All The Year Round, *lacking wrapper, in crimson full morocco slip-case, gilt lettering*
48 pages 8vo. Office of All The Year Round [1860]

Presentation copy with inscription on page one: "Wilkie Collins Esquire / from Charles Dickens."

A.25   GREAT EXPECTATIONS, *3 vol. First Edition, 32 pages of advertisements dated May 1861 on pp. 1, 2 and 5, original purple cloth, gilt backs*
8vo. Chapman and Hall [1861]

On the title-page of each volume appears the signature "J. Forster" but the writing is not that of Dickens's biographer.

With Vol. 1 is a single typed sheet of unknown authorship describing the "points" of a genuine first edition of *Great Expectations* and remarking, "This is the freshest and finest copy I have ever seen and . . . is guaranteed genuine in every respect".

A.26 OUR MUTUAL FRIEND. With illustrations by Marcus Stone *2 vols., full brown contemporary russia elaborately gilt, in brown full morocco slip-case*
8vo. Chapman and Hall [1865]

The Dedication Copy specially bound for presentation to Sir James Emerson Tennent. Dickens has inscribed his signature and the date "Friday Seventeenth November, 1865" beneath the printed dedication to Tennent. Pasted into the front of vol. 1 is an A.L.s. from Dickens to Tennent dated 24 January 1865 (see H.391) together with the autograph envelope.

With these volumes is an A.L.s. (1 March 1937) from Charles Retz, of Retz & Storm, Inc., New York, accepting the Comte de Suzannet's offer for the item.

A.27 HOLIDAY ROMANCE. Collection of the issues of *Our Young Folks. An Illustrated Magazine for Boys and Girls* (published Boston: Ticknor and Fields) for January, February, March, April and May 1868. Instalments of *Holiday Romance* appeared in each issue except for the February one, which has a note that the second part "is not inserted, because the illustrations could not be finished in time". The illustrations are by S. Eytinge, jr., G. G. White and John Gilbert. The collection has been bound up by Henderson & Bisset, Edinburgh, in dark olive-green morocco, gilt.

A.28 THE READINGS OF MR. CHARLES DICKENS AS CONDENSED BY HIMSELF. With Original Illustrations [by S. Eytinge, jr.].
12mo. Boston: Ticknor & Fields [1868]

Owner's name inscribed on fly-leaf: "Lizzie D. Waters Philadelphia".

A.29 THE GREAT INTERNATIONAL WALKING MATCH. Broadside, 19½ by 22 inches, with the signatures of Dickens, George Dolby, James R. Osgood, James T. Fields and William S. Anthony.

This humorous "Sporting Narrative" of a burlesque walking-match between Dickens's manager, Dolby ("the Man of Ross"), and Osgood ("the Boston Bantam"), a junior partner in the firm of Dickens's American publishers, was written by Dickens who, with Fields, umpired the contest which took place in Boston on 29 February 1868. In it he refers to himself as "the Gad's Hill Gasper" on account of his "surprising performances (without the least variation), on that truly national instrument, the American Catarrh". Published in the Nonesuch Edition of Dickens's Works (*Collected Papers*, vol. 1, pp. 110-114). This copy, acquired by Suzannet in 1932, is a specimen of the original printing of the broadside (see the note by Herbert T. F. Cahoon in *The Papers of the Bibliographical Society of America*, vol liii, 1959, p.78).

A.30 THE PLAYS AND POEMS OF CHARLES DICKENS with a few Miscellanies in Prose now first collected edited prefaced and annotated by Richard Herne Shepherd *2 vols., original blue cloth*   *8vo. W. H. Allen & Co.* [1882]

"With the Publishers' Compliments" stamped on title-page of Vol. 1. In his unpublished Catalogue the Comte de Suzannet notes of this edition: "Elle fut supprimée, après la mise en circulation d'un petit nombre d'exemplaires, à la requête de Wilkie Collins, le drame intitulé *No Thoroughfare* ayant été incorporé dans le recueil sans son autorisation. La bibliographie des Oeuvres de Dickens qui se trouve à la fin du second volume est assez complète et renferme des renseignements inédits."

A.31 THE POSTHUMOUS PAPERS OF THE PICKWICK CLUB. With illustrations by R. Seymour, R. W. Buss, Hablot K. Browne ("Phiz") and J. Leech. *2 vols., green cloth, gilt* *8vo. Chapman and Hall* [1887]

The "Victoria Edition" limited to 2,000 copies, edited by Charles Plumptre Johnson, who notes in his Preface: "The illustrations in this Edition include all those used for the original Edition, but, instead of taking impressions from worn plates, the original drawings by the artists have been carefully reproduced in facsimile, by a beautiful method of Photogravure . . .".

A.32 BLEAK HOUSE. With Forty Illustrations by Phiz and Facsimile of Wrapper to First Part. A reprint of the original edition, with an introduction, biographical and bibliographical by Charles Dickens the Younger. *Green cloth.* *8vo. Macmillan and Co.* [1896]

A.33 THE PICKWICK PAPERS. With an Introduction by George Gissing and Notes by F. G. Kitton. Illustrated by E. H. New. *2 vols., red cloth* *8vo. Methuen & Co.* [1899]

Vols. 1 and 2 of the Rochester Edition of the Works of Charles Dickens.

A.34 WACKFORD SQUEERS AND PECKSNIFF. An Unpublished Letter by Charles Dickens to Mrs. S. C. Hall, 29 December 1838 (see H.59). Foreword by Clement Shorter. *Bound in white half-vellum for the Library at La Petite Chardière, original wrappers preserved.* *4to. Privately printed* [1915]

No. 19 of a limited edition of 25 copies, signed by Shorter on verso of title-page.

A.35 AN AMERICAN NOTE never intended for General Circulation although issued at the Seat of Government in March 1842 by Charles Dickens. *Bound in white half-vellum for the Library at La Petite Chardière, original wrappers preserved.* *16mo. Privately printed* [1924]

This pamphlet gives the text of a letter from Dickens to Charles Sumner dated from Washington 13 March 1842 (". . . We are now in the regions of slavery, and spittoons, and senators. All three are evils in all countries, but the spittoon is the worst . . ."). There is an unsigned introduction by George Parker Winship who has added in manuscript at the end of it his initials and the words "For Miss Longfellow".

A.36 DICKENS: POSITIVELY THE FIRST APPEARANCE. A Centenary Review with a Bibliography of Sketches by Boz *green half-cloth* *8vo. The Argonaut Press* [1933]

Reprints the text of "A Dinner at Poplar Walk" (included subsequently in *Sketches by Boz* as "Mr. Minns and his Cousin") from the *Monthly Magazine* of December 1833. With a "Prologue" and "Epilogue" by F. J. Harvey Darton. Inscribed by the publishers to the Comte de Suzannet.

Dickens' Reading Copies

B.1 THE HAUNTED MAN AND THE GHOST'S BARGAIN. A Fancy for Christmas-time. By Charles Dickens. *188 pages (excluding title-page and list of illustrations) red half-morocco gilt, in a cloth slip-case, olive-green morocco gilt back*
16mo, each leaf inlaid to 8vo size, Bradbury & Evans [1848]

Philip Collins suggests (in his "The Dickens Reading-Copies in Dickens House", *The Dickensian*, lxviii, September 1972, pp. 173-79) that Dickens probably began preparing this reading in 1858 for his first "paid" series of public readings. He cut up two copies of the first edition of this Christmas Book and pasted the pages on to larger sized paper. He then worked through to p. 137 deleting many passages, and several entire pages, in blue or red water-colour, making smaller deletions in the text in ink. After p. 137 the text is untouched; at that point Dickens presumably decided that the story was not suitable for the object he had in view and abandoned it (Charles Kent comments, in his *Dickens As A Reader*, that *The Haunted Man* is "about the least likely of all his stories one would have thought to have been thus selected [for reading purposes]"). Further discussion of this and the following items in this section will appear in Professor Collins's forthcoming edition of Dickens's Public Readings for the Clarendon Press.

This volume, which has Dickens's book-plate, was offered for sale in Sotheran's catalogue for January 1879 at £3 10s. Purchased by the Comte de Suzannet from Walter T. Spencer in May 1934.

With the book is a sheet of Gad's Hill headed notepaper on which is written in Dickens's hand: "Faithfully yours Charles Dickens at Liverpool Saturday Twenty Eighth April 1866".

B.2 THE STORY OF LITTLE DOMBEY. *121 pages (no title-page), red half morocco gilt, in a cloth slip-case, olive-green morocco gilt back 8vo. Bradbury & Evans* [1858]

Dickens first read *The Story of Little Dombey* in London on 10 June 1858 and its enormous popularity caused him to keep it in his repertoire for the rest of his reading career. The earliest stage of his preparation of this reading is represented by the scrap of manuscript listed in this catalogue at I.6. The first version of a full prompt-copy is in the Gimbel Collection at Yale University (described by Philip Collins in his "The Texts of Dickens' Readings", *Bulletin of the New York Public Library*, lxxiv, June 1970, pp. 360-80). The Suzannet copy was undoubtedly the one actually used by Dickens, however; the text has been carefully worked over by him, once in black and once in blue ink, major deletions have been painted out with red water colour, and in one place the printed text has been cut up and new manuscript copy pasted in; throughout, there are profuse manuscript alterations written in the margins, much underlining of words to be emphasised, and at least one stage-direction. Collins notes

(*The Dickensian*, lxviii, p. 176) that a rough draft of a later version (*circa* 1862) of *Little Dombey* exists in the Berg Collection but observes that neither this nor the Gimbel copy "could ever have been used for performance".

This copy was purchased by the Comte de Suzannet at the Cortlandt Bishop sale in April 1938. With it is preserved a letter to the Comte from the American Art Association, Anderson Galleries Inc., dated 13 November 1935, concerning their preparation of a sale catalogue of Bishop's library, and one page of a further letter from the Association giving more details about the reading copies to be featured in the sale; also, a cutting from *The Times* of 20 September 1940, describing the presentation of the Howe Collection (including several of Dickens's reading-copies) to New York Public Library by Dr. Albert Berg.

Bookplates of Dickens and Cortlandt Bishop and a Gad's Hill label pasted inside front cover.

B.3   BARDELL AND PICKWICK. MR. CHOPS, THE DWARF. MR. BOB SAWYER'S PARTY. Three Readings. Each in one Chapter. Privately printed. *82 pages (including title), red half morocco gilt in a cloth slip-case, olive-green gilt back*
8vo. William Clowes and Sons [?1861]

The traditional date assigned to this volume is 1866 but Philip Collins has argued (*The Dickensian*, lxviii, p. 176) that it was "almost certainly printed in 1861, during the summer of which Dickens had a great burst of activity, devising a number of new readings for his forthcoming autumn and winter tour".

Bardell and Pickwick (more commonly referred to as *The Trial from "Pickwick"*) was first given in 1858 but the prompt-copy used then seems to have disappeared. The text printed in the volume here listed has no manuscript alterations or additions. Collins observes: "By 1861, [Dickens] doubtless knew the text so well that he did not need to consult his copy; and, being one of the shorter readings already, it did not need, and would not stand, any further abbreviation." *Bardell and Pickwick* was the most popular item of all Dickens's repertoire and was the one most frequently given by him.

Mr. Chops, the Dwarf (adapted from the story, "Going into Society", published in the 1858 Christmas number of *Household Words*) was apparently not performed until 1868 and only infrequently thereafter. The text printed here shows numerous deletions, additions and alterations in Dickens's hand throughout.

Mr. Bob Sawyer's Party was first performed in December 1861 and became a great favourite with audiences. The text printed here has been thoroughly worked over by Dickens at least twice (once in black, and once in blue, ink) and exhibits numerous deletions, alterations and additions throughout, e.g. the insertion of the word "neck-lace" five times on p. 67, in an anecdote told by Jack Hopkins to Mr. Pickwick. In his *Dickens As a Reader* Charles Kent writes of this passage:

> . . . To hear Dickens say this in the short, sharp utterances of Jack Hopkins, to see his manner in recounting it, stiff-necked, and with a glance under the drooping eyelids in the direction of Mr. Pickwick's listening face, was only the next best thing to hearing him and seeing him, still in the person of Jack Hopkins, relate the memorable anecdote about the child swallowing the necklace – pronounced in Jack Hopkins's abbreviated articulation of it, *neck-luss* – a word repeated by him a round dozen times at least within a few seconds in the reading version of that same anecdote . . .

Although not listed in J. H. Stonehouse's 1935 reprint of *Sotheran's Prices Current of Literature*, New Series, Nos. 174-75, this volume has Dickens's book-plate and a Gad's

Hill label, and it appears on the page from Henry Sotheran's original (1878) valuation of Dickens's library which Stonehouse reproduces in facsimile. It has also the bookplates of George Gurney and Edward Arnold. It was bought by the Comte de Suzannet at Sotheby's on 26 March 1937, the vendor being Arnold's son.

With the volume is the following autograph note (on paper headed 8 Devonshire Place, Eastbourne): "To my friend Andrew Arnold as a remembrance of his friend George Gurney also as a tribute for his filial affection and an appreciation of his literary taste December 1901". Also, a printed slip of Arnold's authorship:

> N.B. I should have said that the little "Bardell v. Pickwick" stands in a quite different category from any of the other books. It was not in my father's Library. It was not inherited. Had I not written, and by the advice of my kind friend and master, the late Archibald Forbes, published "The Attack on the Farm", I should never have got it. Mr. Gurney gave it to me because he was so pleased with what I had written; for from his kind heart he was always willing to help young artists and writers, &c. Therefore, as it was a personal gift, it will not be sold.

Also, a collection of newspaper cuttings relating to the trial episode in *Pickwick Papers* made by Arnold, and a cutting from *The Daily Telegraph* 27 March 1937, recording the sale of the volume at Sotheby's.

B.4   THE BASTILLE PRISONER. A Reading. From "A Tale of Two Cities". In Three Chapters. Privately Printed. *45 pages (including title), red half morocco gilt, in a cloth slip-case, olive-green morocco gilt back*   8vo. W. Clowes & Sons [1861]

Dickens devised this reading (derived from Book One of the novel) in 1861 but it was apparently never performed. The text has, however, been carefully worked over by Dickens and there are several deletions, underlinings for emphasis and manuscript additions, as well as numerous stage-directions written into the margins ("Kissing hand", "Knocking", "Beckoning", "Sigh", "Moan", etc.). See Michael Slater's article, "*The Bastille Prisoner:* a Reading Dickens never gave", *Etudes Anglaises*, xxiii (1970), 190-96.

Like the preceding item, this volume does not appear in Stonehouse's 1935 reprint but is listed on the facsimile page of Sotheran's 1878 valuation of the Gad's Hill Library. It has Dickens's book-plate and the Gad's Hill label, also the book-plate of Cortlandt Bishop. Purchased by the Comte de Suzannet at the Bishop Sale in April 1938.

B.5   NICHOLAS NICKLEBY AT THE YORKSHIRE SCHOOL. A Reading. In Four Chapters. Privately printed. *71 pages (including title) red half-morocco gilt in a green cloth slip-case, olive-green morocco gilt back*
                    8vo. William Clowes and Sons [1861]

Dickens first gave this reading on 29 October 1861 and it remained a favourite item in his repertoire. His original prompt-copy, sold for £21 by Sotheran's in 1878, is now in the Berg Collection at the New York Public Library. The volume here catalogued has the words "Short Time" stamped on its spine and is a revision of the 1861 text made in 1866 when "Dickens decided to give a shorter version which could fit into the same two-hour programme as his new reading *Dr. Marigold*, which took about 80 minutes" (Collins, *The Dickensian*, lxviii, p. 177). Throughout there are numerous manuscript alterations, cancellations, underlinings, additions (sometimes on pasted-on slips) and marginal stage-directions ("Breakfasting", "Slapping the desk", etc.). The main change is the suppression of Chapter Three (describing Fanny Squeers's tea-party), Dickens having tied the pages of this chapter together with a red ribbon

24   NICHOLAS NICKLEBY

left unpaid, and so forth. This solemn proceeding
always took place in the afternoon of the day
succeeding his return. So, in the afternoon, the
boys were recalled from house-window, garden,
stable, and cow-yard, and the school were assembled in full conclave, when Mr. Squeers, with
a small bundle of papers in his hand, and Mrs. S.
following with a pair of canes, entered the room
and proclaimed silence.

Slapping the desk

"Let an boy speak a word without leave,"
said Mr. Squeers, "and I'll take the skin off that
boy's back."

This special proclamation had the desired effect,
and a deathlike silence immediately prevailed.

"Boys, I've been to London, and have returned
to my family and you, as strong and as well
as ever."

According to half-yearly custom, the boys gave
three feeble cheers at this refreshing intelligence.
Such cheers.

"I have seen the parents of some boys," continued Squeers, turning over his papers, and

B.5

so that they cannot be opened. The Gimbel Collection at Yale University contains another and quite different "short-time" printed version of this episode entitled *Nicholas Nickleby at Dotheboys Hall* (see Philip Collins, *Yale University Library Gazette*, xl, pp. 153-58). It does not feature any manuscript alterations or deletions by Dickens and it must be considered very doubtful whether he had anything to do with the preparation of this version.

The copy catalogued here was bought by the Comte de Suzannet from Bernard Quaritch in 1937 and a letter to the Comte from Quaritch dated 31 May 1937 is preserved with the volume.

Book-plates of Dickens, Lucy Wharton Drexel and Boies Penrose II and Gad's Hill label pasted in front cover and endpapers.

B.6 SIKES AND NANCY: A Reading. By Charles Dickens. *47 pages (including title) red half morocco gilt, in a cloth slip-case, olive-green morocco gilt back*

8vo. C. Whiting [1868-69]

A READING.   39

It was a ghastly figure to look upon. The
murderer staggering backward to the wall, and
shutting out the sight with his hand, seized
a heavy club, and struck her down. !.' *Action*

The bright sun burst upon the crowded
city in clear and radiant glory. Through
costly-coloured glass and paper-mended window,
through cathedral dome and rotten crevice, it *Mystery*
shed its equal ray. It lighted up the room
where the murdered woman lay. It did. He
tried to shut it out, but it would stream in.
If the sight had been a ghastly one in the
dull morning, what was it, now, in all that
brilliant light!.'.' / *Terror to the End* /

He had not moved; he had been afraid
to stir. There had been a moan and motion
of the hand; and, with terror added to rage,
he had struck and struck again. Once he

B.6

Dickens first prepared this most sensational of all his readings in 1868 and gave
a trial private performance of it on 14 November that year. The prompt-copy used
then is now in the Berg Collection at the New York Public Library and has been
described by Philip Collins in the Library's *Bulletin* (June 1970). He then extended
the reading to include a description of the flight and hunting down of Sikes and had
a new text privately printed, of which the copy listed here is an example. His personal
prompt-copy of this new text seems to have disappeared but all his underlinings,
emendations and numerous stage-directions ("Shudder", "Look round with Terror",
"Cupboard Action", "Sleepy Action", "Murder coming", "Mystery", "Terror to
the End", etc.) have been transcribed into this copy by the actress, Adeline Billington,
to whom he gave it after being deeply moved by her performance as The Veiled Lady
in *No Thoroughfare* (jointly written by Dickens and Wilkie Collins) at the Adelphi
Theatre in 1868 (". . . I never thought I would have cried or shed a tear at my work
as I have been made to do by Mrs. Billington's performance . . .").

Mrs. Billington, whose autograph appears on page one of the text, gave a reading

Sketches of Dickens reading *Sikes and Nancy* by Alfred Thompson, published in *Tinsley's Magazine*, February 1869 (See B.6)

of *Sikes and Nancy* at the Gaiety Theatre in 1872. She subsequently presented her book to John Hollingshead who in turn eventually gave it to Sir Henry Irving. On the title-page is a pencilled note to Irving from Hollingshead dated 1885: "I don't quite know whether B. gave me this or lent it; but will ask when you have done with it— I have had it for years." The volume realised £16.5.6d at the Irving sale at Christie's on 16 May 1906 and was purchased by the Comte de Suzannet at Sotheby's in July 1937.

Book-plates of Sir Henry Irving and Herbert S. Leon.

With the volume is a copy of the 1921 reprint of *Sikes and Nancy* edited by J. H. Stonehouse and published by Henry Sotheran & Co. (no. 6 of a limited edition of 275 copies); a four-page pamphlet entitled *Mr. Charles Dickens's Farewell Readings*, printed by J. Mallett, undated, which reprints a selection of newspaper reviews of Dickens's performance of *Sikes and Nancy*; and a manuscript check-list of the Dickens Reading Editions compiled by the Comte de Suzannet (4 pages, foolscap).

The Dickens House Library includes one other copy (lacking title-page and cover) of the revised edition of the *Sikes and Nancy* reading. This was given by Dickens's daughter, Mary, to John Billington (husband of Adeline) and, after passing through various hands, was acquired by the artist George W. Morrow who presented it to the Dickens House in May 1947.

Dickens' Speeches (Printed Texts)

C.1   Report of the Dinner given to Charles Dickens, in Boston, February 1st, 1842. Reported by Thomas Gill and William English, Reporters of the Morning Post. Most of the Speeches revised by their Authors. *In half-morocco slip-case*
16mo., Boston: William Crosby and Company [1842]

C.2   Report of the Speeches delivered at the Opening Soirée of the Glasgow Athenaeum, held on Tuesday, 28th December, 1847, Charles Dickens, Esq., in the Chair; to which is prefixed a Sketch of the Rise and Progress of the Institution. Published at Request. *Bound in modern half-vellum*
8vo. Glasgow: John Mackie, 106, Queen Street [1848]

On p.2 appears the printed note: "The following Report of the Opening Soirée of the Glasgow Athenaeum, has been reprinted from the columns of the 'Glasgow Chronicle,' with certain additions from the 'North British Mail', in order to meet the wishes of many of the Members who are desirous of possessing a record of so interesting an event, in a form more convenient than that of a Newspaper. It has been corrected throughout with considerable care, and the Speech of Mr. Dickens, in particular, has undergone careful revision."

C.3   Proceedings at the Second [and Fourth, Fifth, Sixth, Seventh, Ninth, Tenth, Eleventh, Twelfth, Thirteenth, Eighteenth, Twenty-First] Anniversary Festival of the [Royal] General Theatrical Fund

12mo	*Brewster & West, Hand Court, Dowgate,*					*1847*
,,	*,,* *,,* *,,*	*,,*	*,,*	*,,*		*1849*
,,	*Edward Brewster,*	*,,*	*,,*	*,,*		*1850*
,,	*,,* *,,*	*,,*	*,,*	*,,*		*1851*
,,	*Kezia* *,,* *,,*	*,,*	*,,*	*,,*		*1852*
,,	*S. G. Fairbrother, 31 Bow Street, Covent Garden*					*[1853]*
,,	*Frederick Ledger, Catherine Street, Strand*					*1855*
,,	*,,*	*,,*	*,,*	*,,*	*,,*	*1856*
,,	*,,*	*,,*	*,,*	*,,*	*,,*	*1857*
,,	*,,*	*,,*	*,,*	*,,*	*,,*	*1858*
,,	*,,*	*,,*	*,,*	*,,*	*,,*	*[1863]*
,,	*,,*	*,,*	*,,*	*,,*	*,,*	*1866*

In his unpublished Catalogue Suzannet notes: "Collection, que je crois complète, des comptes-rendus des soirées annuelles . . . auxquelles Dickens assista et au cours desquelles il prit la parole". In fact, Dickens also attended, and spoke at, the First and Third Anniversary Festivals, 1846 and 1848, (see *The Speeches of Charles Dickens,* ed. K. J. Fielding, 1960, pp. 73 and 92). He was in the chair for the Sixth and Eighteenth meetings, 1851 and 1863, whilst Thackeray presided at the Thirteenth, 1858, when his health was proposed by Dickens.

The pamphlet reporting the proceedings of the Thirteenth Anniversary is specially bound in red cloth, gilt. The word "Royal" first appears before "General Theatrical Fund" on the 1853 pamphlet, which was erroneously entitled *Proceedings at the Ninth* [instead of *Eighth*] *Anniversary Festival*.

With the collection, housed in a green half-morocco slip-case, is an A.L.s. from I. Kyrle Fletcher to Suzannet, dated 15 July 1937, forwarding "five of the Theatrical Fund pamphlets" (. . . I am not sending the issue for 1854 because . . . I was unable to find anything relating to Dickens in it . . . In the circumstances I have reduced the price to £140 . . .").

C.4   Speech of Charles Dickens, Esq., delivered at the meeting of the Administrative Reform Association, at the Theatre Royal, Drury Lane, Wednesday, June 27, 1855. *Bound in modern half-morocco.*

8vo., London: M. S. Rickerby, Printer, 73, Cannon Street, City [1855]

Presentation Copy inscribed on front cover: "Charles Dickens to Frank Stone Tenth July, 1855."

For later issues of this pamphlet see Lot no. 114 in the Sale Catalogue.

C.5   Speech of Charles Dickens, Esq. at the First Festival Dinner of the Playground and General Recreation Society on Tuesday, June the 1st 1858.   *8vo.*

Dickens took the chair at this dinner as well as proposing the main toast of the evening, "Prosperity to the Playground Society". For a full account of the meeting see K. J. Fielding's edition of *The Speeches of Charles Dickens*, pp. 169-75.

C.6   Royal Dramatic College, for Aged and Infirm Actors and Actresses, and for the Maintenance and Education of the Children of Actors, 1858.

16mo. Printed by William Clowes & Sons [1858]

Report of a meeting held at the Princess's Theatre on 21 July 1858, under the chairmanship of Charles Kean, "for the purpose of establishing homes for aged and infirm actors and actresses, and, subsequently, to provide the requisite funds for maintaining and educating children of actors". The immediate cause of the meeting, Kean explained, was the offer by Henry Dodd to the General Theatrical Fund (of which Dickens was a Trustee) of five àcres of land in Berkshire "for the purpose of building certain charitable houses for the reception of aged and worn-out brothers and sisters of the stage". Dickens moved the resolution "joyfully accepting and gratefully acknowledging" Dodd's gift. Other speakers included J. P. Harley and Benjamin Webster.

C.7   Opinion of the Commercial Travellers' Schools, kindly expressed by Charles Dickens, Esq., at the London Tavern, 12th Month 22, 1859.

Broadsheet, printed in blue

Extract from Dickens's speech at the Anniversary Festival of the Charity when he once more agreed to preside (having taken the chair at the 1854 dinner). The text varies slightly from that found in the full version of the speech printed by K. J. Fielding in *The Speeches of Charles Dickens*, pp. 288-93.

With the broadsheet is a circular letter of invitation to the Festival from the Secretary to the Charity, dated from 81 Cheapside, 9 December 1859, printed on the back of which are "Particulars of the Simultaneous Collection [in various towns] on the 'Orphan's Day' ", and a letter to the Comte de Suzannet from Ifan Kyrle Fletcher, dated 14 February 1939, promising to search for a pamphlet giving Dickens's speech (" . . . but, of course, we have no proof that his speech was printed . . . "). Evidently Suzannet acquired the circular letter before locating a copy of the broadsheet.

C.8　Speech of Charles Dickens as Chairman of the Anniversary Festival Dinner of the Royal Free Hospital, held at the Freemasons' Tavern, on the 6th of May, 1863.
16mo. Wyman & Sons, Great Queen Street [1870]

Two footnotes commenting on developments at the Hospital since the date of Dickens's speech have been added. The putative date of publication of the pamphlet is that given by Suzannet in his unpublished catalogue.

C.9　The Charles Dickens Dinner. An Authentic Record of the Public Banquet given to Mr. Charles Dickens at the Freemasons' Hall, London, on Saturday, November 2, 1867, prior to his departure for the United States. With a Report of the Speeches from special shorthand notes.
8vo. London: Chapman and Hall, 193, Piccadilly; Tickner and Field, Boston, [1867]

The reports of the speeches are prefaced by an account of the occasion by Charles Kent, Hon. Secretary of the Dinner Committee. Bulwer Lytton was in the chair and proposed the toast of the evening, "The Health of Charles Dickens" (in the course of which he found occasion handsomely to compliment Matthew Arnold, one of those present, as "distinguished for the manner in which he has brought together all that is most modern in sentiment with all that is most scholastic in thought and language"). Among other speeches reported in this pamphlet is a vigorous one by Anthony Trollope, replying to the toast to "Literature"; he attacked Carlyle's criticism of fiction as having a "perilous and close" cousinship to lying

> . . . Now those were very hard words to us who are engaged in writing fiction, hard words to us who do our teaching by the telling of tales instead of by the speaking of prophecies. Was Colonel Newcome – that finest gentleman of past days – was he a lie? Were the words which Jane Eyre addressed to her lover when he demanded whether she would take from him his one drop of water – a lie? Was the sermon which Dinah preached upon the green – was that a lie? Was the story of Eugene Aram a lie? (Cheers) Gentlemen, do you remember – who here does not remember – the walk which Sykes [*sic*] took with his dog after the murder? (Renewed cheering) . . .

C.10　Address delivered at the Birmingham and Midland Institute, on the 27th September, 1869. By Charles Dickens, Esquire, President. *Bound in modern half-morocco, original cover preserved.*
8vo., Printed by Josiah Allen, jun., Birmingham

C.11　Speeches Literary and Social by Charles Dickens. Now First Collected. With Chapters on "Charles Dickens as a Letter Writer, Poet and Public Reader", *bound in modern full morocco, gilt, original cover and spine preserved.*
12mo., John Camden Hotten, Piccadilly [1870]

For the disreputable origins and textual inadequacy of this literary piracy (on which all subsequent editions of Dickens's speeches were based until 1960) see the "Textual Introduction" to K. J. Fielding's edition of *The Speeches of Charles Dickens* (Clarendon Press, 1960).

W. Brunton's sketch of Dickens's last speech for the Newsvendor's Benevolent Institution, published in *Fun*, 23 April 1870 (See C.12)

C.12   The Newsvendors' Benevolent and Provident Institution. Speeches in behalf of the Institution by the late Mr. Charles Dickens, President.
16mo. London: Printed by Buck and Wootton [1871]

Reports of speeches made by Dickens on 21 November 1849, 27 January 1852, 20 May 1862, 9 May 1865, and 5 April 1870, together with transcript of a letter from him to the Institution dated 13 April 1854. In his unpublished catalogue, where he supplies a publication date, Suzannet notes: "Dans un second tirage une lettre de Dickens datée du 17 juin 1865 fut inserée page 12".

Collected Editions

D.1 DICKENS (CHARLES) Works. *First Cheap Edition, 6 volumes bound as 5, crimson half-morocco, elaborately gilt, frontispieces by C. R. Leslie, T. Webster, Frank Stone, George Cruikshank (2) and Clarkson Stanfield; in two maroon full morocco slip-cases, gilt.*
16mo. Chapman and Hall [1847-50]

Presentation copy with inscription on half-title of *Sketches by Boz* (which is bound up with *American Notes*): "Charles Dickens / to his Godson Alfred Charles / January 1851. / With the rest of the 'Cheap Edition', as being of a convenient size for his youthful reading, and bound (at the back) to match his rosy face". The other volumes in this set are *Pickwick Papers, Oliver Twist, Nicholas Nickleby* and *Martin Chuzzlewit*. Alfred (born 1847) was the son of one of Dickens's younger brothers, Alfred Lamert Dickens.

Acquired by the Comte de Suzannet from Sawyer's in May 1934 (three A.L.ss. from Sawyer to Suzannet are preserved with the books).

D.2 DICKENS (CHARLES) Works, vol. 1, 2, 14, 15, 21-24 and 33, *Gadshill Edition. With Introductions, General Essay, and Notes by Andrew Lang. 9 volumes out of a total issued of 34, viz.: Pickwick Papers (2 vols.); David Copperfield (2 vols.); A Tale of Two Cities, Great Expectations, Our Mutual Friend (2 vols.); The Mystery of Edwin Drood & Master Humphrey's Clock; original crimson cloth, gilt* *8vo. Chapman and Hall* [n.d.]

D.3 DICKENS (CHARLES) Works, 40 vol., *National Edition, original green cloth, gilt*
8vo. Chapman and Hall [1906-08]

This edition was limited to 750 copies.

Charles Dickens

To his Godson Alfred Charles

January 1857.

SKETCHES BY BOZ.

With the rest of the "Cheap Edition", as being of a convenient size for his youthful reading, and bound (at the back) to match his rosy face.

SECTION E

Dickensiana, Biography and Criticism

E.1 Actors by daylight, and pencilings in the pit Nos. 1–55 (3 March 1838– 16 March 1839), together with one issue of *Actors by Gaslight, or "Boz" in the Boxes* (2 June 1838), 2 vols. bound as one.   *J. Pattie and W. M. Clarke* [n.d.]

The sub-title for vol. 1 reads as follows: "Containing Correct Memoirs of upwards of Forty of the most celebrated London performers; Original Tales, Poetry, and Criticisms: the whole forming a faithful account of the London stage for the last twelve months." The sub-title of vol. 2 reads as follows: "Miscellany of the Drama, Music, and Literature. Containing correct memoirs of the most celebrated London performers Original Tales, Poetry, and Criticisms." A woodcut portrait appears in each issue.

E.2 An American lady [i.e. Henry Wood], Change for the American Notes: in Letters from London to New York.   *8vo. Wiley & Patnam* [1843]

Rebound with the original front cover and spine preserved.

E.3 Anon. More hints on etiquette for the use of society at large, and young gentlemen in particular. By παιδ αγωγος with cuts, by George Cruikshank, *crimson morocco slip-case*   *Charles Tilt* [1838]

Loosely inserted is a cutting from the *Athenaeum* 23 May 1903 of a letter from F. G. Kitton arguing against the traditional attribution of this little parody to Dickens and giving reasons for supposing that it may be the work of Thackeray (see note 7 on p. 515 of G. N. Ray's *Letters and Private Papers of Thackeray*, vol. 1).

E.4 Bass (Michael T., M.P.), Street Music in the Metropolis. Correspondence and observations on the existing law, and proposed amendments.
8vo. John Murray [1864]

Rebound with the original front cover and spine preserved.

E.5 Boz Club Papers. Reports of Annual Meetings held in 1906, 1907, 1908, 1911, 1912 and 1914, containing texts of speeches by Augustine Birrell, Henry Fielding Dickens, Percy Fitzgerald, Harry Furniss, Mrs. Perugini (Kate Dickens), W. Pett Ridge, Clement Shorter, and others, *six pamphlets, varying in length from 28 to 34 pages, original green wrappers.*

With these pamphlets (which belonged to Sir John Martin Harvey) is the list of members dated 1904 sent to Martin Harvey together with an A.L.s. (8 November 1905) from the Club Secretary, A. Llewellyn Roberts informing Martin Harvey of his election to the Club; also a set of souvenir dinner menus for 1907–1912 and 1914, with original

25

illustrations by Luke Fildes, Harry Furniss, Marcus Stone and others, portraits of Dickens, facsimile reproductions of MSS. in the Forster Collection and of original drawings for the novels, etc., etc.

E.6   Chesterton (Gilbert Keith), Charles Dickens Fifty Years After, *bound in white half vellum for the library at La Petite Chardière*

4to. privately printed by Clement Shorter [1920]

No. 6 of 25 copies signed by Shorter. Chesterton's essay first appeared in *The Observer*, 6 June 1920.

E.7   Chesterton (Gilbert Keith) Appreciations and criticisms of the works of Charles Dickens, *plates*   *8vo., J. M. Dent* [1911]

E.8   Collier (John Payne), An old man's diary, forty years ago for the first [and last] six months of 1832 [and 1833] *Four parts bound in one volume with original wrappers preserved*   *4to. for strictly private circulation* [1871 – 72]

Inscribed by the author to G. L. Grenfell on fly-leaf of part one. Loosely inserted into the volume is an A.L.s (*3 pages, 8vo. Riverside, Maidenhead, 19 June 1875*) from Collier to George Cruikshank (" . . . my friend Mr. Cosens tells me that you wish for a copy (one of only 50) of my 'Old Man's Diary'. I send you the only complete copy I have left . . . You are mentioned in it, and in terms that I hope you will not disapprove . . . ").

E.9   Collins (Wilkie), The Frozen Deep. A Drama in Three Acts, *46 pages, modern half-morocco, original wrapper preserved*

sm 4to. Not published, imprint on verso of title-page: Watford, S. A. Bradley [n.d.]

Sketch of Dickens (the figure on the ground) acting in *The Frozen Deep*, published in *The Illustrated London News*, 17 January 1857 (See E.9)

The manuscript of Collins's drama, extensively revised by Dickens and called by him "The Prompt Book" was sold at Sotheby's in June 1890 for £300 and is now in The Pierpont Morgan Library. This text was used for the first production by Dickens at Tavistock House in January 1857 and was first published by R. L. Brannan in his *Under the Management of Mr. Charles Dickens* (1966). A version of the play revised by Collins alone was privately printed by him in 1866 when it was produced at the Olympic Theatre (Collins's own copy of this edition is in the library of Mr. Leslie C. Staples). The copy described above, like that in the Sale Catalogue (Lot 132), is undated and differs in format and printer from the 1866 edition. According to an autograph note inserted in this copy, it was "privately issued for Sir Hubert Herkomer, R.A. [1849–1914], for his theatre at Bushey, but was never performed. Very few copies were done and this issue is almost unknown to Dickensians". It may be that the Bushey production never came off because Collins, discouraged by the failure of the 1866 revival, "refused numerous requests from amateur group for permission to produce it" (Brannan, p.2). Writing to a Mr. Kent [? Charles Kent] in 1881 Collins says, " . . . no amateur company that I ever saw or heard of *can* perform the piece. Let me see a new amateur company with two such *born actors* in it as Charles Dickens and Mark Lemon, and they shall have the piece directly . . . " (Letter quoted in *The Dickensian*, vol. 5 [1909], p. 161).

E.10   Cruse (Amy) The Victorians and their books, *plates*
8vo. George Allen & Unwin [1935]

E.11   Dana (Henry Wadsworth Longfellow), Longfellow and Dickens. The story of a trans-Atlantic friendship, *plates, bound in white half-vellum for the library at La Petite Chardière*   *4to. Cambridge (Mass.) Historical Society* [1943]

Extract from vol. 28 (*Proceedings for the Year 1942*) of the Society's Publications.

E.12   Darton (F. J. Harvey, *Ed.*), Essays of the year (1929–1930)
8vo. The Argonaut Press [1930]

No. 202 of a large paper edition limited to 250 copies with Harvey Darton's signature on verso of title-page and J. C. Squire's signature at the end of his prefatory "Essays on Essays". This collection includes "The Grand Manner: Thoughts upon 'A Tale of Two Cities'" by John Drinkwater and "Oliver Twist" by Arthur Symons, both published here for the first time.

E.13   Darton (F. J. Harvey), Dickens: positively the first appearance. A centenary review with a bibliography of "Sketches by Boz", *plates*
8vo. The Argonaut Press [1933]

E.14   Delattre (Floris), Dickens. Traduction, Introduction et Notes
16mo. Paris: La Renaissance du Livre [1924]

Published in the series "Les Cent Chefs-d'oeuvre étrangers". Book-plate of William Miller.

E.15   Ellis (S. M.) Wilkie Collins, Le Fanu and Others
8vo. Constable & Co. [1931]

E.16   Elwin (Malcolm), Victorian Wallflowers   *8vo. Jonathan Cape* [1934]

OLIVER AND LITTLE DICK.

E.17

E.17   Eytinge (Sol., Jr.), Child-pictures from Dickens. With illustrations by S. Eytinge, Jr.   *Boston: Ticknor & Fields* [1868]

E.18   Field (Kate), Pen photographs of Charles Dickens's Readings. Taken from life by Kate Field, an American   *8vo., Trübner & Co.* [1871]

E.19   Fitzgerald (Percy), Pickwickian Manners and Customs
                                                 8vo., The Roxburgh Press [1897]

E.20   Fitzgerald (Percy), Pickwickian Studies
                                                8vo., The New Century Press [1899]

28

E.21   Forster (John), The Life and Adventures of Oliver Goldsmith. A Biography: in four books   *8vo., Bradbury & Evans* [1848]

The dedication copy, specially bound. Inscribed on half-title: "Charles Dickens / from his affectionate friend / John Forster." Book-plate of Charles Dickens and Gad's Hill Sale ticket. In green morocco slip-case.

E.22   Fritz and Liolett (eds.), The Looker-On; a Literary Miscellany, No. 1, Vol. II, January 1851.   *8vo., W. and T. Piper* [1851]

This issue includes: "Half Hours with Charles Dickens. No. 6 – Mr. Micawber".

E.23   [Garrick Club] Correspondence   *4to.,* [n.d.]

In his unpublished catalogue the Comte de Suzannet notes: "Cet imprimé renferme les lettres échangées entre Thackeray, Yates et le comité du Garrick du 19 juin au 1er juillet 1858. Il fut adressé par les soins du comité à tous les membres du cercle avant l'assemblée générale du 10 juillet, qui jugea l'affaire en dernier ressort". Book-plate of John A. Spoor. See E.53, below.

E.24   Gummer (Ellis N.), Dickens' Works in Germany
                    8vo., Oxford: Clarendon Press, [1940]

E.25   Hopkins (Albert A.) and Read (Newbury Frost), A Dickens Atlas including Twelve Walks in London with Charles Dickens.
         4to fascicules New York: the Hatton Garden Press; London: Spurr & Swift [1923]

No. 265 of a limited edition of 300 copies.

E.26   Horne (R. H.), A New Spirit of the Age   *8vo., Smith, Elder & Co.* [1844]

E.27   Kingsmill (Hugh i.e. Hugh Kingsmill Lunn), The Sentimental Journey. A Life of Charles Dickens   *8vo., Wishart & Co.,* [1934]

Pencilled annotations by the Comte de Suzannet.

E.28   Knight (Charles), Passages of a working life during half a century: with a prelude of early reminiscences, 3 vols.   *8vo., Bradbury & Evans* [1864–65]

Inscribed on title-page of vol. 1 to Sir George Nicholls, one of the original Poor Law Commissioners. Pasted into the front of vol. 2 is an A.L.s *(2 pages, 8vo., South Cottage, Kingston on Thames, 24 June 1864)* from Knight to Sir George. The latter has annotated p. 246 of this volume and has also supplied chapter-titles on the contents page of vol. 3. Loosely inserted into the front of vol. 1 is an A.L.s *(5m. 8vo., 2 pages, Examiner Office, 30 March 1865)* from Henry Morley to Knight, accepting for publication a memorial notice of Sir George.

E.29   Langton (Robert), The Childhood and youth of Charles Dickens with retrospective notes, and elucidations, from his Books and Letters.
         8vo., Manchester: published by the Author at Albert Chambers [1883]

No. 57 of a limited subscribers' edition. Initialled by the author on half-title.

E.30   Lann (Eugene),   Диккенс,   *Bound in white half-vellum for the library at La Petite Chardière*
         12mo., Moscow: Gosudarstvyennoy Izdatyelstvo Khudozhestvyennoy Literatury, [1946]

E.31   Macready (William Charles), The diaries of William Charles Macready 1833–1851. Edited by William Toynbee. 2 vols   *8vo., Chapman and Hall* [1912]

E.32   Macready (William Charles), Macready's Reminiscences, and Selections from his Diaries and Letters. Edited by Sir Frederick Pollock, Bart., one of his executors. 2 vols.   *8vo., Macmillan & Co.,* [1875]

E.33   Maurois (André), Dickens   *8vo., John Lane, The Bodley Head* [1934]

With the book are two cuttings of reviews published in *The Times* and *The Daily Telegraph.*

E.34   Meynell (Viola), A Memoir   *8vo., Jonathan Cape* [1929]

E.35   Pollock's Juvenile Drama. Oliver Twist or the Parish Boy's Progress. A Drama in three acts. 6 Plates of Characters, 13 Scenes, 1 Set Piece, 3 Wings. Total 23 Plates. Adapted only for Pollock's Scenes and Characters.   *16 pages, B. Pollock* [n.d.]

The plates in the set accompanying this booklet have been hand-coloured; some of them bear the imprint of Pollock's father-in-law and predecessor in the business, J. Redington.

A Christmas gift to the Comte de Suzannet from Leslie C. Staples.

E.35

30

E.39

E.36   Powell (Thomas), The living authors of England
8vo., New York : D. Appleton & Co. [1849]

E.37   Powell (Thomas), Pictures of the living authors of Britain
16mo., Partridge & Oakey [1851]

E.38   Pontavice de Heussy (Robert Du), L'Inimitable Boz. Etude historique et anecdotique sur la vie et l'oeuvre de Charles Dickens
8vo., Paris : Maison Quantin [1889]

E.39   Quiz [? Edward Caswall], Sketches of Young Ladies: in which these interesting members of the Animal Kingdom are classified according to their several Instincts, Habits and General Characteristics. By "Quiz". With six illustrations by "Phiz". *Original boards, in red half-morocco slip-case* ⸱ *sm. 8vo., Chapman and Hall* [1837]

Inserted into this copy (from the library of Ogden Goelet) are Phiz's original drawings for the illustrations (see G.4).

E.40   Sadleir (Michael), Blessington – D'Orsay. A Masquerade.

8vo., Constable & Co. [1933]

E.41   Sala (George Augustus), Things I have seen and people I have known, 2 vols., *portrait*   *12mo., Cassell & Company* [1894]

Specially bound presentation copy inscribed on title-page of vol. 1 "To Bessie my Beloved Wife from George Augustus Sala Brighton June 1894".

E.42   "Sampson Short-and-Fat", Quozziana: or Letters from Great Goslington, Mass., giving an account of the Quoz Dinner, and other matters

8vo., Boston: William White & H. P. Lewis [1842]

A burlesque of the reports of the great "Boz Ball" given in Dickens's honour at the Park Theatre, New York, 14 February 1842. Book-plate of William Miller.

E.43   Savonarola (Don Jeremy) [i.e. F. S. Mahony], Facts and Figures from Italy by Don Jeremy Savonarola, Benedictine Monk, addressed during the last two winters to Charles Dickens, Esq. being an Appendix to his "Pictures".

8vo., Richard Bentley [1847]

Rebound with the original front cover and spine preserved.

E.44   Seymour (Mrs.), An account of the origin of the "Pickwick Papers" by Mrs. Seymour widow of the distinguished artist who originated the work

4to., privately printed [1901]

No. 8 (signed by F. J. Kitton) of a limited reprint of 50 copies of Mrs. Seymour's 1854 pamphlet. With a preface and notes by F. G. Kitton.

E.45   Thackeray (William Makepeace), The letters and private papers of William Makepeace Thackeray. Collected and edited by Gordon N. Ray. 4 vols.

8vo., Cambridge, Mass.: Harvard University Press [1945–46]

With a copy of the prospectus for the edition written by Howard Mumford Jones (8pp.), a circular and publicity leaflet (4pp.) issued on the publication of vols. 1 and 2. Tipped into vol. 4 is a one-page A.L.s. from Arthur Pforzheimer to the Comte de Suzannet dated 3 February 1947 mentioning Professor Ray's plans for further work on Thackeray and a memorandum in the Comte's hand (4pp.) listing passages of Dickensian interest in the edition.

E.46   Thackeray (William Makepeace), "The Count's Adventures." An offprint from volume one of *The Letters and Private Papers of William Makepeace Thackeray*, edited by Gordon N. Ray   *8vo. Cambridge Mass.: Harvard University Press* [1945]

E.47   Toole (J. L.), Reminiscences of J. L. Toole related by himself, and chronicled by Joseph Hatton. Illustrated by Alfred Bryan and W. H. Margetson. 2 vols.

8vo., Hurst and Blackett [1889]

Pasted into the front of vol. 1 is the Pay List of the Theatre Royal, New Adelphi, for the week ending 15 March 1867, showing that Toole received £30 for his performances that week. Pasted into the front of vol. 2 is the Nightly Return for the Adelphi Theatre for 20 February 1866 (total receipts were £81.15.6). Book-plate of T. C. Venables in both volumes.

MR. TOOLE AS "THE ARTFUL DODGER."

E.47

E.48   Townshend (Chauncy Hare), The Three Gates. In verse.

8vo., Chapman and Hall [1859]

Dedicated to Charles Dickens.

E.49   Ward (Sir Adolphus William), Dickens. Library edition re-issue of 1882 volume in English Men of Letters series.   *8vo., Macmillan & Co.* [1905]

E.50   Wills (William Henry), Old Leaves: gathered from Household Words. Bound in crimson half-morocco with gilt lettering on spine.   *Chapman and Hall* [1860]

Inscription on title-page: "Charles Dickens from his faithful friend/and fellow labourer/W.H.W." Pasted in end-papers is a cutting of an obituary notice of Wills from the *Athenaeum* 4 September 1880. Book-plate of Charles Dickens inside front cover, also Gad's Hill Sale Ticket and book-plates of R. Milne Redhead and John A. Spoor.

Acquired by the Comte de Suzannet in May 1939.

E.51   Wright (Thomas), The Life of Charles Dickens   *8vo., Herbert Jenkins* [1935]

E.52   Wright (Thomas), Thomas Wright of Olney. An Autobiography.

8vo., Herbert Jenkins [1936]

E.53   Yates (Edmund), Mr. Thackeray, Mr. Yates, and The Garrick Club. The correspondence and facts. Stated by Edmund Yates.

8vo., Printed for private circulation [1859]

Yates's personal copy, signed by him on the title-page (printer's error on p. 14 also corrected by hand). Book-plates of Yates, Stephen George Holland and John A. Spoor. See E.23, above.

BIBLIOGRAPHY

E.54   Bay (J. Christian), The Pickwick Papers. Some bibliographical remarks. An address delivered before the Caxton Club 16 January 1937

8vo., Chicago: The Caxton Club [1938]

One of a limited edition of 250 copies.

E.55   Calhoun (Philo) and Heaney (Howell J.), Dickensiana in the Rough, *bound in white half-vellum for the library at La Petite Chardière*

8vo., The Bibliographical Society of America [1947]

Extract from vol. 41 of *The Papers of the Bibliographical Society of America.*

E.56   Calhoun (Philo) and Heaney (Howell J.), Dickens' *Christmas Carol* after a hundred years: a study in bibliographical evidence, *bound in white half-vellum for the library at La Petite Chardière*   *8vo., The Bibliographical Society of America* [1945]

Extract from vol. 39 of *The Papers of the Bibliographical Society of America.* Pencilled annotations throughout by the Comte de Suzannet.

E.57   Cohn (Albert M.), A few notes upon some rare Cruikshankiana, *plates*

8vo., Karslake & Company [1915]

No. 32 of a limited edition of 250 copies. Signed by the author.

E.58   Forster Collection. A Catalogue of the printed books bequeathed by John Forster, Esq., Ll.D [to the South Kensington Museum]. With Index

8vo., H.M. Stationery Office [1888]

E.59   Forster Collection. A Catalogue of the Paintings, Manuscripts, Autograph Letters, Pamphlets, etc. bequeathed by John Forster, Esq., Ll.D [to the South Kensington Museum]. With Indexes.   *8vo., H.M. Stationery Office* [1893]

E.60   Smith (Harry B.), A Sentimental Library comprising Books formerly owned by famous writers, presentation copies, manuscripts and drawings. Collected and described by Harry B. Smith. With 56 illustrations.

large 8vo., privately printed [1914]

E.61   Suzannet (Le Comte Alain de), Catalogue des Manuscrits, Livres Imprimés et Lettres Autographes composant la Bibliothèque de la Petite Chardière. Oeuvres de Charles Dickens. 3 vols.   *8vo., Lausanne* [1934]

Copy presented by Suzannet to the Dickens House in 1934.

E.62   Wilkins (William Glyde), First and Early American editions of the works of Charles Dickens.   *8vo., privately printed* [1910]

Inscription on fly-leaf: "Mr. C. Van Noorden With Compliments of Wm. Glyde Wilkins."

Playbills and Programmes

F.1 Private Theatricals. Stage Manager, Mr. Charles Dickens. On Saturday Evening, April 27, 1833, at Seven o'clock precisely.
J. & G. Nichols, Printers, Earl's Court, Cranbourn Street, Soho

For another copy see Sale Catalogue, Lot 153. This copy belonged, according to the Comte de Suzannet, to Maria Beadnell's friend, Mary-Anne Leigh. The copy in the Sale Catalogue belonged to Thomas Beard.

F.2 New Strand Theatre. Near Somerset House. Licensed by Authority of the Right Hon. the Lord Chamberlain. Triumphant Success! – SAM WELLER Every Night. On Monday, July 24th, 1837, and during the Week, will be presented for the 13th time, with New and Extensive Scenery, Dresses and Decorations, &&., an Entirely New Peregrinating Piece of Incident, Character and Manners; interspersed with Vaudevilles, called SAM WELLER! or the PICKWICKIANS Founded on "Boz's" Posthumous Papers of the PICKWICK CLUB, by the Author of "TOM & JERRY." [William Moncrieff) *Printed in blue type throughout*

On this bill (the bottom part of which has been removed) is printed Moncrieff's apologia for his bold plagiarism of Dickens:

> . . . To meddle with so extraordinary a writer, therefore, is as dangerous as it is enticing; the desultory nature of the adventures in which he has revelled, & the absence of that continuity of plot so essential in a dramatic piece, has also been the subject of much embarassment and has led the adapter to draw on his own resources very frequently, when he would more gladly have availed himself of the superior material of his master . . . Late experience has enabled him to bring Mr. Pickwick's affairs to a conclusion rather sooner than his gifted biographer has done, if not so satisfactorily as could be wished, at all events quite legally . . .

F.3 Theatre Royal, Bath. First Night of SAM WELLER! *Or, The PICKWICK-IANS*, and HERCULES, The King of Clubs. First Night of the Engagement of Mr. W. J. Hammond, of the Theatre-Royal Covent-Garden, and Proprietor of the New Strand Theatre, London. On Tuesday Evening, December 26th, 1837, And Every Night in the Christmas Week, . . .
2 pages, folio, John and James Keene, Printers, Bath Journal Office, Kingsmead Street, Bath

On the bill is printed a synopsis of the three acts of *Sam Weller* and the announcement of an interlude to be presented between that play and the "entirely Original, Classical, Comical, Sculpturesque, and Pantomimic Burletta, called HERCULES!": "Procession of Her Gracious Majesty, QUEEN VICTORIA, on the occasion of her Royal Visit to the City to Dine With the Lord Mayor and Corporation of London on the 9th of November."

Private Theatricals.

STAGE MANAGER, MR. CHARLES DICKENS.

ON SATURDAY EVENING, APRIL 27, 1833,

At Seven o'clock precisely. The performances will commence with

AN INTRODUCTORY PROLOGUE;

THE PRINCIPAL CHARACTERS BY

MR. EDWARD BARROW; MR. MILTON; MR. CHARLES DICKENS; MISS AUSTIN;
AND MISS DICKENS.

IMMEDIATELY AFTER WHICH WILL BE PRESENTED THE OPERA OF

CLARI.

The Duke Vivaldi	MR. BRAMWELL,
Rolamo, a Farmer, (Father to Clari)	MR. C. DICKENS,
Jocoso, (Valet to the Duke)	MR. H. AUSTIN,
Nicolo	MR. MILTON,
Geronio	MR. E. BARROW,
Nimpedo	MR. R. AUSTIN,
Pages to the Duke	MASTERS F. DICKENS & A. DICKENS.
Clari	MISS DICKENS,
Fidalma (her Mother)	MISS L. DICKENS,
Vespina	MISS AUSTIN,
Ninette	MISS OPPENHEIM.

CHARACTERS IN THE EPISODE.

The Nobleman	MR. HENRY KOLLE,
Pelgrino, a Farmer	MR. JOHN DICKENS,
Wife of Pelgrino	MISS URQUHART,
Leoda	MISS OPPENHEIM.

AFTER WHICH THE FAVOURITE INTERLUDE OF

The Married Bachelor.

Sir Charles Courtall	MR. C. DICKENS,
Sharp	MR. JOHN URQUHART,
Lady Courtall	MISS L. DICKENS,
Grace	MISS DICKENS.

TO CONCLUDE WITH THE FARCE OF

Amateurs & Actors.

David Dulcet, Esq. (a Musical Dramatic Amateur, who employs Mr. O. P. Bustle, and attached to Theatricals and Miss Mary Hardacre)	MR. H. AUSTIN,
Mr. O. P. Bustle, (a Provincial Manager, but engaged to superintend some Private Theatricals)	MR. BRAMWELL,
Wing, (a poor Country Actor)	MR. C. DICKENS,
Berry, (an Actor for the heavy Business)	MR. BOSTON,
Elderberry, (a retired Manufacturer, simple in wit and manners, and utterly unacquainted with Theatricals)	MR. J. DICKENS,
Timkins, (Elderberry's Factotum)	MR. R. AUSTIN,
Geoffry Muffincap, (an elderly Charity Boy, let out as a Servant at Bustle's Lodging)	MR. E. BARROW,
Miss Mary Hardacre, (a fugitive Ward of Elderberry's)	MISS DICKENS,
Mrs. Mary Goneril, (a Strolling Tragedy Actress, and a serious evil to her Husband)	MISS OPPENHEIM

The Scenery by Messrs. H. Austin, Milton, H. Kolle, and Assistants.——The Band which will be numerous and complete, under the direction of Mr. E. Barrow.

J. & G. Nichols, Printers, Earl's Court, Cranbourn Street, Soho.

F.1

Private Theatricals.

COMMITTEE.

Mrs. TORRENS. | Mrs. PERRY.
W. C. ERMATINGER, Esq. | Captain TORRENS.

THE EARL OF MULGRAVE.

STAGE MANAGER—MR. CHARLES DICKENS.

QUEEN'S THEATRE, MONTREAL.

ON WEDNESDAY EVENING, MAY 25TH, 1842,

WILL BE PERFORMED,

A ROLAND FOR AN OLIVER.

MRS. SELBORNE.
MARIA DARLINGTON.
MRS. FIXTURE.

MR. SELBORNE.
ALFRED HIGHFLYER.
SIR MARK CHASE.
FIXTURE.
GAMEKEEPER.

AFTER WHICH, AN INTERLUDE IN ONE SCENE, (FROM THE FRENCH,) CALLED

Past Two o'Clock in the Morning.

THE STRANGER.
MR. SNOBBINGTON.

TO CONCLUDE WITH THE FARCE, IN ONE ACT, ENTITLED

DEAF AS A POST.

MRS. PLUMPLEY.
AMY TEMPLETON.
SOPHY WALTON.
SALLY MAGGS.
CAPTAIN TEMPLETON.
MR. WALTON.
TRISTRAM SAPPY.
CRUPPER.
GALLOP.

Montreal, May 24, 1842.   GAZETTE OFFICE,

Playbill of the Private Theatricals
Montreal, 25 May 1842

Forster's copy of the playbill for *A Roland for an Oliver (Courtesy of the
Victoria and Albert Museum)* (See F 5)

F.4   Theatre Royal, Bath. Sam Weller, or the Pickwickians, and Hercules,
King of Clubs, having turned up trumps! will be repeated for the third, fourth and
fifth times, this present Thursday, Dec. 28th, and on Friday and Saturday next.
2 pages, folio, John and James Keene, Printers, Bath Journal Office, 7, Kingsmead Street.
Blue Paper.

Details of contents of bill as for preceding item.

F.5   Private Theatricals, Stage manager Mr. Charles Dickens. Queens Theatre,
Montreal, On Wednesday Evening, May 25th 1842.

Montreal May 24 1842 Gazette Office

37

Together with officers of the Coldstream Guards, Dickens organised and acted in these theatricals for the benefit of charity. The programme consisted of *A Roland for an Oliver,* an interlude called *Past Two O'clock in the Morning* and a farce called *Deaf as a Post* (in which Catherine Dickens played). The actors' names have been added to this copy in an unknown hand. Another copy, annotated by Dickens, is in the Forster Collection, Victoria & Albert Museum. With the copy listed here are two invitation cards to the soirée issued to Mr. and Mrs. Rogers and Mr. Ricardo.

F.6   Strictly Private. Amateur Performance, at Miss Kelly's Theatre 73 Dean St., Soho. On Saturday Evening, September 20th, 1845.

Printed in green, red and gold by Bradbury and Evans

The programme consisted of Jonson's *Every Man in his Humour* followed by a one-act farce, *A Good Night's Rest or, Two O'clock in the Morning.* Another copy of this bill in the Forster Collection, Victoria & Albert Museum, is adorned with sketches by Maclise of Dickens and Forster in the roles of Captain Bobadil and Kitely.

F.7   Strictly Private. Miss Kelly's Theatre No. 73 Dean St., Soho Square. Miss Kelly has the honor to announce to the nobility, gentry, her subscribers and friends that her benefit is fixed for Saturday, January the 3rd, 1846, upon which occasion the distinguished amateurs whose performances have created such extraordinary interest, and confirmed the still existing taste for the Legitimate Drama will (as a tribute of regard for which she cannot express too much her gratified feelings and deep sense of obligation) appear for the last time.

The programme consisted of a Prologue specially written by Dickens for delivery by Miss Kelly, Fletcher's comedy *The Elder Brother* ("altered for this representation") and a farce by Peake entitled *Comfortable Lodgings.*

F.8   Amateur Performance, for the Benefit of Mr. Leigh Hunt, who, after years of ill health and hard struggle, is not, without this assistance, released from difficulty, by a pension granted late in life.

3 pages, 4to

Programme for a performance at the Theatre Royal, Liverpool on 28 July 1847. Dickens, Cruikshank, Forster, Douglas Jerrold, G. H. Lewes and other literary and artistic celebrities are among the cast. The plays performed were *Every Man in his Humour,* Poole's interlude, *Turning the Tables* (Poole was also to benefit from the proceeds) and Peake's *Comfortable Lodgings: or, Paris in 1750.* A preliminary address, written for the occasion by Bulwer Lytton, was delivered by Forster. In his *Autobiography,* chapter 25, Leigh Hunt writes:

> . . . Simultaneous with the latest movement about the pension, was one on the part of my admirable friend Dickens and other distinguished men—Forsters and Jerrolds—who, combining kindly purpose with an amateur inclination for the stage, had condescended to show to the public what excellent actors they could have been, had they so pleased,—what excellent actors, indeed, some of them were. They were of opinion that a benefit for myself at one of the metropolitan theatres would be a dishonour on neither side . . . and preparations were being accordingly made, when the grant of the pension seemed to render it advisable that the locality of the benefit should be transferred from London to a provincial stage, in acknowledgment to the superior boon, and for the avoidance of all appearance of competing with it. The result was still of great use to me, and my name was honoured in a manner I shall never forget by an address from the pens of Mr. Serjeant (late Justice) Talfourd and Sir Edward Bulwer, and the plaudits of Birmingham and Liverpool . . .

STRICTLY PRIVATE.

Amateur Performance,

AT MISS KELLY'S THEATRE, 73, DEAN STREET, SOHO,

On Saturday Evening, September 20th, 1845,

WHEN WILL BE PERFORMED

BEN JONSON'S COMEDY OF

EVERY MAN IN HIS HUMOUR.

CHARACTERS.

KNOWELL	*An Old Gentleman.*	THOMAS CASH	*Kitely's Cashier.*
EDWARD KNOWELL	*His Son.*	OLIVER COB	*A Water Bearer.*
BRAINWORM	*The Father's Man.*	JUSTICE CLEMENT	*An old merry Magistrate.*
GEORGE DOWNRIGHT	*A plain Squire.*	ROGER FORMAL	*His Clerk.*
WELLBRED	*His half-brother.*	WILLIAM	*His Servant.*
KITELY	*A Merchant.*	JAMES	*Wellbred's Servant.*
CAPTAIN BOBADIL	*A Paul's man.*	DAME KITELY	*Kitely's Wife.*
MASTER STEPHEN	*A Country Gull.*	MISTRESS BRIDGET	*His Sister.*
MASTER MATHEW	*The Town Gull.*	TIB	*Cob's Wife.*

TO CONCLUDE WITH THE FARCE IN ONE ACT, CALLED

A GOOD NIGHT'S REST

OR, TWO O'CLOCK IN THE MORNING.

CHARACTERS.

SNOBBINGTON. THE STRANGER.

Previous to the Comedy . . . . . . The Overture to *Masaniello.*
Previous to the Farce . . . . . . The Overture to *La Gazza Ladra.*

The Cards of those who are presentable at the Theatre, from Seven o'Clock. The performance will commence at Half-past Seven exactly: by which time it is requested that the whole of the Company may be seated.

EVENING DRESS.

Forster's copy of the playbill for *Every Man in his Humour*, adorned with Maclise's sketches of Dickens and Forster *(Courtesy of the Victoria and Albert Museum)* (See F.6)

F.9   Theatre Royal, Haymarket. Amateur Performance in aid of the Fund for the Endowment of a Perpetual Curatorship of Shakespeare's House, to be always held by some one distinguished in literature, and more especially in dramatic literature; the profits of which it is the intention of the Shakespeare House Committee to keep entirely separate from the fund now raising for the purchase of the House.

2 pages, folio, printed in blue, red and green by Bradbury and Evans

The productions for 15 May 1848 were *The Merry Wives of Windsor* (with Dickens as Shallow) and Mrs. Inchbald's Farce, *Animal Magnetism* (Dickens as the Doctor). The productions for 17 May, also announced on this programme, were *Every Man in his Humour* (Dickens as Bobadil) and Mr. Kenney's farce of *Love, Law and Physic* (Dickens as Flexible). Cruikshank also acted in all four plays and Suzannet notes in his unpublished catalogue that this copy of the programme belonged to the artist.

F.10   Theatre Royal, Edinburgh. Amateur Performance by the Gentlemen from London connected with Literature and Art . . . On Monday evening, July 17th, 1848 will be presented Shakespeare's Comedy of the Merry Wives of Windsor . . . To be followed by Mr. Kenney's Farce, in one act of Love, Law, and Physic . . . To conclude with a Comic Scene from the French called Two O'clock in the Morning . . . Stage manager Mr. Charles Dickens.

James Brydone, Printer, 17 South Hanover Street, Edinburgh

For Dickens's autograph draft of this bill see H.166.

F.11   Theatre Royal, Manchester, Amateur Performance, by the Members of the Manchester Shakesperian Society, on Thursday, May 16th, 1850, in aid of the Funds of the Juvenile Refuge & Night Asylum.   *gold print on blue silk*

Dickens's name appears among the list of distinguished patrons printed on this programme.

F.12   Devonshire House. On Friday evening, May 16th, 1851, The Amateur Company and the Guild of Literature & Art, will have the honor of performing, for the first time, in the presence of Her Majesty the Queen, and His Royal Highness the Prince Albert, a new comedy . . . Not So Bad As We Seem . . . The whole produced under the direction of Mr. Charles Dickens . . .

Printed in red and black by W. S. Johnson "Nassau Steam Press" 60, St. Martin's Lane

With this playbill is a copy of the programme for the performance printed by "Bradbury & Evans (Printers Extraordinary to the Queen) Whitefriars".

F.13   Hanover Square Rooms. On Wednesday Evening, June 1, 1851, The Amateur Company of the Guild of Literature and Art; to encourage Life Assurance and other Provident habits among Authors and Artists; to render such assistance to both as shall never compromise their independence; and to found a new Institution where honorable rest from arduous labour shall still be associated with the discharge of congenial duties; will have the honor of performing, for the third time, A New Comedy, in Five Acts, by Sir Edward Bulwer Lytton, Bart., called *Not So Bad As We Seem; or, Many Sides to a Character.*

Printed by W. S. Johnson, 60, St. Martin's Lane, Charing Cross

This handbill shows that the public performances of *Not So Bad As We Seem* were followed by a one-act farce by Dickens and Mark Lemon, *Mr. Nightingale's Diary.*

DEVONSHIRE HOUSE.

ON FRIDAY EVENING, MAY 16th, 1851,
THE AMATEUR COMPANY
OF THE

GUILD OF LITERATURE AND ART,
WILL HAVE THE HONOR OF PERFORMING, FOR THE FIRST TIME,
IN THE PRESENCE OF

HER MAJESTY THE QUEEN,
AND

HIS ROYAL HIGHNESS THE PRINCE ALBERT,
A NEW COMEDY, IN FIVE ACTS, BY SIR EDWARD BULWER LYTTON, BART.,
CALLED

NOT SO BAD AS WE SEEM:
OR,
MANY SIDES TO A CHARACTER.

THE DUKE OF MIDDLESEX	*Peers attached to the Son of James II., commonly called the First Pretender*	Mr FRANK STONE.
THE EARL OF LOFTUS		Mr. DUDLEY COSTELLO.
LORD WILMOT	*A Young Man at the head of the Mode more than a Century ago, Son to Lord Loftus,*	Mr. CHARLES DICKENS.
Mr. SHADOWLY SOFTHEAD	*A Young Gentleman from the City, Friend and Double to Lord Wilmot*	Mr. DOUGLAS JERROLD.
Mr. HARDMAN	*(A Rising Member of Parliament, and Adherent to Sir Robert Walpole)*	Mr. JOHN FORSTER.
SIR GEOFFREY THORNSIDE	*(A Gentleman of good Family and Estate)*	Mr. MARK LEMON.
Mr. GOODENOUGH EASY	*(in Business, Highly Respectable, and a Friend of Sir Geoffrey)*	Mr. F. W. TOPHAM.
LORD LE TRIMMER		Mr. PETER CUNNINGHAM.
SIR THOMAS TIMID		Mr. WESTLAND MARSTON.
COLONEL FLINT		Mr. R. H. HORNE.
Mr. JACOB TONSON	*(A Bookseller)*	Mr. CHARLES KNIGHT.
SMART	*(Valet to Lord Wilmot)*	Mr. WILKIE COLLINS.
HODGE	*(Servant to Sir Geoffrey Thornside)*	Mr. JOHN TENNIEL.
PADDY O'SULLIVAN	*(Mr. Fallen's Landlord)*	Mr. ROBERT BELL.
Mr. DAVID FALLEN	*(Grub Street Author and Pamphleteer)*	Mr. AUGUSTUS EGG.
LORD STRONGBOW, SIR JOHN BRUIN, Coffee-House Loungers, Drawers, Watchmen, Newsman.		
LUCY	*(Daughter to Sir Geoffrey Thornside)*	Mrs. HENRY COMPTON.
BARBARA	*(Daughter to Mr. Easy)*	Miss ELLEN CHAPLIN.
THE SILENT LADY OF DEADMAN'S LANE		Mrs. COE.

SCENERY.

Lord Wilmot's Lodgings	Painted by Mr. PITT.
"The Murillo"	,, Mr. ABSOLON.
Sir Geoffrey Thornside's Library	,, Mr. PITT.
Will's Coffee House	,, Mr. PITT.
The Streets, and Deadman's Lane	,, Mr. THOMAS GRIEVE.
The distrest Poet's Garret (after Hogarth)	,, Mr. PITT.
The Mall in the Park	,, Mr. TELBIN.
An open space near the River	,, Mr. STANFIELD, R.A.
Tapestry Chamber in Deadman's Lane	,, Mr. LOUIS HAGHE.
The Act Drop	,, Mr. ROBERTS, R.A.

The Proscenium by Mr. CRACE. The Theatre constructed by Mr. SLOMAN, Machinist of the Royal Lyceum Theatre.
The Costumes (with the exception of the Ladies' Dresses, which are by Messrs. NATHAN, of Titchbourne Street) made by Mr BARNETT, of the Theatre Royal, Haymarket.
UNDER THE SUPERINTENDENCE OF MR. AUGUSTUS EGG, A.R.A.
Perruquier, Mr. WILSON, of the Strand. Prompter, Mr. COE.

THE WHOLE PRODUCED UNDER THE DIRECTION OF MR. CHARLES DICKENS.

THE DUKE OF DEVONSHIRE'S PRIVATE BAND WILL PERFORM DURING THE EVENING,
Under the Direction of MR. COOTE, who has composed an OVERTURE for the occasion.

TO COMMENCE, BY HER MAJESTY'S COMMAND, AT NINE O'CLOCK,
THEREFORE, THE WHOLE OF THE AUDIENCE ARE PARTICULARLY REQUESTED TO BE SEATED, AT LEAST A QUARTER OF AN HOUR BEFORE THAT TIME.

W. J. Johnson, "Nassau Steam Press," 60, St. Martin's Lane

F.12

F.14 Free Trade Hall, Manchester on Wednesday Evening, February 11th, 1852, the Amateur Company and the Guild of Literature & Art; will have the honor of performing, for the twelfth time, a new comedy, in Five Acts, by Sir Edward Bulwer Lytton, Bart., called *Not so Bad As We Seem:* . . . The performance to conclude with (for the ninth time) an Original Farce, in One Act, by Mr. Charles Dickens and

A scene from *Not So Bad As We Seem (Mary Evans Picture Library)* (See F.13)

Mr. Mark Lemon, entitled Mr. Nightingale's Diary . . . The whole produced under the direction of Mr. Charles Dickens. *Printed in red and black*

Suzannet has annotated this playbill: "presented by I. Kyrle Fletcher 1940." Present also are two other copies of this playbill.

F.15   Theatre Royal, Tavistock House. On Twelfth Night, Friday evening, the sixth of January, 1854. Will be presented Fielding's Burlesque Tom Thumb.
3 pages, Sm. folio. Printed in gold, red and green by Bradbury and Evans

These family theatricals were held in honour of Charles Dickens Junior's 16th Birthday and the list of the "powerful and unequalled cast" show that Dickens and Mark Lemon both performed in *Tom Thumb* under the names of "The Modern Garrick" and "The Infant Phenomenon" respectively. The programme includes "at the request of several Persons of Quality" the words of three songs specially written by Dickens to be sung by his son Henry (not yet 5 years old) who played Tom Thumb.

F.16   The Smallest Theatre in the World. Tavistock House. Lessee and Manager Mr. Crummles. On Monday Evening, June 18th, 1855, will be presented at exactly eight o'clock, an entirely new and original domestic melo-drama in two acts by Mr. Wilkie Collins called The Lighthouse . . . To conclude with the Guild-Amateur Company's Farce in one act by Mr. Crummles and Mr. Mark Lemon; Mr. Nightingale's Diary. *Printed in red and black*

F.17   Tavistock House Theatre. Under the Management of Mr. Charles Dickens. On Twelfth Night, Tuesday, January 6th, 1857, at a quarter before 8 o'clock, will be presented an entirely new Romantic Drama, in three acts, by Mr. Wilkie Collins, called THE FROZEN DEEP . . . To conclude with Mrs. Inchbald's Farce, in Two Acts, of ANIMAL MAGNETISM *Printed in red and black*

Present also are two other bills, for the performances of *The Frozen Deep* on 12 and 14 January 1857, identical with the above except that on the 14 January bill Buckstone's *Uncle John* is substituted for *Animal Magnetism*.

F.18   In Remembrance of the Late Mr. Douglas Jerrold   *4 pages, large folio*

Programme of the lectures and theatrical performances organised in London 7–29 July 1857 for the benefit of Jerrold's widow and children. The events detailed in this programme are a lecture by W. H. Russell on his experiences as *Times* correspondent in the Crimea; a lecture by Thackeray on "Week-day Preachers"; revivals of four of Jerrold's most successful plays with all-star casts; three performances of *The Frozen Deep* by Dickens's amateur company (with *Two O'clock in the Morning* as a concluding farce); and a reading by Dickens of *A Christmas Carol*.

F.19   In Remembrance of the late Mr. Douglas Jerrold. Gallery of Illustration, Regent Street. Under the Management of Mr. Charles Dickens. On Saturday evening, July 11th, 1857 . . . will be presented . . . The Frozen Deep.   *Printed in red and black*

Present also is another playbill for this performance of *The Frozen Deep* identical with the above except that the concluding farce has been altered from *Two O'clock in the Morning* to *Uncle John*. A third bill, for the performances on 18 and 25 July (also showing *Uncle John* as the concluding farce) has the surnames of some of the actors added in Dickens's hand.

F.20   Theatre-Royal, Bath . . . On Saturday, March 15, 1862, . . . the Historical Drama, in Two Acts, and a Prologue, adapted from the Celebrated Story by Charles Dickens, Esq., called A Tale of Two Cities . . . To conclude with the favourite Burlesque . . . called The Maid and the Magpie.

F.21   "Prologue", 34 lines in rhymed couplets beginning: "Prologues and Epilogues, in good old days / Were things of course, wherever there were plays", *printed in blue on one side of an octavo sheet*   *No date or imprint*

Purchased by Maggs for the Comte de Suzannet at the sale of letters and relics of Dickens, (formerly the property of Anne Brown) at Sotheby's 23 July 1935. It is listed in the Sale Catalogue (Lot 305) as possibly by Dickens with the following note: "Apparently a General Prologue to three plays produced by Dickens's Company of Amateurs. It contains references to the *"Housekeeper"* (probably Douglas Jerrold's 2-act Comedy), the *"Windmill"* (probably Edward Morton's 1-act Farce), and *"Husbands"* (which may be "Husbands at Sight", J. B. Buckstone's 2-act Farce). If this prologue is by Dickens it seems to be entirely unrecorded. It is similar in form and manner to that written by him for Westland Marston's Play "The Patrician's Daughter"."

Paintings, Prints and Drawings

G.1   ANON., "Arrival of the Great Western Steam Ship, off New York on Monday 23rd April, 1838", *hand-coloured aquatint, cut* (15.7 *in. by* 7.6 *in.*), *mounted*
W. & H. Cave [1838]

Among the figures in the foreground, gathered to welcome the vessel, are Mr. Pickwick, Sam Weller and other characters from the novel. Another figure is carrying a board inscribed "W. & H. Cave Engravers Printers Pattern Card Makers &c. New Market Lane Manchester".

G.2   BARNARD (FRED), Thirty-eight original sepia wash designs depicting various scenes and characters from Dickens's novels, signed.

In his unpublished catalogue the Comte de Suzannet notes "Ces compositions ont été exécutées aux environs de 1884". Many of them, however, feature in Chapman and Hall's "Household Edition" of Dickens's Works (1871-79). Others appeared in *A Series of Character Sketches from Dickens from original drawings by Fred Barnard* (Cassell, 1885) and in *A Series of Character Sketches from Dickens. In colour from original drawings by Fred Barnard* (Waverley Book Company, 1913). The portraits and scenes in the Suzannet Collection relate to the following novels: *Nicholas Nickleby* (6), *The Old Curiosity Shop* (2), *Barnaby Rudge* (3), *Martin Chuzzlewit* (6), *Dombey and Son* (12), *David Copperfield* (7), *Bleak House* (2).

G.3   BARROW (JANET), [maternal aunt of Charles Dickens], Miniature on ivory (2.9 *in. by* 2.2 *in.*) contemporary inscription (probably in the hand of the artist) on back: "Charles Dickens. Painted by Janet Barrow. 1830", *contemporary gilt frame with oval opening, in silk covered case (upper cover detached)*

Presented to The Dickens House by the Comte de Suzannet in 1938.

G.4   BROWNE (HABLOT K.), [Phiz.], Seven original pencil and wash drawings for "Sketches of Young Ladies" *in reverse, bound into a copy of the first edition* (see E.39):   [1837]

(1)   Design for front cover (6.2 *in. by* 3.7 *in.*) *heightened in white, differing substantially from the published design*

(2)   "The Musical Y[oun]g Lady" (*title of published sketch:* "The Young Lady who Sings") (3.8 *in. by* 3.4 *in.*) *Pencilled notes above and below the sketch:* "The lamp is only a *reflection* in the mirror so must not be made prominent" *and* "I have altered the effect in the etching from the above – vide back". *On verso another pencil sketch of the central figures* (2.4 *in. by* 2.8 *in.*)

(3)   "The Evangelical Y[oun]g Lady" (3.7 *in. by* 3.5 *in.*)

G.1

G.3

(4) "The Manly Y[oun]g Lady" (3.5 *in. by* 3.5 *in.*) *Notes in ink and pencil above and below the drawing:* "put a rebating ground on so that I may etch the head in. HKB" *and* "stop out the young lady's hat and veil".

(5) "The Interesting Young Lady", *drawing untitled, heightened with white* (3.7 *in. by* 3.3 *in.*). *Notes in ink above and below the drawing:* "Do not bite the dotting upon the faces and about the eyes & ears &c. *coarsely*" and "Bite the face of the girl between the two old women *slightly* – & let me have it back to touch upon HKB."

(6) "The abstemious Young Lady" (4.2 *in. by* 3 *in.*)

(7) "The Natural Y[oun]g Lady" (3.9 *in. by* 3.7 *in.*)

G.5 BROWNE (HABLOT K.), Six original pencil and wash drawings for "Sketches of Young Gentlemen, "*all in reverse except for* (1), *bound into a copy of the first edition* (see A.6): [1838]

(1) "Military Young Gentlemen" (4 *in. by* 3.4 *in.*), *tracing on verso which reverses the drawing*

(2) "Out and out Young Gentlemen" (4.5 *in. by* 3.5 *in.*)

(3) "The Domestic Young Gent[lemen]" (3.4 *in. by* 3.2 *in.*), *alternative title,* "Mr. Felix Nixon", *written below and deleted.*

(4) "The Funny Y[oun]g Gentleman" (3.5 *in. by* 3.2 *in.*)

(5) "The Poetical Y[oun]g Gentleman" (3.4 *in. by* 3 *in.*)

(6) The Y[oun]g Ladies Y[oun]g Gent[leman]" (3.7 *in. by* 3.5 *in.*). "Wanted back immediately" *written below drawing in pencil.*

G.6 BROWNE (HABLOT K.), Five original pencil and wash drawings for "Nicholas Nickleby" *in reverse, mounted* [1·838–39]

(1) "The Yorkshire Schoolmaster at the Saracen's Head" (4.3 *in. by* 4.3 *in.*). *The figure of Master Belling differs from that shown in the published plate.*

(2) "Kate Nickleby sitting to Miss La Creevy" (4.3 *in. by* 4.3 *in.*) *Title added by Dickens in ink, pencilled note beneath drawing:* "[Will] you have the kindness to send back –– (either home or C & H) *early* to[morrow mor]ning? – HKB".

(3) "Madame Mantalini introduces Kate to Miss Knag" *heightened in white* (4.5 *in. by* 4.5 *in.*). *Title added by Dickens in ink, earlier title in another hand,* "Madame Mantalini's Establishment / No. 1", *deleted.*

(4) "Nicholas recognises the Young Lady unknown" (4.6 *in. by* 4.2 *in.*). *The figure of Madeline Bray differs from that in the published plate; here she wears a bonnet and veil, has no ringlets and is looking down – three pencil sketches beneath the drawing show Browne working towards the published version.*

(5) "A sudden recognition unexpected on both sides" (5 *in. by* 4.5 *in.*). *Pencilled note (partly obscured by mount) in Dickens's hand above the drawing:* "I don't think Smike is frightened enough or that Squeers is earnest enough – for my purpose".

With (5) is a manuscript note, signed "Robson & Kerslake", stating that the drawing was bought by them at the sale of Frederick Chapman's property in July 1880, and sold by them the following month to M. H. Spielmann, also a typewritten description of the item by Mr. Spielmann. The Comte de Suzannet purchased the drawing from Ernest Maggs in 1933.

G.7 BROWNE (HABLOT K.), Seven original pencil and wash drawings for "Martin Chuzzlewit" *all in reverse of the published plates except where otherwise stated, mounted* [1843–44]

G.6(4)

(1) Title-page vignette (5 *in.* by 3.7 *in.*)
(2) "Mark begins to be jolly under creditable circumstances" (6 *in.* by 4.5 *in.*)
(3) "Martin meets an acquaintance at the house of a mutual relation" (5.5 *in.* by 4.5 *in.*)
(4) "Martin is much gratified by an imposing ceremony" (6 *in.* by 4.7 *in.*), *differing markedly from the published plate in many details*
(5) "Mr. Moddle is led to the contemplation of his destiny" (5.5 *in.* by 4.2 *in.*)

G.7(6)

(6) "Mrs. Gamp proposes a toast" (*7in. by 4.5 in.*), *coloured chalks and wash over preliminary pencil, facing same way as published plate, signed:* "Phiz", *sketches for faces of the figures above the drawing*

(7) "reception of Mr. Pecksniff by his venerable friend" (*5.2 in. by 4.3 in.*) *facing same way as published plate, title added, not in Dickens's hand.*

48

G.10

G.8   BROWNE (HABLOT K.), Two original pencil and wash drawings for "Dombey and Son" *in reverse, mounted*   [1847-48]

(1)   "The Midshipman boarded by the enemy" (5 *in. by* 4.5 *in.*)
(2)   "An Arrival" (5.3 *in. by* 5.6 *in.*)

Acquired by the Comte de Suzannet in March 1936. In point of detail these drawings, except for Susan Nipper's reticule which does not appear in (2), are closer to the published plates than the drawings for the same plates now in the Free Library of Philadelphia (which has a complete set of Browne's drawings for all but one of the Dombey plates).

G.9   BROWNE (HABLOT K.), Original design, water- and body-colour, for the title-page vignette of vol. 2 of "Nicholas Nickleby" in the Library Edition of Dickens's Works, "The Gentleman next door declares his passion for Mrs. Nickelby".
                                                                                        [1858]

G.10   BRYAN (ALFRED), Caricature, "Dickens and Fechter" (13.5 *in. by* 9 *in.*), sepia wash heightened with Chinese white.   [n.d.]

This drawing seems not to have been published. Another caricature of "The Two Charles's", by the same artist, appeared in *The Entr'acte*, 23 August 1879 (see K.10 (7)). The published version is less flattering to Dickens.

Presented to The Dickens House by the Comtesse de Suzannet in 1966.

G.11

G.11   D'ORSAY (ALFRED, COMTE), Original pencil drawing, touched with chalk, of Dickens's head and shoulders shown in profile (5.5 *in.* *by* 4 *in.*), signed and dated in pencil, "A. D'Orsay fecit 16 Dec^b 1841", signed in ink by the sitter.

G.12   D'ORSAY (ALFRED, COMTE), Original pencil drawing, touched with chalk, of Dickens's head and shoulders shown in profile (6.2 *in.* *by* 5.5 *in.*), signed and dated in pencil "d'Orsay fecit 28 Dec^b 1842". Beneath the drawing D'Orsay has written in pencil: "Dickens. the Best of the two".

In his unpublished catalogue the Comte de Suzannet notes of this and the preceding item that they were acquired by Sir Thomas Phillips at the Blessington Sale at Gore House in May 1849. Purchased by the Comte at the Sotheby's Phillips Sale in January/February 1950.

G.13   FILDES (LUKE), Original pencil and wash drawing, heightened with white, "The Grave of Charles Dickens" (*sight measurement:* 6 *in.* *by* 4 *in.*), signed and dated: "L.F. 1873".

On the mount is pencilled "To Mrs. Forster from L. F." and (in the same hand) "The Grave of Charles Dickens. Original sketch for Forster's Life of Dickens". Fildes's

G.12

water-colour version of the same scene is in the Forster Collection, Victoria and Albert Museum.

Presented to The Dickens House in 1935 by the Comte de Suzannet, who had purchased it at Sotheby's in July of that year.

G.14   FRITH (WILLIAM POWELL), Original oil painting, "Charles Dickens" *(sight measurement: 16 in. by 21 in.)*, signed and dated: "W. Frith 1886".

With the portrait is an autograph note by M. H. Spielmann stating: "This is the early replica [of his 1859 portrait now in the Forster Collection, Victoria & Albert Museum] painted by Frith for Mr. Cozens which he, and Mrs. Perugini (Charles Dickens's daughter) and Sir Henry Dickens declared to be a better likeness than that in the Victoria & Albert Museum, and the best of all likenesses of Dickens . . . " In a letter to *The Times* of 6 March 1919 (reprinted in *The Dickensian*, xv, April 1919, p. 95) Mr. Spielmann, then owner of the 1886 replica painting, called attention to the existence of two other, later, copies of the painting also by Frith (the first of these "was what might have been expected from an aged hand" and in the second "the failing of the hand was even more apparent"); he noted also that the 1886 replica

G.16

"differs from the Forster original in the substitution of a neutral for the showy colour . . . of the jacket-cuffs worn by the novelist . . . ".

A preliminary study in oils for the original 1859 portrait, signed and dated "W. P. Frith. 1859", is now in the Free Library of Philadelphia.

Presented to The Dickens House by the Comte de Suzannet in 1934.

G.15 GREEN (CHARLES), Original water-colour, "Pickwick addresses the Club" *(sight measurements : 20 in. by 27 in.)*, signed and dated "C. Green 1890".

Presented to The Dickens House by the Comte de Suzannet in 1934.

G.16

G.16   HANNAH (ROBERT), Two original oil paintings of Dickens giving Public Readings *(sight measurements of each : 10 in. by 7.2 in.)*

Walter Dexter notes in *The Dickensian* (XXXVII, June 1941, pp. 134-35) that these paintings "were given to Georgina Hogarth in January, 1904, by the artist, Robert Hannah, and bear inscriptions by both the artist and Miss Hogarth. Both paintings were made from memory the morning after the artist had been present at the Readings . . . ". The inscriptions mentioned by Dexter seem no longer discoverable.

Presented to The Dickens House by the Comte de Suzannet and Mr. Ifan Kyrle Fletcher in 1941.

G.19

G.17 LEECH (JOHN), Original pencil and water-colour sketch of Trotty Veck, the hero of "The Chimes" (5 *in. by* 4 *in.*), *signed, mounted*   [?1844]

G.18 SEYMOUR (ROBERT), Original pencil and wash drawing for the illustration to Chapter 3 of "Pickwick Papers" entitled "The Dying Clown" (4 *in. by* 3.6 *in.*), *facing same way as the published plate, mounted.*   [1836]

Purchased from Dr. A. S. W. Rosenbach by the Comte de Suzannet in November 1931. With the drawing is an A.L.s. from Rosenbach to the Comte (" . . . I want to congratulate you on obtaining this, the most famous drawing known to me for Dickens's works . . . [it] came originally from Sir Stuart Samuel. I remember seeing it in his house in London . . . "). Dickens requested Seymour to make certain alterations to this design (see Pilgrim Edition of the Letters, vol. 1, p. 145-46) and the artist had begun working on these just before he committed suicide; his unfinished second drawing, formerly owned by Augustine Daly, is now in the Widener Collection at Harvard University, together with Dickens's letter.

Also with the drawing catalogued here is a photograph (5 *in. by* 4.5 *in.*) of Taylor's portrait of Seymour.

G.19 STANFIELD (CLARKSON), Original water-colour for the "The Carrier's Cart" ("The Cricket on the Hearth") (5 *in. by* 3.2 *in.*), *mounted.*   [?1845]

Some words from the text, "Mrs. Peerybingle then went running to the door", are pencilled beside the water-colour.

G.20 STONE (MARCUS), Original water-colour, "The Happy Pair" ("Our Mutual Friend", Book One, Chapter 10) *(sight measurement:* 6.3 *in. by* 11.2 *in.*) signed and dated "Marcus Stone / 64", *mounted*   [1864]

SECTION H

Autograph Letters and Documents
of Charles Dickens

H.1 A.L.s. to Mary Anne Leigh, friend of Maria Beadnell, *3 pages, 8vo, 21 George Street Monday [7 march 1831]*, apologising for not keeping a promise the previous evening ("... that fact is I was so exceedingly tired from my week's exertions that I slept on the Sofa the whole day...."), *on pink paper, addressed on fourth page of sheet* ("Miss Leigh / Clapton"), *postmarked 8 March 1831 (a Tuesday)*.

Purchased at auction (Sotheby's) by the Comte de Suzannet, 20 December 1939.

H.2 A.L.s. to Thomas Beard, 1 page, 8vo, n.p., Saturday [1832], inviting Beard and "'a Brother or two' to look in and take a Glass of Punch and a Cigar tomorrow Evening", *integral address leaf, endorsed, presumably by Beard:* "C.D. 1832".

Above the address is a note "apparently in the hand of John Dickens" (Pilgrim Edition of the *Letters*, vol. 1, p. 12). See J.23. *Dexter Gift.*

H.3 A.L.s. to Thomas Beard, *1 page, 8vo, 18 Bentinck St. 2 February* [1833], enclosing an invitation from his mother to attend his coming of age party, *addressed on verso of sheet, endorsed, presumably by Beard:* "C.D. Bentinck St. Feb. 2 1833."

With the letter is the invitation–see J.32. Letter mounted in a cardboard frame. *Dexter Gift.*

H.4 A.L.s. to Thomas Beard, *1 page, 4to, 18 Bentinck St. Monday Morning [?22 April 1833]*, sending him a copy of the playbill for the Dickens family's private theatricals on 27 April 1833 (see F.1), *addressed on verso of sheet, endorsed. Dexter Gift.*

H.5 A.L.s. to "My dear Bird", *viz* Thomas Beard, *2 pages, 8vo, Bentinck Street Saturday Morng. [?February 1834]*, postponing a meeting "in consequence of my mother's illness (to say nothing of the calomel) ...", *addressed on fourth page, endorsed.*

For dating see Pilgrim Edition of the *Letters*, vol. 1, p. 36. *Dexter Gift.*

H.6 A.L.s. to Thomas Beard, *4 pages, 4to, Bentinck Street. Saturday Evening [29 November 1834]*, informing Beard that the Dickens household is about to be dispersed "for a time, at all events" owing to "the state of my father's affairs, and his want of attention to them" and that he himself, taking his brother Frederick with him "to instruct and provide for as I best can", is going to move into chambers in Furnival's Inn, *separate address leaf, endorsed.*

... My mother appears most anxious that your sister and yourself should be made acquainted with the situation in which she is placed ....

For dating see Pilgrim Edition of the *Letters*, vol. 1, p. 46. *Dexter Gift.*

56

H.7   A.L.s. to Thomas Beard, *4 pages, 8vo, Bentinck Street. Thursday Morning* [*?4 December 1834*], asking for a loan, *separate address leaf, endorsed.*

> . . . My salary for a week or two is so completely mortgaged by the expences consequent on our removal, that I really have no resource but your kind offer. If your expectation of receiving some money has been realized, will you lend me £5 for a short time? . . . .

For dating see Pilgrim Edition of the *Letters*, vol. 1, p. 48. *Dexter Gift.*

H.8   A.L.s. to Thomas Beard, *3 pages, 8vo, Furnivals Inn Tuesday Evening* [*16 December 1834*], postponing a projected convivial evening, *addressed on fourth page, endorsed, postmarked 17 December 1834.*

> . . . As I have *no dishes*, no curtains, and no french polish, I think we had better, for all our comforts, defer the projected flare until Saturday . . . .

> . . . Pray tell your father, that I place implicit reliance upon him; and be kind enough to remember on your own account that I have got some really EXTRA-ORDINARY french brandy . . . .

Dexter Gift.

H.9   A.L.s. to Thomas Beard, *4 pages, 4to, Black Boy Hotel – Chelmsford Sunday Morning* [*11 January 1835*], describing his journey to Colchester, Braintree and Chelmsford to report for the *Morning Chronicle* on nominations for the General Election, *address panel on fourth page, endorsed, postmarked 11 January 1835.*

> . . . Yesterday I had to start at 8 OClock for Braintree . . . being unable to get a Saddle Horse, I actually ventured on a gig . . . . I wish to God you could have seen me tooling in and out of the banners, drums, conservative Emblems, horsemen, and go-carts with which every little Green was filled as the processions were waiting for Sir John Tyrell and Baring. Every time the horse heard a drum he bounded into the hedge, on the left side of the road; and every time I got him out of that, he bounded into the hedge on the right side . . . .
> If any one were to ask me what in my opinion was the dullest and most stupid spot on the face of the Earth, I should decidedly say Chelmsford. . . . There is not even anything to look at in the place, except two immense prisons, large enough to hold all the Inhabitants of the county – whom they can have been built for I can't imagine . . .

Letter has been mounted in a cardboard frame. *Dexter Gift.*

H.10   A.L.s. to Thomas Beard, *3 pages, 4to, Wincanton Saturday Morng 2 May 1835,* describing how he and Unwin, a colleague on the *Morning Chronicle,* have gained the lead of the *Times* reporters in the race back to London with news of Lord John Russell's speech at Exeter, *addressed on fourth page* ("Thos Beard Esqre / Exeter / Favored by John Neilson Esqre"), *endorsed.*

> . . . I arrived here (57 miles from Exeter) at 8 yesterday evening having finished my whack at the previous stage. . . . I have now not the slightest doubt (God willing) of the success of our Express. On our first stage we had very poor horses; at the termination of the second, The Times and I changed Horses together; they had the start two or three minutes: I bribed the post boys tremendously & we came in literally neck and neck – the most beautiful sight I ever saw . . . .

For dating see Pilgrim Edition of the *Letters*, vol. 1, p. 58. *Dexter Gift.*

H.11   A.L.s. to Thomas Beard, *2 pages, 4to, Furnivals Inn Monday Morng* [*4 May 1835*], telling Beard that the *Morning Chronicle's* account of Lord John Russell's Exeter speech was the first to appear and was "*much much* longer . . . than any other paper", complaining of rheumatism and deafness as a result of the journey from Exeter, and asking after his bag (". . . For Heaven's sake, forward it immediately, for I have not a clean shirt to put on . . . "), *addressed on fourth page* ("Thomas Beard Esq. / New London Inn / Exeter"), *endorsed, postmarked 4 May 1835. Dexter Gift.*

H.12   A.L.s. to Thomas Beard, *1 page, 4to, Brompton, Saturday Morning* [*8 August 1835*], sending Beard "the proof we spoke of" and asking for its return "some day, as it belongs to Mr. Hogarth . . . ", *separate address leaf, endorsed, postmarked 8 August 1835. Dexter Gift.*

H.13   A.L.s. to Thomas Beard, *2 pages, 8vo, Furnival's Inn, Wednesday Morning* [*?14 October 1835*], asking for a loan and reporting that his fiancée and her mother are both ill with scarlet fever which is causing him "great distress of mind", *separate leaf, endorsed.*

> . . . . If you are in cash at present, and can lend me a couple of sovereigns until *Saturday Week*, you will oblige me very greatly . . . .

For dating see Pilgrim Edition of the *Letters*, vol. 1, p. 76. *Dexter Gift.*

H.14   A.L.s. to Thomas Beard, *1 page, 4to, 13 Furnivals Inn. Saturday Morning* [*?24 October 1835*], repaying a loan "with many thanks for your friendly readiness both on this and on a former occasion, when I had not an equally early opportunity of acknowledging it . . . ", *addressed on fourth page, endorsed.*

For dating see Pilgrim Edition of the *Letters*, vol. 1, p. 80. Letter mounted in a cardboard frame. *Dexter Gift.*

H.15   A.L.s. to Thomas Beard, *3 pages, 8vo, Furnivals Inn   Tuesday Afternoon* [*2 February 1836*], concerning a dispute over their conditions of employment as reporters on *The Morning Chronicle, separate address leaf, endorsed, postmarked 2 February 1836. Dexter Gift.*

H.16   A.L.s. to Chapman and Hall, *1 page, 8vo, Furnivals Inn Saturday* [*?6 August 1836*].

> . . . When you have quite done counting the sovereigns, received for Pickwick, I should be much obliged to you, to send me up a few . . . .

> . . . I see honorable mention of myself, and Mr. Pickwick's politics, in Fraser this month. They consider Mr. P. a decided Whig . . . .

For dating see Pilgrim Edition of the *Letters*, vol. 1, p. 161.

H.17   A.L.s. to John Leech, *2 pages, 4to, 15 Furnival's Inn. Wednesday Morning* [*?24 August 1836*], thanking Leech for his specimen illustration to *Pickwick Papers* and explaining that there is no possibility of Leech's being commissioned to illustrate the work, *integral address leaf* ("– Leech esq") *signed and inscribed by Dickens:* "*This gentleman will call*" *(underlined twice).*

For dating see Pilgrim Edition of the *Letters*, vol. 1, p. 168.

Furnivals Inn
Saturday

Of Sir —

When you have quite done
counting the Sovereigns received for
Pickwick, I should be much
obliged by you, to send me up a
few. I have lamed myself, and
am a Prisoner, or I should have
looked in myself. I hope Mr
Chapman is better.

I see honorable mention of
myself, and Mr. Pickwick's politics,
in Fraser this month. They
consider, Mr P a decided Whig.

Ever Yours faithfully
Charles Dickens

I suppose you know that a second
Edition of "Boz", is advertised.

H.16

H.18   A.L.s. to Thomas Beard, *1 page, 8vo, Petersham. Firiday Morning.* [*23 September 1836*], saying that he wishes Beard to accompany him to the first night of his play *(The Strange Gentleman)* at the St. James's Theatre and inviting him to dinner, *integral address leaf, endorsed, postmarked 23 September 1836.*

Letter mounted in a cardboard frame. *Dexter Gift.*

H.19   A.L.s. to George Cruikshank, *1 page, 8vo, Furnivals Inn. Monday Morning* [*?3 October 1836*], altering an appointment ("... I am so engaged with Pickwick...") and ending, "Macrone bid me ask you for the MS. if you have done with it...".

For dating see Pilgrim Edition of the *Letters,* vol. 1, p. 179.

H.20   A.L.s. to Thomas Beard, *1 page, 4to, 15 Furnivals Inn. Wednesday Morning* [*5 October 1836*], inviting Beard to dine ("... We shall all go to the Saint James's in the evening; and I hope you will join us...."), *integral leaf, endorsed, postmarked 5 October 1836.*

Letter mounted in a cardboard frame. *Dexter Gift.*

H.21   A.L. (subscription and signature cut away) to Thomas Beard, *1 page, 4to, Furnivals Inn Saturday Night* [*?15 October 1836*], enclosing tickets and asking Beard to dinner with "my old Editor Holland", *addressed on second page, endorsed.*

For dating see Pilgrim Edition of the *Letters,* vol. 1, p. 182. *Dexter Gift.*

H.22   A.L. (fragment only) to Thomas Beard, *1 page, 8vo, Furnivals Inn. Friday Morning* [*28 October 1836*], inviting Beard to call ("... I should like to have a chat and a glass of grog with you....") and mentioning his plans regarding his reporting work, *separate address leaf, endorsed, postmarked 28 October 1836.*

> ... I have not been able to bring that Sunday Times affair to bear :- I could not get enough, and I saw no reason for doing it *cheap.* As matters stand at present, there-fore, I think I shall exhibit in the Gallery next session – till Easter at all events, unless I see cause, good and sufficient, to change my mind, between this and then ....

Dexter Gift.

H.23   A.L.s. to Thomas Beard, *2 pages, 8vo, Furnivals Inn Wednesday Night* [*? December 1836*], inviting Beard to a turkey dinner and jocularly warning him not to rely on "our excellent friend Warburton" ("... I arrived home at one o clock this morning dead drunk, & was put to bed by my loving missis ..."), *addressed on fourth page, endorsed.*

For dating see Pilgrim Edition of the *Letters,* vol. 1, p. 217. *Dexter Gift.*

H.24   A.L.s. to Thomas Beard, *2 pages, 8vo, Furnival's Inn, Saturday Night* [*28 January 1837*], arranging a meeting and sending a copy of "the forthcoming Miscellany, with my glance at the new poor Law Bill ...", *endorsed, with the autograph envelope, signed.*

For dating see Pilgrim Edition of the *Letters,* vol. 1, p. 231.

H.25   A.L.s. to Chapman and Hall, *1 page, 8vo, Furnivals Inn. Tuesday Morning* [*? January 1837*], concerning the return of some magazines he has borrowed and ending, "Hard at work, at Pickwick", *integral address leaf.*

For dating see Pilgrim Edition of the *Letters,* vol. 1, p. 232.

H.26   A.L.s. to George Cruikshank, *2 pages, 4to, Furnival's Inn Wednesday Morning* [*?8 February 1837*], sending MS. of next chapter of *Oliver Twist* and suggesting a subject for illustration, *addressed on fourth page.*

For dating see Pilgrim Edition of the *Letters*, vol. 1, p. 234.

H.27   A.L.s. to Thomas Beard, *2 pages, 4to, Mrs. Nash's. Chalk. Near Gravesend. Wednesday Morning* [*22 February 1837*], inviting Beard to come down to Gravesend for a weekend (" . . . We can give you a bed, and shall feel much disappointed if you do not comply with our requisition . . . "), *integral address leaf, signed, postmarked 22 February 1837, endorsed.*

H.28   A.L.s. to Thomas Chapman, brother of Edward Chapman of Chapman & Hall, *1 page, 8vo, Furnivals Inn. Tuesday Morning* [*?March 1837*], refusing an invitation (" . . . I have solemnly pledged myself to Mrs. Dickens to-night . . . "). *1950 Gift.*

H.29   A.L. (subscription and signature cut away) to Thomas Beard, *1 page, 8vo, Upper Norton Street Thursday* [*30 March 1837*], informing Beard of the date fixed for the dinner given by Chapman & Hall to celebrate the success of *Pickwick Papers*, *integral address leaf signed and endorsed.*

For dating see Pilgrim Edition of the *Letters*, vol. 1, p. 244.

H.30   A.L.s. to Thomas Beard, *1 page, 8vo, 48 Doughty Street Wednesday Morning* [*?12 April 1837*], inviting Beard to dine and explaining why he could not see Edward Barrow (his uncle) when he called (" . . . I was sitting for my portrait to George Cruikshank . . . and George being a ticklish subject could not leave him . . . "), *integral address leaf, endorsed.*

For dating see Pilgrim Edition of the *Letters*, vol. 1, p. 248. *Dexter Gift.*

H.31   A.L.s. to George Cruikshank, *1 page, 8vo, 48 Doughty Street. Thursday Evening* [*?20 April 1837*], concerning *Bentley's Miscellany, integral address leaf signed and inscribed in Dickens's hand*, "WAIT"

> . . . Mr Bentley is here, and it is a matter of life and death to us, to know whether you have got Ainsworth's MS. yet. Oliver you shall have tomorrow . . . .

Various sketches and notes in Cruikshank's hand on the verso of this sheet (see J.12). For dating see Pilgrim Edition of the *Letters*, vol. 1, p. 249.

H.32   A.L.s. to George Cruikshank, *2 pages, 8vo, 48 Doughty Street Monday Morning* [*?24 April 1837*], enclosing corrected proofs of material to be published in *Bentley's Miscellany* and asking for the return of a portion of *Oliver Twist, endorsed.*

For dating see Pilgrim Edition of the *Letters*, vol. 1, p. 252.

H.33   A.L.s. to Thomas Beard, *4 pages, 8vo, Collins's Farm, North End Hampstead Wednesday Evening* [*17 May 1837*], concerning the death of Mary Hogarth (" . . . the very last words she whispered were of me . . . ") and his own and her family's grief (" . . . I am so shaken and unnerved . . . that I have been compelled to lay aside all thought of my usual monthly work, for once . . . "), *mourning paper, separate address leaf signed, postmarked 19 May 1837 (a Friday) and endorsed.*

H.34   A.L.s. to Thomas Beard *1 page, 4to, Doughty Street Friday Morning* [*?2 June 1837*], informing Beard that the christening of Charles Dickens Junior has had to be postponed and that Catherine Dickens has now recovered from the miscarriage brought on by her "grief and agitation" over Mary's death, *mourning paper, endorsed on fourth page.*

Letter has been mounted in a cardboard frame. *Dexter Gift.*

H.35   A.L.s. to Thomas Haines, reporter at the Mansion House police office, *2 pages, 4to, 48 Doughty St. – Mecklenburgh Square Saturday 3 June 1837,* asking for Haines's assistance in "smuggling" him into the Hatton Garden magistrate's office to study Mr. Laing as a model for a harsh and insolent magistrate to appear in *Oliver Twist, mourning paper, separate address leaf, signed.*

H.36   A.L. (subscription and signature cut away) to Mrs. George Hogarth, *3 pages, 8vo,* [*? June 1837*], concerning arrangements for meeting his wife's grandparents, Mr. and Mrs. Thomson and expressing anxiety about Mrs. Hogarth's health (" . . . I wish I could hear that you had been out to walk. You cannot think how much it would please me. It is really time you made the effort . . . "), *mourning paper.*

For dating see Pilgrim Edition of the *Letters,* vol. 1, p. 275. *1950 Gift.*

H.37   A.L.s. to Thomas Beard, *1 page, 8vo, Doughty Street. Friday Morning* [*21 July 1837*], enclosing a loan (" . . . and let me intreat you not to turn your thoughts to this small enclosure until you have devoted every ten pounds you have, to every demand that presses upon it . . . "), *mourning paper, endorsed, with the autograph envelope, signed and postmarked 21 July 1837. Dexter Gift.*

H.38   Autograph Document, *1 page, 4to, 26 July 1837,* rhymed postscript to a letter to Charles Hicks, foreman-printer of Bradbury and Evans, headed "To Mr. Hicks."

> Oh Mr. Hick
>   –S, I'm heartily sick
> Of this sixteenth Pickwick
> Which is just in the nick
>   For the publishing trick,
> And will read nice and slick,
>   If you'll only be quick.
>   I don't write on tick,
> That's my comfort, Avick!

For dating see Pilgrim Edition of the *Letters,* vol. 1, p. 287. The first two pages of this document, on which the letter was written, have been removed.

H.39   A.L.s. to George Beadnell, father of Maria Beadnell, *4 pages, 8vo, Doughty Street. Monday Evening* [*?Late July 1837*], explaining why he declines to incorporate into *Pickwick Papers* material sent to him by correspondents, *mourning paper.*

> . . . If I were in the slightest instance whatever, to adopt any information so communicated, however much I invented upon it, the World would be informed one of these days, – after my death, perhaps –, that I was not the sole author of the Pickwick Papers; that there were a great many other parties concerned; that a gentleman in the Fleet Prison perfectly well remembered stating in nearly the same words – &c &c &c. . . .

H.38

For dating see the Pilgrim Edition of the *Letters*, vol. 1, p. 289. In his 1934 Catalogue (vol. 2, p. 55) the Comte de Suzannet notes, "Cette lettre ainsi que les autres lettres à George Beadnell et à Mrs Winter, imprimées dans le présent catalogue, proviennent de la succession de Margaret Lloyd, la fille aînée de George Beadnell".

H.40 A.L.s. to Thomas Beard, *3 pages, 8vo, Doughty Street. Monday Morning* [*14 August 1837*], asking Beard to act as an intermediary in his dispute with the publisher Richard Bentley, *mourning paper, endorsed* "C. D. Doughty St. 1837 Dispute with Bentley", *with the autograph envelope, signed.*

For dating see Pilgrim Edition of the *Letters*, vol. 1, p. 295. *Dexter Gift.*

H.41 A.L.s. ("CD.") to Thomas Beard, *1 page, 4to, Wednesday Morng ½ p 11* [*16 August 1837*], concerning the quarrel with Bentley, *mourning paper, endorsed* "C D

'George Cruikshank', by Daniel Maclise (See H.43)

1836 This refers to a disputed agreement with Bentley about 'Barnaby Rudge' ", *addressed on verso of sheet.*

> . . . I have just received the inclosed. As I do not recollect one word in the agreement, for God's sake do nothing until they shew you the original with my signature . . . .

For dating see Pilgrim Edition of the *Letters*, vol. 1, p. 296. *Dexter Gift.*

H.42   A.L.s. to George Cruikshank, *2 pages, 8vo, Doughty Street Wednesday Night* [*30 August 1837*], informing Cruikshank that "There will be no Oliver Twist next month" and suggesting alternative subjects for Cruikshank to illustrate from material to be published in that number of *Bentley's Miscellany, mourning paper.*

For dating see the Pilgrim Edition of the *Letters*, vol. 1, p. 301.

H.43   A.L.s. to George Cruikshank, *1 page, 8vo, Doughty Street Friday Night* [*?13 October 1837*], sending some "slips" of *Oliver Twist* and suggesting "a very good subject at page 10, which we will call 'Oliver's reception by Fagin and the boys' ".

For dating see Pilgrim Edition of the *Letters*, vol. 1, p. 319.

H.44   A.L.s. to William Harrison Ainsworth, *3 pages, 4to, Doughty Street Monday 30 October* [*1837*], concerning Abraham Hayward and his review of Dickens in the *Quarterly*, Forster, and Ainsworth's "flattering and kind-hearted" mention of himself in the new Preface to *Rookwood, mourning paper, signature and address on fourth page, postmarked 31 October 1837.*

H.45   A.L.s. to Charles Hicks, *1 page, 8vo, Doughty Street Monday Evening* [*13 November 1837*], inviting Hicks to the dinner given by Chapman and Hall to celebrate the completion of *Pickwick Papers, mourning paper.*

Letter mounted in a cardboard frame. For dating see Pilgrim Edition of the *Letters*, vol. 1, p. 330.

H.46   A.L.s. to Thomas Beard, *1 page, 8vo, Doughty Street. Wednesday Morning* [*6 December 1837*], inviting Beard to the christening of Charles Dickens, Junior, *endorsed, with autograph envelope signed and postmarked 6 December 1837. Dexter Gift.*

H.47   A.L.s. to William Harrison Ainsworth, *3 pages, 8vo, Doughty Street, Monday Evening* [*11 December 1837*], sending Ainsworth a specially-bound complimentary copy of *Pickwick Papers, mourning paper.*

For dating see Pilgrim Edition of the *Letters*, vol. 1, p. 341.

H.48   A.L.s. to William Howison (of 2 Lothian Road, Edinburgh), *3 pages, 4to, 48 Doughty Street London Thursday 21 December 1837,* expressing his pleasure at learning of the institution of an "Edinburgh Pickwick Club", *signature and address on fourth page.*

> . . . my most cherished recollections are of a dearly loved friend and companion who drew her first breath in Edinburgh and died beside me . . . .
>
> . . . every hearty wish that I can muster for your long-continued welfare and prosperity, is freely yours. Mr. Pickwick's heart is among you always. . . .

H.49   A.L.s. to Chapman and Hall, *1 page, 8vo, Doughty Street. Wednesday Evening* [*? December 1837 | January 1838*], concerning some hostile notice of his work, *endorsed, integral address leaf.*

> . . . Don't get the attack; at least don't spend the twopence on my account. Forster has shewn it to me, and I am quite satisfied . . . .

Letter pasted into front of a copy of the first volume edition of *Pickwick Papers* (see A.4). Endorsed on page 4: "Refers to an attack on Pickwick in some Periodical – Forster is the Author of The Life of Eliot in Lardner's Cyclopedia. E.M.". Provisional dating suggested by Editors of the Pilgrim Edition of the *Letters* (to whom this letter was not known when they were preparing vol. 1).

H.50   A.L.s. to George Cruikshank, *1 page, 8vo,* [*? Mid-January 1838*], concerning an illustration for *Oliver Twist,* "Mr. Bumble and Mrs. Corney taking tea", *integral address leaf, signed.*

On the address leaf Cruikshank has drawn a small sketch of a man's head. For dating of this letter see Pilgrim Edition of the *Letters*, vol. 1, p. 353.

H.51   A.L.s. to William Harrison Ainsworth, *4 pages, 8vo, Doughty Street. Thursday Morning* [*25 January 1838*], inviting Ainsworth to dinner, mentioning a projected joint work on London, his own and Forster's literary labours, and difficulties between Macready and Talfourd over the latter's new play *(The Athenian Captive)*.

> . . . my month's work has been dreadful – Grimaldi, the anonymous book for Chapman and Hall, Oliver and the Miscellany. They are all done, thank God, and I start on my pilgrimage to the cheap schools of Yorkshire (a mighty secret of course) next Monday Morning . . . .
> . . . The Mogul is in the last agonies of procrastinated composition – hunted down by that prince of humbugs Lardner, baited by Longmans, and bullied by the Printers. He related dreadful and mysterious anecdotes of not having been in bed for a fortnight, and is reduced to such a fearful ebb of nervous exasperation that Mrs. Cooper has temporalily [*sic*] fled No. 58 and resigned her duties to a deputy who is under a course of violence . . . .

Letter presented to Mr. John Greaves by the Comtesse de Suzannet in 1966 and presented by him to The Dickens House in 1973. For dating see Pilgrim Edition of *The Letters*, vol. 1, p. 358.

H.52   A.L.s. to [Thomas Gaspey], journalist and novelist, *3 pages, 8vo, Doughty Street   Monday Morning* [*?29 January 1838*], concerning a contribution by Gaspey to *Bentley's Miscellany* (" . . . As you have long since ceased to be a 'colt' in the periodical paddock, you will not be surprised at my not having been able to find room in the next No. for that same paper . . . ."), *endorsed "Mr Charles Dickens – Boz."*

For dating and identification of Gaspey see Pilgrim Edition of the *Letters*, vol. 1, p. 363. *1950 Gift.*

H.53   A.L.s. to George William Lovell, dramatist, *3 pages, 8vo, 48 Doughty Street   Thursday Evening* [*?15 February 1838*], thanking Lovell for his "most kind exertions in Mrs Macrone's behalf" and asking for his contribution (to *The Pic-nic Papers*) "by the end of the first week in March", *with the autograph envelope, signed.*

For dating see the Pilgrim Edition of the *Letters*, vol. 1, p. 374.

H.54   A.L.s. to Thomas Beard, *1 page, 8vo, Doughty Street   Friday Evening* [*23 February 1838*], altering a dinner date (" . . . I have had a note from Bulwer begging me to dine with him next Sunday. As I have repeatedly disappointed him of late, I fear I must do so . . . ."), *endorsed and with autograph envelope, signed, and postmarked 24 February 1838.*

Letter and envelope have been mounted in a cardboard frame. *Dexter Gift.*

H.55   A.L.s. to Thomas Beard, *3 pages, 8vo, Twickenham Park   Tuesday Morning* [*12 June 1838*], inviting Beard to visit him and Catherine (" . . . the longer you stay, the better you will please us . . . "), *endorsed, with the autograph envelope, signed and postmarked 12 June 1838. Dexter Gift.*

H.56   A.L.s. to James Henry Leigh Hunt, *3 pages, 8vo, 48 Doughty Street   Friday Evening* [*?13 July 1838*], sending Hunt copies of "a portion of Oliver Twist", an American edition of *Pickwick Papers* and the first four numbers of *Nicholas Nickleby* (" . . . I have directed the publishers to send you all future numbers regularly . . . ").

> . . . If you can only find it in that green heart of yours to tell me one of these days that you have met, in wading through the accompanying trifles, with any thing that felt like a vibration of the old chord you have touched so often and sounded so well, you will confer the truest gratification on, My Dear Sir, / Your faithful friend / Charles Dickens.

H.57   A.L.s. to George Cruikshank, *1 page, 8vo, Doughty Street Saturday Morning* [*?6 October 1838*], concerning an illustration for *Oliver Twist*.

> . . . I find on writing it, that the scene of Sikes's escape will not do for illustration. It is so very complicated, with such a multitude of figures, such violent action, and torch-light to boot, that a small plate could not take in the slightest idea of it . . . .

For dating see Pilgrim Edition of the *Letters*, vol. 1, p. 440.

H.58   A.L.s. to the Hon. James Erskine Murray, author of *A Summer in the Pyrenees* (1837), *2 pages, 4to, 48 Doughty Street London 27 November 1838*, thanking Murray for his contribution to "Mrs Macrone's book" (*The Pic-Nic Papers*) and inviting him to contribute to *Bentley's Miscellany, integral address leaf, signed*.

H.59   A.L.s. to Mrs. Samuel Carter Hall, *4 pages, 8vo, Doughty Street 29 December 1838*, concerning the Yorkshire schools, particularly William Shaw's, and describing his visit to Bowes earlier in the year, the graveyard inscription that inspired him with the idea of Smike, etc.

> . . . Depend upon it that the rascalities of those Yorkshire schoolmasters *cannot* easily be exaggerated, and that I have kept down the strong truth and thrown as much comicality over it as I could, rather than disgust and weary the reader with its fouler aspects. . . .
>
> . . . the first grave-stone I stumbled on that dreary winter afternoon was placed above the grave of a boy, eighteen years old, who had died – suddenly, the inscription said; I suppose his heart broke – the Camel falls down 'suddenly' when they heap the last load on his back – died at that wretched place, I think his ghost put Smike into my head, upon the spot. . . .

Letter bound in a red morocco album, gilt, with calligraphic title-page and transcript and the following items: cutting of B. W. Matz's article on the letter, *The Dickensian*, September 1915; John Suddaby's "The Shaw Academy Trials", *The Dickensian*, October 1915; coloured postcard of "Kyd's" sketch of Squeers; various newspaper cuttings (*The Times, Pall Mall, Telegraph*) commenting on the discovery of the letter; Margaret Hunt's article on Bowes, *The Art Journal*, September 1887; Clement Shorter's "A Literary Letter: Wackford Squeers and Pecksniff", *The Sphere*, 16 October 1915.

H.60   A.L.s. to Samuel Laman Blanchard, poet and journalist, *3 pages, 8vo, 48 Doughty Street Saturday Morning 9 February* [*1839*], thanking Blanchard for a sight of "Mr. Colburn's letter", confirming that Colburn "is quite right in supposing that Barnaby Rudge has nothing to do with factories, or negroes – white, black or particoloured" and alluding to Colburn's method of advertising Mrs. Trollope's novel *Michael Armstrong, the Factory Boy*.

Letter mounted on card. For dating see Pilgrim Edition of the *Letters*, vol. 1, p. 506.

H.61   A.L.s to Thomas Beard, *2 pages, 8vo, Doughty Street, Wednesday Night* [*13 March 1839*], inviting him to dinner (". . . I haven't seen anything of you (except at the buttonless party) for time out of mind. . . ."), *endorsed, separate address leaf, signed and postmarked 14 March 1839. Dexter Gift.*

H.62   A.L.s. to William Harrison Ainsworth, *4 pages, 4to, Doughty Street. Tuesday*

George Taylor's gravestone in Bowes churchyard (See H.59)

Morning 26 March 1839, vehemently urging Ainsworth to exonerate Forster in Bentley's eyes from any charge of having caused mischief between Bentley and himself.

In crimson morocco slip-case, gilt, with typed transcript of the letter on the notepaper of Chas. J. Sawyer Ltd.

H.63   A.L.s. to Thomas Beard, *2 pages, 8vo, Doughty Street   Thursday Morning* [*11 April 1839*], altering a dinner date (" . . . I am in a manner obliged to dine with Lord Jeffrey next Sunday . . . "), *integral address leaf, endorsed, signed and postmarked 12 April 1839 (a Friday). Dexter Gift.*

H.64   A.L.s. to Thomas Beard, *1 page, 8vo, Petersham   Friday Morning* [*7 June 1839*], telling Beard to come down to Petersham at his own time and in his own way, to avoid mistakes, *with the autograph envelope signed and postmarked 7 June 1839.*

Letter and envelope have been mounted in a cardboard frame. *Dexter Gift.*

H.65   A.L.s. ("CD.") to Charles Hicks, *3 pages, 8vo, 40 Albion Street, Broadstairs. Sunday Morning (I mean afternoon)* [*15 September 1839*], sending copy for *Nicholas Nickleby* and arranging about proofs, *address on fourth page.*

For dating see Pilgrim Edition of the *Letters*, vol. 1, p. 580.

H.66   A.L.s. to Thomas Beard, *2 pages, 8vo, 40 Albion Street Broadstairs 21 September 1839*, informing Beard of the date of the Nickleby Dinner, *endorsed.*

> . . . I have been so hard as work here, and we are so delightfully situated in a bay-windowed house in front of the sea, that we don't return to town until Tuesday week . . .

H.67   A.L.s. to George Cattermole, *2 pages, 8vo, 40 Albion Street Broadstairs 21 September 1839*, inviting Cattermole to "make one at the little table" at the Nickleby Dinner on 5 October, *endorsed, presumably by Cattermole, on fourth page "Dickens. Nickleby Dinner".*

H.68   A.L.s. to Charles Hicks, *1 page, 8vo, 40 Albion Street Broadstairs 21 September 1839*, inviting Hicks to the Nickleby Dinner.

Letter mounted in a cardboard frame.

H.69   A.L.s. to Thomas Hill, bibliophile and patron of literature, *1 page, 8vo, 40 Albion Street Broadstairs. 21 September 1839*, inviting Hill to the Nickleby Dinner (" . . . I could not possibly dispense with your attendance . . . ").

Pasted on to fourth page is Cruikshank's illustration "Oliver asking for more".

H.70   A.L.s. to William Charles Macready, *2 pages, 4to, 40 Albion Street Broadstairs 21 September 1839*, asking permission to dedicate *Nicholas Nickleby* to Macready to show the world "that I was a friend of yours and interested to no ordinary extent in your proceedings at that interesting time when you showed them such noble truths in such noble forms . . . , " *integral address leaf signed and with an endorsement in Macready's hand.*

Letter bound in red morocco album, gilt, with calligraphic title-page and transcript of the letter, a specimen of Finden's engraving of Maclise's portrait of Dickens, a proof of the dedication page and the half-title, title-page and dedication page from a first edition of the novel. The typography and lay-out of the published title-page differ from the proof.

H.71   A.L.s. to Sir David Wilkie, *2 pages, 4to, 40 Albion Street Broadstairs 23 September 1839,* inviting Wilkie to the Nickleby Dinner on 5 October (" . . . I cannot tell you how happy I should be to see you, and how much true pleasure and delight your company will afford me . . . ") *integral address leaf, signed, with Ramsgate and London postmarks (23 and 24 September) and an endorsement.*

H.72   A.L.s. to George Cruikshank, *1 page, 8vo, Doughty Street Thursday Morning* [*?3 October 1839*], informing Cruikshank that the writing of *Nickleby* is finished (" . . . I am going tooth and nail at Barnaby, and shall have MS by the middle of the month for your exclusive eye . . . ").

For dating see Pilgrim Edition of the *Letters,* vol. 1, p. 589.

H.73   A.L.s. to Thomas Beard, *2 pages, 8vo, 1 Devonshire Terrace Tuesday Morning* [*17 December 1839*], inviting Beard to dine and alluding to his quarrel with Bentley (" . . . War to the knife and with no quarter on either side, has commenced with the Burlington Street Brigand . . . "), *endorsed, with the autograph envelope postmarked 18 December 1839. Dexter Gift.*

H.74   A.L.s. to Frederick Henry Yates, actor and manager of the Adelphi Theatre, *1 page, 8vo, 1 Devonshire Terrace Wednesday Afternoon* [*?15 January 1840*], asking for a box at the theatre that evening for himself and Forster.

For dating see Pilgrim Edition of the *Letters,* vol. 2, p. 10. *1950 Gift.*

H.75   A.L.s. to Richard Henry (or Hengist) Horne, poet and journalist, *2 pages, 16mo, At Forster's Saturday Night* [*?February 1840*], expressing his indignation at having been accused "by some jolter-headed enemies" of having written in *Oliver Twist* "a book after Mr. Ainsworth's fashion" and regretting that he cannot, for reasons of delicacy connected with this charge, sign a petition (against the monopoly of the Patent Theatres) drawn up by Horne.

For dating see Pilgrim Edition of the *Letters,* vol. 2, p. 20.

H.76   A.L.s. to Thomas Beard, *1 page, 8vo, 1 Devonshire Terrace, Wednesday 1 July* [*1840*], inviting Beard to dine, *endorsed with the autograph envelope signed and postmarked 1 July 1840.*

H.77   A.L.s. to Henry Colburn, publisher, *2 pages, 8vo, Devonshire Terrace Wednesday 19 August* [*1840*], urging Colburn to expedite the publication of *The Pic-Nic Papers* for the benefit of Mrs. Macrone and her "fatherless children" (" . . . For God's sake do not delay it beyond November . . . ").

For dating see Pilgrim Edition of the *Letters,* vol. 2, p. 118.

H.78   A.L.s. to Chapman and Hall, *1 page, 8vo, Broadstairs. Friday 2 October 1840,* sending "eleven slips of MS [of *The Old Curiosity Shop*]", complaining of some facial trouble (" . . . whether rheumatism, tic doloreux or what not Heaven knows . . . ") and signing himself "Yours inflammatorily and despondingly" with a postscript stating "I haven't the heart to flourish".

Letter in crimson cardboard folder, gilt.

H.79   A.L.s. to George Cruikshank, *1 page, 8vo, 1 Devonshire Terrace   Tuesday 17 November [1840]*, announcing his intention of calling on Cruikshank "about Mrs Macrone's book".

For dating see Pilgrim Edition of the *Letters*, vol. 2, p. 151.

H.80   A.L.s. to Thomas Beard ("or Miss Beard"), *1 page, 8vo, Devonshire Terrace 21 January 1841*, inviting Beard and his sister to dinner, *with the autograph envelope, signed and inscribed, in Dickens's hand*, "Wait". *Dexter Gift.*

H.81   A.L.s. to Thomas Beard, *2 pages, 8vo, Devonshire Terrace. Saturday Night 23 January 1841*, postponing the dinner arranged in the preceding letter on account of Catherine Dickens's sudden indisposition, *endorsed and with the autograph letter, signed. Dexter Gift.*

H.82   A.L.s. to [?Edward Chapman), *1 page, 8vo, Devonshire Terrace. Wednesday 10 March 1841*, thanking him for pointing out an anachronism in *Barnaby Rudge*.

For tentative identification of correspondent see Pilgrim Edition of the *Letters*, vol. 2, p. 228. *1950 Gift.*

H.83   A.L.s. to Thomas Beard, *1 page 8vo, Devonshire Terrace. 2 June 1841*, telling Beard that he feels he ought not to attend "the Newspaper Dinner" but should work that evening instead (". . . I have much to do before going to Edinburgh . . . "), *endorsed, with the autograph letter, signed. Dexter Gift.*

H.84   A.L.s. ("Boz" to Thomas Beard, *1 page, 8vo, Devonshire Terrace Sunday 25 July 1841*, announcing his imminent departure for Broadstairs (" . . . You have not changed your mind, I hope, in respect of your weekly visits, dips and airings? . . . "), *endorsed, with the autograph envelope, signed and inscribed, in Dickens's hand* "Free". *Dexter Gift.*

H.85   A.L.s. to Thomas Beard, *2 pages, 8vo, Broadstairs 2 August 1841*, giving Beard instructions for the journey by boat from London to Broadstairs, *endorsed with the autograph envelope, signed and stamped. Dexter Gift.*

H.86   L.s. (the whole, including the signature, in the hand of Catherine Dickens) to Thomas Beard, *2 pages, 8vo, 1 Devonshire Terrace   Tuesday Morning [12 October 1841]*, telling Beard that he has been very ill and has had to undergo "a cruel operation, and the cutting out root and branch of a disease caused by working over much which has been gathering it seems for years . . . ", *endorsed, with the autograph envelope, also in Catherine Dickens's hand and marked* "Free". *Dexter Gift.*

H.87   A.L.s. ("CD.") to George Hogarth, *1 page, 8vo, Devonshire Terrace. 23 December 1841*, altering an appointment.

Letter endorsed on back: Phillips MS. 36460 (2). *1950 Gift.*

H.88   A.L.s. to Daniel Maclise, *3 pages, 4to, Adelphi Hotel Liverpool Monday 2 January 1842*, expressing his strong affection for Maclise and giving an amusing description of the smallness of the Dickenses' cabin on board the ss. Britannia (". . . It is more like one of those cabs where you get in at the back: but I think you could put on a shirt in one of those: and you certainly couldn't in this chamber . . . "), *signature and address on fourth page, postmarked 4 January 1842 (date of receipt in London)*.

A lengthy postscript to this letter has been added by Forster (see J.40).

The New York 'Boz Ball' (See H.89)

H.89   A.L.s ("CD.") to Daniel Maclise, *2 pages, 4to, Carlton House, New York 27 February 1842*, expressing his distrust and detestation of Transatlantic steam-ships, mentioning the "Boz Ball" given in his honour in New York on 18 February (" . . . the most splendid, gorgeous brilliant affair you . . . can possibly conceive . . . ") and emphasising his fatigue and intense homesickness, *addressed and signed on fourth page with, in Dickens's hand, the direction "By Packet Ship 'Garrick' from N. York", stamp of the Carlton House, Broadway, postmarked 20 March (Liverpool) and 21 March (London).*

On the bottom of p. 2 and on p. 3 Dickens has pasted cuttings from a New York newspaper describing the "Boz Ball", the refreshments, room-decorations, etc., and another newspaper cutting purporting to be a portrait of his wife, underneath which he has written seven exclamation marks and the words, "All this information is exclusive".

H.90   A.L.s. to Daniel Maclise, *2 pages, 4to, Baltimore, 22 March 1842*, facetiously denouncing Royal Academicians in general and Martin Archer Shee in particular, describing his travels (" . . . the railroads go through the low grounds and swamps, and it is all one eternal forest . . . ") and complaining of the fatigue of being constantly fêted and of the impertinent lengths to which the Americans go to gratify their curiosity about him, *signed and addressed on fourth page.*

Page 3 is occupied by a letter from Catherine Dickens (see J.16).

H.91 A.L.s. to Thomas Beard, *3 pages, 8vo, Devonshire Terrace. 11 July 1842,* concerning the engineering career of his brother, Alfred, whom Beard may have an opportunity of assisting, and mentioning the eccentricities of Cruikshank, *endorsed and with the autograph envelope, signed and postmarked.*

> . . . You are acquainted with the business that kept my away from the Chronicle last Saturday. George Cruikshank came home in my phaeton, on his head – to the great delight of the loose Midnight Loungers in Regent Street. He was last seen, taking Gin with a Waterman . . . .

Dexter Gift.

H.92 A.L.s. to Thomas Beard, *2 pages, 8vo, Devonshire Terrace. 19 July 1842,* inviting Beard to dinner and to hear "the Falstaffic F" read "our passage out, which I have just finished writing", *endorsed, and with the autograph envelope, signed. Dexter Gift.*

H.93 A.L.s. to Thomas Beard, *2 pages, 8vo, Devonshire Terrace. 21 July 1842,* postponing the dinner suggested in previous letter, *endorsed and with the autograph envelope, signed.*

> . . . I have consulted Mr. Groves of Charing Cross. His suggestive mind gave birth to this remarkable expression – "then why not consider this here breast o' wenson off – and let me git another prime 'un in good eatin' order for you, for Sunday week? What" – continued Mr Groves – "is the hodds to a day?" . . . .

Dexter Gift.

H.94 A.L.s. to Thomas Beard, *2 pages, 8vo, Broadstairs. Thursday 4 August 1842,* thanking Beard for his "thoughtfulness and consideration in the matter of Alfred" and pressing him to take a month's holiday at Broadstairs (" . . . This place is most beautiful just now . . ."), *endorsed and with the autograph envelope, signed, stamped and postmarked. Dexter Gift.*

H.95 A.L.s. to Thomas Beard, *1 page, 8vo, Broadstairs Thursday 8 September 1842,* cataloguing the delights of Broadstairs and expressing impatience for Beard's visit, *endorsed, and with the autograph envelope, signed and stamped. Dexter Gift.*

H.96 A.L.s. to Thomas Beard, *1 page, 8vo, Devonshire Terrace Saturday 5 November [1842],* inviting him to dinner (" . . . there is a Leg of delicate Welsh Mutton in the Pantry . . . which deserves attention . . . "), *endorsed, and with the autograph envelope, signed. Dexter Gift.*

H.97 A.L.s. to Thomas Beard, *2 pages, 8vo, Devonshire Terrace 15 November 1842,* explaining that he cannot help to secure a post for someone recommended to him via Beard by W. G. Greenhill because his "sympathy and interest" have already been enlisted "in behalf of a niece of Miss Edgeworth" and reporting that he is working at his new book "like a brick" (" . . . I don't know why it is, but that popular simile *seems* a good one . . . "), *endorsed, and with the autograph envelope, signed, stamped and postmarked.*

With the letter is the letter from Greenhill to Beard that the latter forwarded to Dickens (see J.46).

'The Girl at the Waterfall', by Maclise *(Courtesy of the Victoria and Albert Museum)* (See H.99)

H.98   A.L.s. to Thomas Beard, *1 page, 8vo, Devonshire Terrace 18 November 1842*, postponing a projected "Prison Trip", *endorsed, and with the autograph envelope, signed, stamped and postmarked. Dexter Gift.*

H.99   A.L.s. ("CD.") to Thomas Beard, *4 pages, 8vo, n.p., Sunday 18 December* [*1842*], asking Beard to help him in a "pious fraud" whereby he can purchase from Maclise a picture that Maclise is painting of a girl at a waterfall without the painter's suspecting who the purchaser is, *endorsed, and with the autograph envelope, signed and inscribed, in Dickens's hand,* "Wait". (Georgina Hogarth posed for this painting.)

> . . . I know very well that if I were to say [that I wanted the painting], he would either insist upon giving it to me, or would set some preposterous price upon it, which he can by no means afford to take . . . .

With the letter is Beard's shorthand draft of his letter to Maclise about this matter (see J.5). *Dexter Gift.*

H.100   A.L.s. ("CD.") to Thomas Beard, *1 page, 8vo, Devonshire Terrace 22 December 1842*, inviting him to dinner to meet a gentleman from Quebec, *endorsed, and with the autograph envelope, signed and stamped. Dexter Gift.*

H.101   A.L.s. to William Makepeace Thackeray, *1 page, 8vo, Devonshire Terrace 26 January 1843*, reminding Thackeray of a dinner engagement with him.

H.102   A.L.s. to Ebenezer Johnstone, *3 pages, 8vo, Devonshire Terrace 15 February 1843*, saying that Catherine Dickens is still too unwell to go out visiting and that he himself is "in agonies peculiar to February – a month which, by reason of its shortness, ought to be blotted out of the almanacks . . . ". *1950 Gift.*

H.103   A.L.s. to Thomas Beard, *1 page, 8vo, Devonshire Terrace 13 March 1843*, sending Beard "the unforgotten Drury Lane order", *endorsed, and with the autograph envelope, signed and stamped. Dexter Gift.*

H.104   A.L.s. to Thomas Beard, *4 pages, 8vo, Devonshire Terrace 21 March 1843*, amusingly reporting the failure of his dog, Timber, when taken to mate with a bitch belonging to "a Finchley Postman", *endorsed, and with the autograph envelope, signed and stamped.*

> . . . He was absent one hour and a half.
> He returned covered with disgrace and mortification. He had done *nothing*. The official report was, that he had tried, but was considered to be weak in the loins. . . .

Dexter Gift.

H.105   A.L.s. ("CD.") to Thomas Beard, *1 page, 8vo, Finchley Friday 31 March 1843*, inviting Beard to a "wedding feast at Richmond" (the seventh anniversary of his marriage) with a postscript concerning his dog ("I am happy to report that Timber runs into a corner and stands on 2 legs, at the word of command"), *endorsed.*

Letter mounted in a cardboard frame. *Dexter Gift.*

H.106   A.L.s. to John Pritt Harley, actor, *1 page, 8vo, Devonshire Terrace 6 April 1843*, thanking Harley for consulting him "in the matter of our friend's note."

> . . . He must be rather a rum customer, I take it, for he *had* written to me before, forwarding a book of Poems (?) of his writing: the which I graciously acknowledged. Therefore I should have thought he needed no other Introduction . . .

1950 Gift.

H.107   A.L.s. ("CD.") to Thomas Beard, *1 page, 8vo, Devonshire Terrace 7 April 1843*, suggesting a dinner in town the following day, *endorsed. Dexter Gift.*

H.108   A.L.s. to Frederick Wilkinson, *1 page, 8vo, London 1 Devonshire Terrace York Gate Regents Park 30 June 1843*, apologising for misreading a note from Wilkinson (" . . . I am quite as much obliged by your polite communication as if you had offered me a Hundred Translations . . . . "). *1950 Gift.*

H.109   A.L.s. ("CD.") to Thomas Beard, *4 pages, 8vo, Devonshire Terrace 18 July 1843*, urging Beard, apparently convalescent, to come and spend "eight undisturbed weeks" with the Dickenses at Broadstairs and explaining the difficulty of entering into arrangements with Mr Blackburn about the sale of his books in India, *endorsed and with the autograph envelope, signed, stamped and postmarked.*

> . . . The bedroom you had last year is ready for you. The bathing machine beckons its wooden finger, and cocks its preposterous eye on the sands. The tide rushes in, demanding to be breasted. Dick is all joviality, and very brown in the face from northern toasting . . . Forster asserts with dignified emphasis that "it is the very sort of thing, my dear boy, that Beard requires to set him on his legs." . . .

Beard's London address has been crossed out on the envelope and the letter redirected to Lewes, Sussex. With the letter is a letter from Blackburn to Beard (see J.6). *Dexter Gift.*

H.110   A.L. (in the third person) to Margaret Gillies, painter, *1 page, 8vo, Devonshire Terrace 21 July 1843,* making an appointment for a sitting.

Letter mounted in a cardboard frame. *1950 Gift.*

H.111   A.L.s. to Thomas Mitton, Dickens's solicitor, *4 pages, 8vo, Broadstairs 28 September 1843,* complaining bitterly of his father from whom he has received a "threatening letter" and discussing the possibility of employing his brother Alfred as his secretary.

> . . . I am amazed and confounded by the audacity of his [John Dickens's] ingratitude. He, and all of them, look upon me as a something to be plucked and torn to pieces for their advantage . . . .

H.112   A.L.s. to Mrs. David Laing, wife of the chaplain to the Middlesex Hospital, *2 pages, 8vo, 1 Devonshire Terrace. 2 February 1844,* agreeing to attend a dinner given in aid of the Governesses' Benevolent Institution and expressing his appreciation of Mr. Laing's work as founder of the Institution, *with the autograph envelope, signed.*

For the text of Dickens's speech at the dinner see *The Speeches of Charles Dickens,* ed. K. J. Fielding, 1960, pp. 65-67. (The date of Dickens's letter to Mrs. Laing is here erroneously given as 1 February 1844.) *1950 Gift.*

H.113   A.L.s. to Thomas Beard, *3 pages, 8vo, Devonshire Terrace 14 February 1844,* explaining his reluctance to introduce a friend of Beard's to Chapman and Hall for the purpose of obtaining translation work (" . . . I am in this difficulty, that I have recently stood in relations towards Chapman and Hall, which are not perfectly agreeable . . . "), *endorsed, and with the autograph envelope, signed, stamped and postmarked. Dexter Gift.*

H.114   A.L.s. ("CD.") to Daniel Maclise, *3 pages, 8vo, Devonshire Terrace 2 March 1844,* sending a Liverpool newspaper and promising to "add the munificent gift of a Birmingham paper", with a postscript consisting of a copy of the verses written by Dickens in Christiana Weller's album ("I put in a book, once, by hook and by crook / The whole race (as I thought) of a 'feller,' / Who happily pleas'd the town's taste, much diseas'd / – And the name of this person was Weller . . . ").

H.115   A.L.s. to Thomas Beard, *2 pages, 8vo, 9 Osnaburgh Terrace, 10 June 1844,* expressing his great satisfaction with the report of a charity dinner on behalf of the

Sanatorium in the *Morning Herald,* mentioning two concerts to be given by Christiana Weller, and inviting Beard to dinner, *endorsed and with the autograph envelope, stamped. Dexter Gift.*

H.116   A.L.s. to Thomas Beard, *1 page, 8vo, Osnaburgh Terrace. Friday [28 June 1844],* informing Beard that "Sunday's dinner is transferred to Forster's", *endorsed, with the autograph envelope signed and postmarked 28 June 1844.*

On the flap of the envelope Dickens has written, "It is particularly requested that if Sir James Graham should open this he will not trouble himself to seal it again." Letter and envelope mounted in a cardboard frame. *Dexter Gift.*

H.117   A.L.s. to Charles Black, a relation by marriage of George Cattermole's, *2 pages, sm. 8vo, Hotel Meloni [Rome] Friday Evening 10 o'clock [February/March 1845],* making arrangements for a pleasure trip to a lake the following day. *1950 Gift.*

H.118   A.L.s. to Frederick Oldfield Ward, sub-editor of *Hood's Magazine, 1 page, 8vo, Devonshire Terrace Saturday 12 July 1845,* giving permission for his name to be used as a Member of the Committee of the Hood Fund, *endorsed. 1950 Gift.*

H.119   A.L.s. to Thomas Beard, *2 pages, 8vo, Devonshire Terrace 6 August 1845,* enquiring about the expenses of the Foreign Department of the *Morning Herald* and the *Morning Chronicle, endorsed. Dexter Gift.*

H.120   A.L.s. to George Cruikshank, *1 page, 8vo, Devonshire Terrace 13 August 1845,* regretting that he cannot at present assist a friend of Cruikshank's who is suffering misfortune, and hoping that he will see Cruikshank at Margate the following week. *1950 Gift.*

H.121   A.L.s. to Thomas Beard, *1 page, 8vo, Devonshire Terrace. Monday 12 October 1845,* saying that he has a "confidential question" to ask Beard that may "rather amaze" him, *endorsed, and with the autograph envelope signed.*

12 October 1845 was a Sunday so this letter was probably written on 13 October. *Dexter Gift.*

H.122   A.L.s. to Thomas Beard, *3 pages, 8vo, Devonshire Terrace. Thursday 4 September 1845,* introducing to Beard Sydney Blanchard, son of Samuel Laman Blanchard, who is seeking a reporting job in the *Morning Herald, endorsed, and with the autograph envelope, signed.*

With the letter is a letter to Beard from Douglas Jerrold, also recommending Blanchard for an engagement (see J.52), *Dexter Gift.*

H.123   A.L.s. to J. Montgomery, *2 pages, 8vo, London. 1 Devonshire Terrace York Gate Regents Park 28 August 1845,* regretting that "special reasons for anxiety at home" prevent him from visiting Sheffield after going to Manchester, *with the autograph envelope, signed, London and Sheffield postmarks. 1950 Gift.*

H.124   A.L.s. ("CD.") to Thomas Beard, *1 page, 8vo, Devonshire Terrace. 20 October 1845,* arranging a dinner at the Parthenon (" . . . Kate being in a state of tribulation . . . ") *endorsed, and with the autograph envelope, signed and postmarked. Dexter Gift.*

H.125   A.L.s. to Thomas Beard, *3 pages, 8vo, Devonshire Terrace Sunday Night* [*26 October 1845*], asking Beard (addressed as "My Dear Master Beard") about the *Morning Herald's* arrangements regarding certain foreign correspondents, mentioning his wife's pregnancy (". . . I call her Joanna Southcote . . . ") and preparations for a forthcoming charity performance of *Every Man in his Humour* by The Amateur Players (". . . Forster is already getting deep dents in his nose by reason of the workings of the coming Kitely . . . "), *endorsed and with the autograph envelope, signed, stamped and postmarked 27 October 1845. Dexter Gift.*

H.126   A.L.s. to Thomas Beard, *2 pages, 8vo, Devonshire Terrace Friday Night* [*31 October 1845*], postponing a dinner (". . . On five minutes notice, I am obliged to go into Derbyshire . . . "), *endorsed, and with the autograph envelope, signed.*

The Comte de Suzannet notes in his catalogue (vol. 2, p. 159), "Cette lettre a dû être écrite par Dickens le 31 octobre 1845, trois jours après la naissance de son fils Alfred." *Dexter Gift.*

H.127   A.L.s ("CD.") to Thomas Beard, *1 page, 8vo, Devonshire Terrace Saturday,* [*8 November 1845*], asking Beard's opinion about the appropriate remuneration for a journalist taken from the *Morning Chronicle, endorsed and with the autograph envelope, signed, marked "Prepaid" and postmarked 8 November 1845. Dexter Gift.*

H.128   A.L.s. ("CD.") to "Bardolph" *viz.* Thomas Beard, *3 pages, 8vo, 90 Fleet Street. New Year's Day 1846,* sending him a ticket for the performance of *The Elder Brother* by the Amateur Players on 3 January, *separate address leaf marked "Private", endorsed.*

> . . . When I am bullied through those Four Acts, always regard me as being ready (in serious earnest) to stab Forster to the heart. It makes me so damned savage that I could rend him limb from limb . . . .

Dexter Gift.

Forster acting in *The Elder Brother*, sketched by Clarkson Stanfield (See H.128)

H.129   A.L.s. ("CD.") to Thomas Beard, *2 pages, 8vo, 90 Fleet Street 9 January 1846,* introducing his secretary, Wills, who is conveying a "business enquiry" from him to Beard, *endorsed and with the autograph envelope, marked* "Private" *and signed. Dexter Gift.*

H.130   A.L.s. ("CD.") to Thomas Beard, *2 pages, 8vo, 90 Fleet Street Monday Morning* [*January 1846*], explaining that the only connection between *Punch* and the *Daily News* is that Douglas Jerrold is engaged to work for both publications, *endorsed, and with the autograph envelope (marked* "Private" *in Dickens's hand).*

The Comte de Suzannet notes in his catalogue (vol. 2, p. 165), "Cette lettre a dû être écrite dans les premiers jours de janvier 1846". *Dexter Gift.*

H.131   A.L.s. ("CD.") to Thomas Beard, *1 page, 8vo, Offices of the Daily News Whitefriars Saturday Evening* [*January 1846*], informing Beard that he has "altered the plan very much and made it one that is more likely, I think, to suit you" and asking him to call at Devonshire Terrace before seeing his "Governor" (presumably, Edward Baldwin, proprietor the *Morning Herald), with the autograph envelope, signed and inscribed, in Dickens's hand,* "Wait". *Dexter Gift.*

H.132   A.L.s. to Thomas Beard, *3 pages, 8vo, Offices of the Daily News Whitefriars 16 January 1846,* informing Beard of the *Daily News's* plan to commission a special train to bring its reporters from Norwich with their account of a Free Trade meeting there (" . . . I don't think we should do this, but for a preliminary splash . . . "), *with the autograph envelope, signed. Dexter Gift.*

H.133   A.L.s. ("CD.") to Thomas Beard, *2 pages, 8vo, Offices of the Daily News Whitefriars Saturday Afternoon* [*17 January 1846*], outlining the *Daily News's* plans for getting reports of Peel's speech rapidly to every part of the country and enquiring whether the *Morning Chronicle* would be interested in joining in these plans, *endorsed, with the autograph envelope, signed and inscribed by Dickens* "Immediate".

Parliament reassembled, in an excited atmosphere, on 19 January 1846. It was strongly rumoured that Peel, the Prime Minister, would recommend the repeal of the Corn Laws, a measure vigorously supported by the new-born *Daily News*. Peel began outlining his revolutionary proposals in his speech (opening the debate on the Queen's Speech) on 22 January.

Letter and envelope mounted in a cardboard frame. *Dexter Gift.*

H.134   A.L.s. ("CD.") to Thomas Beard, *1 page, 8vo, Devonshire Terrace Thursday* [*22 January 1846*], concerning the second issue of the *Daily News, endorsed* "C.D. 1846. The Daily News just started".

> . . . I am delighted to say we have a capital paper today. I sat at the stone, and made it up with my own hands.

The first issue of the *News* appeared on Wednesday 21 January and it was, the Comte de Suzannet notes in his 1934 catalogue (vol. 2, p. 169) "très mal executée". *Dexter Gift.*

H.135   A.L.s. ("CD.") to Thomas Beard, *1 page, 8vo, Whitefriars* [*January 1846*], regretting that he has missed seeing Beard (" . . . I had the Leader-Writing Men here, and could not get rid of them . . . ''), *endorsed, and with the autograph envelope signed and inscribed, in Dickens's hand* ''Wait''. *Dexter Gift.*

H.136   A.L.s (''CD.'') to Thomas Beard, *1 page, 4to, D.N. Office Sunday Night* [*January 1846*], concerning the *Daily News* and its co-operation regarding Expresses with the *Morning Herald* ('' . . . by our influence at Birkinhead we detained the Irish Mail *one hour* . . . ''), *separate address leaf, endorsed, signed and marked in Dickens's hand* ''Delivery''. *Dexter Gift.*

H.137   A.L.s. (''CD.'') to Thomas Beard, *1 page, 8vo, Offices of the Daily News Whitefriars Thursday Night* [*January 1846*], jocular note concerning *News* business ('' . . . Think of OUR having a Bombay Times from our Alexandrian agent – posted at Kennington Cross too! . . . ''), *endorsed and with the autograph envelope, signed and inscribed, in Dickens's hand,* ''Deliver''. *Dexter Gift.*

H.138   A.L.s. to Thomas Beard, *1 page, 8vo, Offices of the Daily News Whitefriars Monday Afternoon 2 February 1846*, informing Beard that the *News* intends ''expressing the whole Corn Law Debate down the Great Northern Railways'' and asking if the *Herald* would wish to share in this, *endorsed and with the autograph envelope, signed. Dexter Gift.*

H.139   A.L. (subscription and signature cut away) to Professor John Wilson [''Christopher North'' of *Blackwood's Magazine*], *2 pages, 8vo, London. 1 Devonshire Terrace York Gate Regents Park Friday 27 February 1846*, recalling the great pleasure he derived from becoming acquainted with Wilson ''three and a half years ago'' and introducing Macready ''one of my dearest and most cherished friends''. *1950 Gift.*

H.140   A.L.s. to Thomas Beard, *1 page, 8vo, Devonshire Terrace Thursday 5 March 1846*, asking Beard to call on him the following day or on Saturday, *endorsed, and with the autograph envelope, signed and postmarked. Dexter Gift.*

H.141   A.L.s. to Thomas Beard, *1 page, 8vo, Devonshire Terrace Saturday 11 April 1846*, concerning a meeting of the proprietors of the *Daily News, endorsed, and with autograph envelope, signed and postmarked.*

> . . . Forster attended the last meeting, which lasted *six hours*. Some of the dissenters,
> I believe, fell prostrate on the floor, and foamed at the mouth with exhaustion . . .

Dexter Gift.

H.142   A.L.s. (''CD.'') to Thomas Beard, *1 page, 8vo, Devonshire Terrace Wednesday 22 April 1846*, telling Beard that he must alter an appointment, *endorsed, and with the autograph envelope, signed and postmarked. Dexter Gift.*

H.143   A.L.s. to Thomas Beard, *2 pages, 8vo, Devonshire Terrace. Friday Morning* [*24 April 1846*], inviting Beard to dinner and asking for an opinion of a horse that he is considering buying, *endorsed, and with the autograph envelope inscribed, in Dickens's hand,* ''Wait''.

The Comte de Suzannet notes in his catalogue (vol. 2, p. 176), ''Cette lettre a été écrite le 24 avril 1846'' but does not give his evidence for this date. *Dexter Gift.*

ROSEMONT VILLA

Rosemont Villa, Lausanne (See H.146)

H.144 A.L.s. ("CD.") to Thomas Beard, *1 page 8vo, Devonshire Terrace Saturday 25 April [1846]*, a covering note sent to Beard with the horse mentioned in the previous letter, *endorsed and with the autograph envelope, signed and inscribed, in Dickens's hand*, "with a quadruped". *Dexter Gift.*

H.145 A.L.s. ("CD.") to Thomas Beard, *1 page, 8vo, Devonshire Terrace Friday [22 May 1846]*, cancelling "that Derby engagement" because of pressure of other commitments, *endorsed and with the autograph envelope, signed and postmarked 22 May 1846.*

Dexter Gift.

H.146 A.L.s. to Daniel Maclise, *1 page, 4to, Hotel Gibbon, Lausanne Switzerland Sunday Night 14 June 1846*, describing the villa he has hired at Lausanne (" . . . a kind of beautiful bandbox . . . ") and "a little fête, in honor of the Republican Independence of this Canton" that he has enjoyed attending that day. *Addressed on verso of sheet, postmarked.*

H.147 Autograph memorandum to Hablot K. Browne ("Phiz"), *1 page, 4to [Paris, December 1846]*, giving very detailed instructions for the design of one of the plates to appear in the fourth monthly number of *Dombey and Son* and supplying title for this illustration, "Doctor Blimber's young gentlemen as they appeared when enjoying themselves".

The number of *Dombey* containing this illustration was published in January 1847.

H.148 A.L.s. to [Messrs. Coutts and Co.], *1 page, 8vo, 48 Rue de Courcelles, Paris 3 February 1847*, acknowledging receipt of circular notes and saying he will write for a letter of credit when he knows how much money he will require in Paris. *1950 Gift.*

Major Bagstock is delighted to have that opportunity.

H.149

H.149   A.L. to Hablot K. Browne ("Phiz"), *1 page, 4to, 1 Chester Place, Regent's Park 10 March 1847,* giving detailed instructions for one of the plates to appear in the seventh monthly number of *Dombey and Son* ("Major Bagstock is delighted to have that opportunity").

> . . . The Major presents them [Mrs. Skewton and Edith] to Mr. Dombey, gloating within himself over what may come of it, and over the discomfiture of Miss Tox. Mr. Dombey (in deep mourning) bows solemnly. Daughter bends. The Native in attendance, bearing a camp-stool and the Major's greatcoat. Native evidently afraid of the Major and his thick cane.

If you like it better, the scene may be in the street or in a green lane. But a great deal will come of it; and I want the Major to express that, as much as possible, in his apoplectic Mephistophilean observation of the scene, and in his share in it . . . .

H.150   A.L.s. ("CD.") to Hablot K. Browne ("Phiz"), *1 page, 4to, 1 Chester Place Monday Night 15 March 1847,* commenting on Browne's sketch for the illustration requested in the preceding letter, *addressed and signed on verso of sheet, inscribed, in Dickens's hand,* "Immediate".

H.151   A.L. (in the third person) to Percy Boyd (30 South Frederick Street Dublin), *1 page, 8vo, Devonshire Terrace, London 18 March 1847,* thanking Boyd for his "most obliging and welcome note, and the flattering tribute sent with it" and explaining that he has been abroad for a long time, to account for his belatedness in writing, *with the autograph envelope, postmarked 19 and 20 March 1847.*

With the letter is a forged version endorsed in pencil on p. 4, "Forgery. Arthur Rogers 4 Eldon Place Newcastle". See Humphry House, "A Dickens Letter: a copy or a forgery?", *The Dickensian,* xlix, March 1953, pp. 69–73. *1950 Gift.*

H.152   A.L.s. ("CD.") to Thomas Beard, *2 pages, 8vo, 1 Chester Place, Regents Park 22 March 1847,* inviting him to dine with John Henry Barrow and commenting on the *Times's* literary critic, Samuel Phillips, *with the autograph envelope signed and postmarked.*

> . . . I understand you have got for a leader writer at the Herald, a Jew of the name of Phillips, who wrote (but he little thinks I know it) the attacks on me in the Times – and volunteered them, I am told, in return for old acts of good nature on my part. I have a mighty mind to break down the anonymous, resolutely and fiercely, in that kind of stabbing, – and if I *do* nail up said Phillips by name on the cover of Dombey, I'll be damned if it shall be easy to take him down again . . .

Letter and envelope mounted in a cardboard frame. *Dexter Gift.*

H.153   A.L.s. ("CD.") to John Forster, *5 pages, 8vo, Athenaeum Wednesday night 9 June 1847,* giving a full account of his interview with Sir A. Duff-Gordon relative to a dispute between Thackeray and Forster (see J.65) and reporting Gordon's opinion that Forster's letter to Thackeray did him "great credit", being "full of good sense and manly dealing", *endorsed on sixth page, in Forster's hand,* "Letter A".

H.154   A.L.s. ("CD.") to Frank Stone, artist, *2 pages, 8vo, Broadstairs, Kent 4 July 1847,* giving rehearsal times for the production by the Amateur Players of *Every Man in his Humour,* in which Stone took the part of Downright, and dates for the performances in Liverpool and Manchester, and asking Stone to forward an enclosure to Augustus Egg (also a member of the Players).

H.155   A.L.s. ("CD.") to Thomas Beard, *2 pages, 8vo, Broadstairs 14 July 1847,* telling Beard that he will be away from Broadstairs until 1 August, *endorsed and with the autograph envelope, signed and stamped.*

> . . . That you should have been and gone and missed last Saturday! Wild beasts too, at Ramsgate, and a young lady in armour, as goes into the dens, while a rustic keeper who speaks through his nose, exclaims, "Beold the abazick power of woobbud!".

Dexter Gift.

H.156   A.L.s. ("CD.") to Thomas Beard, *1 page, 8vo, Broadstairs Monday 2 August 1847*, informing Beard of his return to Broadstairs and urging him to come down on a visit, *endorsed and with the autograph envelope, stamped. Dexter Gift.*

H.157   A.L.s. ("CD.") to Thomas Beard, *2 pages, 8vo, Broadstairs. 12 August 1847*, urging Beard to visit Broadstairs and mentioning the Margate Theatre, *endorsed, and with the autograph envelope, signed and postmarked. Dexter Gift.*

H.158   A.L.s. ("CD.") to Thomas Beard, *2 pages, 8vo, Broadstairs Wednesday 8 September 1847*, asking Beard to bring down to Broadstairs with him some "essence of Wormwood" from a chemist's and a diary left behind in Devonshire Terrace, *endorsed, and with the autograph envelope, postmarked.*

On p. 3 Dickens has written a note to a servant at Devonshire Terrace authorising her to admit Beard into his study (see next item). *Dexter Gift.*

H.159   A.L.s. to Josephine, servant at Devonshire Terrace, *1 page, 8vo, Broadstairs 8 September 1847*, authorising her to admit Thomas Beard into his study at Devonshire Terrace to fetch a book for him.

Written on page 3 of preceding item. *Dexter Gift.*

H.160   Autograph Document, Signed, *2 pages, 8vo, 1 May 1848*, setting out rules and regulations for the conduct of the Amateur Players' rehearsals.

This document was published in part by Forster in his *Life of Dickens* (Ley's edition, pp. 468-69). In his unpublished catalogue the Comte de Suzannet notes that this copy of the regulations was the one sent by Dickens to Frank Stone.

H.161   A.L.s. ("CD.") to Thomas Beard, *3 pages, 8vo, Devonshire Terrace Wednesday 10 May 1848*, inviting Beard to dinner, describing some "frightful and horribly unnatural tokens of virility" at last manifested by his dog, Timber, "in connexion with an insignificant, drivelling, blear-eyed little tame rabbit of the female sex", and reporting comically on the strenuous rehearsals of the Amateur Players, *endorsed, and with the autograph envelope, signed and postmarked.*

> . . . Stone is affected with congestion of the kidneys, which he attributes to being forced to do the same thing twenty times over, when he forgets it once. Beads break out all over Forster's head, and *boil* there, visibly and audibly . . . Leech is limp with being bullied . . .

Dexter Gift.

H.162   A.L.s. to an unknown Correspondent, *1 page, 8vo, Birmingham 27 May 1848*, saying that he would write out a passage from *Dombey* were he able to recollect one but he cannot do so. *1950 Gift.*

H.163   A.L.s. to W — Smith junior, *2 pages, 8vo, London, 1 Devonshire Terrace York Gate Regents Park 10 June 1848*, declining an invitation to preside at a forthcoming soirée of the Sheffield Athenaeum (" . . . I do some violence to my own inclinations, I assure you, in excusing myself from compliance with a requisition so agreeable and interesting to me . . . "). *1950 Gift.*

H.160

H.164   A.L.s. to Angus Fletcher, Comptroller of Inland Revenue for Scotland and cousin of the sculptor Angus Fletcher who executed a bust of Dickens in 1839, *5 pages, 8vo, London, 1 Devonshire Terrace York Gate Regent's Park 10 June 1848*, seeking Fletcher's advice about the possibility of the Amateur Players doing a one-night stand in Edinburgh in July and asking for Fletcher's assistance in organising the event.

H.165   A.L.s. to Angus Fletcher, *7 pages, 8vo, Devonshire Terrace 22 June 1848*, sending a draft of the playbill for the Edinburgh performance of *The Merry Wives of Windsor* (see next item) and giving very detailed instructions regarding tickets, arrangements for the orchestra, the preparation of the stage, etc.

H.166   Autograph Document, *1 page, foolscap* [*Devonshire Terrace, 22 June 1848*], draft of playbill advertising the Edinburgh performance of *The Merry Wives of Windsor*.

Enclosed in letter to Angus Fletcher. (See preceding item and F.10.)

H.167   A.L.s. ("CD.") to Thomas Beard, *3 pages, 8vo, Devonshire Terrace. Friday 28 July 1848,* informing Beard that "for a novelty" the Dickens family are going to Broadstairs for "the next eight or ten weeks", inviting him to visit them regularly there, and mentioning his sister Fanny's illness, *endorsed and with the autograph envelope, signed and postmarked. Dexter Gift.*

H.168   A.L.s. to Richard Henry (or Hengist) Horne, *3 pages, 8vo, Broadstairs, Kent 10 August 1848,* describing an accident suffered by his wife.

> . . . Mrs. Dickens being in an *un*interesting condition, has besought me to bring her out of that stagnant air of London for two months . . . And yesterday she was all but frightened to death by that pony running away with her headlong, down hill; our footman, who had been trusted to drive her, "losing his head" as they call it, and jumping out directly the said pony set off, – in return for which the wheels went over his legs; and here he lies plastered all over like Mr. Squeers "a brown-paper parcel chock-full of nothing but groans" . . .

With the letter is a print of a Daguerreotype portrait of Horne with a facsimile of Horne's signature beneath it.

H.169   A.L.s. ("CD.") to Peter Cunningham, Treasurer of The Shakespeare Society, author of *A Handbook to London* (1849) and editor of Walpole's Letters (1857). *2 pages, 8vo, Broadstairs, Kent 27 August 1848,* forwarding a business letter concerning the fund established to endow a perpetual curatorship of Shakespeare's house, *pencilled endorsement.*

Letter mounted in a cardboard frame. *Dexter Gift.*

H.170   A.L.s. ("CD.") to Thomas Beard, *2 pages, 8vo, Devonshire Terrace 6 September 1848,* expressing the hope that Beard will stay "at least a fortnight" at Broadstairs and mentioning the date of his sister's funeral (" . . . I begin to think, like the Monk who spoke to Wilkie, that we are the shadows, and Pictures the more robust realitities . . . "), *mourning paper, endorsed, and with the autograph envelope, signed and postmarked. Dexter Gift.*

H.171   A.L.s. ("CD.") to Thomas Beard, *1 page, 8vo, Devonshire Terrace Tuesday 12 December 1848,* telling Beard that he wants to ask him a question and asking him to call at Devonshire Terrace on his way to "Shoe Lane and the great Propogator", *mourning paper, endorsed, and with the autograph envelope, signed. Dexter Gift.*

H.172   A.L.s. to Peter Cunningham, *1 page, 8vo, Devonshire Terrace 28 February 1849,* accepting an invitation to dinner, *mourning paper, pencilled endorsement.*

Letter mounted in a cardboard frame. *Dexter Gift.*

H.173   A.L.s. to Thomas Beard, *3 pages, 8vo, Devonshire Terrace 21 June 1849,* referring to "the villain Bentley", inviting Beard (here addressed as "My Dear ould Mas'r Beard") to dinner, and discussing plans for a summer holiday, *endorsed and with the autograph envelope, signed and postmarked. Dexter Gift.*

H.174   A.L.s. to Thomas Beard, *4 pages, 8vo, Devonshire Terrace. Wednesday 18 July 1849*, giving Beard his holiday address at Bonchurch, Isle of Wight (" . . . There is a Waterfall in the grounds which I have driven a Carpenter almost mad by changing into a – SHOWER BATH – with a fall of 150 feet! . . . ") and describing an encounter with "the Baldwinian Twins" on the beach at Broadstairs, *endorsed.*

> . . . Oh the apparent age of those young Codgers! They were on the sands, in the blue stage of rickets, with their small noses very red, and pinched up sharp at the ends. They slobbered as they dangled over the nurse's shoulder, and, feebly crooning, looked out to sea, as if they were expecting the Marine Goblins who had changed them at their birth, to come and fetch them away to bowers of slime and seaweed. It was a dreadful spectacle – with a vague smell of cheese about it – and one I can never forget . . .

Dexter Gift.

H.175   A.L.s. to Frederick Mullett Evans, of Bradbury and Evans, *2 pages, 8vo, Devonshire Terrace 19 July 1849*, asking for £100 to be paid into his bank account, giving his holiday address on the Isle of Wight, inviting Evans to visit him there (quoting Mr. Pecksniff's phrase, "A favorable opportunity now offers"), and complaining about the printers' failure to return all of his manuscript. *1950 Gift.*

H.176   A.L.s. ("Flaster Floby") to "The Editor of The Morning Herald", *viz* Thomas Beard, *1 page, 8vo, Bonchurch, Isle of Wight. 20 August 1849*, facetiously asking to be informed of "the date of birth of the lively young colt, Holiday, got by Beard out of Baldwin, *endorsed, and with the autograph envelope signed, stamped and postmarked. Dexter Gift.*

H.177   A.L.s. to Thomas Beard, *2 pages, 8vo, Bonchurch, Isle of Wight. Sunday 9 September 1849*, expressing pleasure at Beard's forthcoming visit to Bonchurch and giving instructions for the journey, *endorsed, and with the autograph envelope, signed, stamped and postmarked. Dexter Gift.*

H.178   A.L.s. ("CD.") to John Leech, *Punch* cartoonist and one of the illustrators of Dickens's Christmas Books, *1 page, 8vo, Devonshire Terrace 7 November 1849*, telling Leech that he has decided against going to witness the Mannings' execution, *with the autograph envelope, signed.*

H.179   A.L.s. ("CD.") to John Leech, *2 pages, 8vo, Devonshire Terrace Monday 12 November 1849*, concerning arrangements for witnessing the Mannings' execution, *with the autograph envelope, signed and inscribed in Dickens's hand "Wait".*

> . . . We have taken the whole of the roof (and the back kitchen) for the extremely moderate sum of Ten Guineas, or two guineas each . . .

H.180   A.L.s. to Charles F. Ellerman, poet and sanitary reformer, *2 pages, 8vo, Devonshire Terrace 16 November 1849*, telling Ellerman that he has been obliged to make a rule about not helping dramatists to get their plays produced or published because of the "enormous number" of such applications made to him but offering to meet Ellerman provided that he understands this rule to be unbreakable. *1950 Gift.*

H.181 A.L.s. to Edward Chapman, of Chapman and Hall, *1 page, 8vo, Devonshire Terrace 13 February 1850*, approving the choice of Cruikshank to supply the frontispiece for the Cheap Edition of *Oliver Twist*.

H.182 A.L.s. ("CD.") to Thomas Beard, *2 pages, 8vo, Devonshire Terrace 22 March 1850*, asking Beard to arrange swimming lessons at the Holborn Baths for Charles Dickens, Junior ("Charley"), *endorsed, and with the autograph envelope, signed and inscribed, in Dickens's hand* "Favored by Charley". *Dexter Gift.*

H.183 A.L. (in the third person) to Charles F. — Ellerman, *1 page, 8vo, Devonshire Terrace 22 May 1850*, acknowledging receipt of Ellerman's play (*Alphonso Barbo; or, the Punishment of Death*, a verse tragedy in three acts) and his "obliging note". *1950 Gift.*

H.184 A.L.s. to Edward W. — Cole, *1 page, 8vo, Devonshire Terrace 22 May 1850*, saying that he has been much gratified by the members of the Newsvendors' Benevolent and Provident Institution's "generous remembrance" of him at their last annual meeting and expressing his willingness to render them any service that he can. *1950 Gift.*

H.185 A.L.s. to Rev. R. — Baring Claiborne, *2 pages, 8vo, Devonshire Terrace 7 June 1850*, explaining why he feels that a poem Claiborne has sent him is unsuitable for publication. *1950 Gift.*

H.186 A.L.s. ("CD.") to Thomas Beard, *2 pages, 8vo, Devonshire Terrace. 8 July 1850*, regarding holiday plans (" . . . Fort House, Broadstairs, *until the end of October ! ! !* . . . "), inviting Beard to dinner and sending remembrances from Fraser whom he has just seen in Paris, *endorsed and with the autograph envelope, signed and stamped. Dexter Gift.*

H.187 A.L.s. to Elizabeth Cleghorn Gaskell, *1 page, 4to, Devonshire Terrace 7 August 1850*, declining to reprint in *Household Words* an old sermon (" . . . the best [of its kind] I ever saw or heard in my life . . . ") that Mrs. Gaskell has sent to him, *addressed on verso of sheet, postmarked.*

> . . . It would be ungrateful to say that anything in your pleasant handwriting could disappoint me. I only thought when I saw it, outside the letter, that there might be a tale by you, within. *That* I couldn't help, you know . . .

Half of the sheet has been removed so that the address is incomplete. *Dexter Gift.*

H.188 A.L. to Georgina Hogarth, *1 page, 8vo, Office of Household Words Saturday 31 August 1850*, concerning some domestic arrangements, *endorsed by Kate Perugini on fourth page.*

Letter pasted into a paper folder endorsed on the outside by Kate Perugini. *1938 Gift.*

H.189 A.L. to "T.B.", *viz.* Thomas Beard, *1 page, 8vo, [Broadstairs], [15 September 1850]*, humorously protesting against the non-arrival of Beard in Broadstairs (" . . . Why do you try the feelings of your friends by prolonged absence? . . . "), *endorsed, and with the autograph envelope, stamped. Dexter Gift.*

H.190   A.L.s. to Thomas Beard, *2 pages, 8vo, Broadstairs Tuesday 1 October 1850,* concerning a forthcoming visit by Beard to Broadstairs, *endorsed and with the autograph envelope, signed and stamped.*

> . . .You will probably find a few "Household Words" here: to wit Wills and his wife, and Horne and his wife; but we have laid on a supplementary cottage, and have plenty of room . . .

Dexter Gift.

H.191   A.L. (in the third person) to J— W— Blockley, *1 page, 8vo, Broadstairs, Kent 3 October 1850,* acknowledging receipt of a "very pretty song", *with the autograph envelope, stamped and postmarked. 1950 Gift.*

H.192   A.L.s. to Thomas Beard, *2 pages, 8vo, Broadstairs, Kent Friday Night 18 October 1850,* forwarding a "hideous and infernal-looking document "that has arrived for Beard from his employer, Baldwin, *endorsed and with the autograph envelope, signed and stamped.*

> . . . I have written back, to the father of those prematurely ripe little Stiltons (the Twins), that I have sent it after you . . .

Dexter Gift.

H.193   A.L.s. to J— Moncrieff, *2 pages, 8vo, Devonshire Terrace, London Thursday Night 28 November 1850,* thanking Moncrieff for sending him a souvenir of a beloved mutual friend, expressing keen appreciation of the terms in which Moncrieff writes of the friend and saying that he hopes he may become personally acquainted with Moncrieff. *1950 Gift.*

H.194   Prompt-Books of: (1) Bourcicault (Dion) USED UP: A PETIT COMEDY IN TWO ACTS *(12mo, Acting National Drama Office, n.d.),* interleaved with manuscript notes, stage directions, etc., also diagram of stage, list of actors and inscription on fly-leaf, "at Rockingham Castle 13th & 15th Jany 1851", numerous underlinings and alterations to text throughout, all in Dickens's hand; (2) Inchbald (Mrs.) ANIMAL MAGNETISM: A FARCE IN THREE ACTS *(12mo, G. H. Davidson, Peter's Hill, Doctors' Commons, n.d.),* interleaved with manuscript notes, stage directions ("Knocker ready", etc), etc., by Dickens and Thomas Coe, text amended throughout in Dickens's hand with substitution of Spanish names for the French ones of dramatis personae, new dialogue added at the end by Dickens, cast list in Dickens's hand, also inscription on fly-leaf, "at Rockingham Castle 13th and 15th Jany 1851" (signature at end of text: "Thos. Coe Prompter 1850". Coe has also written on fly-leaf "Charles Dickens Esqre 1850"); (3) Dance (Charles) A WONDERFUL WOMAN. A COMIC DRAMA, IN TWO ACTS *(12mo, Thomas Hailes Lacy, n.d.)* diagram of stage in Dickens's hand, facing title-page, also interleaved with manuscript notes, stage directions, etc., all in the hand of Thomas Coe.
  With the above books is a fourth one, John Poole's TURNING THE TABLES; AN ORIGINAL FARCE IN ONE ACT *(12mo, John Duncombe, n.d.).* This is inscribed on the fly-leaf in Coe's hand, "Charles Dickens Esqre. 1850" and below this appears the signature "Syd S. Dickens Gad's Hill June 1866"; the book is interleaved with manuscript notes and stage directions all in the hand of Coe whose signature, "Thos. Coe Prompter 1850" appears at the end of the text.

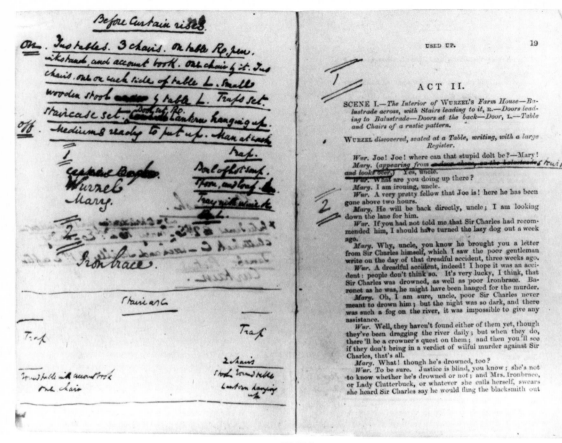

H.194

These prompt-books were given by Georgina Hogarth to Sir Henry Fielding Dickens and sold by his son, Admiral Sir Gerald Dickens, at Sotheby's on 31 May 1949, the purchaser being the Comte de Suzannet.

H.195   A.L.s. to Thomas Beard, *2 pages, 8vo, Devonshire Terrace Monday 31 March 1851*, informing Beard of his father's death (" . . . He didnt know me, or any one, and quietly declined until he died . . . ") *mourning paper, endorsed, and with the autograph envelope, signed and stamped. Dexter Gift.*

H.196   A.L.s. to Thomas Beard, *3 pages, 8vo, Devonshire Terrace Saturday 19 April 1851*, alluding to the death of his infant daughter, Dora, and enclosing a corrected proof of an advertisement for the first performance of *Not So Bad As We Seem* to be inserted in the *Morning Herald, mourning paper, endorsed, and with the autograph envelope, signed.*

> . . . If you will give some notice of the enclosed prospectus, and call attention to it,
> you will serve a cause of the highest importance, to which we are all zealously bound . . .

Dexter Gift.

H.197   A.D. Corrected proof of advertisement for first performance of *Not So Bad As We Seem*, enclosed in letter to Beard of 19 April 1851 (see preceding item). *Dexter Gift.*

H.198   Corrected Proofs of Bulwer Lytton's comedy, *Not So Bad As We Seem* (produced by Dickens's Amateur Players in aid of the Guild of Literature and Art, May 1851). These proofs, revised throughout in Dickens's hand and Forster's, were bound up in green cloth for his use as actor, stage manager and producer. Further alterations were made by him to the text during rehearsals and these are also marked. His book-plate appears inside the front cover.

A small number of copies, incorporating Dickens's earliest revisions and with "[Private and Confidential]" printed at the head of the first page of the text, were printed for the use of the other actors and three specimens of these, the copies that belonged to Douglas Jerrold, Frank Stone and F. W. Topham, are also present. Each copy bears its owner's signature and has passages marked and deleted and stage directions written in by him throughout.

Each of the four copies is in a dark blue morocco slip-case.

Another copy of the private edition exists in the William M. Elkins Collection in the Free Library of Philadelphia. This is described in the exhibition catalogue (*The Life and Works of Charles Dickens* 1812-1870), Free Library of Philadelphia, 1946, item no. 15) as a "prompter's copy" with the cast list of the first performance (at Devonshire House, 30 April 1851) written in in Dickens's hand.

H.199   A.D.s. Notice concerning the Amateur Players, *1 page, folio, Devonshire House, 28 April 1851,* proposing that the Company should dine at the Bedford Hotel, Covent Garden [altered in pencil, not in Dickens's hand, to "Household Words Office"] the following Wednesday "in order that the whole of the dresses [for *Not So Bad As We Seem*] may be tried on there, after dinner, while there is yet ample time before the Dress Rehearsal for making any needful alterations" and requesting all "gentlemen who assent to this arrangement" to sign their names.

Document signed in pencil by: J. Forster, D. Jerrold, R. H. Horne, P. Cunningham, T. W. Topham, Dudley Costello, F. Stone, Charles Knight, Wilkie Collins, Augustus Egg, Mark Lemon, Robert Bell.

H.200   A.L.s. ("CD.") to Thomas Beard, *4 pages, 8vo, Devonshire Terrace Tuesday 13 May 1851,* concerning the preparations for the first performance of *Not So Bad As We Seem* at Devonshire House, *mourning paper, endorsed, and with the autograph envelope, signed.*

> . . . You have no idea of the work I have had. My legs swell so, with standing on the stage for hours together, that my stockings won't come off. I get so covered with sawdust among the carpenters, that my Infants don't know me. I am so astonishingly familiar with everybody else's part, that I forget my own. I roar to the Troupe in general, to that extent that the excellent Duke (who is deaf) thinks in the remoteness of his own little library that the wind is blowing hard . . .

Dexter Gift.

H.201   A.L.s. ("CD.") to Thomas Beard, *1 page, 8vo, Guild of Literature and Art, 10, Lancaster Place, Strand, Tuesday 17 June 1851,* offering Beard three tickets for the performance of *Not So Bad As We Seem* at the Hanover Square Rooms the following day, *endorsed and with the autograph envelope, signed. Dexter Gift.*

H.202   A.L.s. to Thomas Beard, *3 pages, 8vo, Sherborne, Dorsetshire Wednesday Evening 25 June 1851,* written from Macready's home, inviting Beard to join him on a visit to Charles Dickens, Junior, at Eton, *endorsed, and with the autograph envelope, signed and stamped.*

> . . . I have promised Charley that I will appear at 11 that morning at Slough, armed with a hamper from Fortnum and Mason's, and take him and three other young Etonian shavers up the river . . . .

Dexter Gift.

Charles Dickens, Junior (See H.202)

H.203   A.L.s. ("CD.") to Thomas Beard, *3 pages, 8vo, H.W. Office Monday 30 June 1851,* concerning the forthcoming visit to Eton to see his son and mentioning his acting in *Not So Bad As We Seem* (" . . . I am so burnt, that I cannot calculate the amount of cold cream and powder that will have to be applied to my visage on Wednesday night, before I can 'go on' as a youthful Lord . . . "), *endorsed, and with the autograph envelope, signed. Dexter Gift.*

H.204   A.L.s. ("CD.") to Thomas Beard, *2 pages, 8vo, Broadstairs, Kent Monday 6 October 1851,* mentioning the alterations being made to Tavistock House, preparatory to the Dickens family's moving there and describing a succession of guests at Broadstairs, *mourning paper, endorsed, and with the autograph envelope, signed and stamped.*

. . . Here has Horne been here (with a guitar) bathing at "Dumblegap", the flesh-colored Horror of maiden ladies. Here has Forster been and gone, after patronising with suavity the whole population of Broadstairs, and impressing Tom Collins with a profound conviction that he (F) did the Ocean a favor when he bathed . . . .

Dexter Gift.

H.205　A.L.s. ("CD.") to Thomas Beard, *2 pages, 8vo, Broadstairs, Thursday 9 October 1851*, concerning a forthcoming visit to Broadstairs by Beard, *mourning paper, endorsed, and with the autograph envelope, signed and stamped.*

. . . You will find Pump (Stone) mooning about here, and also. Egg. They are at present in a fearful state of idleness in the Drawing Room . . . flushed, tousled, and crumpled with intensest laziness . . .

Letter and envelope mounted in cardboard frame. *Dexter Gift.*

H.206　A.L.s. to Peter Cunningham, *2 pages, 8vo, Guild of Literature and Art, 10, Lancaster Place, Strand, Friday 31 October 1851*, informing Cunningham that he has pledged the Amateur Players to a second performance at Bristol, all seats for the only performance scheduled so far having been taken "though the room where we perform at that city is of immense size", *pencilled endorsement.*

Letter mounted in a cardboard frame. *Dexter Gift.*

H.207　A.L. (in the third person) to Thomas Beard, *1 page, 8vo, Tavistock House, Tavistock Square Wednesday 26 November 1851*, a humorously-worded invitation to dinner, *endorsed and with the autograph envelope, signed. Dexter Gift.*

H.208　A.L.s. ("CD.") to Thomas Beard, *1 page, 16mo, Tavistock House Thursday 5 February 1852*, inviting Beard to dine with him on his birthday. *Dexter Gift.*

H.209　A.L. (in the third person) to Charles F. Ellerman, *1 page, 8vo, Tavistock House, Tavistock Square 3 March 1852*, saying that he will be pleased to accept a compliment that Ellerman wishes to pay him (i.e. the dedication to him of Ellerman's poem, "The Tale of a Keg; or a Singular Relic of Columbus", eventually published in *Anglo-Belgic Ballads and Legends*, 1864). *1950 Gift.*

H.210　A.L.s. to Thomas Beard, *1 page, 8vo, Tavistock House Monday Evening 8 March 1852*, concerning the non-receipt by Beard of a book from Bradbury and Evans (presumably a copy of the first number of *Bleak House*), *endorsed.*

With this letter is a note from Frederick Evans to Dickens (see J.39). *Dexter Gift.*

H.211　A.L.s. ("CD.") to William Woodley Frederick de Cerjat, of Lausanne, *4 pages, 8vo, London, Tavistock House, Tavistock Square Saturday 8 May 1852*, a long, gossiping letter, mentioning a project, concerted with the Watsons, "to make a dash over to Lausanne at midsummer, performances of *Not So Bad As We Seem* (" . . . the whole such a perfect picture of the time of George the Second . . . ") the birth of his youngest son, Edward, and the death of his infant daughter, Dora, (" . . . called Dora, in remembrance of 'Copperfield'. It was an ill-omened name, and she followed her predecessor to the land of Shadows . . . ''), the progress of *Bleak House* (" . . . a most enormous success . . . ''), and various London topics and personalities, *with the autograph envelope, signed and postmarked.*

> . . . I saw the Duke of Wellington last . . . a week ago. You cannot imagine how old he looks (it was his 83rd birthday) or how long he was in jerking a short speech out of himself like a series of words of command! Rogers (five years older) is lamed by an accident . . . In all other respects he is the same as ever. Vivacious enough, and vicious enough, – tells the same stories, to the same people, in the same words, twenty times in a day, and has his little dinner parties of four, where he goes mad with rage if anybody talks to anybody but himself . . .

H.212   A.L.s. to John Bate Cardale, minister of the Catholic Apostolic ("Irving-ite") Church, and Dickens's neighbour in Tavistock Square, *1 page, 8vo, Tavistock House Thursday 27 May 1852,* telling Cardale that he has taken back into his own keeping the key of a gate which his servant and others have apparently, to Cardale's annoyance, been using a short cut. *1950 Gift.*

The last few lines of this letter are written inside the flap of the accompanying envelope.

H.213   A.L.s. ("CD.") to Thomas Beard, *1 page, 8vo, Tavistock House Tuesday 22 June 1852,* inviting Beard to accompany him and Mark Lemon to Eton, to take Charley Dickens and his friends on a "water party", *endorsed, and with the autograph envelope, signed and stamped. Dexter Gift.*

H.214   A.L.s. to Elizabeth Cleghorn Gaskell, *2 pages, 8vo, Tavistock House Tuesday 29 June 1852,* commenting on some papers that Mrs. Gaskell has sent him (" . . . I cannot say that the impression they leave on me is quite satisfactory. I doubt if Mr Gaskell would teach children in that way . . . ") and discussing which plays the Amateur Players will perform in Manchester.

> . . . *You* have made such an impression on me as to the repetition of Bulwer's Comedy at Manchester, that I have resolved *not* to play it. We shall act Used Up, Charles The Twelfth, and Mr Nightingale's Diary. The two former are excellent little pieces – especially the first, which is by far the best thing we have ever done. It is a French story, and the idea of it is quite delightful . . .

Dexter Gift.

H.215   A.L.s. ("CD.") to Thomas Beard, *3 pages, 8vo, Tavistock House Tuesday Evening 29 June 1852,* concerning the forthcoming expedition to Eton and mentioning his dog, Timber, (" . . . He has given up all idea of handing down his name and race . . . "), *endorsed, and with the autograph envelope, signed, stamped and inscribed, in Dickens's hand,* "Private". *Dexter Gift.*

H.216   A.L.s. ("CD.") to Thomas Beard, *2 pages, 8vo, 10 Camden Crescent, Dover 22 July 1852,* inviting Beard to visit Dover and mentioning the "Baldwinian twins" (" . . . two small green objects with an ancient and fish-like smell proceeding from the surfaces . . . having been seen on the beach at Broadstairs . . . "), *endorsed. Dexter Gift.*

H.217   A.L.s. to Thomas Beard, *2 pages, 8vo, 10 Camden Crescent Dover 2 October*

1852, making arrangements for Beard to visit the Dickens family in Boulogne during the following fortnight, *endorsed*.

Letter mounted in a cardboard frame. *Dexter Gift.*

H.218   A.L.s. ("CD.") to Thomas Beard, *1 page, 8vo, Tavistock House Saturday 23 October 1852*, informing Beard that the Dickens family "have now come home for good" and hoping that they will see him "soon and often", *endorsed, and with the autograph envelope, signed, stamped and postmarked. Dexter Gift.*

H.219   A.L.s. to Charles Manby, manager of the Adelphi Theatre, *1 page, 8vo, Tavistock House, Tavistock Square Friday 29 October 1852*, asking for a box at the Adelphi for himself and Clarkson Stanfield the following Tuesday. *1950 Gift.*

H.220   A.L.s. to John Bate Cardale, *2 pages, 8vo, Junction Parade, Brighton Thursday Evening 10 March 1853*, concerning some shared building expenses, about which he has written to Messrs. Cubitt. *1950 Gift.*

H.221   A.L.s. to Dr. Johann Jakob Guggenbuhl, Swiss writer on cretinism, *2 pages, 8vo, Tavistock House Wednesday Morning 30 March 1853*, inviting Guggenbuhl to dinner that evening to meet Dr. John Elliotson, the mesmerist, and another English friend of his, just returned from Switzerland, who takes a keen interest in the sort of work that Guggenbuhl is engaged in.

Letter mounted on card. *1950 Gift.*

H.222   A.L.s. to Thomas Beard, *3 pages, 8vo, Villa des Moulineaux, Boulogne Sunday 28 August 1853*, inviting Beard to Boulogne (" . . . We have a charming doll's country-house here, of many rooms, with large and extremely pretty gardens . . . ") and giving domestic news (" . . . the Inimitable wears a satanic and gloomy moustache . . . "), *endorsed. Dexter Gift.*

H.223   A.L. (in the third person) to Thomas Weddle ("Inland Revenue Office, Coventry"), *1 page, 8vo, Boulogne 29 August 1853*, saying that he has no leisure to comply with a request made to him by Weddle, *with the autograph envelope (imperfect), stamped. 1950 Gift.*

H.224   A.L.s. ("CD.") to Thomas Beard, *4 pages, 8vo, Boulogne, Sunday 18 September 1853*, giving instructions for getting to the Villa des Moulineaux, *endorsed*.

> . . . At a few miles' distance you will be waylaid by three implacable Gauls who will lay hold of your greatcoat, and ask "Est-ce que Monsieur ait quelque chose a declarer?" Hereupon you will blandly smile, and reply "Rien" – (therein not imitating Forster, who, the other day, not at all understanding the enquiry, said after a moment's reflection with the sweetness of some choice wind instrument "Bon jour!" – and was immediately siezed) . . . .

Dexter Gift.

H.225   A.L.s. to the Editor of *The Times*, *1 page, 8vo, Boulogne, 18 September 1853*, denying statements published in "a country paper" and copied by *The Times* that he has drawn on the experiences of "that excellent Police Officer, Mr. Inspector Field" in *Bleak House* and that he was going to write Field's biography.

H.226 A.L.s. ("CD.") to Georgina Hogarth, *4 pages, 8vo, Hotel de la Ville, Milan. Tuesday 25 October 1853,* vivaciously describing various incidents of his journey through Switzerland to Italy with Wilkie Collins and Augustus Egg, *with the autograph envelope, signed, postmarked and endorsed* "Italian Tour 1853 with Wilkie and Mr. Egg".

> . . . The next thing you will be interested in hearing of is the progress of the cumulative moustaches of the two other members of the Triumvirate. They are more distressing, more comic, more sparse and meagre, more straggling, wandering, wiry, stubbly, formless – more given to wandering into strange places and sprouting up noses and dribbling under chins – than anything in that nature ever produced, as I believe, since the Flood. Collins has taken to wiping his (which are like the Plornish-ghenter's eyebrows) at dinner; and Egg's are not near his nose, but begin at the corners of his mouth, like those of the Witches in Macbeth. I have suffered so much from the contemplation of these terrific objects from grey dawn to night in little carriages, that this morning, finding myself with a good-looking glass and a good light, I seized my best razor, and, as a great example shaved off the the whole of the Newgate fringe from under my chin! . . . .

Letter pasted into a paper folder endorsed by Mrs. Perugini. *1938 Gift.*

H.227 A.L.s. ("CD.") to Thomas Beard, *2 pages, 8vo, Tavistock House Thursday 2 February 1854,* inviting Beard to celebrate his birthday with him at Gravesend, *endorsed, and with the autograph envelope, signed and stamped. Dexter Gift.*

H.228 A.L.s. ("CD.") to Thomas Beard, *1 page, 8vo, Tavistock House 5 February 1854,* concerning arrangements for the expedition to Gravesend, *endorsed, and with the autograph envelope, signed and stamped. Dexter Gift.*

H.229 A.L.s. ("CD.") to Peter Cunningham, *1 page, 8vo, Tavistock House Saturday 18 March 1854,* enclosing an off-print of his obituary notice of Thomas Noon Talfourd, to be published in *Household Words* (see Lot No. 112 in Sale Catalogue), *pencilled endorsement and note,* "Talfourd's Death".

Letter mounted in a cardboard frame. *Dexter Gift.*

H.230 A.L.s. to Henry Morley, staff journalist on *Household Words, 2 pages, 8vo, Tavistock House Saturday Evening 15 April 1854,* concerning an article Morley has written – Dickens forwards to him a communication from a "sensible and serviceable man", saying that he feels sure that, if there is something to be said to the credit of "The Society in question" (to which he himself belongs) Morley will not neglect to feature it in the next suitable paper he writes for *Household Words,* and telling Morley that he has been deeply moved by the article, which could not have been better done.

The article in question is presumably Morley's harrowing description of the sufferings of the desperately poor inhabitants of Bethnal Green ("The Quiet Poor", *HW*, vol. 9, pp. 201-06 [15 April 1854]) in which he makes some criticism of the Society for Improving the Dwellings of the Poor. *1950 Gift.*

H.231 A.L.s. ("CD.") to Thomas Beard, *1 page, 8vo, Villa du Camp de droite, Boulogne Friday 14 July 1854,* inviting Beard to dine with him at the Garrick, to hear about "the glories of this eagle's nest", *endorsed. Dexter Gift.*

H.232 A.L.s. to Thomas Beard, *4 pages, 8vo, Villa du Camp de droite, Boulogne*

Saturday 23 September 1854, giving directions for Beard's forthcoming journey to visit the Dickens family in Boulogne, mentioning his youngest son, Edward (" . . . the Plornish Maroon is in a brilliant state . . . "), and describing certain bizarre military happenings in the vicinity, *endorsed*.

> . . . He ["Plorn"] thinks you will be interested with the camp, in reference to which the most ridiculous thing I know is the practice of the Trumpeters – of whom there appear to be about two to every Private. These unfortunates have been dispersed, all through the summer, in lonely corn-fields, bean crops, pasture-lands, and bye-places of all sorts, incessantly blowing their lives away and never doing any one of the calls right. One weazen little burnt up youth from the South, practised on the road outside our garden gate, all through July and August, when the heat was intense. Two shaggy and immense creatures with enormous beards – so broad across the chest that you couldn't take into your eye their two rows of buttons at once – instructed him. They marched up and down gravely, with him between them. Without the least effort, they blew such prodigious blasts that the old High Tower shook to every note. Then they left off, eyed this Imbecile severely, and he broke into a miserable little cracked abortion of a brazen wheeze, and trembled with the effort. I suppose him to have gasped himself into the Hospital, and to be now no more . . . .

Dexter Gift.

H.233   A.L.s. to John Bate Cardale, *4 pages, 8vo, Villa du Camp de droite, Boulogne Saturday 23 September 1854*, expressing the regret of the Dickens family at losing the Cardales as neighbours, offering to lease or rent a piece of ground belonging to Cardale that is overlooked by the window of his study, and mentioning Cardale's son, on active service in the Crimea. *1950 Gift.*

H.234   A.L.s. ("CD.") to Thomas Beard, *1 page, 8vo, Tavistock House Tuesday 26 December 1854*, inviting Beard to dine with him on New Year's Eve, *endorsed*. *Dexter Gift.*

H.235   A.L.s. to Messrs. Letts Son and Steer, *1 page 8vo, Tavistock House 3 January 1855*, thanking the firm for once again sending him a complimentary diary and praising the enduring quality of the "old cover". *1950 Gift.*

H.236   A.L.s. ("CD.") to Bradbury and Evans, *2 pages, 8vo, Tavistock House 5 January 1855*, forwarding a letter from a would-be translator of Dickens's works into French and calling the attention of Bradbury and Evans to a legal point with regard to which he himself and they seem to be in the wrong. *1950 Gift.*

H.237   A.L.s. ("CD.") to Thomas Beard, *2 pages, 8vo, Tavistock House 30 January 1855*, inviting Beard to celebrate his birthday with him, again at Gravesend, *endorsed, and with the autograph envelope, signed and stamped. Dexter Gift.*

H.238   A.L.s. ("CD.") to Peter Cunningham, *1 page, 8vo, Office of Household Words, Thursday 1 February 1855*, inviting Cunningham to join a dinner-party at Gravesend, to celebrate his birthday, *pencilled endorsement*.

Letter mounted in a cardboard frame. *Dexter Gift.*

H.239   A.L.s. to Jules Benedict, composer and conductor, *1 page, 8vo, Tavistock House Wednesday Evening 28 February 1855*, inviting Benedict to dine the following day to meet Dickens's German publisher, Tauchnitz of Leipzig. *1950 Gift.*

Ella Maria Winter (see H.240)

H.240   A.L.s. to Ella Maria Winter, daughter of Maria Beadnell, *4 pages, 8vo, Tavistock House Tuesday Evening 13 March 1855,* replying to her letter of thanks for a brooch he has given her, and mentioning his raven (" . . . He breaks all the kitchen-windows every day, and flies at Everybody except the Cook . . . ") and his youngest son, whose birthday it is (" . . . and he says he don't want many happy returns of the Measles – which he has got at present . . . "), *with the autograph envelope, stamped.*

H.241   A.L.s. ("CD.") to Thomas Beard, *1 page, 8vo, Tavistock House Tuesday 20 March 1855,* inviting Beard to join himself, Mark Lemon and W. H. Wills on an expedition to Ashford where he is going to read the *Christmas Carol* "to the Railway workpeople" there, *endorsed and with the autograph envelope, signed and stamped. Dexter Gift.*

H.242   A.L.s. to Frank Stone, *1 page, 8vo, Tavistock House 29 May 1855,* sending him details of times fixed for rehearsals of *The Lighthouse.*

H.243   A.L.s. ("CD.") to Thomas Beard, *4 pages, 8vo, Tavistock House Friday 6 July 1855,* suggesting that Beard operate the wind machine at the forthcoming performances of *The Lighthouse* at Camden House, *endorsed, and with the autograph envelope, signed and stamped.*

. . . in order to blow with distinguished merit, it will be necessary on Monday Evening (when there is a Dress Rehearsal) to rehearse the storm before the people come in, under the auspices of Charley whom I have trained to the government of the Elements . . . .

Dexter Gift.

H.244   A.L.s. to "My Dear Boreas", *viz*. Thomas Beard, *2 pages, 8vo, Folkestone Thursday 23 August 1855*, extolling the charms of the district and inviting Beard to visit him, *endorsed*.

> . . . The host of Boreas, having nothing particular to do – except a new book twenty months long – Household Words – and other trifles – has taken to expend his superfluous vitality in swarming up the face of a gigantic and precipitous cliff in a lovely spot overhanging the wild sea-beach. He may generally be seen (in clear weather) from the British Channel, suspended in mid-air with his trousers very much torn, at fifty Minutes past 3 P.M. . . .

Letter mounted in a cardboard frame. *Dexter Gift.*

H.245   A.L. (in the third person) to Mrs. — Jennings, *2 pages, 8vo, Folkestone, Kent. 26 July 1855*, concerning a servant-girl, in trouble for stealing, whom Mrs. Jennings is seeking to place in Miss Burdett-Coutts's home for delinquent girls at Shepherd's Bush. Dickens explains that the Home is not primarily intended to deal with such cases and requests details of the theft, and of the girl's parentage and education, so that he can decide whether he should interview her as a candidate for admission to the Home. *1950 Gift.*

H.246   A.L. (in the third person) to Mrs. — Jennings, *2 pages, 8vo, Folkestone, Kent. 26 August 1855*, saying that he cannot give an opinion about the suitability of a certain girl (see preceding item) for admission into Miss Burdett-Coutts's Home without some knowledge of her demeanour and appearance, and that he has asked the Superintendent of the Home, Mrs. Marchmont, to be ready to interview the girl and report to him since he does not know when he will next be in London. *1950 Gift.*

H.247   A.L.s. to Thomas Beard, *3 pages, 8vo, Folkestone, Sunday 7 October 1855*, making plans for Beard to visit Folkestone and describing the stormy weather in the Channel, braved by Frank Stone and Augustus Egg, *endorsed. Dexter Gift.*

H.248   A.L.s. to Elizabeth Cleghorn Gaskell, *2 pages, 8vo, Paris, 49 Avenue des Champs Elysées 2 January 1856*, informing Mrs. Gaskell that measures have been taken to reserve the right of translation of material appearing in *Household Words* and enquiring about an unfinished story, *with the autograph envelope, signed (the stamp has been removed)*.

> . . . I have been going on, hoping to see the end of the story you could not finish (which was not your fault or anybody's) in time for Christmas. When will it be forthcoming, I wonder! You have not deserted it. You cannot be such an unnatural mother . . . .

Dexter Gift.

H.249   A.L.s. ("CD.") to Georgina Hogarth, *1 page, 8vo, Household Words (Just before dinner) 7 February 1856*, saying he has just received both her letters and telling her to "take the Pavilion" (" . . . I have no doubt of its being the best place . . . ").

Letter pasted into a paper folder endorsed by Mrs. Perugini. *1938 Gift.*

H.250 A.L.s. to Georgina Hogarth, *3 pages, 8vo, Household Words Friday 8 February 1856*, describing a dinner held the previous evening to celebrate his birthday (" . . . Charley was in great force and floored Peter Cunningham and the Audit Office on a question about some bill transaction with Barings . . . ") and mentioning that "the first No of Little Dorrit has gone to 40,000, and the others are fast following".

Letter pasted into a paper folder endorsed by Mrs. Perugini. *1938 Gift.*

H.251 A.L.s. ("CD.") to Georgina Hogarth, *2 pages, 8vo, H.W. Office Tuesday 11 March 1856,* concerning some negotiations with a French landlady and joking about Forster's forthcoming marriage.

> . . . Tell Catherine that I have the most prodigious, overwhelming, crushing, astounding, blinding, deafening pulverizing, scarifying secret of which Forster is the hero, unimaginable by the united efforts of the whole British population. It is a thing of that kind, that after I knew it (from himself) this morning, I lay down flat, as if an Engine and Tender had fallen upon me . . . .

1938 Gift.

Georgina Hogarth (See H.252)

H.252 A.L.s. ("CD.") to Georgina Hogarth, *3 pages, 8vo, Household Words Friday 14 March 1856,* describing a visit to the Olympic Theatre to see *Still Waters Run Deep* (" . . . I laughed [in a conspicuous manner] to that extent at Emery when he received the dinner-company, that the people were more amused by me than by the Piece . . . ") and reporting that he has that day paid the purchase-money (£1790) for Gad's Hill Place.

Letter pasted into a paper folder endorsed by Mrs. Perugini. *1938 Gift.*

H.253 A.L.s. to Bradbury and Evans, *1 page, 8vo, Paris, 49 Champs Elysées Friday 4 April 1856,* forwarding £100 due to *Household Words* from the German publisher Tauchnitz. *1950 Gift.*

H.254   A.L.s. ("CD.") to Georgina Hogarth, *4 pages, 8vo, Tavistock House Monday 5 May 1856,* describing Stanfield's enthusiasm for putting on a new play at Tavistock House (" . . . Mark had a farce ready for the Managerial perusal – but it won't do . . . "), an argument with Miss Coutts's companion, Mrs. Brown, a "good dialogue" with the landlady of the Ship Hotel at Dover, a depressing visit to the theatre there, and "a painful picture of a great deal of merit" *(The Death of Chatterton)* at the Academy Exhibition.

> . . . I went to the Dover Theatre on Friday night, which was a miserable spectacle. The pit is boarded over, and it is a drinking and smoking place. It was "for the Benefit of Mrs A. Green", and the town had been very extensively placarded with "Don't forget Friday." I made out Four and ninepence (I am serious) in the house, when I went in. We may have warmed up in the course of the evening, to twelve shillings. A Jew played the Grand Piano, Mrs A. Green sang no end of songs (with not a bad voice, poor creature), Mr Green sang comic songs fearfully, and danced clog hornpipes capitally, and a miserable woman, shivering in a shawl and bonnet, sat in the side boxes all the evening, nursing Master A. Green, aged 7 months. It was a most forlorn occasion, and I should have contributed a Sovereign to the Treasury if I had known how . . . .

1938 Gift.

H.255   A.L.s. ("CD.") to Georgina Hogarth, *1 page, 8vo, Household Words Office Friday 9 May 1856,* giving Georgina instructions about getting a new passport either in Paris or Boulogne and describing a dinner-party given by him the previous evening, visits to theatres, etc.

Letter pasted into a paper folder endorsed by Mrs. Perugini. *1938 Gift.*

H.256   A.L.s. to Peter Cunningham, *1 page, 8vo, Office of Household Words, Friday 6 June 1856,* praising a book that Cunningham has sent him.

Letter mounted in a cardboard frame. *Dexter Gift.*

H.257   A.L.s. to Thomas Beard, *4 pages, 8vo, Villa des Moulineaux, Boulogne S/M. Saturday 21 June 1856,* describing life at the Villa, a new cook, etc., and giving an account of the distressed state of the Cattermole family, also resident in Boulogne, and the kindness towards them of their landlord, Beaucourt (also Dickens's landlord), *endorsed, and with the autograph envelope, signed and stamped. Dexter Gift.*

H.258   A.L.s. ("CD.") to Thomas Beard, *1 page, 8vo, H.W. Office 1 July 1856,* inviting Beard to dine at the office the following day (" . . . Turtle and a steak . . . "), *endorsed and with the autograph envelope, signed. Dexter Gift.*

H.259   A.L.s. ("CD.") to Thomas Beard, *2 pages, 8vo, Tavistock House Monday 8 September 1856,* announcing the Dickens family's sudden return from Boulogne because of a "dangerous Epidemic" at Paris and suggesting a walk and "a dinner of consolation at Gravesend", *endorsed, and with the autograph envelope, signed and stamped. Dexter Gift.*

H.260   A.L.s. ("CD.") to Thomas Beard, *1 page, 8vo, Tavistock House 1 October 1856,* enquiring after Beard's health, *with the autograph envelope, signed and stamped. Dexter Gift.*

101

H.261 A.L.s. ("CD.") to Thomas Beard, *1 page, 8vo, Tavistock House Tuesday 14 October 1856,* saying that he will write to "poor old Guy, telling him . . . that I have no influence with the Barnacles", *with the autograph envelope, signed and stamped. Dexter Gift.*

H.262 A.L.s. ("CD.") to Thomas Beard, *1 page, 8vo, Tavistock House Tuesday 23 December 1856,* suggesting "a walk at Gad's Hill" the following Sunday, *with the autograph envelope, signed and stamped. Dexter Gift.*

H.263 A.L.s. to David Hastings, Music Critic of the *Morning Herald, 2 pages, 8vo, Tavistock House Tuesday 30 December 1856,* concerning the forthcoming private production of *The Frozen Deep* at Tavistock House, to which Hastings has been invited (" . . . if you should think it of any public interest or merit I beg you to use your own free discretion as to noticing it . . . ").

H.264 A.L.s. ("CD.") to Thomas Beard, *1 page, 8vo, Tavistock House Wednesday 28 January 1857,* inviting Beard to dinner on his birthday either at Tavistock House or at Gravesend, depending on the weather, *with the autograph envelope, signed and stamped. Dexter Gift.*

H.265 A.L.s. ("CD.") to Thomas Beard, *1 page, 8vo, Tavistock House Thursday 5 February 1857,* informing Beard that the birthday dinner will be held at Tavistock House, *with the autograph envelope, signed and stamped. Dexter Gift.*

H.266 A.L.s. ("CD.") to Thomas Beard, *2 pages, 8vo, Tavistock House Tuesday Night 24 February 1857,* sympathising with Beard over some difficulties that have arisen between him and his employer (Edward Baldwin of the *Morning Herald*), and inviting him to dine at the Garrick (". . . A glass of good wine may take the taste of that Scum out of our mouths . . ."), *with the autograph envelope, signed and stamped.*

> . . . If I were you, I would above all things leave a card for Delane without a day's delay . . . .

Dexter Gift.

H.267 A.L.s. to Henry Morley, *2 pages, 8vo, Tavistock House, Tuesday Night 24 February 1857,* thanking Morley for a book which he looks forward to reading (" . . . The 'dead men' are not buried here, believe me . . . ") and readily agreeing to his request to be allowed to reprint some of his *Household Words* articles in volume form.

The book Morley sent Dickens was probably a copy of his *Cornelius Agrippa* (1856). His *Gossip . . . Reprinted from Household Words* appeared later in 1857. *1950 Gift.*

H.268 A.L.s. ("CD.") to Thomas Beard, *2 pages, 8vo, Tavistock House 1 March 1857,* postponing a projected "theatrical trip", *with the autograph envelope, signed and stamped. Dexter Gift.*

H.269 A.L.s. ("CD.") to Thomas Beard, *2 pages, 8vo, Tavistock House Sunday 15 March 1857,* concerning the prospects for Beard's future (" . . . I am now confirmed in my hopes, that whatever becomes of the Paper, your position is permanently improved . . . ") and arranging for a visit to a theatre, *with the autograph envelope, signed, stamped and inscribed, in Dickens's hand,* "Private". *Dexter Gift.*

H.270   A.L.s. ("CD.") to Thomas Beard, *1 page, 8vo, Tavistock House Thursday 23 April 1857,* informing Beard that he has invited Delane to dinner the following Saturday and asking him to hold himself engaged accordingly, *with the autograph envelope, signed and stamped. Dexter Gift.*

H.271   A.L.s. ("CD.") to Thomas Beard, *1 page, 8vo, Office of Household Words, Tuesday 12 May 1857,* inviting Beard to dine that afternoon at the office with Bradbury and Evans, Lemon and Forster (" . . . It is our half yearly Audit Day . . . "), *with the autograph envelope, signed. Dexter Gift.*

H.272   A.L.s. to Thomas Beard, *2 pages, 8vo, Waites's Hotel Gravesend Sunday 17 May 1857,* giving travelling directions for a forthcoming visit to Gad's Hill by Beard (referring to Gad's Hill as "my Numble abode"), *with the autograph envelope, signed and stamped.*

Letter and envelope mounted in a cardboard frame. *Dexter Gift.*

H.273   A.L.s. to William Howard Russell, *1 page, 8vo, Tavistock House Thursday 21 May 1857,* promising to meet Russell next day at the Gallery of Illustration, Regent Street, (no doubt in connection with Russell's lecture on his experiences as the *Times's* correspondent in the Crimea, one of the events organised by Dickens for the benefit of Douglas Jerrold's widow and her children). *1950 Gift.*

H.274   A.L.s. to Mrs. R. H. Horne, *2 pages, 8vo, Tavistock House 29 May 1857,* enthusing about Gad's Hill Place and expressing the hope that Mrs. Horne will shortly visit him there. *1950 Gift.*

H.275   A.L.s. to William Howard Russell, *2 pages, 8vo, Tavistock House Saturday 30 May 1857,* explaining why his wife cannot accept an invitation for the following day and checking the date of an appointment. *1950 Gift.*

H.276   A.L.s. ("CD.") to Daniel Maclise, *2 pages, 8vo, Tavistock House 8 July 1857,* replying to Maclise's congratulations on his acting of Richard Wardour in *The Frozen Deep* (" . . . the interest of such a character to me is that it enables me, as it were, *to write a book in company* . . . ") and mentioning Queen Victoria's approbation of the performance.

H.277   A.L.s. ("CD.") to Thomas Beard, *1 page, 8vo, Tavistock House Thursday Evening 9 July 1857,* asking Beard if he would like to see a performance of *The Frozen Deep* "from the Proscenium Wing" (" . . . If you would, managerial potentiality can achieve it . . . "), *with the autograph envelope, signed and stamped. Dexter Gift.*

H.278   A.L.s. to William Jerdan, former Editor of the *Literary Gazette, 4 pages, 8vo, Gad's Hill, Higham by Rochester Tuesday 21 July 1857,* describing Hans Christian Andersen's five-week sojourn with the Dickens family.

> . . . whenever he got to London, he got into wild entanglements of cabs and Sherry, and never seemed to get out of them again until he came back here, and cut out paper into all sorts of patterns, and gathered the strangest little nosegays in the woods . . . .
>
> One day he came home to Tavistock House, apparently suffering from corns that had ripened in two hours. It turned out that a cab driver had brought him from the City, by way of the new unfinished thoroughfare through Clerkenwell. Satisfied

Hans Christian Andersen (See H.278)

that the cabman was bent on robbery and murder, he had put his watch and money into his boots – together with a Bradshaw, a pocket-book, a pair of scissors, a penknife, a book or two, a few letters of introduction, and some other miscellaneous property . . . .

H.279   A.L.s. to Professor Attwell, *2 pages, 8vo, Gad's Hill Place, Higham, by Rochester 27 July 1857,* thanking Attwell for some poems he has sent and making an appointment to see him, *with the autograph envelope, stamped (address:* "Professor Attwell / Romford / Essex").

Possibly this correspondent was Henry Attwell, translator and teacher of languages, who published a volume entitled *Poems* in 1856. *1950 Gift.*

H.280   A.L.s. ("CD.") to Georgina Hogarth, *2 pages, 8vo, Office of Household Words, Wednesday 29 July 1857,* asking Georgina to send to Wilkie Collins a collection of "odd cuttings, pamphlets and pictures" relating to Newgate from his study. *1938 Gift.*

H.281   A.L.s. to William Bodham Donne, Examiner of Plays in the Lord Chamberlain's Office, *1 page, 8vo, Gallery of Illustration Regent Street 11 August 1857,* asking Donne to licence *The Frozen Deep* so that the Amateur Actors can perform it in Manchester, for the benefit of the Jerrold Fund. *1950 Gift.*

H.282   A.L. (in the third person) to Mr. Hoole, *1 page, 8vo, Gad's Hill, Higham, by Rochester [? summer 1857],* saying that he was, in fact, aware that the window in St. George's Church, Southwark, referred to at the end of *Little Dorrit,* was not as old as the date of the story but considered this minor anachronism unimportant since the window "appropriately carried out the spirit of the tale at its conclusion".

The Editors of the Pilgrim Edition of Dickens's Letters suggest a tentative dating of this letter to the summer of 1857 on the evidence of the handwriting. *1950 Gift.*

H.283   A.L.s. to Thomas German Reed, musician and co-organiser of Mr. and Mrs. German Reed's "Entertainments", *1 page, 8vo, Gad's Hill Place, Higham, by Rochester Wednesday 12 August 1857,* inviting Reed and his wife to come to Gad's Hill when Macready will also be there. *1950 Gift.*

H.284   A.L. (in the third person) to the Master of the Angel Hotel, Doncaster, *2 pages, 8vo, Tavistock House, London Thursday 3 September 1857,* booking a sitting-room and two bedrooms for himself and Wilkie Collins for 13 September and informing the Master that he may remain in Doncaster for the whole of the races week. *1950 Gift.*

H.285   A.L.s. to Thomas Beard, *1 page, 8vo, Tavistock House Thursday 19 November 1857,* inviting Beard to dinner the following Sunday, *with the autograph envelope, signed and stamped. Dexter Gift.*

H.286   A.L.s. ("CD.") to William Makepeace Thackeray, *2 pages, 8vo, Tavistock House, Tuesday 2 February 1858,* explaining that the Guild of Literature and Art is hampered by law "*from doing any thing* until it shall have existed in a perfectly useless condition for Seven Years" so that it cannot assist in a case referred to him by Thackeray.

With the letter is a four-page extract from the February 1864 number of the *Cornhill Magazine* containing Dickens's "In Memoriam" notice of Thackeray.

H.287   A.L.s. to Thomas Beard, *2 pages, 8vo, Tavistock House, Tavistock Square, London, W.C. Monday 5 April 1858,* sending tickets for a charity reading of the *Christmas Carol,* saying that he has "all but decided" to give readings for his own profit and reporting the success of a reading at Edinburgh, *with the autograph envelope, signed and stamped. Dexter Gift.*

H.288   A.L.s. ("CD.") to Thomas Beard, *1 page, 8vo, Tavistock House, Tavistock Square, London. W.C. Saturday Morning 17 April 1858,* telling Beard that he has asked his manager, Arthur Smith, to send Beard tickets for each of his readings (" . . . and I hope I shall never miss my old friend's face . . . "), *with the autograph envelope, signed and stamped. Dexter Gift.*

H.289   A.L.s. to Thomas Beard, *2 pages, 8vo, Tavistock House, Tavistock Square, London W.C. Saturday 1 May 1858,* discussing his readings, *with the autograph envelope, signed and stamped.*

> . . . I think some people are a little afraid of the Chimes. To tell you the truth, I am – as yet – a little so myself, for I *can not* yet (and I have been at it all the morning) command sufficient composure at some of the more affecting parts, to project them with the necessary force, the requisite distance.
>
> I must harden my heart, like Lady Macbeth . . . .

Dexter Gift.

H.290   A.L.s. ("CD.") to Thomas Beard, *2 pages, 8vo, Tavistock House, Tavistock Square, London. W.C. Friday Evening 7 May 1858,* mentioning Gad's Hill and reporting on the success of a reading of *The Chimes, with the autograph envelope, signed and stamped. Dexter Gift.*

H.291   A.L.s. ("CD.") to Georgina Hogarth, *1 page, 8vo, n.p., Monday 10 May 1858,* concerning domestic matters.

Letter pasted into a paper folder endorsed by Mrs Perugini. *1938 Gift.*

H.292   A.L.s. to Bernard Homer Dixon, *1 page, 8vo, Tavistock House, Tavistock Square, London W.C. Saturday Evening 15 May 1858,* thanking Dixon for a book and saying that he is always gratified to receive marks of attention from Americans travelling·in England.

The book sent to Dickens by Dixon was possibly a copy of his *Surnames* (privately printed in Boston, Mass., in 1855, new edition 1857). *1950 Gift.*

H.293   A.L.s. ("CD.") to Angela Georgina Burdett-Coutts, *2 pages, 8vo, Household Words Office 19 May 1858,* concerning his decision to separate from his wife (" . . . nothing on Earth – no, not even you – no consideration, human or Divine, can move me from the resolution I have taken ' . . ") and warning her that he cannot discuss with her anything that she may already have talked about in the presence of his "wicked" mother-in-law.

H.294   A.L.s. to Cornelius Conway Felton, Professor of Greek at Harvard University, *3 pages, 8vo, Tavistock House, Tavistock Square, London W.C. 22 May 1858,* informing Felton of his separation from his wife and inviting him to visit "my little place in Kent" before leaving England (" . . . Don't be disturbed by the news I give you. It is all for the best . . . ").

H.295   Autograph Transcript (unsigned) of the first portion of a letter to Arthur Smith dated 25 May 1858 (later called by Dickens, after its publication, the "Violated Letter"), *2 pages, 8vo, Tavistock House, Tavistock Square, London W.C., n.d.,* stating the personal and temperamental incompatibility of his wife and himself.

> . . . An attached woman – more a friend to both of us than a servant – who lived with us 16 years, and is now married, and who was, and still is, in Mrs. Dickens's confidence and in mine has had the closest familiar experience of this unhappiness – in London – in the country – in France – in Italy – wherever we have been – year after year, month after month, week after week, day after day.

Dickens apparently copied out this portion of the letter for the information of the woman referred to in it, Anne Cornelius (née Brown). The document was sold at Sotheby's on 23 July 1935 for £88 by Mrs. Cornelius's grand-daughter, Miss F. K. Romer, the purchaser being the Comte de Suzannet who, later in the year, presented it to The Dickens House.

A few words representing an earlier attempt at transcribing these paragraphs appear on page 4 of this document.

H.296   A.L.s. to Thomas Beard, *2 pages, 8vo, Gad's Hill Place, Higham by Rochester, Kent. Tuesday Evening 6 July 1858,* inviting Beard to come and take "a little country

> **Tavistock House,**
> **Tavistock Square, London. W.C.**
>
> *[facsimile of autograph letter in Dickens's hand]*

H.295

idleness" at Gad's Hill before he goes away on a long Reading Tour, *with the autograph envelope, signed and stamped. Dexter Gift.*

H.297   A.L.s. to John Palgrave Simpson, dramatist and novelist, *3 pages, 8vo, Tavistock House, Tavistock Square, London W.C. 3 July 1858,* mocking the absurdity of the behaviour of the Garrick Club Committee with regard to Thackeray's complaint against Edmund Yates and advising Simpson not to make any protest until Yates has ascertained what the legal position is.

H.298   A.L.s. ("CD.") to Thomas Beard, *1 page, 8vo, Gad's Hill Place, Higham by Rochester, Kent. Sunday 1 August 1858,* concerning a "little writing-case" which Beard has left behind at Gad's Hill, *with the autograph envelope, signed and stamped. Dexter Gift.*

H.299   A.L.s. to John T. Lawrence, *2 pages, 8vo, Wolverhampton Wednesday 11 August 1858,* courteously declining an invitation from some friends of Lawrence's, Mr. and Mrs. Potts, on the grounds that he is obliged to deny himself "all social pleasures" during his Reading tours because of the exhausting nature of these, and saying that he could not, in any circumstances, dine out on a day when he was due to give a reading. *1950 Gift.*

H.300   A.L.s. ("CD.") to Georgina Hogarth, *1 page, 8vo, Tavistock House, Tavistock Square, London WC Wednesday Morning 18 August 1858,* reporting that his cold has improved and that he has recovered his voice (" . . . I think I sang half the Irish Melodies to myself as I walked about, to test it . . . ").

Letter pasted into a paper folder endorsed by Mrs. Perugini. *1938 Gift.*

H.301   A.L.s. ("CD.") to Georgina Hogarth, *4 pages, 8vo, Adelphi Hotel, Liverpool Friday Night, 20 August 1858,* reporting on the great success of his Readings.

> . . . What Arthur's state has been tonight – he, John, Berry and Boycett, all taking money and going mad together – you can*not* imagine. They turned away hundreds, sold all the books, rolled on the ground of my room knee deep in checks, and made a perfect Pantomime of the whole thing . . . .

Letter mounted in a cardboard frame. *1938 Gift.*

H.302   A.L.s. ("CD.") to Georgina Hogarth, *6 pages, 8vo, Morrisons' Hotel Dublin Sunday Night 29 August 1858,* reporting the success of his Readings in Belfast, mentioning Landor, saying that he has bought an Irish jaunting car, etc.

> . . . The success at Belfast has been equal to the success here. Enormous. We turned away half the town. I think them a better audience on the whole than Dublin; and the personal affection there, was something overwhelming. I wish you and the dear girls could have seen the people look at me in the street – or heard them ask me, as I hurried to the hotel after the reading last night to "do me the honor to shake hands Misther Dickens and God bless you Sir; not only for the light you've been to me this night; but for the light you've been in mee house Sir (and God love your face!) this many a year" . . . .

Letter pasted into a paper folder endorsed by Mrs. Perugini. *1938 Gift.*

H.303   A.L. (signature cut away) to Georgina Hogarth, *2 pages 8vo, Office of Household Words, Tuesday 7 September 1858,* concerning a school bill that he has forgotten to pay.

Letter pasted into a paper folder endorsed by Mrs. Perugini. *1938 Gift.*

H.304   A.L.s. to Bradbury and Evans, *1 page, 8vo, Office of Household Words Tuesday 7 September 1858,* requesting that the bearer of the note be given copies of the Reading Editions of the *Carol, Chimes, Dombey,* the *Poor Traveller,* etc.

Letter preserved with a set of these Reading Editions (see A.22).

H.305   A.L. (fragment only) to G— Holsworth, *1 page, 8vo, Station Hotel York. Friday 10 September 1858,* asking Holsworth to extract for him from *Household Words* a complete version of "The Lazy Tour of Two Idle Apprentices" (serialised in the magazine 3–31 October, 1857) and to send it to him.

The signature and conclusion of the letter have been removed. *1950 Gift.*

H.306   A.L.s. ("CD.") to Georgina Hogarth, *6 pages, 8vo, Royal Hotel, Scarborough Sunday 11 September 1858,* concerning a suitor of his daughter Kate's, describing his travels and audiences at his readings, *with the autograph envelope, signed (stamp removed).*

> . . . There was a remarkably good fellow of 30 or so, too, who found something so very ludicrous in Toots that he *could not* compose himself at all, but laughed until he sat wiping his eyes with his handkerchief and whenever he felt Toots coming again, he began to laugh and wipe his eyes afresh; and when he came, he gave a kind of cry, as if it were too much for him. It was uncommonly droll, and made me laugh heartily.

Letter and envelope in paper folder endorsed by Mrs. Perugini. *1938 Gift.*

H.307   A.L.s. ("CD.") to Georgina Hogarth, *3 pages, 8vo, King's Head, Sheffield Friday 17 September 1858,* concerning his Readings at Halifax and Sheffield.

Letter pasted into a paper folder endorsed by Mrs. Perugini. *1938 Gift.*

H.308   A.L.s. ("CD.") to Thomas Beard, *1 page, 8vo, Tavistock House, Tavistock Square, London. W.C. Thursday 14 October 1858,* sending Beard an advertisement that might interest him and reporting on the success of the Reading Tour (" . . . Between ourselves, the clear profits of the Readings, after payment of all the charges, which are necessarily heavy – one thousand pounds per month! . . . "), *with the autograph envelope, signed and stamped.*

With the letter is the newspaper cutting sent by Dickens to Beard (an advertisement by the National Newspaper League Company seeking a General Manager for a projected new paper, *The Dial*) and the printed programme for Dickens's provincial Reading Tour of autumn 1858. *Dexter Gift.*

H.309   A.L.s. to Thomas Beard, *2 pages, 8vo, Hen and Chickens, Birmingham Wednesday 20 October 1858,* urging Beard to apply to the Government for some kind of public employment and describing a reading of the Trial from Pickwick (" . . . when Mr. Serjeant Buzfuz said: 'Call Samuel Weller' they gave a great thunder of applause, as if he were really coming in . . . "), *with the autograph envelope, signed and stamped. Dexter Gift.*

H.310   A.L.s. to Georgina Hogarth, *4 pages, 8vo, Wolverhampton Wednesday 3 November 1858,* reporting a successful Reading at Leamington, mentioning the son of Mr. and Mrs. Watson (of Rockingham Castle) and anticipating a good house at his Wolverhampton reading that evening.

Letter pasted into a paper folder endorsed by Mrs. Perugini. *1938 Gift.*

H.311   A.L. (subscription and signature cut away) to Georgina Hogarth, *2 pages, 8vo, Tavistock House, Tavistock Square, London WC Monday 8 November 1858,* forwarding a letter from the Hon. Mrs. Richard Watson and sending cheques for housekeeping and other expenses.

Letter pasted into a paper folder endorsed by Mrs. Perugini. *1938 Gift.*

H.312   A.L.s. to Ella Maria Winter, *1 page, 8vo, Tavistock House, Tavistock Square, London W.C. 15 December 1858,* thanking her for her gift of a "pretty book-marker" and saying that it "will often and often carry my mind back to the days when your Mamma was a girl, and I was a boy, and very few people knew the name of / your affectionate / Charles Dickens."

H.313   A.L.s. to Peter Cunningham, *2 pages, 8vo, Tavistock House, Tavistock Square, Friday 11 February 1859*, thanking Cunningham for a copy of "the concluding Walpole volume" and gently reproaching him for repeating "monomaniacal nonsense" about Dickens's actions and motives in the Garrick Club affair (" . . . such preposterous statements as that I pay Mr. Yates's costs against the Garrick club . . . ").

H.314   A.L.s. to Francis Carr Beard, brother of Thomas Beard, *2 pages, 8vo, Tavistock House, Tavistock Square, London. W.C. Monday 14 February 1859*, asking Beard to become the Dickens household's regular medical attendant. *Dexter Gift.*

H.315   A.L.s. ("CD.") to Thomas Beard, *2 pages, 8vo, Gad's Hill Place, Higham by Rochester, Kent. Saturday 30 April 1859,* saying that he has written to Bulwer-Lytton on Beard's behalf regarding some "office" to which Beard aspires, *with the autograph envelope, signed and stamped. Dexter Gift.*

H.316   A.L.s. ("CD.") to Thomas Beard, *1 page, 8vo, Office of All the Year Round, Tuesday 3 May 1859,* enclosing Bulwer-Lytton's reply to his letter on Beard's behalf (" . . . the place, unfortunately, is not in his gift . . . ") and suggesting that Beard apply to "that Jackass Ld Malmesbury", *with the autograph envelope, signed and stamped. Dexter Gift.*

H.317   A.L.s. to Francis Carr Beard, *1 page, 8vo, Office of All the Year Round, Saturday 25 June 1859,* saying that he wants to see Beard about a minor ailment which has been caused by his "bachelor state", *with the autograph envelope inscribed in Dickens's hand* "Wait Answer".

The version of this letter printed in the Nonesuch Edition of the Letters (vol. 3, p. 108) has been bowdlerised. *Dexter Gift.*

H.318   A.L.s. to Francis Carr Beard, *1 page, 8vo, Office of All the Year Round, Friday 2 July 1859,* asking Beard to call on him (" . . . What I principally want to know is, whether your medicine irritates my skin . . . "), *with the autograph envelope, signed. Dexter Gift.*

H.319   A.L.s. to Francis Carr Beard, *1 page, 8vo, Gad's Hill Place, Higham by Rochester, Kent. Friday 29 July 1859,* concerning his health (" . . . I am very little better – really very little . . . "), *with the autograph envelope, signed and stamped. Dexter Gift.*

H.320   A.L.s. ("CD.") to Thomas Beard, *1 page, 8vo, Office of All the Year Round, Tuesday 2 August 1859,* concerning a forthcoming visit by Beard to Gad's Hill, *with the autograph envelope, signed and stamped. Dexter Gift.*

H.321   A.L.s. ("CD.") to Francis Carr Beard, *1 page, 8vo, Gad's Hill Place, Higham by Rochester, Kent. Saturday 6 August 1859,* anticipating a definite improvement in his health. *Dexter Gift.*

H.322   A.L.s. ("CD.") to Georgina Hogarth, *1 page, 8vo, Norwich (Royal Hotel) Wednesday Evening 12 October 1859,* reporting the "*Immense Success*" of his Reading the previous evening, *with the autograph envelope, signed and stamped.*

H.323   A.L.s. ("CD.") to Georgina Hogarth, *1 page, 8vo, Eagle Hotel, Cambridge*

Monday 17 October 1859, telling her the time of the Oxford train and commenting on Cambridge (" . . . I don't very much like the look of the place. It seems what Plorn would call 'ortily' dull. . . . "), *with the autograph envelope, signed and stamped. 1938 Gift.*

H.324   A.L.s. ("CD.") to John Forster, *3 pages, 8vo, Tavistock House, Tavistock Square, London W.C. Monday 24 October 1859,* arranging to meet Thornton Hunt to discuss with him allegations in the press that his father, Leigh Hunt, was Dickens's model for Harold Skimpole in *Bleak House.*

> . . . What I said to his poor father in your presence, I will say in any way Thornton Hunt likes; – that there are many remembrances of Hunt in little traits of manner and expression, in that character and especially in all the pleasantest parts of it, but that is all . . . .

H.325   A.L. (signature cut away) to Thornton Leigh Hunt, *1 page, 8vo, Tavistock House, Tavistock Square, London W.C. Monday 4 December 1859,* concerning the article "Leigh Hunt. A Remonstrance" which he is proposing to publish in *All The Year Round.*

A note on p. 3, presumably in Hunt's hand, reads: "T.L.H. gave signature of Dickens to Glyde".

H.326   A.L.s. to Thornton Leigh Hunt, *1 page, 8vo, Office of All The Year Round Wednesday 7 December 1859,* asking Hunt to call at the office the following day and look over the proof of "Leigh Hunt. A Remonstrance" with him.

H.327   A.L.s. to Thomas Beard, *1 page, 8vo, Tavistock House, Tavistock Square, London W.C. Saturday Night 31 December 1859,* sending New Year good wishes and some "old liqueur brandy not easy to get", *with the autograph envelope, signed and inscribed, in Dickens's hand,* "With Half a Dozen Bottles". *Dexter Gift.*

H.328   A.L.s. ("CD.") to Georgina Hogarth, *2 pages, 16mo, Office of All the Year Round, Tuesday New Years' Day 1860,* forwarding a letter for his son Sydney from the son of Sir Richard Bromley and giving instructions about a greenhouse.

Letter pasted into a paper folder. *1938 Gift.*

H.329   A.L.s. to Lord Chancellor Paget, *2 pages, 8vo, Tavistock House, 5 January 1860,* about obtaining a nomination as a naval cadet for his son, Sydney Smith Dickens (with draft of a reply on a blank page).

This letter is recorded as forming part of the Comte de Suzannet's 1950 Gift to The Dickens House but has subsequently been mislaid. A transcript made before its disappearance is in the files of the Editors of the Pilgrim Edition of Dickens's Letters.

H.330   A.L.s. to Sir Alexander Cornewall Duff-Gordon, *1 page, 8vo, Tavistock House, Tavistock Square, London, W.C. Friday 30 March 1860,* enclosing an invitation to Gad's Hill which he wishes Duff-Gordon to forward to "the Ninevite" (Sir Austen Henry Layard) before Layard comes to lecture in Rochester under his presidency. *1950 Gift.*

H.331   A.L.s. to Count Strzelecki, (Sir Paul Edmund Strzelecki, K.C.M.G., F.R.S.), explorer and scientist, author of *A Physical Description of New South Wales and Van Diemen's Land* (1845), *2 pages, 8vo, Tavistock House, Tavistock Square, London. W.C.*

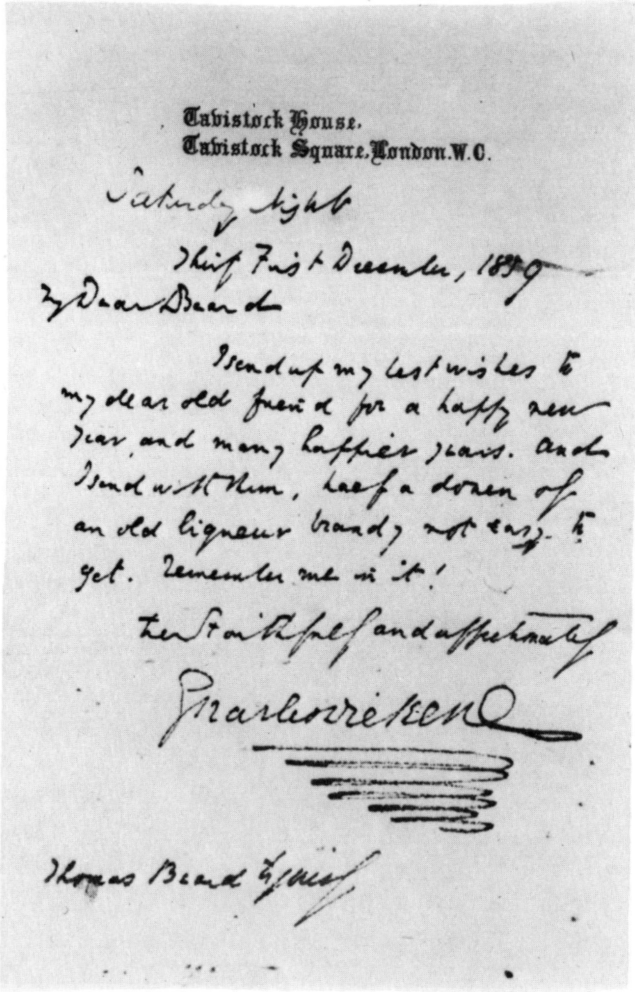

Tavistock House.
Tavistock Square, London. W.C.

Saturday Night

Thirty First December, 1859

My Dear Beard

I send up my best wishes to
my dear old friend for a happy new
Year, and many happier Years. And
I send with them, half a dozen of
an old liqueur brandy not easy to
get. Remember me in it!

Ever Faithful and affectionate

Charles Dickens

Thomas Beard Esquire

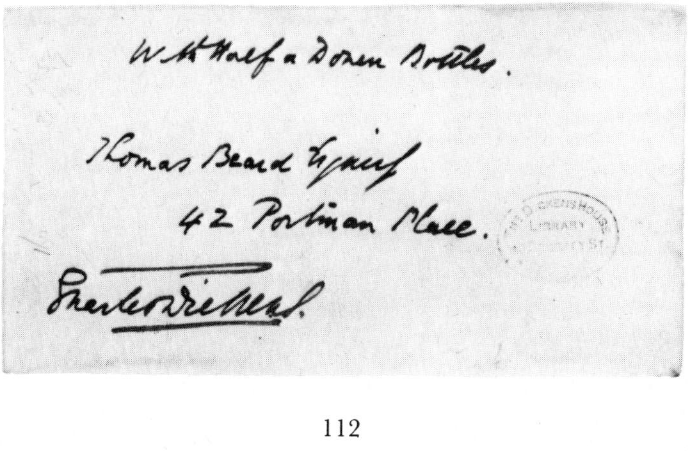

With Half a Dozen Bottles.

Thomas Beard Esquire
42 Portman Place

Charles Dickens

Friday 20 April 1860, declining on principle to associate himself with some testimonial to the memory of a writer which Strzelecki is organising and expressing the opinion that, until the memory of such men is publicly honoured by the nation, "their best Monument is in their own Works." *1950 Gift.*

H.332   A.L.s. to Thomas Beard, *1 page, 8vo, Tavistock House, Tavistock Square, London. W.C. 28 April 1860,* sending a ticket for a dinner to be held in honour of Charles Dickens Junior, *with the autograph envelope, signed and stamped. Dexter Gift.*

H.333   A.L.s. to Lieutenant-Colonel Edward Bruce Hamley, writer and Professor of Military History at Sandhurst College, *1 page, 8vo, Gad's Hill Place, Higham by Rochester, Kent. Friday 8 June 1860,* regretting that he will be unable to dine with Hamley on 15 June since ill-health has compelled him to leave London for the country earlier than usual this year.

With the letter is an "outline" of the Maclise portrait of Dickens. *1950 Gift.*

H.334   A.L.s. ("CD.") to Thomas Beard, *2 pages, 8vo, Gad's Hill Place, Higham by Rochester, Kent. Tuesday 12 June 1860,* inviting Beard to the wedding of his daughter Kate with Charles Collins, *with the autograph envelope, signed and stamped. Dexter Gift.*

H.335   A.L.s. ("CD.") to Thomas Beard, *1 page, 8vo, Gad's Hill Place, Higham by Rochester, Kent. Thursday 11 July 1860,* giving instructions for proceeding to Gad's Hill on the day of Kate Dickens's wedding, *with the autograph envelope, signed and stamped. Dexter Gift.*

H.336   A.L.s. ("CD.") to Georgina Hogarth, *2 pages, 8vo, [The Reform Club] Tuesday Evening (Dining here with Wills) 21 August 1860,* announcing the completion of his sale of Tavistock House and mentioning his search for a house for his widowed sister-in-law, Helen Dickens.

Letter pasted into a paper folder endorsed by Mrs. Perugini. *1938 Gift.*

H.337   A.L.s. ("CD.") to Georgina Hogarth, *2 pages, 16mo, Office of All the Year Round, Tuesday Night 21 August 1860,* concerning the house for Helen Dickens (" . . . John has seen some houses by the Orphan Working School at Haverstock Hill . . . of which, one that has been inhabited four years and from which the people *ran away,* seems to me, the thing . . . ").

Letter pasted into a paper folder endorsed by Mrs. Perugini. *1938 Gift.*

H.338   A.L.s. ("CD.)) to Georgina Hogarth, *1 page, 16mo, Office of All the Year Round, Wednesday 31 October 1860,* asking Georgina to forward some enclosed letters to the manager of his Reading Tours, Arthur Smith.

Letter pasted into a paper folder endorsed by Mrs. Perugini. *1938 Gift.*

H.339   A.L.s. ("CD.") to Georgina Hogarth, *2 pages, 8vo, Bideford, North Devon Thursday Night 1 November 1860,* reporting his safe arrival in Bideford "in a Beastly Hotel" and detailing his future movements.

> . . . We had stinking fish for dinner, and have been able to drink nothing—
> though we have ordered wine, beer, and brandy and water. There is nothing in the
> house but Two Tarts and a pair of snuffers. The landlady is playing cribbage with

the landlord in the next room (behind a thin partition), and they seem quite comfortable . . . .

1938 Gift.

H.340   A.L.s. ("CD.") to Georgina Hogarth, *2 pages, 8vo, Office of All the Year Round, Wednesday 14 November 1860*, concerning his son Sydney's illness, mentioning Madame Celeste and Wilkie Collins, and describing Forster and his wife at a dinner party (" . . . In the previous proceedings at the Bank of England, Forster had amazed and terrified that establishment – but still had impressed it . . . ").

Letter pasted into a paper folder endorsed by Mrs. Perugini. *1938 Gift.*

H.341   A.L.s. ("CD.") to Georgina Hogarth, *2 pages, 8vo, Office of All the Year Round, Tuesday 27 November 1860*, describing a visit to his mother, mentioning Wilkie Collins, etc.

> . . . I found my mother yesterday, much better than I had supposed. She was not in bed but downstairs. Helen and Laetitia were poulticing her poor head, and, the instant she saw me, she plucked up a spirit and asked me for "a pound" . . .

Letter pasted into a paper folder endorsed by Mrs. Perugini. A passage of about four or five lines has been excised following the paragraph quoted above. *1938 Gift.*

Dickens's mother photographed in 1860 (See H.341)

H.342   A.L.s. ("CD.") to Georgina Hogarth, *2 pages, 16mo, Office of All the Year Round, Wednesday 28 November 1860,* reporting progress on the compilation of the Christmas Number of *All The Year Round* (" . . . Mrs Gaskell being much too long for the purpose, I have put Charley Collins into the Xmas No. . . .").
Letter pasted into a paper folder endorsed by Mrs. Perugini. *1938 Gift.*

H.343   A.L.s. ("CD.") to Thomas Mitton, *1 page, 8vo, Gad's Hill Place, Higham by Rochester, Kent., Sunday 2 December 1860,* telling Mitton that he will not be at the *All the Year Round* Office until Tuesday week since he is feeling overworked and in need of rest. *1950 Gift.*

H.344   A.L.s. ("CD.") to Georgina Hogarth, *2 pages, 8vo, Office of All the Year Round, Friday 28 December 1860,* concerning his health (" . . . I have delivered myself over to be physicked . . . ") and sending various instructions about domestic matters at Gad's Hill.
Letter pasted into a paper folder endorsed by Mrs. Perugini. *1938 Gift.*

H.345   A.L.s. ("CD.") to Georgina Hogarth, *2 pages, 8vo, Office of All the Year Round, Wednesday 2 January 1861,* describing a visit, with Wilkie Collins, to "Buckley's Serenaders" at the St. James's Hall (" . . . They do the most preposterous things, in the way of Violin Solos, Deeply Sentimental Songs, and Lucrezia Borgia Music, sung by a majestic female in black velvet and Jewels, *with a blackened face! . . .* ") and reporting on his health (" . . . Frank Beard thinks me decidedly better today . . . ").
Letter pasted on to loose sheet. *1938 Gift.*

H.346   A.L.s. ("CD.") to Georgina Hogarth, *1 page, 16mo, Office of All the Year Round, Saturday 5 January 1861,* forwarding a letter which he has "not the heart to open" (" . . . will you make me out a list of that affectionate contribution towards my ruin . . . "). *1938 Gift.*

H.347   A.L.s. ("CD.") to Georgina Hogarth, *2 pages, 16mo, Office of All the Year Round, Monday 7 January 1861,* expressing approval of "the Theatrical arrangements" and reporting on his improved health (" . . . I have not taken the objectionable medecine since last Friday . . . ").
Letter pasted into paper folder endorsed by Mrs. Perugini. *1938 Gift.*

H.348   A.L.s. ("CD.") to Georgina Hogarth, *1 page, 16mo, Office of All the Year Round, Wednesday 9 January 1861,* concerning an invitation he has received from the Lady Mayoress of London (Lady Oliffe) to a "Family dinner" at the Mansion House (" . . . Shall we go? Perhaps it might be well to take the opportunity. . . . ").
Letter pasted into a paper folder endorsed by Mrs. Perugini. *1938 Gift.*

H.349   A.L.s. ("CD.") to Georgina Hogarth, *1 page, 8vo, Office of All the Year Round, Thursday 17 January 1861,* arranging to come down to Gad's Hill and saying that he has had his "Vapour Bath" (" . . . and, strange to add, have positively enjoyed it!!!"), *with the autograph envelope, signed, stamped and endorsed* "Various 1860-1".
Letter pasted into a paper folder endorsed by Mrs. Perugini. *1938 Gift.*

H.350 A.L.s. ("CD.") to Francis Carr Beard, *1 page, 16mo, Office of All the Year Round, Tuesday 29 January 1861,* asking Beard to visit him (" . . . I should like to be inspected – though I hope I can offer no new attractions . . . "), *with the autograph envelope, initialled and stamped. Dexter Gift.*

H.351 A.L.s. ("CD.") to Thomas Beard, *1 page, 8vo, Office of All the Year Round, Tuesday Evening 29 January 1861,* inviting Beard to dine with him at No. 3 Hanover Terrace on his next birthday. *Dexter Gift.*

H.352 A.L.s. ("CD.") to Georgina Hogarth, *3 pages, 16mo, Office of All The Year Round, Saturday 2 February 1861,* enclosing money and giving detailed instructions concerning the moving of the household into No. 3 Hanover Terrace.
    Letter pasted into a paper folder endorsed by Mrs. Perugini. *1938 Gift.*

H.353 A.L.s. ("CD.") to Thomas Beard, *1 page, 8vo, 3 Hanover Terrace, Sunday 3 March 1861,* enquiring how many tickets Beard would like for the Readings at St. James's Hall that month, *with the autograph envelope, initialled and stamped. Dexter Gift.*

H.354 A.L.s. ("CD.") to Francis Carr Beard, *1 page, 8vo, 3 Hanover Terrace Tuesday 12 March 1861,* concerning some complimentary tickets for one of his Readings.
    Letter mounted in a cardboard frame. *Dexter Gift.*

H.355 A.L.s. ("CD.") to Thomas Beard, *2 pages, 8vo, 3 Hanover Terrace 25 March 1861,* suggesting that Beard abstract a pamphlet on Prison Discipline for *All the Year Round* and asking why Beard doesn't visit him in his retiring-room at the St. James's Hall during intervals in his Readings, *with the autograph envelope, signed and inscribed, in Dickens's hand,* "Private". *Dexter Gift.*

H.356 A.L.s. to Thomas Beard, *1 page, 8vo, 3 Hanover Terrace Thursday 18 April 1861,* praising the way in which Beard has carried out the task suggested in a previous letter (see above, 25 March 1861), *with the autograph envelope, initialled and stamped.*

> . . . The condensation, and slight touch here and there, which I think will improve it, I will mark in the proof . . . The changes that occur to me are certainly no greater than I make in five out of every six papers that go in . . .

Dexter Gift.

H.357 A.L.s. to Elizabeth Cleghorn Gaskell, *1 page, 8vo, All the Year Round 22 April 1861,* saying that he will attempt to retrieve a letter written by Mrs. Gaskell to Miss Burdett Coutts (" . . . It is quite likely that it has never been opened, as no human creature can imagine how impossible it is for that lady to keep pace with her correspondents . . .") and mentioning the secretarial and charitable work done for Miss Coutts by W. H. Wills. *Dexter Gift.*

H.358 A.L.s. ("CD.") to Georgina Hogarth, *1 page, 8vo, Lord Warden Hotel Dover Sunday 26 May 1861,* sending money for housekeeping expenses and reporting on his health (" . . . My face aches at times, but very little . . . ").
    Letter pasted into a paper folder endorsed by Mrs. Perugini. *1938 Gift.*

H.359   A.L.s. ("CD.") to Georgina Hogarth, *2 pages, 16mo, Office of All the Year Round, Wednesday 17 July 1861,* asking Georgina to bring him a "white Dress Shirt" and commenting on various friends and acquaintances.

> . . . I have a horrible idea upon me at times, that Bartlett will not turn out grateful. I don't know what it is that whispers the suspicion to me – something in her cheek bone, I think – but it comes over me occasionally, like the whiff of some disagreeable Factory . . . .

Letter pasted into a paper folder endorsed by Mrs. Perugini. *1938 Gift.*

H.360   A.L.s. ("CD.") to Georgina Hogarth, *2 pages, 16mo, Office of All the Year Round, Wednesday 31 July 1861,* concerning domestic arrangements, visitors to Gad's Hill, etc.

Letter pasted into a paper folder endorsed (with incorrect date) by Mrs. Perugini. *1938 Gift.*

H.361   A.L.s. ("CD.") to Georgina Hogarth, *1 page, 8vo, Office of All the Year Round, Thursday 19 September 1861,* concerning his wardrobe and also the engagement of Thomas Headland as Manager for his Reading Tour, in succession to Arthur Smith.

Letter pasted into a paper folder endorsed by Mrs. Perugini. *1938 Gift.*

H.362   A.L.s. ("CD.") to Georgina Hogarth, *2 pages, 16mo, Office of All the Year Round, Wednesday 9 October 1861,* concerning the death of his brother-in-law, Henry Austin. *1938 Gift.*

H.363   A.L.s. ("CD.") to Thomas Beard, *1 page, 8vo, Office of All the Year Round, Friday 11 October 1861,* making arrangements to attend the funeral of his brother-in-law, Henry Austin, *with the autograph envelope, signed and stamped. Dexter Gift.*

H.364   Autograph Envelope (fragment only), Signed, addressed to: "Miss Hogarth / Gad's Hill Place / Higham / by / Rochester", *black-bordered, stamped and postmarked: Ipswich 1 November 1861.*

The letter belonging to this envelope is printed in the Nonesuch Edition of the Letters, vol. 3, p. 248. *1938 Gift.*

H.365   A.L.s. to Thomas Beard, *1 page, 8vo, Gad's Hill Place, Higham by Rochester, Kent, Sunday 3 November 1861,* mentioning a gift of "some birds" sent by him to Beard from Norwich and expressing his understanding of Beard's desire to attend the marriage of Charles Dickens, Junior, to the daughter of Frederick Evans (" . . . But I must add the expression of my earnest hope that it is not your intention to enter Mr. Evans's house on that occasion . . . "), *mourning paper, with the autograph envelope signed and stamped. Dexter Gift.*

H.366   A.L.s. ("CD.") to Georgina Hogarth, *4 pages, 8vo, Bedford Hotel, Brighton, Thursday 7 November 1861,* reporting the great success of his Readings at Hastings and Dover, mentioning the appearance among the audience of his former brother-in-law, Henry Burnett (" . . . His imbecility was overwhelming . . . "), describing a great storm at Dover (" . . . The sea came in like a great sky of immense clouds, for ever breaking suddenly into furious rain . . . "), commenting on his audience's reactions, mentioning his brother, Frederick, and discussing plans for forthcoming Readings (" . . . I am trying to get off Manchester and Liverpool: both of which I strongly doubt, in the present state of American affairs . . . "), *mourning paper*.

> . . . The most delicate audience I have seen in any provincial place, is Canterbury. The audience with the greatest sense of humour, certainly is Dover. The people in the stalls set the example of laughing, in the most curiously unreserved way; and they really laughed when Squeers read the boys' letters, with such cordial enjoyment, that the contagion extended to me. For, one couldn't hear them without laughing too. . . .

Letter mounted in a cardboard frame. *1938 Gift.*

H.367   A.L.s. ("CD.") to a member of his staff, *1 page, 16mo, Office of All the Year Round, Friday 15 November 1861,* concerning proofs of the 1861 Christmas Number of *All The Year Round* ("Tom Tiddler's Ground").

Letter mounted on card. With it is a copy of the Christmas Number referred to. *1950 Gift.*

H.368   A.L.s. ("CD.") to Georgina Hogarth, *4 pages, 8vo, Queen's Head, Newcastle Friday 22 November 1861,* lamenting the incompetence of his tour manager, Thomas Headland, *mourning paper. 1938 Gift.*

H.369   A.L.s. ("CD.") to Thomas Beard, *2 pages, 8vo, Gad's Hill Place, Higham by Rochester, Kent. Thursday 26 December 1861,* reciprocating Christmas greetings, mentioning his Readings (" . . . As to the new Readings, I rather think myself that Copperfield is A1 . . . ") and describing the departure, for service in the Navy, of his son Sydney, *mourning paper, with the autograph envelope, stamped.*

> . . . Sydney got appointed to the Orlando (a ship that everyone in the service seemed to be trying for), and has sailed for Halifax. He looked very very small when he went away with a chest in which he could easily have stored himself and a wife and family of his own proportions . . . .

Dexter Gift.

H.370   A.L.s. ("CD.") to Thomas Beard, *2 pages, 8vo, Office of All the Year Round, Saturday 1 February 1862,* making plans for celebrating his birthday and mentioning the "dazzling" success of his Readings at Manchester and Liverpool, *with the autograph envelope, black-bordered, stamped. Dexter Gift.*

H.371   A.L. (in the third person) to an Unknown Correspondent, *1 page, 16mo, Office of All the Year Round, 24 February 1862,* rejecting a manuscript entitled "The Eldest Daughter" submitted for publication in *All The Year Round.*

The date and the title of the manuscript have been written in another hand, the rest of the note being in Dickens's own hand. *1950 Gift.*

H.372   A.L.s. ("CD.") to Thomas Beard, *2 pages, 8vo, Office of All the Year Round, Saturday 5 April 1862,* concerning (presumably) the work of a would-be contributor to *All The Year Round,* discussing audiences at his Readings (" . . . they are so much more quick and so much more delicate than they used to be . . . ") and inviting

Sydney Dickens as a Midshipman (See H.369)

Beard to dine at the "nastiest little house in London (16, Hyde Park Gate South)",
with the autograph envelope, stamped.

With the letter is a letter to Beard from C. J. Cottingham (see J.11) concerning
the would-be contributor to Dickens's journal. *Dexter Gift.*

H.373   A.L.s. ("The Inimitable") to Thomas Beard, *2 pages, 8vo, Paris, Rue du
Faubourg St. Honoré 27 4 November 1862,* asking Beard if he would consider accompanying him to Australia if he should decide to go there for a Reading Tour (" . . . I
am wavering between reading in Australia, and writing a book at home . . . "), *with
the autograph envelope, stamped.*

> . . . The work would be, seconding the Inimitable in the ring, delivering him at
> the scratch in fine condition, keeping off the crowd, polishing him up when at all
> punished and checking the local accounts . . .

Dexter Gift.

119

H.374   A.L.s. ("CD.") to Thomas Beard, *2 pages, 8vo, Paris, Rue du Faubourg St. Honoré 27 Saturday 15 November 1862,* further discussing the possibility of his going to Australia on a Reading Tour and of Beard's accompanying him, *with the autograph envelope, stamped.*

> . . . I have a notion that I could perhaps see that country in its present early state of transition, from some point of view (for after-use in fiction) that has not yet struck any man's fancy. I spoke to Bulwer about it, here, the other day; and his un-limited confidence in this possibility was almost absurd–It certainly was immensely greater than mine . . . .

Dexter Gift.

H.375   A.L.s. ("CD.") to Thomas Beard, *1 page, 8vo, Office of All the Year Round, Thursday 26 February 1863,* announcing his return from Paris (" . . . I wish you could have seen and heard a Reading *there! . . .* "), inviting Beard to Gad's Hill, and giving details of some forthcoming London Readings, *with the autograph envelope, stamped. Dexter Gift.*

H.376   A.L.s. ("CD.") to Thomas Beard, *1 page, 8vo, Office of All the Year Round, Friday 13 March 1863,* making arrangements for Beard to visit Gad's Hill and men-tioning Charles Fechter, *with the autograph envelope, signed and stamped. Dexter Gift.*

H.377   Signed cheque drawn on Coutts & Co. for £12.9.9, dated 9 April 1863 and made payable to Mr. Lewis Jacobs. The amount, date and payee's name all in Dickens's hand. Mounted in a cardboard frame. *Dexter Gift.*

H.378   A.L.s. ("CD.") to Dr. James Sheridan Muspratt, chemist, *1 page, 8vo, Gad's Hill Place, Higham by Rochester, Kent. Thursday 28 May 1863,* thanking Muspratt for a photograph and mentioning Wilkie Collins, *with the autograph envelope, stamped.*
The bottom half of the page (presumably blank, unless there was a postscript) has been removed. *1950 Gift.*

H.379   A.L.s. to John Bate Cardale, *1 page, 8vo, Gad's Hill Place, Higham by Rochester, Kent. Friday 19 June 1863,* telling Cardale that he will use a personal anecdote that Cardale has sent him either in *All The Year Round,* when the subject of "Undevel-oped Impressions" (see *ATYR*, vol. 9, pp. 366-69) is reverted to, or elsewhere, and sending a cheque for £20 in respect of the final year of his tenancy of ground in Tavis-tock Square belonging to Cardale (see above, H. 233). *1950 Gift.*

H.380   A.L.s. to Lady Rose Fane, daughter of Dowager Countess of Westmor-land, *2 pages, 8vo, Gad's Hill Place, Higham by Rochester, Kent. Friday 24 July 1863,* apologising for being unable to vote for a protégé of hers, applying for admission to the Hospital for Incurables, because his vote is already pledged to a candidate of Fanny Kemble's. *1950 Gift.*

H.381   A.L.s. to Charlotte Smith (the writer "Kenner Deene"), *1 page, 8vo, Gad's Hill Place, Higham by Rochester, Kent. Monday 5 October 1863,* thanking her for sending him her novel, *The Schoolmaster of Alton,* and praising some aspects of it but commenting also on the "inexperience and precipitation" that mark it, and hoping that she "will some day write a much better story."

Charlotte Smith's surname has been twice deleted. *1950 Gift.*

H.382   A.L.s. ("CD.") to Thomas Beard, *6 pages, 8vo, Office of All the Year Round, Thursday 29 October 1863,* a long detailed account of the plot of a melodrama which Fechter is about to produce at the Lyceum Theatre (with himself in the leading rôle) and which Dickens is anxious Beard should give some favourable notice to, *with the (black-bordered) autograph envelope, signed and stamped. Dexter Gift.*

H.383   A.L.s. to Thomas Beard, *2 pages, 8vo, Gad's Hill Place, Higham by Rochester, Kent. Saturday 16 January 1864,* congratulating Beard on a new appointment (as "Court Newsman") and suggesting possible new apartments for his residence, *mourning paper, with the autograph envelope, signed and stamped. Dexter Gift.*

H.384   A.L.s. ("CD.") to Thomas Beard, *1 page, 8vo, The Athenaeum Tuesday Night 19 January 1864,* giving details of his movements during the two following days and advising Beard on the choice of new apartments (" . . . you could not do better than in the old Guild rooms. They are the snuggest little chambers I know – a complete little house – and thoroughly cheerful . . . "), *with the autograph envelope, black-bordered, signed and stamped.*

Letter and envelope mounted in a cardboard frame. *Dexter Gift.*

H.385   Autograph Envelope, Signed, addressed to: "Thomas Beard Esquire / F. Carr Beard Esquire / 44 Welbeck Street / Cavendish Square / W.", *black-bordered, stamped and postmarked 21 January 1864. Dexter Gift.*

H.386   A.L.s. to Henry Gardiner Adams, *1 page, 8vo, 57 Glos'ter Place, Hyde Park Gardens. Thursday 25 February 1864,* agreeing to comply with a request from Adams's Committee (presumably the Committee of the Chatham Mechanics' Institution), congratulating Adams on his son's new appointment in the Civil Service, and mentioning the death in India of his own son, Walter Landor Dickens, *mourning paper. 1950 Gift.*

H.387   A.L.s. ("CD.") to Francis Carr Beard, *1 page, 8vo, 57 Gloster Place, Monday 9 May 1864,* making an appointment, *mourning paper, with the autograph envelope signed. Dexter Gift.*

H.388   A.L.s. ("CD.") to Lady (Andalusia) Molesworth, widow of the politician, Sir William Molesworth, *1 page, 8vo, Gad's Hill Place, Higham by Rochester, Kent. Tuesday 21 June 1864,* promising that he will sign an autograph-book for someone at Lady Molesworth's request, and saying that he will consult his daughter Mary, when she returns from race-going in Hampshire, about meeting in July. *1950 Gift.*

H.389   A.L.s. to Sir James Emerson Tennent, Secretary to the Board of Trade, *2 pages, 8vo, Gad's Hill Place, Higham by Rochester, Kent. Friday 22 August 1864,* regretting that he must postpone visiting Tennent and expressing his pleasure that Tennent sets "so much store by the dedication", *mourning paper, with the autograph envelope, signed, stamped and addressed to Tennent at:* "Tempo House / Tempo / Co: Fermanagh / Ireland."

... It is not the length of time consumed, or the distance traversed, but it is the departure from a settled habit and a continuous sacrifice of pleasures that comes in question. This is an old story with me. I have never divided a book of my writing with anything else, but have always wrought at it to the exclusion of everything else; and it is now too late to change ...

Letter tipped into the Dedication Copy of *Our Mutual Friend* (see A.26).

H.390   A.L.s. to Chapman and Hall, *1 page, 16mo, Office of All the Year Round, Monday 10 October 1864*, requesting the delivery of one copy of *A Child's History of England* to the bearer of the note, *addressed on second page. 1950 Gift*.

H.391   A.L.s. to Sir James Emerson Tennent, *1 page, 8vo, Gad's Hill Place, Higham by Rochester, Kent. Tuesday 24 January 1865*, explaining that "Trade requirements necessitate the publication at this time of the first 10 Nos. of Our Mutual Friend, as the first volume of that story" but that he will not be sending Tennent a copy of the book until it is complete, even though the first volume does contain the Dedication, *with the autograph envelope, black-bordered, signed, stamped, inscribed* "Private" *and addressed to Tennent at the Board of Trade*.

Letter and envelope pasted into the front of the Dedication Copy of *Our Mutual Friend* (see A.26).

H.392   A.L.s. ("CD.") to Peter Cunningham, *1 page, 8vo, Gad's Hill Place, Higham by Rochester, Kent. 15 February 1865*, mentioning his brother Frederick (" ... I ... earnestly hope he is doing well ... ") and *Our Mutual Friend*, and signing himself "Ever Your faithful Manager" (in allusion to their former association in the Amateur Players), *mourning paper*.

Letter mounted in a cardboard frame. *Dexter Gift*.

H.393   Visiting card printed with Dickens's name and Gad's Hill Place address, inscribed by Dickens: "16 Somers Place Hyde Park – *till the* 5th *June*." Presumably sent by Dickens to Beard in February or March 1865. Mounted in a cardboard frame together with a small coloured slip advertising Dickens's Readings at St. Martin's Hall in May and June 1858, and an autograph envelope (Office of *Household Words* stationery) addressed to Beard by Dickens and signed by him. *Dexter Gift*.

H.394   A.L.s. ("CD.") to Francis Carr Beard, *1 page, 8vo, 16 Somers Place Tuesday Morning 21 March 1865*, reporting a recurrence of his foot trouble (" ... We are now at work at the Poppy fomentations again ... "), *with the autograph envelope, black-bordered, signed*.

Letter and envelope mounted in a cardboard frame. *Dexter Gift*.

H.395   A.L.s. ("CD.") to Francis Carr Beard, *2 pages, 16mo, Office of All the Year Round, Saturday 10 June 1865*, telling Beard about his involvement in the Staplehurst railway disaster.

... I was in the carriage that did not go down, but hung in the air over the side of the broken bridge. I was not touched – scarcely shaken. But the terrific nature of the scene makes me think that I should be the better for a gentle composing draught or two ....

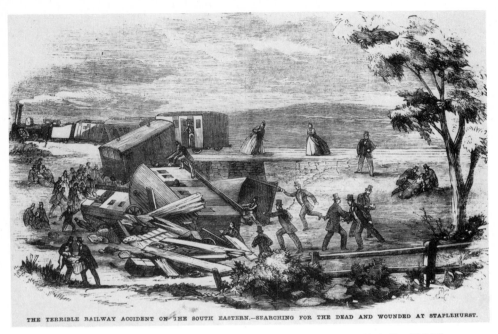

THE TERRIBLE RAILWAY ACCIDENT ON THE SOUTH EASTERN.—SEARCHING FOR THE DEAD AND WOUNDED AT STAPLEHURST.

The Staplehurst Railway Disaster *(The Illustrated Police News*, 17 June 1865) (See H.395)

Pencilled endorsement, "The Railway Accident", on p. 4, presumably by Francis Beard. *Dexter Gift*.

H.396   A.L.s. to "My dear Arnold", *1 page, 8vo, Gad's Hill Place, Higham by Rochester, Kent. Monday 12 June 1865,* describing the Staplehurst railway accident of 9 June and its after-effects on him which have caused his doctor to forbid him all social engagements (otherwise he would gladly have dined with Arnold and his brother). *1950 Gift*.

H.397   A.L.s. ("CD.") to Francis Carr Beard, *1 page, 8vo, Office of All the Year Round, Wednesday 21 June 1865,* concerning the after-effects of his Staplehurst shock (" . . . My pulse is still feeble and I am unfit for noise and worry . . . "). *Dexter Gift*.

H.398   A.L.s. to Rev. W. Brackenbury, Headmaster of Wimbledon School, *2 pages, 8vo, Gad's Hill Place, Higham by Rochester, Kent. Monday 18 September 1865,* asking for Brackenbury's advice about the academic ability of his sixth son, Henry Fielding Dickens, who has declared he "did not wish to enter the Indian Civil Service", and saying that he would be willing to send Henry to Cambridge only if he could be sure of his being successful there. "I told him", writes Dickens,

> . . . that many of us have many duties to discharge in life which we do not wish to undertake, and that we must do the best we can to earn our respective livings and make our way. I also clearly pointed out to him that I bear as heavy a train as can well be attached to any one working man, and that I could by no means afford to send a son to College who went there for any other purpose than to work hard, and to gain distinction . . . .

In *Crockford's Clerical Directory* for 1868 Brackenbury's Christian names are given as John Matthew. *1950 Gift.*

H.399 A.L.s. to Thomas Beard, *1 page, 8vo, Office of All the Year Round, Thursday 21 September 1865,* inviting Beard to visit Gad's Hill, *with the autograph envelope, signed and stamped. Dexter Gift.*

H.400 A.L.s. ("CD.") to Francis Carr Beard, *1 page, 8vo, Office of All the Year Round, Thursday 8 February 1866,* arranging to be "thoroughly examined" by Beard and to dine afterwards with him and Wilkie Collins at Verey's restaurant, *with the autograph envelope, signed.*

With the letter and envelope is an initialled note to Beard from Wilkie Collins (see J. 9). *Dexter Gift.*

H.401 A.D. Draft of letter to Frederic Ouvry, Dickens's solicitor, in the hand of W. H. Wills, corrected and amended by Dickens, *2 pages, 8vo, Office of All the Year Round, 16 February 1866,* strongly denying that "Messrs. Kings and Co." have any grounds for complaint about an article concerning Broughams published in *All The Year Round,* and positively declining to give them any free advertisement in the pages of the journal in the form of a note saying they were not the firm alluded to in the article in question.

The *Business Directory* for 1862/63 lists "W. King & Co. Coach-builders" at 101 Long Acre. The article in which King's conceived themselves to be slandered must have been "Carriages and their Changes" *(All The Year Round,* vol. 15, pp. 11-16, 13 January 1866). On p. 15 appears the passage: "A certain class of carriage-builders use green wood of any quality, relying on paint to cover all defects, not expecting or caring to see any customer twice. There are some advertising fabricators of diminutive Broughams who are especially to be avoided." *1950 Gift.*

H.402 A.L.s. to Francis Carr Beard, *1 page, 8vo, Office of All the Year Round, Friday 16 February 1866,* saying that when he has anything wrong with him he is "so surrounded on all sides by anxious people" that he does not like Beard to have to bear the full responsibility for his "being out of sorts" and suggesting therefore that, if Beard does not find him to be " 'picking up' " on Monday, they should call in a second opinion (" . . . I have a notion of Brinton of Brook Street . . . "), *with the autograph envelope, signed and stamped. Dexter Gift.*

H.403 A.L.s. to Frederick Chapman, *1 page, 8vo, Office of All the Year Round, Thursday, 31 March 1866,* commiserating with Chapman on a bereavement.

Letter pasted on card. *1950 Gift.*

H.404 A.L.s. to Chandos Wren Hoskyns, writer on agriculture, *1 page, 8vo, Glasgow Tuesday 17 April 1866,* saying that he would certainly have voted for Wren Hoskyns's admission to a club if he had been in London.

Wren Hoskyns was elected to membership of the Athenaeum in 1866. *1950 Gift.*

H.405 Autograph signature on sheet of Gad's Hill headed notepaper: "Faithfully yours / Charles Dickens / at Liverpool Saturday Twenty Eighth April 1866".

This sheet is tipped into the Reading Copy of *The Haunted Man* (see B.1).

H.406   A.L.s. to Francis Carr Beard, *1 page, 8vo, Gad's Hill Place, Higham by Rochester, Kent. Sunday 10 June 1866,* saying that he has asked Dolby to send Beard a ticket for a good seat at his Reading on Tuesday (" . . . and I hope you may like your brother doctor . . . " [i.e. Dr. Marigold in Dickens's Reading]), *with the autograph envelope, signed and stamped. Dexter Gift.*

H.407   A.L.s. to Frederick Chapman, *2 pages, 8vo, Gad's Hill Place, Higham by Rochester, Kent. Tuesday 17 July 1866,* sending copy for the dedication page (to "E.L.T.") of Frances Eleanor Ternan's novel, *Aunt Margaret's Trouble* (anonymously published by Chapman and Hall, 1866) and asking for proofs of the book to be sent to him. *1950 Gift.*

H.408   A.L.s. ("CD.") to Georgina Hogarth, *2 pages, 8vo, on Gad's Hill notepaper with the printed address scored through, Wednesday 1 August 1866,* asking Georgina to reply to a letter he has received, telling the sender (stated by Walter Dexter in the Nonesuch Edition of the *Letters* to be Catherine Dickens) "that you are absolutely certain that I never will go to her house, and that it is my fixed purpose (without any abatement of kindness otherwise), to hold as little personal communication with her as I possibly can . . . ".

> . . . It is pretty clear to me that she very well knows what is amiss, and has been put up by somebody to trying to get hold of me . . . .

1938 Gift.

H.409   A.L.s. to Francis Carr Beard, *2 pages, 8vo, Gad's Hill Place, Higham by Rochester, Kent. Thursday 6 September 1866,* asking for a prescription and describing one given to him ten years previously by Dr. John Elliotson, *with the autograph envelope, signed and stamped. Dexter Gift.*

H.410   A.L.s. to Francis Carr Beard, *1 page, 8vo, Office of All the Year Round, Monday 10 September 1866,* mentioning certain side-effects of the prescription sent to him by Beard in response to H.409 and asking if all is as it should be, *with the autograph envelope, signed and stamped. Dexter Gift.*

H.411   A.L.s. ("CD.") to William Charles Kent, Editor of *The Sun, 1 page, 16mo, Office of All the Year Round, Thursday Evening 4 October 1866,* concerning the proposing of Kent for membership of the Athenaeum Club, *with the autograph envelope, signed and inscribed in Dickens's hand "Private", typed endorsement. 1950 Gift.*

H.412   A.L. (in the third person) to Benjamin Phillips, Lord Mayor of London, *1 page, 8vo, Gad's Hill Place, Higham by Rochester, Kent. Tuesday 30 October 1866,* regretting that a bad cold will prevent him from dining with the Lord Mayor and Lady Mayoress that evening.

A photograph of Dickens seated in a chair has been pasted on to the letter. *1950 Gift.*

H.413   A.L.s. to William Bonham, *1 page, 8vo, Gad's Hill Place, Higham by Rochester, Kent. Monday 12 November 1866,* giving Bonham permission to reprint in a anthology either the opening of the "Seven Poor Travellers" or "the story of old

Cheeseman" but regretting that he cannot extend the permission to include the story of Richard Doubledick since he receives so many requests of this nature.

The stories entitled *The Seven Poor Travellers* formed the 1854 extra Christmas Number of *Household Words*. "Old Cheeseman" is the hero of "The Schoolboy's Story" in the 1853 Christmas Number. *1950 Gift.*

H.414   A.L.s. ("CD.") to William Charles Kent, *1 page, 8 vo, Office of All the Year Round, Monday 26 November 1866,* sending Kent a promised early proof of the Christmas Number of *All The Year Round, with the autograph envelope, signed and inscribed in Dickens's hand,* "Private". *1950 Gift.*

H.415   A.L.s. ("The Boy (at Mugby)") to Thomas Beard, *1 page, 8vo, Office of All the Year Round, Saturday 15 December 1866,* concerning an appeal which has been made to him to assist a former journalistic colleague (" . . . Can you enlighten me touching a vague and misty impression I have that he was a bad subject altogether? . . . "). *Dexter Gift.*

H.416.   A.L.s. ("CD.") to Francis Carr Beard, *2 pages, 8vo, Carrick's Royal Hotel, Glasgow Monday 18 February 1867,* asking Beard's advice as to what he should do about losing blood as a result of taking some pills to counteract piles, *with the autograph envelope, signed and stamped. Dexter Gift.*

H.417   A.L.s. ("CD.") to Georgina Hogarth, *2 pages, 16mo, Office of All the Year Round, Friday 10 May 1867,* sending a cheque, mentioning the pressure of his many commitments (" . . . Last night I was so tired, that I could hardly undress for bed . . . ") and hinting at a return to America, *with the autograph envelope, signed and stamped.*

> . . . expenses are so enormous, that I begin to feel myself drawn towards America, as Darnay in the Tale of Two Cities was attracted to the Loadstone Rock, Paris . . . .

1938 Gift.

H.418   A.L.s. to Francis Carr Beard, *1 page, 8vo, Great Western Hotel Tuesday 21 May 1867,* arranging to dine that evening with Beard and Wilkie Collins. *Dexter Gift.*

H.419   A.L.s. ("CD.") to Johnson, *2 pages, 8vo, Gad's Hill Place, Higham by Rochester, Kent. Wednesday 29 May 1867,* directing Johnson to send him some clothes from his wardrobe at Gad's Hill and to send an enquiry to the Great Western Hotel about some keys which may have been left behind in his bedroom there. *1950 Gift.*

H.420   A.L.s. to Francis Carr Beard, *1 page, 8vo, Gad's Hill Place, Higham by Rochester, Kent. Monday 14 October 1867,* saying that he has received "the medecine" and has "stuck to it", *with the autograph envelope, signed and stamped. Dexter Gift.*

H.421   A.L.s. ("CD.") to Thomas Beard, *1 page, 8vo, Office of All the Year Round, Thursday 14 May 1868,* inviting Beard to come and spend the weekend at Gad's Hill, *with the autograph envelope, signed. Dexter Gift.*

H.422   A.L.s. to Alfred Hermant, manager of the Vaudeville Theatre, Paris, *1 page, 8vo, Hôtel du Helder, 9 & 10 Rue du Helder, Paris, Mardi 2 June 1868,* thanking

Cartoon by Alfred Thompson commenting
on the Parisian production of *No Thoroughfare*
(See H.422)

Hermant for "la libéralité avec laquelle vous avez mis les ressources de vôtre excellent Théâtre au service d'un écrivain Anglais" and expressing his gratitude "aux artistes qui m'ont prêté leurs concours dans la représentation de 'L'Abîme' ce soir".

With the letter is a cutting from a French sale-catalogue describing the item and the Parisian production of *L'Abîme (No Thoroughfare)*.

H.423   A.L.s. to Madame Charlotte H. Sainton, sister of George Dolby, *1 page, 8vo, Gad's Hill Place, Higham by Rochester, Kent. 21 June 1868,* accepting an invitation and mentioning his great affection for, and trust in, Dolby. *1950 Gift.*

H.424   A.L.s. ("CD.") to James Birtles, printer, *1 page, 8vo, Office of All the Year Round, Saturday 4 July 1868,* sending a poem for setting up in type and directing that the proof should be sent to Charles Mackay, saying that Mackay will also be supplying copy for a prose article on "Ice" for the next number, and arranging a date for making up the next issue of *All The Year Round, with the autograph envelope, signed.*

The poem was, possibly, "At a Club Dinner" published in *ATYR*, vol. 20, pp. 108-09 (11 July 1868). Mackay's article, "Ice", was not, in fact, published until 1 August (vol. 20, pp. 180-82). *1950 Gift.*

H.425   A.L.s. ("CD.") to Francis Carr Beard, *2 pages, 8vo, Adelphi Hotel, Liverpool Sunday 11 October 1868,* reporting that Beard's latest prescription, although it helps his voice, causes nausea (" . . . If I were living another kind of life than a Reading one, this might not be . . . "). *Dexter Gift.*

H.426   A.L.s. ("CD.") to Georgina Hogarth, *2 pages, 8vo, Adelphi Hotel, Liverpool Thursday 29 October 1868,* concerning some domestic matters, mentioning Wilkie Collins and a certain "poor Stephen", and reporting on his health (". . . *I cannot get right internally, and have begun to be as sleepless as sick* . . . ").

> . . . Wilkie's affairs defy all prediction. For any thing one knows, the whole matrimonial pretence may be a lie of that woman's, intended to make him marry her, and (contrary to her expectations) breaking down at last . . . .

1938 Gift.

H.427   A.L.s. to Thomas Beard, *1 page, 16mo, Office of All the Year Round Tuesday 10 November 1868,* inviting Beard to an experimental private reading of *Sikes and Nancy, with the autograph envelope, signed.*

> . . . I am going to do an odd thing on Saturday. I cannot make up my mind whether to read the murder from Oliver Twist, or no. So I am going to have a handful of private friends in St. James's Hall, to try how it affects them and so decide . . .

With the letter is a *laissez-passer* written for Beard by Dickens's manager, George Dolby (see J.37).

H.428   Autograph Envelope, Signed, Addressed to: "Thomas Beard Esquire", *endorsed in pencil: 16 Dec. 1868. Dexter Gift.*

H.429   Printed itinerary headed "Mr Charles Dickens's Farewell Readings. Addresses for Correspondents" and covering the period 4 January – 27 March 1869. 4 page leaflet printed on the 2 centre pages with many emendations in Dickens's hand and inscribed by him on p.1 "Readings Winter and Spring 1869". Presumably sent to Beard by Dickens in December 1868. Mounted in a cardboard frame. *Dexter Gift.*

H.430   A.L.s. to Frederick Lehmann, nephew by marriage of Mrs. W. H. Wills, *1 page, 8vo, Office of All the Year Round, Tuesday 2 February 1869,* refusing an invitation because of pressure of work and mentioning his *Sikes and Nancy* Readings.

Letter pasted on stiff sheet. *1950 Gift.*

H.431   A.L.s. ("CD.") to Francis Carr Beard, *1 page, 16mo Office of All the Year Round, Tuesday 13 April 1869,* reporting a recurrence of his trouble with piles (see H.416) and announcing that "the foot is growling again . . . ", *with the autograph envelope, signed and stamped.*

H.432   A.L.s. ("CD.") to Francis Carr Beard, *1 page, 8vo, Blackburn Monday 19 April 1869,* expressing anxiety over his health and asking Beard to write to him at Blackpool.

> . . . Is it *possible* that anything in my medecine can have made me extremely giddy, extremely uncertain of my footing (especially on the left side) and extremely indisposed to raise my hands to my head? These symptoms made me very uncomfortable on Saturday night, and all yesterday . . . .

Dexter Gift.

H.433   A.L.s. ("CD.") to Francis Carr Beard, *1 page, 8vo, Blackpool Wednesday afternoon 21 April 1869*, reporting some improvement in his health, *with the autograph envelope, signed and stamped.*

> . . . The said symptoms have greatly moderated since Sunday; but there they are, and they are all *on the left side*. Six weeks will carry me through the Readings, if you can fortify me a little bit . . . .

Letter and envelope mounted in a cardboard frame. *Dexter Gift.*

H.434   A.L.s. to Sol Eytinge, American artist, *1 page, 8vo, Office of All the Year Round, Friday 15 May 1869*, inviting Eytinge to visit Gad's Hill to "make some sketches for yourself of Mr. Pickwick's early scenery at your leisure" and also to accompany himself and Inspector Field on a forthcoming expedition "to have a glimpse of the darker side of London life."

Date should be 14 May (15 May 1869 was a Saturday). Letter mounted on card.

H.435   A.L.s. ("CD.") to James T. Fields, Dickens's American publisher, *1 page, 8vo, St. James's Hotel 18 May 1869*, advising Fields on a suitable price to give for a painting (apparently a portrait of Molière), *with the autograph envelope, signed. 1950 Gift.*

H.436   A.L.s. to Mr. Day, printer, *1 page, 16mo, Office of All the Year Round, Thursday 2 September 1869*, concerning the printing of a book (probably *The Religious Opinions of the late Reverend Chauncey Hare Townshend*; edited by Dickens). *1950 Gift.*

H.437   A.L.s. to the Rev. Dr. Thomas Fisher Redhead, Perpetual Curate of Higher Bebington, Birkinhead, *1 page 8vo, Gad's Hill Place, Higham by Rochester, Kent. Thursday 23 September 1869*, returning and commenting on some paper, apparently concerning a clergyman, that Redhead has sent him (" . . . If any spiritual pastor and master could amaze me, this shining pillar of the Church would; but I am past the state of mind in that connexion . . . "), *with the autograph envelope, signed and stamped.*

With the letter and envelope are two cuttings from Liverpool newspapers, one of an article by J. R. Eastwood occasioned by the death, in 1900, of Dickens's former Readings Manager, George Dolby, and the other of three or four articles (including one on "Charles Dickens's Welsh Schoolmaster") saluting the centenary of Dickens's birth. *1950 Gift.*

H.438   A.L.s. ("CD.") to William Charles Kent, *1 page, 8vo, Gad's Hill Place, Higham by Rochester, Kent. Wednesday 29 September 1869*, sending Kent a circular he has received and saying that he has replied that he cannot intervene in the matter, *with the autograph envelope, signed, stamped and inscribed in Dickens's hand* "Private".

According to a pencilled note on the dealer's envelope in which this item is housed the circular Dickens refers to concerned the Editorship of the *Literary Gazette. 1950 Gift.*

H.439   A.L.s. to—Hills, *1 page, 8vo, 5 Hyde Park Place W. Thursday 10 February 1870*, accepting an invitation to dinner. *1950 Gift.*

H.440   A.L.s. to Sir Roderick Impey Murchison, geologist and traveller to Russia, *1 page, 8vo, 5 Hyde Park Place W. Sunday 3 April 1870*, saying that he has discovered that he is already engaged for the date for which he has accepted an invitation from Murchison (letter signed: "Your faithful friend and admirer"). *1950 Gift.*

H.441 A.L.s. ("CD.") to Francis Carr Beard, *1 page, 8vo, 5 Hyde Park Place Tuesday 5 April 1870,* reporting an improvement in his health.

> . . . I am getting better "nicely", as the Nurse's phrase is. Tomorrow I am going to the Levee, and shall be absent (in a Fancy Dress) at our usual time. Let us say Friday, if convenient to you . . . .

Dexter Gift.

H.442 A.L.s. ("CD.") to Charles Mackay, *1 page, 16mo, Office of All the Year Round, Thursday 21 April 1870,* concerning contributions to *All the Year Round.*

> . . . The prose paper, The False Friend, has lingered, because it seems to me that the idea is to be found in an introduced story of mine (called the Baron of Grogzwig) in Pickwick . . . .

The story of the Baron of Grogzwig appears, in fact, in *Nicholas Nickleby*, not *Pickwick Papers.*

H.443 A.L.s. to Dr. Thomas Harrington Tuke, alienist, *1 page, 8vo, Gad's Hill Place, Higham by Rochester, Kent. Thursday 26 May 1870,* regretting that he cannot accept an invitation owing to indisposition.

> . . . I am occasionally subject to a Neuralgic (or whatever else it may be) attack in the foot, which originated a few years ago, in over-walking in deep snow, and was revived by a very hard winter in America; and it has so plagued me, under the dinings and other engagements of this London Season, that I have been lame these three weeks, and have resolved on an absolute rest in Kent here, and an avoidance of hot rooms, and an unbroken quiet training, for some months . . . .

SECTION I

Literary Manuscripts
of Charles Dickens

I.1   THE ALBUM OF MARIA BEADNELL, containing four original contributions in verse by Dickens and a transcript in his hand of a poem by Thomas Moore, all written 1830/31, *contemporary green straight-grained morocco, with lock, in green half morocco slip-case.*

Dickens's contributions to the album are as follows:

(i)   Acrostic on the name of Maria Beadnell, 13 lines, ending:
    "Life has no charms, no happiness, no pleasures now for me
    Like those I feel, When 'tis my lot Maria, to gaze on thee."
    unsigned [?1830]

(ii)   "The Devil's Walk", a satirical poem of eight 8-line stanzas,
    signed "CD" *and dated* Nov. 1831.

(iii)   "The Churchyard", a poem of eight 8-line stanzas,
    signed "C.D." *and dated* Nov. 1831.

(iv)   "Lodgings to Let", a poem of three 6-line stanzas ending:
    "Still I'm most proud amongst these pickings
    To rank the humblest name. — Charles Dickens"
    Written to match a watercolour illustration on the opposite page (see below)

(v)   "Written in an Album by T. Moore", 10 lines transcribed by Dickens,
    initialled "C.D. 1831".

The contents of the album as a whole are as follows:

Inscription: "Miss Maria Beadnell from a sincere friend Nov. 17th 1827"
Frontispiece (watercolour): an arrangement of imaginary leaves from books of plates

Pictorial title-page (drawn in ink) showing a bee-hive and signed "H. Austin 1831"
    (Henry Austin married Dickens's younger sister, Letitia, in 1837)

"Time's Swiftness. By B. W. Spencer" Three 4-line verses signed "J.B.W."

"On a Lady. Throwing Snow Balls at her Lover", 8 lines signed A.B.M.

"The star, which glints so fair at e'en", two 8-line verses and 2 4-line verses alternating, signed "M.P."

"There's a bliss beyond all that the minstrel has told" By Moore, 8 lines signed "M.P."

"Love", 22 lines attributed to Southey and signed "E.S."

"What is Life?", 21 lines, signed "J.B.W."

Pencil and wash drawing of the Acropolis signed "R.B." with transcript of verse from *Childe Harold* below ("Son of the morning, rise! approach you here!") signed "R.B. 1827".

131

I.1

"Les Fleurs", 16 lines attributed to Boisjohn, signed "G.F. 1830".

"On hearing the Sounds of an Aeolian Harp", 14 lines, signed "J.W."

"Song" ("If thou wouldst have thy charms enchant our eyes") three 4-line verses attributed to Moore and signed "B.W.K."

"A Mother's Love" "From the German of Wernicke", 3 lines. Unsigned but same handwriting as preceding item.

"Love, when 'tis true, needs not the aid" attributed to Sedley and signed "G. H. G."

"Why should I blush to own I love?", three 4-line stanzas, signed "J. W."

"England, with all thy faults I love thee still", 49 lines, attributed to Cowper and signed "E.F."

"Oh were it not for this sad voice", 10 lines, attributed to "the Epicurean" and signed "E.M."

"The Soldier's Dream", six 4-line stanzas, signed "E.S. 1829"

"Oh! ever thus, from childhood's hour", 8 lines attributed to "Lallah Rook" and signed "E.M."

"There is an hour I love to stray", four 6-line stanzas, attributed to "Volti" and signed "B.W.K."

"In many a strain of grief and joy", fourteen 4-line stanzas, attributed to "J.M." and signed "M.P." A pencilled note at the head of the verses reads: "The following lines were addressed to a Lady to whom the Author had been much attached, but who during his absence from England was married to another".

"A Reflection at Sea", two 4-line stanzas, signed "M.P."

"How richly grows the water's breast", 16 lines, signed "J.W."

"La Chute des feuilles", 44 lines, attributed to Milleroye and signed "Antoinette D."

"Woman", 40 lines with epigraph from Milton, signed "B.W.K."

"The Forsaken", 59 lines, attributed to "L.E.L." and signed "E.H."

Pencil and wash drawing of a landscape with a church (inserted).

"Farewell, my gentle harp, farewell", three 6-line stanzas, attributed to "Croby" and signed "G.H.G."

"When he who adores thee has left but the name", 16 lines signed "J.W."

Wood engraving of Chillon with ornate hand-painted frame.

"Dreams", four 8-line stanzas, signed "J.S. 1828".

"Good Night", 14 lines, unsigned.

"The West", seven 4-line verses, signed "D.Ll." (i.e. David Lloyd, brother-in-law of Maria Beadnell).

"The Exchange", two 4-line verses, unsigned.

"Appealing language! unto me", 8 lines, attributed to Bernard Barton and signed "L. Moule 1829".

"Address to Memory", 16 lines, attributed to [Samuel] Rogers and signed Louisa [i.e. Louisa Moule] 1829".

"To—", three 4-line stanzas beginning "I turn from pleasures witching form", signed "J.J.B."

"Address to the Moon", 16 lines, signed "J.W."

"Each season possesses a pleasure for me", 16 lines, ending "So I think that for lovers the summer is best", signed S.M.B. (i.e. Sarah Maria Beadnell, the album's owner).

"Since first my soul, with soft alarm, / On fair Maria's beauties hung," 4 lines, signed "W.T.M. [i.e. William Moule, Louisa's brother] 1829".

"Hope", 8 lines, signed "W.T.M. 1829".

"Stanzas to—" six 8-line stanzas beginning "Though the day of my destiny's o'er", attributed to Byron and signed.

"On a Rose", two 4-line stanzas, signed "W.T.M. 1829".

Acrostic on "Maria Beadnell". Pencilled note beneath, "By Dickens".

"Give me a cottage on some Cambrian wild", 14 lines, signed "J.W."

"To Maria", two 4-line verses, signed "T.E.R. February 1832".

Hand-coloured engraving, "Vue du Nant d'Arpenas".

"Home", 12 lines, attributed to Montgomery and signed "M.L.J."

"Fall from your horse and break your neck", 4 lines, signed "J.J.B."

"I cannot sleep! my night's glide on", three 4-line stanzas, signed "S.R."

"The Garland", two 4-line verses, signed "J.H.J."

"à Mademoiselle Maria", 26 lines beginning "Vous savez plaire assurement", signed "Henry".

"To Miss——", four 4-line stanzas beginning "Oh dream it not! Oh dream it not!", attributed to "J.G.D." and signed "J.B.W."

"On a Lady", 6 lines, attributed to Sheridan and signed "J.B.W."

"The Envy of Love", two 4-line verses beginning "Yes, Maria, I truly grant / The charm of —'s eyes I see", signed "T.E.R." (below the verses T.E.R. has written: "Il y'a dans la jalousie plus d'amour propre, que de propre amour").

"To the Lily", two 4-line verses, signed "L.M."

"To the Rose", two 4-line verses, signed "Louisa 1829".

Water-colour painting of a lily and a rose, signed "L. Moule 1829".

"To my Mother", 13 lines, signed "E . . . . W. . . . . . [i.e. Ella Winter, Maria's daughter] 2nd May 1859"
"And canst thou, mother, for a moment think,
That we, thy children, when old age shall shed
Its blanching honours on thy weary head,
Could from our best of duties shrink? . . . "

"The Shrubbery", six 4-line stanzas, attributed to Cowper and signed "D.L." [i.e. David Lloyd]

"On Friendship", two 4-line verses, signed "Julia".

"Say what is she, who steals the heart away / Speaks to deceive and smiles but to betray", 4 lines, signed "T.E.R."

"Amitié, qui sans toi porterait nos malheurs", 6 lines, attributed to Dumas and signed "Mathilde M."

Hand-coloured engraving, "Vue de la cascade du Bonnant".

"Remember thee! yes, while there's life in this heart", three 4-line verses, signed "M.U. Mellington".

"Sympathy", six 4-line verses, signed "Woodbines 12 August 1830".

"Solitude", 18 lines beginning " 'Tis night, when meditation bids us feel" attributed to Byron and signed "H.M."

"Epitaph on a young Lady, who died in a consumption", 16 lines, signed "M.L.J."

"I cannot stain this snowy leaf", 20 lines, unsigned.

"Happy a man may pass his life / If freed from matrimonial chains", 20 lines, signed "S.M.B." [i.e. Sarah Maria Beadnell]. Underneath is written in pencil: "Vide next page. Qy. Is it intended as a demurrer to the foregoing E.S."

"I envy thee, thou careless wind", four 4-line verses, signed "S.R."

"In all the stages of domestic life", 10 lines, signed "H.B."

"They tell me 'tis decided; you depart", six 8-line stanzas signed "M."

"There's not a joy the world can give like that it takes away", five 4-line stanzas, signed "M.Ll." [i.e. Maria's married sister, Margaret Lloyd].

"L'Italie", five 5-line verses, attributed to "Ancelot" and signed "Alexandrine J.B. 1 Décembre 1830".

Five lines of music, signed at the top "S.J. Nov. 1828".

"A un Père, sur la mort de sa fille", six 4-line stanzas, signed "Félicie Notaire 28 9bre 1830".

"Maria", 9 lines beginning "Thou art so fair so excellently framed", signed "J.R.J."

"Oh, think not my spirits are always as light", 12 lines, signed "M. U. Mellington".

"Not in those climes where I have late been straying", 27 lines, attributed to Byron and signed "T.B."

"Memory", 12 lines, signed "E.S. 1830".

Print of Lago Maggiore with hand-painted ornate frame.

"Le Petit Frère", 52 lines, signed "Marie H."

"An Acrostic to Maria" (calligraphic, with ornamental border), 13 lines signed "H.E.H."

"On hearing Maria play on the Harp", 14 lines, signed "T.B. Junr."

"How wonderful is Death", 44 lines, attributed to *Queen Mab* and signed "H.B."

Pencil drawing of a leafy cemetery (inserted).

"A l'Amitié", 60 lines, signed "J. Garnier".

"Le printemps et les fleurs", 28 lines, signed F. D^{ville}

"As on the cold sepulchral stone", two 4-line verses signed "M.A.L." [i.e. Maria's friend, Mary Anne Leigh].

"A sister's birthday! may the theme inspire", four 4-line verses, unsigned.

"Aux mânes de ma fille", 63 lines, signed "Clementine Talma 1830".

"Cupid and my Campaspe play'd", 14 lines, attributed to "John Lyly 1600", unsigned.

"And dost thou ask me what is love", 4 lines, signed "T.E.R."

Water-colour of a basket of fruit.

"Oh weep for those that wept by Babel's stream", three 4-line verses signed "T.H."

"True Love", four 4-line verses, signed "T.E.R."

"Lines that come to nothing", 38 lines, attributed to "Y.Z." and signed "J.B.W."

"Je n'aime pas les grands yeux noirs", 4 lines, unsigned.

"Maria dont le coeur a cet album pour livre", 26 lines, signed "Jules Planch".

Pencil and wash drawing of a lakeside scene.

"With a wreath of violets", 36 lines, signed "A.T.B." [i.e. Anne Thompson Beadnell, Maria's sister].

"L'Espérance", three 4-line verses, signed "Acélie Garnier".

"To Maria", three 8-line verses, signed "H. . . . A. . . . 1832" [i.e. Henry Austin]
"When first on thine angel form so bright
Entranced, I gazed with ravished eye . . . "

" 'Twas ever thus from childhood's hour", 12 lines, attributed to Moore and signed
"M.A.L." [Mary Anne Leigh].
Under these verses is written in another hand:
"What is better than the art of pleasing? Pleasing without art."

"The Devil's Walk" [by Dickens — see above].

"Lines on a Suicide", seven 4-line stanzas, signed "G. . . . e B. . . . . 11 Junr."
[i.e. Maria's younger brother, George].

"Waltz", four lines of music, signed "by C.W.B."

"To — — ", two 8-line verses, signed "T.B. Junr. 1833".

"To Polly" 4 lines (written in pencil), unsigned:
"When I look at your *Album*
Bound up in neat *calf*
I think of the Hottentot Venus
And *Laugh*".

"Thoughts", 8 lines, signed "J.B.W."

"La vie humaine est une mélange", 4 lines, signed "T.E.R. . . y . . "

Pencil drawing of an old church, signed "E.R."

"To Maria", two 8-line verses beginning "When e'er I see those smiling eyes",
signed "E.R."

"J'aime", 4 lines, and "Charade", 6 lines, signed T.E.R. . . y . . "
(written above these lines in same hand: "L'amitié est l'amour sans ailes —
L'absence la fortifie si elle est forte et l'affaiblit si elle est faible").

Pencil and wash drawing, "Mosque d'El Haram à Jerusalem", signed "J.R.F. 1833".

"Sonnet on contemplating the Miniature of a deceased friend", signed "London E.S."

"Careless Love", 10 lines, and "Faithful Love", 10 lines, unsigned but dated "Aug^t.
1830".

"The Churchyard" [by Dickens — see above].

"Le Petit Savoyard", three 8-line verses, calligraphic script, signed "H. . . . A. . . . .
1831" [Henry Austin], with watercolour of the Savoyard on facing page, signed
"H.A. 1831".

"To Maria — ", three 4-line verses, unsigned.

"Mon âme impregnée de langueur", 12 lines, signed "D" and dated "Août 1837".

"Oh, canst thou not", nine 4-line verses, signed "J.G. May 1829".

"Cato's Soliloquy", 31 lines, signed "M.Ll.J."

"Curs'd be the gold and silver which persuade", 16 lines, attributed to Collins and
signed "J.Ll."

"The quality of mercy is not strained", 14 lines, signed "E.A.B."

"Maria Beadnell", 4 lines in French, signed "Achille" and dated "Londres 8 aout
1837".

136

"*Lodgings to Let*"

Lodgings here! a charming place,
The owner's such a lovely face,
The neighbours too seem very pretty
Lively, sprightly, gay, and witty,
Of all the spots that I could find
This is the place to suit my mind.

Then I will say sans hesitation
This place shall be my habitation
This charming spot my home shall be
While, dear Maria keeps the key,
I'll settle here, no more I'll roam
But make this place my happy home.

A great advantage too will be,
I shall keep such good company,
So good, that I fear my composing
Will be considered very prosing
Still I'm most proud amongst these pickings.
To rank the humblest name, – Charles Dickens.

I.1

"Dido", 38 lines, calligraphic script, signed "H. . . . A. . . . . 1832" [Henry Austin];
on facing page a watercolour of Dido and Ascanius, copied from an engraving of
Guenier's 1817 painting, "Aeneas recounting to Dido the fall of Troy":
"As Dido art thou painted here?
Maria, thou art much too fair . . . "

Pencil and wash drawing of a ruin and some buildings, signed "E.A.H."

"Once when no language yet was known", 22 lines, signed "J.G. May 1829".

Three lines of music signed "J.H." [? John Hullah].

"Lodgings to Let" [By Dickens – see above]; on facing page a water-colour painting
of a window displaying a sign "Lodgings Genteely Furnished" – the window
can be raised to reveal a young woman working at a wash-tub with a bottle and
glass by her side.

Pencil drawing of a mountain chapel with figures before it (inserted).

"Flower after flower comes forth in spring", 30 lines, signed "T.B. Junr. 1833".

"The Bride's Farewell", four 8-line verses, attributed to Mrs. Hemans and signed
"F.E.D. 1831" [i.e. Fanny Dickens, Charles's elder sister].

Watercolour entitled "The Sister of Dido Augt. 1830" (fanciful depiction of Anne
Beadnell as Anna in *The Aeneid*).

"March of Intellect in Ireland", 18 lines, signed "M.P."

"To Miss Maria — ", 18 lines, signed "T.B. 20 July 1833".

"Oh bright was the sunshine and fair was the flower", four 4-line verses, signed "J. G. May 1839".

"Written in an Album by T. Moore" [by Dickens – see above].

I.1

Watercolour portrait of Maria Beadnell as a milkmaid. Painted by Henry Austin for Dickens to present to her. The page into which it is slotted is signed "C.D. 1831".

"Pray tell me Dear Jane, says inquisitive Ned / What's the first thing you do when you get into bed", 4 lines in pencil, signed "G.B. Junr. July 26 / 39" [i.e. George Beadnell, Maria's younger brother].

"An Album, 'tis said, dear Maria", four 4-line verses, calligraphic script, signed "H. . . . A. . . . . 1831" [Henry Austin]
    "An Album, 'tis said, dear Maria
    Of the Owner an Emblem should be
    'Tho' thine is most beautiful, still
    It is far from an emblem of thee. . . "

Water-colour of a red flower.

Pencil drawing of a church.

"Love!", 6 lines, unsigned.

"Maria", 4 lines in Italian, attributed to Metastasio, unsigned but same hand as
preceding entry.

"The Fair Sex", 8 lines, unsigned but same hand as preceding two entries.

Four-line verse in German, unsigned but same hand as preceding three entries.

With the Album are two letters to the Comte de Suzannet, dated 21 January and
18 February 1935, from Ernest Maggs, who purchased it (together with two letters
of Dickens's to Maria's daughter, Ella, some Beadnell family photographs and Henry
Winter's bankruptcy certificate—see H.240, 312 and J.69) for the Comte. Maggs quotes
a letter from the Album's vendor, a Mr. Paver:

> The Album passed from Maria Beadnell, upon her death, to her daughter Ella
> Maria Winter . . . Ella Winter became a Mrs. Osmond living at Westbourne, West
> Sussex, and upon her death a certain amount of clothes, books and personal things
> must have been stored and left unclaimed. Recently these were sent for sale to pay
> storage . . . it was only the fact that I had read the life of Charles Dickens and
> remembered the name of Beadnell which made me realize that there might be some-
> thing of value amongst what was, to all intents and purposes, just an interesting album
> and a lot of valueless rubbish . . .

Also present is a letter to the Comte, dated 22 March 1935, from J. H. Stonehouse
concerning the Album and its history (" . . . The Barrells (that is Mrs. Winter's
daughter Ellen and her Husband) were a curious pair – intemperate in habit, and
somewhat given to changing their domicile in a Micawberish kind of way . . . ")
The Album is described by Suzannet in an article in *The Dickensian*, xxxi, Summer
1935, 161-68.

I.2   THE BILL OF FARE. Transcript of Dickens's poem in the hand of Maria
Beadnell's married sister, Margaret Lloyd, *360 lines on 15 pp. 4to. on paper water-marked*
"Tassell and Smith 1839".

This poem, parodying Goldsmith's "Retaliation", concerns the Beadnell family
and their friends and was perhaps recited by Dickens at a dinner given by Mr. and
Mrs. Beadnell. His allusion to the poem in a recently-discovered 1831 letter to Maria
(purchased by the Trustees of the Dickens House at Sotheby's, 28 March 1972) seems
to indicate that he wrote out the poem in Anne Beadnell's Album (see Michael Slater,
"David to Dora: a New Dickens Letter", *The Dickensian*, lxviii, September 1972,
162-66) which has since disappeared. The only other contemporary MS. of the poem
is the copy in the hand of Maria Beadnell now in the Huntington Library; the text
of this copy differs from that of Mrs. Lloyd's.

The MS. catalogued here passed into the possession of Margaret Lloyd's daughter,
Countess Visconti, and was sold by her to J. M. Sotheran in 1908. It was purchased
by the Comte de Suzannet (together with five Dickens letters) in 1934 and presented
by him to The Dickens House in 1938.

With the MS. are the following documents:

(i)   Four letters and a card from Countess Visconti's nephew, Lionel F. Gosling,
to J. H. Stonehouse, 22 August – 8 September 1908, arranging for Stonehouse
to borrow the Dickens letters and MS. of "The Bill of Fare" owned by the
Countess (" . . . With regard to the persons mentioned in the poem my

aunt has recollection only of the 2 Miss Leighs one of whom married a greek called Balli I believe and the other Mary Anne Leigh married a Mr Bach whom my aunt says was rather a vulgar old fellow . . . ").

(ii) A card from Gosling to Stonehouse and a receipt for £21 for "Dickens' Poem" dated 16 May 1908 and signed by the Countess Visconti.

(iii) A letter from Gosling to Stonehouse dated 25 June 1911 agreeing to sell for £50 4 Dickens letters, also a receipt for the amount signed by Gosling dated 26 June 1911.

(iv) Four letters from J. H. Stonehouse to the Comte de Suzannet, 13 – 25 March 1934, concerning the sale to the Comte of 5 Dickens Letters and the MS. of "The Bill of Fare" for £500. Also two receipts for this amount signed by Stonehouse.

I.3 THE PICKWICK PAPERS. The thirteenth page of the Autograph Manuscript of Chapter XXXVII, showing some deletions and minor revisions, *one page 4to, numbered at the top by Dickens, 81.*

This page, which begins with the words, " . . . commanding tone." and ends with " ' . . . I hope gentlemen, I give satisfaction.", follows the twelve pages listed in the Sale Catalogue (Lot 303). It was presented to The Dickens House by the Comte de Suzannet in 1938.

I.4 NICHOLAS NICKLEBY. The Autograph Manuscript of Chapter IX, *39 pages, 4to, numbered by Dickens 38 - 75, numerous revisions and corrections throughout.*

In his unpublished catalogue Suzannet notes that the manuscript belonged successively to C. Foote, W. A. White and Dr. A. S. W. Rosenbach. It was presented to The Dickens House by Suzannet in 1938.

With the manuscript is a photo-copy of the three pages of Chapter XV containing Fanny Squeer's Letter to Ralph Nickleby. See Lot 308 in the Sale Catalogue.

I.5 Mrs. GAMP IN THE PROVINCES. Uncorrected proofs, mounted on four 8vo pages, of a sketch by Dickens that remained unpublished until it appeared in Forster's *Life of Dickens* in 1873. Dickens intended the sketch to be illustrated by Maclise, Egg, Frank Stone, Leech and Cruikshank (see Sale Catalogue, Lot 251) and Suzannet has noted on the envelope containing these proofs that they were the ones sent by Dickens to Frank Stone in August 1847.

This item was acquired from Maggs by the Comte de Suzannet in March 1944.

I.6 THE STORY OF LITTLE DOMBEY. Fragments of the manuscript used for the printing of the "Reading Edition" of *Little Dombey* in 1858, viz. one leaf of the first edition of *Dombey and Son* (pp. 115 and 116) showing numerous deletions and alterations in Dickens's hand, and 37 lines of manuscript (1 page 8vo.) corresponding to the text of pp. 79-82 of *The Story of Little Dombey* ("such spirits as Little Dombey had . . . " to " . . . as long afterwards as Saturday morning.").

These fragments were bought by the Comte de Suzannet at auction (Hodgson's) on 5 May 1948.

I.7 THE SCHOOLBOY'S STORY. The Autograph Manuscript of the story published by Dickens in the 1853 Christmas Supplement to *Household Words*, *10 pages, 8vo, with numerous corrections and deletions in Dickens's hand throughout, light blue paper, in dark blue half-morocco slip-case, gilt.*

In the top left-hand corner of p. 1 appears the name (not in Dickens's hand) "Dampier" – presumably, the compositor responsible for setting up the copy.

In his *Catalogue* (1934) the Comte de Suzannet notes of this item (vol. 1, p. 49): "Ce manuscrit fut offert par Dickens à son ami Dean Bagot d'où il passa par héritage à William A. Traill." Presented to The Dickens House by the Comte de Suzannet in 1938.

I.8 OUR COMMISSION. The Autograph Manuscript of the satirical article published in *Household Words* 11 August 1855, *11 pages, 8vo, with numerous revisions and deletions in Dickens's hand throughout, light blue paper, in green morocco slip-case, gilt.*

The manuscript has been divided into sections, by another hand, for the attention of various compositors whose names have been written in. With the manuscript is a typed transcript and an unsigned prefatory note (also typed), apparently written about 1930, commenting on the article.

Presented to The Dickens House by the Comte de Suzannet in 1938.

Manuscript Dickensiana

J.1   AUTOGRAPHS (MISCELLANEOUS) *2 pages, 4to, n.d.*, comprising the signatures of: Wilkie Collins, Charles Knight, D. F. Ansted, R. H. Horne, W. H. Wills, J. Alfred Novello, Joseph Parker, Robert Bell, Tom Taylor, Edwin Landseer, Charles Dickens, F. O. Ward, George Cruikshank, N. Arnold, P. M. Roget, W. Sharpey, John J. Griffin, J. Chapman, Ebenezer Syme. *Dexter Gift.*

J.2   BEADNELL (NATHANIEL GEORGE, *nephew of Maria Beadnell*). Three A.L.s.s. *6 pages, Chatham and Gosport, all undated except for one dated 20 April 1865, which is accompanied by the autograph envelope, mourning paper*, to Ella Winter, daughter of Maria Beadnell, concerning his love for her and family objections to their marriage

> . . . you must know that my love for you Ella was no common love, it was so strong that even now I feel sure I shall never get the better of it but you know also Ella that the commands of a dying father cannot be cast aside thoughtlessly I feel that were we anything more than we are now to one another, a curse would follow us to the end of the world . . .

J.3   BEARD (FRANCIS CARR, 1814-1893, *Dickens's medical attendant, brother of Thomas Beard*) Autograph notes on Dickens's pulse-rates during the Public Readings given in London on 15 and 22 February and 1, 8 and 15 March 1870, *1 page, foolscap.*

> . . . Tuesday March 8th 1870 / Pulse before reading Boots at the Holly Tree 94 After reading 112. After reading Nancy & Sykes (the murder) 120. After reading Bob Sawyers party 108, 15 minutes after 82 . . .

With this document is an envelope inscribed: "Diagnosis of Dickens's pulse & state of health made by my father, Francis Carr Beard F.R.C.S. during Dickens's last public readings a short time before his death. Nathaniel T. Beard." Dr. Beard's notes were published in *Dickens to his Oldest Friend*, ed. Walter Dexter, 1932, pp. 253-54.

J.4   BEARD (FRANCIS CARR) A.L.s. *2 pages, 8vo, Gad's Hill Place [8 June 1870]* to his sister, Catherine Charlotte Beard asking her to forward his letters (" . . . I must remain here to see the END of this sad story . . . There is no longer a secret of where I am and what I am doing – so let it be known – it will be in all the papers in a few hours . . . "), *with the autograph envelope, signed and inscribed:* "deliver immediately. Wait answer".

With the letter is a note by Beard's son, Nathaniel, headed "Charles Dickens's death 1870", describing and dating this letter and another one from Dr. Russell Reynolds (see below, J.58).

J.5   BEARD (THOMAS, 1807-1891) Autograph draft in shorthand of a letter written to Daniel Maclise at Dickens's request (see H.99), *2 pages, 8vo* [*18 December 1842*]. *Dexter Gift.*

J.6   BLACKBURN (——) A.L.s. *4 pages, 8vo, Colonial Club, St. James' Square, 24 June 1843* to Thomas Beard, asking Beard if he thinks that "Boz" would be willing to allow the republication of his works "as literary extracts" in an Indian periodical, *The Englishman* (" . . . It appears that by a recent enactment of a very stringent nature such piracies are strictly prohibited . . . ").

For Dickens's response to this enquiry see H.109. *Dexter Gift.*

J.7

J.7   CARLYLE (THOMAS, 1795-1881) Autograph inscription, signed, on the back of a carte-de-visite photograph of Dickens reading in his garden at Gad's Hill Place ("Charles Dickens, at the back of his House, Gadshill, reading a Vol. of French Revolut." "6 or 7 Augt 1866" [See *Letters* 1 & 2 of the Phot^r Masson – who sent it june 1870; a thing really touching & tragical to me, & to be kept *private* withal] . . ")

Presented to The Dickens House by the Comte de Suzannet in 1932.

J.8   CHAPMAN AND HALL, L.s., *1 page, 8vo, Strand, 29 March 1837,* to Thomas Beard, inviting him to a dinner "to celebrate the success of the immortal Pickwick", *with the autograph envelope.*

J.9   COLLINS (WILLIAM WILKIE, 1824-1889) A.L.s. ("W.C."), *1 page, 16mo, n.p., Thursday [8 February 1866]*, to Francis Carr Beard confirming that he will meet Beard and Dickens for dinner that evening. For dating see H.400. *Dexter Gift.*

J.10   COLLINS (WILLIAM WILKIE) A.L.s. ("WC"), *1 page, 90, Gloucester Place, Portman Square, W [8 June 1870]* to Catherine Charlotte Beard (" . . . I am shocked and grieved. I will call later to hear if you have got any news . . . ") *with the autograph envelope.*

Pencilled note by the Comte de Suzannet on p. 4.

J.11   COTTINGHAM (C. J.) A.L.s., *2 pages, 8vo, 54 Gracechurch St., 3 April, 1862*, to Thomas Beard, thanking Beard for forwarding a manuscript to *All The Year Round* and offering to send another one by the same author, on "The Inns of Court and The Benchers" ("The writer . . . is a man of extraordinary research in *odd ways*, & I do think he may become a useful contributor to "All the Year Round" . . . ").

For Dickens's comment on this see H.372. The manuscript referred to was entitled "Fanciful Insanity" (published in *ATYR*, 26 April): "Inns of Court" was published in the issue for 10 May. *Dexter Gift.*

J.12   CRUIKSHANK (GEORGE, 1792-1878) Autograph memoranda, signature and sketches, scribbled on the back of a letter from Dickens (see H.31), *2 pages, 8vo, [? 20 April 1837]*. The memoranda outline Cruikshank's early ideas for seasonal subjects to be illustrated in his *Almanack* for 1838.

> . . . Jany.   Dancing the old year out and the New Year in
> Feby.   Frost on Thames
> March   St. Patrick's day – or David's
> April   Low Sunday
> May   Mails going out
> June   Victoria Proclaiming
> July   —

J.13   CRUIKSHANK (GEORGE) Autograph draft, *1 page, 8vo, [? 2 October 1839]* of a letter to Charles Dickens enquiring about *Barnaby Rudge* (" . . . when I saw you last you were in doubt as to having Barnaby illustrated or not but . . . would consider the matter and let me know in a few days . . . ").

Published in The Pilgrim Edition of the *Letters*, vol. 1, p. 589 (footnote 4). On p. 2 of the draft appear some memoranda and sketches of heads by Cruikshank.

J.14   DALBY (John Watson, *poet*) A.L.s. *3 pages, 8vo, Thornbury Cottage, 19 October 1859*, to Thornton Hunt, telling Hunt that his attitude towards Dickens, in the matter of the supposed caricature of his father as Skimpole in *Bleak House*, is too generous.

> . . . When your father so feelingly complained of "the great blow" which came so unexpectedly and so staggeringly upon him, ought not Mr. Dickens to have told the world that it was never aimed? To me his silence, then and now, appears unaccountable, unexplainable, inexcusable. And we see what rascally inferences are drawn from it. To have said, as he did, that "he even made his own father sit to him for some forbidding features" was an aggravation and no contradiction of the wrong . . .

In his privately printed *Leigh Hunt and Charles Dickens. The Skimpole Caricature* (Cedar Rapids, Iowa, 1930) Luther A. Brewer quotes (pages 29-30) from a letter in

Memoranda and Sketches by Cruikshank
(See J.13)

his possession written by Dalby to Leigh Hunt, dated 14 October and written some time between 1853 and 1859:

> . . . It seems to me that you need be under not the least apprehension with respect to the rascally misconception. How could it escape me to mention when we were talking over the painful matter at your house, that when at Buckingham I found the notation to be that Dickens intended Moore to be the original of his Skimpole? No one that I had intercourse with in that place dreamed of you; and those to whom I have spoken here receive the idea with feelings of surprise and disgust. Only last night a very intelligent friend of mine denounced the portrait altogether as inconsistent and unnatural. And, he added, that he could not see the possibility of associating it in any way with you. Oh, that there were some mode of removing the miserable impression from your mind! How Mr. Dickens can rest for a moment without doing his utmost for that purpose I am unable to conceive! . . .

J.15 DALBY (John Watson) A.L.s. *3 pages, 8vo, Thornbury 31 December, 1859* to Thornton Hunt, thanking him for a copy of *All The Year Round* containing Dickens's article, "Leigh Hunt. A Remonstrance":

> . . . Mournfully, rather than agrily, I still find myself saying, "Why so late?" &, like my friend De Wilde, the "Remonstrance" puzzled and puzzles me. Does Mr. Dickens mean that he is "remonstrating" with the "revivers" of the scandal, or has been himself remonstrated with, for having originated, & neglected to silence it? . . .

Maclise's painting of Dickens's children, taken with them by Dickens and his wife on their American Tour *(Courtesy of Cedric C. Dickens)* (See J.16)

J.16   DICKENS (CATHERINE THOMSON, 1815-1879, *wife of the novelist)* A.L.s. *written on p. 3 of Dickens's letter to Maclise (see H.90), Baltimore, 22 March 1842,* to Daniel Maclise (" . . . I only add a word to put you in mind there is such a being in existence which I fear you have forgotten unless that heavenly portrait [see H.90] has awakened some dormant recollections . . . "')

> . . . My beautiful sketch of our darlings is more admired than I can possibly describe. It is in great demand wherever we go and Willis the Author actually asked me to give it to him. Imagine such impudence! and audacity! . . .

J.17   DICKENS (CATHERINE THOMSON), A.L.s., *2 pages, 8vo, 1, Devonshire Terrace, Thursday morning 27 October 1842,* to Thomas Beard, sending him a copy of the second edition of *American Notes* "which Charles who has gone to Cornwall this morning begged me to send you, and also to say that you should have had it before this, but they have sold so quickly he has not had all his own copies until now . . ."

Published in *Dickens to his Oldest Friend,* ed. Walter Dexter, 1932, pp. 266-67. *Dexter Gift.*

J.18   DICKENS (CATHERINE THOMSON), A.L.s., *2 pages, 8vo, Broadstairs*

Portrait of Catherine Dickens in 1842, by Maclise (See J.17)

Monday morning, to Thomas Beard requesting the forwarding of "that parcel which Mr. Forster sent you for me" since it "contains some things of the children's which they are much in want of", *with the autograph envelope, postmarked, and inscribed, in Catherine's hand,* "Free".

Published in *Dickens to his Oldest Friend,* p. 272. *Dexter Gift.*

J.19   DICKENS (CATHERINE THOMSON) Nine A.L.s.s. (one, on mourning paper, in the third person), *18 pages, 8vo and sm. 8vo, 1, Devonshire Terrace and Tavistock House, 1 May 1846 [October 1847], 21 December 1847, 14 November and 21 December 1848, 7 April 1849, "Monday Forenoon", "Tuesday" [1 February 1853] and "Xmas Eve",* to Thomas Beard, inviting him to various dinners; to a wedding breakfast for Dickens's brother, Alfred; to a birthday party for Charles Dickens, Junior; and to a wedding breakfast for Dickens's youngest brother, Augustus (" . . . of course so soon after poor Fanny's death, it is to be very quiet . . . but Charles desires me to say he hopes you will come and assist him in getting through this *trying occasion,* as he knows none of the people (except his own family) who are coming . . . "); the sixth letter is a request to Beard for tickets for Charles Dickens Junior for the Cyclorama at the "Colloseum" and for the Polythenic (" . . . what hard words to spell! . . . "); *with three autograph envelopes, postmarked and inscribed* "Free".

All these letters are published in *Dickens to his Oldest Friend,* pp. 273-277. *Dexter Gift.*

Catherine Dickens in later life (See J.20)

J.20 DICKENS (CATHERINE THOMSON). Autograph message of thanks to Thomas Beard for his sympathy on the occasion of Dickens's death, inscribed on a black-bordered printed acknowledgment card, *with the autograph envelope, stamped and postmarked 19 July 1870.*

Card and envelope mounted in a cardboard frame. *Dexter Gift.*

J.21 DICKENS (CHARLES CULLIFORD BOZ, 1837-1896, *eldest* son of the novelist) Two A.L.s.s., *2 pages, 8vo., n.p. Saturday 26 April and Tuesday 30 December 1851,* to Thomas Beard his godfather requesting a ticket for "the Colosseum and Cyclorama" (first letter) and for the Princesses Theatre (second letter), *earlier letter on mourning paper. Dexter Gift.*

J.22 DICKENS (CHARLES CULLIFORD BOZ) A.L.s., *2 pages, 8vo, mourning paper, Gad's Hill Place 15 June 1870,* to Thomas Beard, expressing regret that it was not possible to invite Beard to attend Dickens's funeral ("... Our hands were ... completely tied by the terms of the will and we found it absolutely impossible ... to ask anyone but members of the family, and Forster, Ouvry, and your brother Frank in their official capacities of executor, solicitor and medical attendant ... "), *with the autograph envelope, stamped.*

J.23   DICKENS (JOHN, ?1785-1851, *father of the novelist*) Autograph note, written on letter from Dickens to Beard (see H.2), to Thomas Beard (" . . . Get me what signatures you can to the book there's a good fellow. If you see Fisher or Mr. Ross there's money in my drawer.").

J.24   DICKENS (JOHN) A.L.s., *4 pages, 8vo, 1 page 4to,n.p., 4 December 1834,* to Thomas Beard, concerning the breaking up of the Dickens family's establishment (" . . . Mrs. Dickens my Daughters Alfred & Boz [i.e. Augustus Dickens], going into more economical apartments somewhere in the vicinity of Fanny's engagements, Charles (taking Frederick with him into Chambers) and your humble servant "to the Winds" . . . "), saying that he can blame no-one but himself for this (" . . . I ought never to have allowed myself to be a party to an arrangement, for appearances sake, which was to lead to my own undoing . . . ") and that the event "has been hastened by Charles's determination to leave home, and that, on the first occasion of his having an *annual engagement*"; and expressing a high regard for every member of Beard's family (" . . . I shall always when I reflect upon the hours I have passed in their society, think on those which have been among the happiest of my life . . . "), *addressed, marked* "Private", *and postmarked on p. 6.*

Published, with one or two errors of transcription, in *Dickens to his Old Friend*, ed. Walter Dexter, 1932, pp. 265-66.

J.25   DICKENS (JOHN) A.L.s. (headed "Confidential") *3 pages, 8vo, n.p., Tuesday 16 December 1834,* to Thomas Beard, asking for the loan of "Two Sovereigns, until the first Proximo" for urgent shoe repairs for his son Alfred who "is walking to & from Hampstead daily in dancing pumps" and for himself and inviting Beard to visit Mrs. Dickens and her children at No. 21 George Street, Adelphi (" . . . if you can comply with my request will you do me the favor to enclose it me by post addressed Mr. Dickens, Mrs. Davis's (Laundress) North End Hampstead . . . "), *addressed, marked* "Private" *and postmarked on p. 4.*

Published in *Dickens to his Oldest Friend*, pp. 266-67.

J.26   DICKENS (JOHN) A.L.s. (headed "Confidential") *2 pages, 8vo, 21 George Street Adelphi 19 January 1835,* to Thomas Beard explaining that he will shortly receive a cheque from Charles Tennyson (the newly-elected M.P. for Lambeth) "for 17 devilish hard days & nights work" helping in the election campaign, and will then repay what he owes to Beard; and inviting Beard to call on him (" . . . The differences which have existed between me & my family are removed . . . "), *addressed, marked* "Private" *and postmarked on p. 4; also on p. 4, Post Office stamp:* "More to Pay, 1d." *and another stamp:* "Paid".

Published in *Dickens to his Oldest Friend*, pp. 267-68.

J.27   DICKENS (JOHN) A.L.s., *1 page, 8vo, n.p., Tuesday 9 May 1837,* to Thomas Beard, informing Beard of the sudden death of Mary Hogarth (" . . . On Saturday Evening we were at the St. James's Theatre poor Mary Hogarth in the highest possible apparent health & spirits. On Sunday at 3 o'clock she was a corpse . . . "), *mourning paper, addressed and marked* "Private" *on p. 4, endorsed.*

Published in *Dickens to his Oldest Friend*, p. 268.

J.28   DICKENS (JOHN) A.L.s. (headed "Confidential"), *3 pages, 8vo, At*

J.25

Mrs. Brennans The Hyde Thursday Morng. [*19 October 1837*], to Thomas Beard, inviting Beard to a meal, *addressed and postmarked on p. 4, endorsed*

> . . . As it is my intention to quit this rural retreat in a few days, I shall on Saturday next, put a bit of supper on table namely, a joint, and a couple of Ducks or Fowls, in order to make a slight return to one or two of my Villager friends for their kindness . . . It will be Yorkshire, after the cloth is withdrawn . . .

Published in *Dickens to his Oldest Friend*, p. 270.

J.29 DICKENS (JOHN) A.L.s., *1 page, sm. 8vo, 34 Edwards Street Saturday*, to Thomas Beard, inviting Beard to dinner the following day (" . . . Charles and Catherine are to be with us . . . ") *integral address leaf, postmarked.*

Published in *Dickens to his Oldest Friend*, p. 270.

John Dickens (See J.30)

J.30   DICKENS (JOHN) A.L.s. (headed "Confidential"), *3 pages, 8vo, 90,
Fleet Street 23 December 1845,* to Thomas Beard, asking for information (" . . . If I'm
guilty of impertinence kick me! . . . ") about the *Morning Herald's* number of Parliamentary reporters for the coming session, the remuneration paid to reporters on legal
circuits, etc.

> . . . We [i.e. The Daily News] must not stand lower than the Herald on the
> Money Market as regards these matters, but at the same time we must not, through
> ignorance, throw money away . . .

J.31   DICKENS (JOHN) A.L.s., *1 page, 8vo, Office of the Daily News 90 Fleet
Street 27 December 1845,* to Thomas Beard (" . . . Charles desires me to say he shall
be most happy to see you tomorrow after Church . . . ").

Published in *Dickens to his Oldest Friend,* p. 273.

J.32   DICKENS (ELIZABETH BARROW, 1789-1863, *mother of the novelist*),
A.L. (in the third person), *1 page, 8vo, 18 Bentinck St. Manchester Square [2 February 1833],*
to Thomas Beard, inviting him to an evening party (" . . . Quadrilles 8 o'clock . . . ")
on 11 February.

This note, enclosed by Dickens in a letter to Beard of 2 February 1833 (see H.3)
has been mounted in cardboard frame. *Dexter Gift.*

J.33   DICKENS (ELIZABETH BARROW) A.L. (in the third person), *1 page,
8vo, 18 Bentinck Street 14 April [1833],* to Thomas Beard inviting him to "witness a
private representation" (see F.1) on 27 April. *Dexter Gift.*

J.34   DICKENS (MARY, 1838-1896, *eldest daughter of the novelist*), Printed invitation card to an "At Home" at 5 Hyde Park Place on Thursday 7 April [1870]. The name of [Thomas] Beard and the date are written in Mary Dickens's hand. Card mounted in a cardboard frame. *Dexter Gift.*

J.35   DICKENS (MARY, 1838-1896) Black-bordered printed acknowledgment card from the Dickens family thanking Thomas Beard for his letter of sympathy on Dickens's death (Beard's name written in in Mary's hand) *with the autograph envelope, stamped and postmarked 8 July 1870.* Card and envelope mounted in a cardboard frame. *Dexter Gift.*

J.36   DICKENS (MARY) Autograph inscription, "Aunt Letitia / With Mamie's dear love. / 1882", written in a copy of *The Charles Dickens Birthday Book. Compiled and edited by his Eldest Daughter. With Five Illustrations by his Youngest Daughter (4to, Chapman & Hall, 1882).*

Suzannet notes in his unpublished catalogue: "Les noms de plus de 50 membres des familles Dickens, Hogarth, Austin, Burnett, Roney, etc., sont inscrits dans cet album. Quelques-unes des signatures sont autographes."

J.37   DOLBY (GEORGE, 18??-1900, *Dickens's Manager for the Public Readings*), Autograph laissez-passer, signed, issued to Thomas Beard, *1 page, 12mo,* [*? 15 March 1870*] headed "St. James's Hall. Mr. Charles Dickens's Farewell Reading" and bearing the instruction "Pass Mr. T. Beard to Mr. Dickens's Room". *Dexter Gift.*

J.38   DUFF-GORDON (SIR ALEXANDER CORNEWALL, 1811-1872), A.L.s., *2 pages, 16mo, n.p.* [*11 June 1847*], to Dickens, a covering note sent with Thackeray's letter to Dickens of 11 June 1847 (see J.66), endorsed by Forster on p. 1.

Published in *The Letters and Private Papers of William Makepeace Thackeray*, ed. G. N. Ray, vol. 2, p. 300.

J.39   EVANS (FREDERICK MULLET, *of Bradbury & Evans*), A.L.s., *2 pages, 8vo, Whitefriars, 8 March 1852,* to Charles Dickens assuring Dickens that Thomas Beard's copy of that month's number of *Bleak House* was sent to Beard from the publishers addressed as usual to the *Morning Herald* office and suggesting that it might in future be better to send the numbers of Beard's private address.

For Dickens's comment on this letter see H.210. *Dexter Gift.*

J.40   FORSTER (JOHN, 1812-1876, *friend and biographer of Dickens*) A.L.s. to Daniel Maclise in the form of a postscript to a letter from Dickens to Maclise of 2 January 1842 (see H.88), confirming Dickens's description of the smallness of the Dickenses' cabin on board the S.S. *Britannia* and praising "Mrs. D's cheerfulness about the whole thing . . . She deserves to be what you know she is so emphatically called – The Beloved . . .".

J.41   FORSTER (JOHN) Autograph memorandum, *2 pages, 4to,* relative to his quarrel with Thackeray in 1847, comprising copies of two letters from himself to Thackeray, one from Thackeray to him (see J.65), two from himself to Tom Taylor, and one from himself to Dickens, together with a list of four related letters, marked A-D, preserved with this memorandum.

The texts of the Forster letters in this memorandum have been published in *The Letters and Private Papers of William Makepeace Thackeray,* ed. G. N. Ray, vol. 2, pp. 294, 295-96, 298-99 and 303-04.

J.42   FORSTER (JOHN) Autograph draft, *3 pages, 4to,* of a letter to Thackeray, recalling earlier quarrels between them ("the old Pendennis charge" and "our dispute relating to the Lectures"), admitting that he may unintentionally have done injustice to Thackeray but insisting that Thackeray has also been unjust to him (calling him "an unfair critic", "Steele's man", etc. and "coming down to quite the other day, too, you told me I am also Stanfield's man . . . ") and concluding with the expression of an earnest wish to "forget as far as possible whatever has been painful in the past" and to renew friendly intercourse with Thackeray.

With the document is a transcript in the hand of the Comte de Suzannet. The draft letter is published in *The Letters and Private Papers of William Makepeace Thackeray,* vol. 1, pp. cxxxv-vii.

J.43   FORSTER (JOHN) A.L.s., *4 pages, 16mo, West Cliff Hotel, Folkestone, 25 October 1859,* to Thornton Hunt, concerning arrangements for Hunt to meet Dickens (see H.324) and enclosing "a letter from Mr. Sotheby" (" . . . if your answer from America shd. not be directly favorable, the suggestion of a sale . . . will be worth considering . . . ").

Mrs Gaskell (See J.44)   Mrs Carlyle (See J.44)

J.44   GASKELL (ELIZABETH CLEGHORN, 1810-1865) A.L.s., *4 pages, 4to, 27 Woburn Square Monday Morning [13 May 1849],* to her friend, Annie Shaen describing a breakfast party at Monckton Milnes's, a visit to the Duke of Sutherland's home, Stafford House, and a dinner party given by Dickens in Devonshire Terrace, *pencilled endorsement:* "Received in Spring 1849" *and dated* 13.5.1849.

. . . Anne sat between Carlyle and Rogers, – I between Dickens and Douglas Jerrold. Anne heard the most sense, and I the most wit; I never heard anyone so witty as Douglas Jerrold, who is a very little almost deformed man with grey, flowing hair, and very fine eyes. He made so many bon-mots, that at the time I thought I could remember; but which now have quite slipped out of my head. After dinner when we went upstairs I sat next to Mrs. Carlyle, who amused me very much with her account of their only servant who comes from Annandale in Scotland, and had never been accustomed to announce titles; so when Count Pepoli called she announced him as Mr. Compilloly; Lord Jeffrey as Lorcherfield and simply repeated it louder & louder each time; till at last Mrs. Carlyle said "What is it – man woman or beast?" to which the servant answered "a little wee gentleman, Ma'am". Miss Fanny Kemble called in a hat and a habit, and when Mrs. C. spoke to the servant about bringing Miss K. in, unannounced, the servant said "I did not know if *it* was a Mr. or Mrs." . . . Mr. Tom Taylor was there too, who writes those comical ballads in Punch; and Anne said we had the whole Punch-bowl, which I believe we had . . . There were some very nice little Dickens' children in the room, – who were so polite and well-trained . . .

This letter is not included in *The Letters of Mrs. Gaskell*, ed. J. A. V. Chapple and Arthur Pollard, 1966. *Dexter Gift.*

J.45   GREEN (JOSEPH) Signed receipt for the sum of £6.19.6 paid for Dickens by Thomas Beard, dated 4 February 1843. *Dexter Gift.*

J.46   GREENHILL (W. G.) A.L.s., *2 pages, 4to, 77 Cannon St., 11 November 1842,* to Thomas Beard, asking Beard to use his influence with Dickens on behalf of an old family friend of the Greenhills who is a candidate for the post of Matron at the Sanatorium. For Dickens's response see H.97. *Dexter Gift.*

J.47   HILL (ROWLAND, 1849-1945, *editor of 'The Bedford Mercury')* Notes on Dickens's Reading of *A Christmas Carol, 32 typed pages, 8 x 6½".*

. . . now written by Rowland Hill, of Bedford, who heard Charles Dickens read his "Christmas Carol in Prose", several times, in St. James's Hall, in London, in 1868, 1869 and 1870, notably at his last reading on March 15, 1870. He seemed well in health at the last Reading and gave a Farewell to his hearers on that unique occasion . . .

I used to take my copy of the book, and note, in pencil, any alterations he made, seemingly on the spur of the moment . . . For instance, on page 2, in line 9, instead of "and sole mourner", he said "HIS sole mourner", with a staccato pause after the word mourner . . .

. . . he constantly omitted phrases describing who spoke and how they spoke, by making marvellous changes of tone and changes of his facial expression . . .

From a remark on p. 28 it is clear that these notes were typed by Hill in 1930. With this document is a photo copy of the obituary notice of Hill published in the *Bedfordshire Times*, 5 October 1945, and a letter to the Comtesse de Suzannet about Hill from Professor Philip Collins.

J.48   HOGARTH (GEORGINA, 1827-1917, *sister-in-law of the novelist)* Five A.L.s.s. (one on mourning paper with the autograph envelope, and one mounted in a cardboard frame), *8 pages, 8vo, 1 Devonshire Terrace, dated only by the day of the week or month,* to Thomas Beard, inviting Beard to dinner on Dickens's birthday [1844];

explaining that Charles Dickens Junior's birthday party must be postponed because of his mother's illness "on her return from Scotland" [1848]; and soliciting tickets for the Panorama and Cyclorama.

The first two letters are published in *Dickens to his Oldest Friend*, ed. Walter Dexter, 1932, pp. 272 and 274. *Dexter Gift.*

J.49   HOGARTH (GEORGINA) Copy in the hand of Nathaniel T. Beard, son of Francis Carr Beard, of a signed letter from Miss Hogarth to Francis Beard, written from Gad's Hill, 22 June [1870], the original of which appears in this Catalogue at K.2. At the end of the copy Nathaniel Beard has appended this signed note: "The inkstand above referred to figures in the print entitled '*The Empty Chàir*'—a view of the interior of Dickens's study at Gad's Hill, published in 'The Graphic' after his death, the inkstand and the illustration being both in my possession (March 1880) at the present time." *Dexter Gift.*

J.50   HOGARTH (GEORGINA) A.L.s., *4 pages, 8vo, Gad's Hill Sunday* [*July 1870*], to Francis Carr Beard, thanking him for his "kind note", mentioning some "Orange Brandy and Cigars" that she has sent to him, enquiring if any of his patients "not well off" would like to have "two Pairs of Elastic Stockings of dearest Charles'— QUITE NEW", and sending a message to Wilkie Collins (". . . I will not fail to write to him after the dreadful trial of leaving this dear place is over . . . "), *mourning paper.*

Published in *Dickens to his Oldest Friend*, pp. 278-79. *Dexter Gift.*

J.51   HUNT (JAMES HENRY LEIGH, 1784-1859, *poet and essayist*) Autograph envelope initialled, addressed to Edmund Ollier, Esqre./6 Bute Street / Old Brompton. Postmarked: Hammersmith 13 February 1855.

J.52   JERROLD (DOUGLAS WILLIAM, 1803-1857, *dramatist and journalist*) A.L.s., *1 page, 8vo, West Lodge, Putney Common, 1 October* [*1845*], to Thomas Beard, recommending Sydney Blanchard, son of his old friend, Laman Blanchard, for the post of reporter on the *Morning Herald* (for Dickens's letter of recommendation see H.122). *Dexter Gift.*

J.53   JERROLD (DOUGLAS WILLIAM) Acting copy of *Not So Bad As We Seem* with autograph signature, stage-directions, passages marked and deleted, etc. See H. 198.

J.54   MORLEY (HENRY, 1822-1894, *journalist and man of letters*) A.L.s., *3 pages, sm. 8vo, 4 Upper Park Road, Haverstock Hill, 24 December 1859,* to Thornton Hunt, concerning Dickens's relations with Leigh Hunt (" . . . you cannot want corroboration of the fact that Mr. Dickens's regard for your father was in all its cordiality sincere . . . ") and referring to an article on Leigh Hunt's poetry written by himself for *Household Words.*

J.55   OLLIER (EDMUND, 1827-1886, *journalist*) A.L.s., *3 pages, 8vo, 10 Victoria Grove, South Kensington, 13 June 1870,* to Thornton Hunt, replying to Hunt's letter of thanks for a letter published by Ollier in the *Daily News*

> . . . I was writing at the D.N. Office, on Friday, the leading article on Dickens which appears in Saturday's paper; & I felt I could not leave the place without, in

my private, personal and non-journalistic capacity, correcting once more . . . the fatal error about Skimpole . . .

˙J.56 PERUGINI (KATE MACREADY, 1839-1929, *younger daughter of the novelist*), Autograph manuscript, signed, of "On Woman Old and New", written for delivery as a speech in 1920 and published in *The Dickensian*, June 1933, *9 pages, 8vo.* In stiff crimson folder.

J.57 PUTNAM (GEORGE WILLIAM, 1812-1896, *Secretary to Dickens on his first visit to America*) A.L.s., *4 pages, 4to, Linden, 28 October 1885*, to Benjamin P. Cheney, one of the founders of the American Express Co., sending Cheney a Dickens letter written to himself in 1842, describing his contacts with the "Great Author", and viciously attacking Forster as unworthy of Dickens's intimate friendship.

> . . . As to Charles Dickens – had he been a temperate man he would no doubt have been living now. I am well convinced from what I *know* of his life and character intemperance was his *only* vice – all the jeers and flings of the world to the contrary notwithstanding . . .

This letter was given by one of Cheney's daughters to F. W. C. Hersey, Instructor in English at Harvard University, and presented by him to the Comte de Suzannet in April 1939. Preserved with it is an A.L.s. *(2 pages, 4to, 14, Gordon Street, Cambridge, Mass., 27 April 1939)*, from Hersey to Suzannet (" . . . I ought to say that my first thought on reading Putnam's letter with its exaggerated charges of Dickens's drinking to excess was that it ought to be destroyed so that no sensational writer should use it to besmirch Dickens's memory. The scandal-mongers have been attacking him so frequently recently, and I understand a new book is coming out this spring with very distressing revelations . . . ").

J.58 REYNOLDS (SIR JOHN RUSSELL, 1828-1896, *physician*) A.L.s., *3 pages, 8vo, 38, Grosvenor Street, W.* [*8 June 1970*], to Catherine Charlotte Beard, informing her that Dickens "has had a most severe apoplectic seizure" and is "now sinking rapidly", *with the autograph envelope, initialled.*

J.59 SMITH (GEORGE, ——) A.L.s., *1 page, 8vo, 65 Cornhill -th December 1859*, to Thornton Hunt, thanking Hunt for a sight of "Mr. Charles Dickens's Note" and assuming that the publication of Leigh Hunt's Autobiography "on the 20th of this month" will be "in accordance with your and Mr. Dickens's wishes . . . "

J.60 STONE (MARCUS, 1840-1921, *first illustrator of Our Mutual Friend*) Autograph notes concerning Dickens. Nine slips, 8vo and·16mo, seven numbered and headed "C.D.", and two more headed "People I met at Dickens's" and "C.D.'s Appearance". The notes concern Dickens's comments on printers, the source for Sam Weller's surname, the scenery of the early part of *Great Expectations*, boyhood memories of Dickens, the scene on which the pauper's funeral in *Oliver Twist* is based and the source for Mr. Venus in *Our Mutual Friend*

> . . . Never make a fair copy of a much corrected manuscript. An M.S. with few or no corrections is always given to the boy beginner to set up, & you will get a proof full of errors. The M.S. which is difficult to decipher is put into the hands of a first rate compositor whose proof will give very little trouble.

. . . at Chatham, on the right side of a hilly street which leads to Fort Pitt there is – or was – a low wall with an iron railing on the top. "I remember" he said, pointing it out to me as we were walking by "my poor mother, God forgive her, put me up on the edge of that wall, so that I might wave my hat and cheer George 4th – then Prince Regent – who was driving by."

These notes, together with the following item (Stone's reminiscences) and the uncorrected proofs of *Mrs. Gamp in the Provinces* (see I.5), were purchased at Sotheby's by the Comte de Suzannet in February 1944. Stone's notes and reminiscences, on which he drew for his speech at the 1910 Boz Club Dinner (reported in *The Dickensian*, vi, March 1910, pp. 61-64), were being edited for publication in *The Dickensian* by Walter Dexter at the time of his death.

Marcus Stone (See J.61)

J.61 STONE (MARCUS) Autograph reminiscences, *105 pages*, *4to*, comprising two chapters of an Autobiography (78 pages), a chapter headed "Two Visits to Boulogne" [1853 and 1854] (21 pages), and an untitled chapter dealing with his early development as an artist (6 pages). Dickens is frequently mentioned and described in these pages which include also copies of several letters from Dickens to Marcus Stone or to his father, Frank. In stiff crimson folder.

. . . From his constant daily habit of taking long walks in all weathers he [Dickens] was bronzed & ruddy . . . His pace was four miles an hour. The afternoon walk was generally a stretch of twelve to fifteen miles, frequently more, he made a practice of increasing his speed when ascending a hill . . .

. . . His eyes, most impressive and wonderful eyes, were of a colour rarely met with, a sort of green hazel grey – steadfast honest, all seeing eyes . . . They were not only seeing, they were also speaking eyes, they could question you, they could assent and sympathise. They could call your attention to an object of interest by a quick glance at you and then with an equally rapid glance at that which he wished you to observe. He moved his eyes without moving his head more than is the habit of most people . . . I have been embarrassed by my intimate understanding of this ocular telegraph on occasions, when it would have been indiscreet to laugh. When I met him in Paris in 1862 I was dining with him, his sister in law, his daughter, and Bulwer, who was not yet Lord Lytton, was the only other guest. Lord Lytton was afflicted with deafness of an intermittent kind . . . that evening he was very hard of hearing . . . After the ladies retired he told us very interesting stories which he had picked up in Florence. He spoke with great deliberation his elegant diction delivered with solemnity. They were dramas of a romantic & tragic kind. As he was describing one of his heroes, Dickens who was a most attentive listener asked, "Was he wealthy?" Bulwer answered "Healthy, one of the healthiest of men, never had a day's illness in his life" whereupon the wonderful eyes turned upon me and a faint rise of colour came to his cheek. I had to get up and look out of window . . .

J.62 STONE (FRANK, 1800-1859, *artist, father of Marcus*) Acting copy of *Not So Bad As We Seem* with autograph signature, passages marked and deleted, etc. See H.198.

J.63 SWINBURNE (ALGERNON CHARLES, 1837-1909) Corrected proofs of his article, "Charles Dickens", published in the *Quarterly Review,* July 1902. 20 pages, 8vo, with numerous manuscript corrections and additions throughout. Bound in crimson half-morocco with a calligraphic title-page.

J.64 TAYLOR (TOM, 1817-1880, *dramatist and journalist, afterwards Editor of "Punch"*) A.L.s., *12 pages, 8vo, The Temple, 11 June 1847,* to John Forster, explaining that he thoughtlessly repeated to Thackeray some words of Forster's that gave great offence and profusely apologising for this, *endorsed on p. 12 by Forster:* "Letter B".

Published in *The Letters and Private Papers of William Makepeace Thackeray,* ed. G. N. Ray, vol. 2, pp. 301-03.

J.65 THACKERAY (WILLIAM MAKEPEACE, 1811-1863) A.L.s., *1 page, 8vo, 13 Young St. Kensington Squ., 9 June 1847,* to John Forster, explaining that his refusal to shake hands with Forster the previous night was because of "words used by yourself many weeks ago when you were pleased to inform a mutual acquaintance that I was 'as false as hell'", *notes in Forster's hand on p. 2 heavily scored through, separate address leaf inscribed:* "J. Forster Esq. Favored by Sir A. Duff-Gordon".

Published in *The Letters . . . . of Thackeray,* ed. G. N. Ray, vol. 2, p. 297.

J.66 THACKERAY (WILLIAM MAKEPEACE) A.L.s., *3 pages, 8vo, 13 Young St. Kensington, 11 July 1847,* to Dickens, concerning the part played by Taylor in causing a breach between himself and Forster, *addressed on p. 4, shorthand notes by Dickens written above address*

. . . the affair seems to me to stand thus, Forster ought not to have used the words: Taylor ought not to have told them: and I ought not to have taken them up. And I for my part am sorry I did . . .

Published in *The Letters . . . . of Thackeray,* ed. G. N. Ray, vol. 2, p. 299.

J.67   THACKERAY (WILLIAM MAKEPEACE) A.L.s., *1 page, sm. 8vo, 36 Onslow Square, Sunday ev⁹. [May 1858]*, to James Wilson concerning the rumours that were circulating at the time of Dickens's separation from his wife

> ... I have a note from Mr Dickens on the subject of the common report derogatory to the honor of a young lady whose name has been mentioned in connection with him. He authorises me to contradict the rumour, on his own solemn word and his wife's authority ...

For dating see *The Letters . . . . of Thackeray*, ed. G. N. Ray, vol. 4, p. 83.

J.68   TOPHAM (FRANCIS WILLIAM, 1808-1877 *artist*) Acting copy of *Not So Bad As We Seem* with autograph signature, passages marked and deleted, etc. See H.198.

J.69   WINTER (HENRY LOUIS, — , *husband of Maria Beadnell*) Six A.L.s.s., *23 pages, 8vo, various addresses, 1858-1863*, to his daughter, Ella Winter, chiefly affectionate letters on domestic matters, one reproaching her for showing temper towards her mother ("... take my experience in life as an earnest of the truth . . . that, nothing in a woman's conduct is so likely to destroy her future happiness in life whether as child wife or mother as an indulgence of bad temper and a want of self dignity even under undeserved reproof . . . "), *with four autograph envelopes, stamped, and a photograph of a portrait of Mrs. George Beadnell, Maria's mother.*

With these letters is a Certificate of Conformity (The Bankruptcy Law Consolidation Act, 1849) signed by Robert George Cecil Fane, Commissioner of the Court of Bankruptcy, and dated 11 March 1859, certifying that Henry Winter has conformed to all the requirements of the Act and "that his Bankruptcy has not arisen wholly from unavoidable losses and misfortunes" (*parchment 39 cm. by 52.5 cm.*); also, a collection of 6 carte-de-visite photographs of Maria Beadnell Winter, Henry Louis Winter and their daughter, Ella Maria Winter. All these documents came into the Collection of the Comte de Suzannet at the same time as the Album of Maria Beadnell (see I.1).

Mr. and Mrs. Henry Winter and their daughter, Ella (See J.69)

SECTION K

Varia

K.1   MARRIAGE LICENCE issued to "Charles John Huffam Dickens of Furnivals Inn in the County of Middlesex Bachelor and Catherine Thomson Hogarth of the Parish of Saint Luke Chelsea in the same County Spinster a Minor" for their wedding at St. Luke's, signed by John Moore, Registrar, and dated 29 March 1836, *in dark blue full morocco case, gilt.*

Endorsed on the back: "Dickens & Hogarth 2nd April 1836 Rev. W. Morice".

This document was sold at Sotheby's on 4 December 1922 by Frederick A. Crisp and bought by the Comte de Suzannet from Dr. A. S. W. Rosenbach in December 1946. Presented to The Dickens House by the Comte in 1947.

K.2   DICKENS'S CIGAR-CASE, leather, lined with watered silk, gilt rim, Dickens's monogram "C.D." on the front in raised gilt letters, gilt plaque on the reverse on which is engraved:

> "A Souvenir of Happy Memories
> Rustling above the dusty growth of years
> Come back green leaves of yesterday.

A Thought from Nicholas Nickleby Ch. 49"

With the case is an A.L.s. *(3 pages, 8vo, Gads Hill 22 June [1870])* from Georgina Hogarth to Frank Beard

> . . . I have the charge under Charles's Will of distributing among his *dear* friends the familiar objects in his study. First of all we think of *you* – & shall never forget you in association with him – in the memory of what you did for him at Preston – & still more in the remembrance of what we all went through together in those last hours – I send you a Cigar Case which was given to him before he went to America – It is a double one – & has an inscription which will make it valuable to you . . .

The case was acquired by Maggs Bros. from Beard's nephew, Mr. Cass, and purchased from Maggs by the Comte de Suzannet in April 1930. Presented by the Comte de Suzannet to The Dickens House in 1933.

K.3   DICKENS'S INK-STAND, large glass bottle with cut glass top sunk in an ebony stand.

The letter to Frank Beard from Georgina Hogarth quoted in relation to K.2 continues:

> . . .Will you tell your brother Tom (to save my writing one note – I have so many to write) that the Inkstand I send him is the one Charles used most of all here & which he used for the books he wrote here . . .

K.1

This relic was acquired by Maggs Bros. from Beard's nephew, Mr. Cass, and purchased from Maggs in April 1930 by the Comte de Suzannet who presented it to The Dickens House that same month.

K.4 BEADNELL (GEORGE, *father of Maria Beadnell*) Last Will and Testament, Copy dated 16 August 1862, *9 pages folio.*

K.5 PHOTOGRAPHS OF CHARLES DICKENS. Collection of eight portrait photographs of Dickens published by the London Stereoscopic Company (3), Tradelle and Young (4) and Robert Thrupp (1), together with seventeen carte-de-visite photographs, also of Dickens, by Mason & Co. (16) and Gurney (1) and one carte-de-visite photograph of Dickens and a group of friends outside Gad's Hill Place.

K.5

K.6　ADMISSION TICKET for the dinner given in Dickens's honour at the Freemason's Hall 2 November 1867, *green card, mounted.*

　　This item formed part of the Beard Collection of Dickensiana. *Dexter Gift.*

K.7　"Mr. Charles Dickens's Final Readings." Advertising leaflet, published by Chappell & Co. announcing that "Mr. Charles Dickens, having some time since become perfectly restored to health, has resumed his interrupted series of Farewell Readings . . . ", *4 pages, printed in red, mounted with an admission ticket (sofa stall) for the Reading on 1 February 1870.*

　　These items formed part of the Beard Collection of Dickensiana. *Dexter Gift.*

K.8　"Catalogue of Drawings, Sketches and Etchings by that Distinguished Artist, George Cruikshank, deceased . . . which . . . will be sold by Auction by Messrs. Christie, Manson & Woods . . . . on Tuesday, July 8, 1879 . . . ", *24 pages, 8vo.* [1879].

K.9　BUCALOSSI (ERNEST). " 'Pickwick' Waltz. On Melodies from Edward Solomon's Dramatic Cantata." Parts for flute and piccolo, oboes, drums, euphonium, trombones, bass trombone, cornets, horns, bassoons and clarinets.

K.10　DICKENSIANA. Envelope containing the following miscellaneous items of Dickensian interest:

　　(1)　Two pages from the weekly miscellany *The Town*, dated in pencil 9 September 1837, containing a description of a "Pickwick Club" held at the Sun Tavern, Long Acre, (" . . . The illustrious 'Boz' himself has deigned to honour it

162

K.10(7)

with more than one visit . . .") and also comment on Mr. Laing of Hatton Garden, the original of Mr. Fang in *Oliver Twist*.

(2) Two pages from the issue of *The Town* for 10 February 1838 containing a sketch of a London "boots" which refers to Sam Weller (" . . . he was anything but a genuine *boots*. As a flash groom, Mr. Weller was a perfect picture – rather out of his place as a footman, and wholly so as a tavern menial . . . ").

(3) Watercolour (5½ *in. by* 10½ *in.*) of a view in Cobham Park signed E. W. B. and dated August 1844; beneath the painting is written in pencil, "The seat of the Earl of Darnley (CD's Neighbour)".

(4) Armytage's engraving of Samuel Lawrence's portrait of Carlyle with facsimile signature beneath, mounted (on reverse of mount are two carte-de-visite size In Memoriam cards issued after Dickens's death).

(5) Pound's engraving of a photograph of Dickens by Mayall, issued as a Supplement to *The Illustrated News of the World*.

(6) In Memoriam notice of Dickens published in *The Tomahawk. A Saturday Journal of Satire*, 25 June 1870, together with double-page pull-out portrait of Dickens and some characters from the novels, entitled "A Memory of the Past".

(7) "The Two Charles's", Caricature of Dickens and Charles Fechter by Alfred Bryan published in *Entr'acte* 23 August 1879, differing considerably from the original drawing listed at G.10.

(8) "What are the Wild Waves saying?" Print (7 *in.* *by* 11.3 *in.*) Nichols's illustration to Chapter VIII of *Dombey and Son*, published by Letts, Son & Co., n.d.

(9) "A Reading in the West" Print (5½ *in.* *by* 8 *in.*) of W. Small's illustration of Bret Harte's poem, "Dickens in Camp" (mounted, with reproduction of Frank Miles's portrait of Bret Harte on reverse of mount).

K.11 NOT SO BAD AS WE SEEM. Contributions by Mrs. Belloc Lowndes, Henry Fielding Dickens, Compton Mackenzie, Hugh Walpole, Stephen Leacock, Alfred Noyes and others; illustrations by Augustus John, George Morrow, H. M. Bateman, Frank Reynolds and others. *32 pages, 4to, The Rolls House Publishing Co. for the Children's Libraries Movement* [1921].

This booklet contains the cast list for the revival of *Not So Bad As We Seem* at Devonshire House, Piccadilly, on 30 November 1921, to raise funds for "David Copperfield's Library" at 13 Johnson Street, Camden Town; the part of Lord Wilmot, created by Dickens in 1851, was played by Ivor Novello. Also included are extracts from the replies of eminent people invited to participate in the production (" . . . If I were unconnected with the theatrical profession I could afford to expose myself to the merited contempt of the actors who work for me by taking part in this deplorable tomfoolery. G. BERNARD SHAW").

With the booklet is an A.L.s. dated 8 October 1921, from the Rev. J. Brett Langstaff, originator of the project, to W. Allen Cunningham, and a typed cast-list.

Letters and Documents Relating
to the Suzannet Collection

L.1   DEXTER (WALTER, Editor of *The Dickensian*, 1925-1944) Five hundred and forty-two A.L.ss. to the Comte de Suzannet (3 February 1931-30 March 1944) dealing with publication of materials from the Comte's Collection and other Dickensian matters.

On 19 February 1945 the Comte de Suzannet wrote to Mr. Leslie C. Staples that in these letters Dexter's views " . . . . on Dickens's life and personality, on his friends, his 'fanatical' admirers and his detractors, are expressed with a frankness, a sincerity, an unprejudiced open-mindedness which very vew of the professional critics have equalled and I am convinced they will prove of great biographical interest and value to Dickensians later on".

L.2   DICKENS FELLOWSHIP. Thirty A.L.ss. to the Comte de Suzannet from officers of the Dickens Fellowship (A. W. Edwards, Percy Merriman, S. J. Rust, T. W. Hill, John Greaves, Lord Hewart of Bury) (8 July 1932-5 October 1949) thanking the Comte for gifts and donations to The Dickens House, etc.

L.3   ECKEL (JOHN C., author of *The First Editions of the Writings of Dickens*), Two A.L.ss. to the Comte de Suzannet (21 September 1928 and 2 December 1932) concerning Eckel's bibliographical work on Dickens, together with a copy of a long A.L. from Suzannet to Eckel (30 November 1932) and other documents relating to the same subject.

L.4   GREEN (C. H., Hon. Secretary of the Dickens Fellowship, 1920 - 1925), Three A.L.ss. to the Comte de Suzannet (28 September 1944-5 September 1946) concerning a projected work on the illustrations to *Pickwick Papers*.

L.5   HATTON (THOMAS, co-author of *A Bibliography of the Periodical Works of Dickens*), Thirty-nine A.L.ss. to the Comte de Suzannet (24 October 1933-3 May 1937) concerning Dickensian bibliography, together with four A.L.ss. to the same correspondent (4 March - 7 May 1934) from A. H. Cleaver on the same subject.

L.6   HILL (T. W., Hon. Secretary of the Dickens Fellowship 1914 - 1919 and Hon. Treasurer 1932 - 1947), Seventeen A.L.ss. to the Comte de Suzannet (20 April 1943 - 8 July 1950), concerning Hill's annotations to Dickens's novels published in *The Dickensian*.

L.7   HOUSE (HUMPHRY, author of *The Dickens World*) Six A.L.ss. to the Comte de Suzannet (25 July 1949 - 14 November 1950), concerning a projected new edition of Dickens's letters (later called The Pilgrim Edition), together with seven

A.L.ss. from Rupert Hart-Davis to the Comte on the same subject (16 December 1948 -
25 May 1950) and a typed prospectus (11 pp.) entitled "Proposed New Edition of
Dickens's Letters".

L.8 JOHNSON (EDGAR, author of *Charles Dickens: His Tragedy and Triumph*),
Six A.L.ss. to the Comte de Suzannet (22 October 1946 - 30 July 1947), concerning
Johnson's biographical work on Dickens.

L.9 KENT (WILLIAM, writer on Dickens), Two A.L.ss. to the Comte de
Suzannet (20 and 28 September 1949), concerning Dickens's biography and the
mistakes of "idolaters" and an annotated copy of a cyclostyled letter from Kent to the
Editor of *The Dickensian* (1 March 1949).

L.10 LEY (J. W. T., Hon. Secretary of the Dickens Fellowship 1904-1909,
Editor of Forster's *Life of Dickens*), Two A.L.ss. to the Comte de Suzannet (22 April
and 11 May 1935) concerning Ley's publications on Dickens.

L.11 MILLER (WILLIAM, author of *The Dickens Student and Collector*),
Fifty-seven A.L.ss. to the Comte de Suzannet (30 July 1933 - 31 January 1950),
concerning Miller's Dickensian researches, together with fifteen photocopies and
prints of Dickens material and a visiting card of Alfred Tennyson Dickens inscribed
to B. W. Matz, founder of the Dickens Fellowship.

L.12 RAY (GORDON N., author of *Thackeray*), Two A.L.ss. to the Comte de
Suzannet (18 September and 28 October 1940) concerning Dickens's relations
with Thackeray.

L.13 SADLEIR (MICHAEL), Four A.L.ss. to the Comte de Suzannet (4
March 1932 - 2 January 1938), concerning Sadleir's work on Count D'Orsay and a
projected work on Dickens's relations with Richard Bentley, the publisher.

L.14 STAPLES (LESLIE C., Editor of *The Dickensian* 1944 - 1968), One
hundred and eighteen A.L.ss. to the Comte de Suzannet (7 February 1940 - 27 July
1950), on Dickensian matters.

L.15 SUZANNET (ALAIN DE), Autograph list of accessions to his Dickens
Collection 1912 - 1945, *33 pages, foolscap.*

L.16 SUZANNET (ALAIN DE), Autograph check-list of "Presentation
Copies of the Works of Charles Dickens, *16 pages foolscap*, together with another
check-list of the same, typed, *6 pages, 8vo.*; draft of an article, "Presentation Copies
of the Works of Charles Dickens. First attempt at a Census", *4 pages, foolscap;* various
notes and memoranda concerning Presentation Copies.

L.17 SUZANNET (ALAIN DE), Autograph list of 514 characters in *Pickwick
Papers* in blue-covered 4to. exercise-book, together with an earlier list of the same
(474 characters), *5 pages foolscap* and a list of Dickens's aristocratic characters, *2 pages
foolscap.*

L.18 SUZANNET (ALAIN DE), Autograph list of temporary or permanent residences of Dickens in chronological order, *27 pages, foolscap*, together with a separate list detailing Dickens's sojourns at Broadstairs, *1 page 8vo.*

L.19 SUZANNET (ALAIN DE), Autograph check-list of "The Writings of Charles Dickens at La Petite Chardière" (including speeches, contributions to periodicals, etc.) in blue-covered 4to. exercise-book.

L.20 SUZANNET (ALAIN DE), Autograph MSS. of articles, reviews, "Letters to the Editor", etc., contributed to *The Dickensian*, 1933-1949; together with notes for a projected article, "The Mysteries of an Unfortunate Friendship" (on Dickens and Thomas Powell), *9 pages foolscap;* facsimile of Dickens's letter to the Editor of *The Sun* (14 December 1849) concerning Powell; and photo-copy of 4-page 4to. pamphlet dealing with Powell's misdemeanours, printed for Dickens in 1849.

L.21 SUZANNET (ALAIN DE), *Catalogue des Manuscrits, Livres Imprimés et Lettres Autographes composant la Bibliothèque de La Petite Chardière: Oeuvres de Charles Dickens, 311 typed pages, foolscap.*

Introductory note by Michael Slater dated February 1970, explaining that this typescript was made, at the request of the Comtesse de Suzannet, from the Comte's manuscript at La Petite Chardière (". . . Internal evidence suggests that the last work was done on this Catalogue in late 1948 or early 1949 . . ."); together with an earlier manuscript Catalogue of the same in four blue-covered 4to. exercise-books.

L.22 Collection of Thirty-four A.L.ss. and telegrams to the Comte de Suzannet from Ernest Maggs, Bernard Quaritch, A. S. W. Rosenbach and other book-dealers (28 December 1921 - 7 December 1949) concerning purchases made by the Comte for his Dickens Collection; together with detailed descriptions of many of the items concerned.

SOTHEBY & CO.
34 & 35 NEW BOND ST., LONDON WI

CATALOGUE

OF

AUTOGRAPH MANUSCRIPTS AND LETTERS, ORIGINAL DRAWINGS AND FIRST EDITIONS OF CHARLES DICKENS

From the collection of
THE LATE COMTE ALAIN DE SUZANNET
(*removed from La Petite Chardière, Lausanne*)

The Property of THE COMTESSE DE SUZANNET

DAYS OF SALE:
MONDAY, 22ND NOVEMBER, 1971   LOTS 1-189
TUESDAY, 23RD NOVEMBER, 1971   LOTS 190-325
AT ELEVEN O'CLOCK PRECISELY EACH DAY

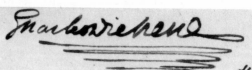

Charles Dickens

Tott. m. Ticknor, His Reading Book 20th April, 1868.

MRS. GAMP.

BY

CHARLES DICKENS.

AS CONDENSED BY HIMSELF, FOR HIS

READINGS.

WITH AN ILLUSTRATION BY S. EYTINGE, JR.

BOSTON:
TICKNOR AND FIELDS.
1868.

CATALOGUE

OF

Autograph Manuscripts and Letters, Original Drawings and First Editions

of

Charles Dickens

from the Collection of
the late Comte Alain de Suzannet
(*removed from La Petite Chardière, Lausanne*)

𝔗𝔥𝔢 𝔓𝔯𝔬𝔭𝔢𝔯𝔱𝔶 𝔬𝔣 𝔱𝔥𝔢 𝔆𝔬𝔪𝔱𝔢𝔰𝔰𝔢 𝔡𝔢 𝔖𝔲𝔷𝔞𝔫𝔫𝔢𝔱

FIRST DAY'S SALE:

Monday, 22nd November, 1971

AT ELEVEN O'CLOCK PRECISELY

All the bound volumes bear the bookplate of the Comte de Suzannet.

FIRST AND EARLY EDITIONS, INCLUDING TRANSLATIONS AND
DRAMATIZED VERSIONS

1   A complete set of the eight contributions to *The Monthly Magazine*, afterwards published in *Sketches by Boz, the first five anonymous, the last three have the pseudonym Boz printed at the end, extracted and bound in 1 vol., green morocco gilt, panelled back*   8vo 1833-35

**   The pieces comprise:
   (1) A Dinner at Poplar Walk (afterwards called Mr. Minns and his Cousin), *this was Dickens' first appearance in print.*
   (2) Mrs. Joseph Porter over the Way.
   (3) Horatio Sparkins.
   (4) The Bloomsbury Christening.
   (5) The Boarding House.
   (6) The Boarding House, No. II.
   (7) The Steam Excursion.
   (8) Passage in the Life of Mr. Watkins Tottle.

The remainder of the pieces afterwards published in "Sketches by Boz" first appeared in *The Evening Chronicle, Bell's Life in London, The Library of Fiction, The Morning Chronicle* and the *Carlton Chronicle.*

171

FIRST AND EARLY EDITIONS

2   The Library of Fiction, 2 vol., *original parts 1-10 and 13, parts 1-4, 6 and 8 in duplicate, plates by R. Seymour, R. W. Buss and others, original wrappers, uncut, lower cover of part 9 missing, in a cloth case; sold not subject to return*
                                                      8vo   *Chapman & Hall*, 1836-37

*** Dickens' two sketches *The Tuggs's at Ramsgate* and *A Little Talk about Sweeps* appeared here for the first time (parts 1 and 3 respectively). They were later included in *Sketches by Boz*, the latter under the title of 'The First of May'.

3   The Library of Fiction, 2 vol., *plates by R. Seymour, R. W. Buss and others, original blue cloth, blocked in blind, uncut*   8vo   *Chapman & Hall*, 1836-37

*** Dickens' two sketches *The Tuggs's at Ramsgate* and *A Little Talk about Spring and Sweeps* appeared here for the first time. They were later included in *Sketches by Boz*, the latter under the title of *The First of May*.

4   SKETCHES BY "BOZ" [*First Series*], 2 vol., FIRST EDITION, *plates by George Cruikshank, mostly slightly discoloured, original dark-green cloth, uncut, re-cased, endpapers stained*; Sketches by Boz . . . the Second Series, FIRST EDITION, FIRST ISSUE (*without the list of illustrations on the lower half of the second page of contents*), *engraved title and plates by George Cruikshank, 10 leaves of advertisements dated Dec., 1836, at end, original pink cloth, blocked in blind, uncut, rebacked, the original back laid down, in a dark-green morocco-backed cloth slip-case*   12mo   *J. Macrone*, 1836-37

*** PRESENTATION COPY TO THOMAS BEARD, VOL. 1 OF THE FIRST SERIES INSCRIBED BY THE AUTHOR: "Thomas Beard Esᵍʳᵉ: From his sincere friend The Author".

Thomas Beard was Dickens' oldest friend.

5   *Sketches by "Boz" [First Series], 2 vol.*, FIRST EDITION, *plates by George Cruikshank, faint off-sets on most plates, original dark green cloth, uncut, new endpapers*; Sketches by Boz . . . the Second Series, FIRST EDITION, *second issue* (*with the list of illustrations on the lower half of the second page of contents*), *engraved title and plates by George Cruikshank, the two additional plates executed for the second edition of the second series are loosely inserted, 10 leaves of advertisements dated Dec., 1836, at end, half-title lacking, original pink cloth, blocked in blind, recased, in 3 dark-green half morocco gilt slip-cases, book-plate of Frederic S. Clarke* 12mo *J. Macrone*, 1836-37

6   SKETCHES BY BOZ, IN THE ORIGINAL 20 MONTHLY PARTS, FIRST EDITION IN ONE VOLUME, *plates by George Cruikshank, with all the advertisements, etc., as listed by Hatton & Cleaver, margins of plates discoloured,* ORIGINAL PINK WRAPPERS, UNCUT, PARTS 11-19 UNOPENED, *in a brown morocco case*   8vo   *Chapman & Hall*, 1837-39

*** Included with this lot are 2 proofs of Cruikshank's design for the upper cover of the wrappers, ONE WITH THE IMPRINT OF J. MACRONE, the other with that of Chapman & Hall. An enclosed note by H. W. Bruton states that the only other copy of the former known to him is in the British Museum.

FIRST AND EARLY EDITIONS

7 CRUIKSHANK (GEORGE) A COMPLETE SET OF PROOFS BEFORE LETTERS ON INDIA PAPER OF THE 28 PLATES TO THE TWO SERIES OF '*Sketches by Boz*', *including the 2 extra plates*, '*The Last Cab-Driver*' *and* '*The First of May*', *which were executed for the second edition of the second series, all undivided (2 plates to a sheet), mounted in an oblong folio volume, dark-green morocco gilt, g.e., bookplate of H. W. Bruton*

** Purchased by H. W. Bruton at the sale of the Dew collection of the works of George Cruikshank, Sotheby's, 19th March, 1872, lot 77 (a copy of the catalogue is loosely inserted, on the title of which the collection is described as "comprising that formed by the artist himself, for the inspection of the Queen and Prince Albert"). Inserted at the beginning are 4 A.Ls.s. from George Cruikshank, the first to Dickens

. . . I just drop this note to apologize for not answering your note before—and to assure you that in two or three days you may rely upon seeg: me with proofs", *n.d.*

the other 3 to John Macrone, the publisher of "Sketches by Boz"

I am sorry that I was not at home when you & friend "Boz" honoured me with a call—Ainsworth had been with me & will come again on Friday at ½ past 3.—perhaps you will also favor me with y^r. presence that we may finally decide upon the number—of subjects &c. &c. . . . 1*st March*, [18]36

As it would not answer my purpose to stand Idle I have commenced another work which *must* be finished before I can take up the Sec^d. Vol of "Boz." I shall be truly sorry should this affect any of y^r. Publishing arrangements but it is clearly no fault of mine—I did expect to see the MS. from time to time in order that I might have the privilege of suggesting any little alterations to suit the Pencil—but if you are printing the book all that sort of thing is out of the question—only thus much I must say that unless I can get good subjects to work upon, I will not work at all, 11*th Oct.*, 1836

I have made arrangements which will enable me to proceed at once with—"Boz"—and shall endeavour to hold a consultation with that gentleman—on Monday or Tuesday 25 as by that time I shall have finished Sketches . . . 15th Oct., [18]36

8 Watkins Tottle, and other Sketches, illustrative of Every-Day Life and Every-Day People. By Boz, 2 vol., FIRST AMERICAN EDITION OF SKETCHES BY BOZ, *first series, original boards, linen backs, with paper labels, in 2 cloth slip-cases, red morocco gilt backs, bookplate of George Barr McCutcheon*
       12mo Philadelphia, Carey, Lea & Blanchard, 1836

9 The Tugg's at Ramsgate, by "Boz". Together with other Tales, by distinguished Writers, FIRST AMERICAN EDITION, *original boards, linen back, with paper label, in a morocco-backed slip-case*, 12mo, *Philadelphia, Carey, Lea & Blanchard*, 1837; The Lamplighter's Story; Hunted Down [etc.], *frontispiece, original cloth, joints splitting, in a cloth slip-case, morocco gilt back*, 8*vo*, *id., T. B. Peterson & Brothers*, 1861; The Atlantic Monthly, nos. 123-125 [CONTAINING THE FIRST PRINTING OF DICKENS' STORY "GEORGE SILVERMAN'S EXPLANATION"], *original wrappers, uncut, in a green half calf slip-case, large* 8*vo*, *Boston, Ticknor & Fields, Jan.-March*, 1868; The Atlantic Monthly, no. 142 [CONTAINING THE FIRST PRINTING OF DICKENS' ARTICLE "ON MR. FECHTER'S ACTING"], *brown morocco gilt, t.e.g., original wrapper preserved, large* 8*vo*, *id., Aug.*, 1869; Old Lamps for New Ones and other Sketches and Essays hitherto uncollected, edited by F. G. Kitton, *original cloth gilt, bookplate of G. W. Redway, in a red morocco pull-off case*, 8*vo*, *New York*, 1897; and three others

FIRST AND EARLY EDITIONS

10　Humoristische Genrebilder aus dem Londoner Alltagsleben von Boz . . . nach dem Englischen von Dr. A. Diezmann, 2 vol. in one, FIRST FDITION IN GFRMAN OF 14 PIECES FROM SKETCHES BY BOZ AND OF THE FIRST CHAPTER OF MUDFOG PAPERS, *2 lithographic frontispieces after G. Cruikshank, that to vol. 2 slightly cropped, contemporary boards, cloth back*　　　　12mo　Brunswick, G. Westermann, 1838-39

11　SUNDAY UNDER THREE HEADS . . . by Timothy Sparks, FIRST EDITION, *3 plates and 3 woodcuts on title by Hablot K. Browne, dark-green half morocco, upper portion of original wrapper preserved (soiled), padded with blank leaves, in a red morocco pull-off case, bookplate of A. Edward Newton*　　　　sm. 8vo　Chapman & Hall, 1836

　　** PRESENTATION COPY TO THOMAS MITTON, THE HALF-TITLE INSCRIBED BY THE AUTHOR IN HIS EARLY HAND: "Thomas Mitton Esqre From The Author".

Thomas Mitton, a solicitor, was one of Dickens' earliest close friends.

12　Sunday under Three Heads . . . by Timothy Sparks, FIRST EDITION, *3 plates and 3 woodcuts by Hablot K. Browne, calf gilt, panelled back, t.e.g., other edges uncut, by F. Bedford, upper portion of original wrapper preserved at end, bookplate of Ralph Clutton*　　　　sm. 8vo　Chapman & Hall, 1836

13　Sunday under Three Heads . . . by Timothy Sparks, FIRST EDITION, *3 plates and 3 woodcuts on title (repeated on upper cover) by Hablot K. Browne, original wrapper, rebacked, bookplate of H. W. Poor, in a red morocco-backed cloth slip-case*
　　　　　　　　　　　　　　　　　　　sm. 8vo　Chapman & Hall, 1836

　　**　A copy of the reprint by Pearson of Manchester is included with this lot.

14　Bentley's Miscellany, vol. 1-6, *plates by George Cruikshank, olive half morocco gilt, t.e.g.; sold as a magazine, not subject to return*　　　　8vo　R. Bentley, 1837-39

　　**　Dickens was editor of this magazine from its commencement till early in 1839. *Oliver Twist* appeared for the first time in vol. 1-5.

FIRST AND EARLY EDITIONS

15   Bentley's Miscellany. Extraordinary Gazette. Speech of His Mightiness on Opening the Second Number of Bentley's Miscellany, edited by "Boz", *4 pages, woodcut by Phiz [H. K. Browne], 8vo [1837], these pages were inserted in the third number of Bentley's Miscellany, bound with various contributions by Dickens to that periodical, red morocco gilt*—The Daily News [edited by Dickens], no. 1 [*containing an editorial and "Travelling Letters", both by Dickens, the second-mentioned later forming the first chapter of "Pictures from Italy"], last leaf defective, large folio, 21st Jan.,* 1846, *in a cloth case, bookplates of John C. Eckel and Morris L. Parrish;* and another   (3)

16   THE VILLAGE COQUETTES: a Comic Opera. In Two Acts. By Charles Dickens. The Music by John Hullah, *libretto,* FIRST EDITION, *title and last page somewhat spotted and dust-soiled, sewed and uncut, in a limp cloth, slip-case*   8vo   R. *Bentley,* 1836

   ✱ PRESENTATION COPY TO J. P. HARLEY TO WHOM THE OPERA IS DEDICATED AND WHO TOOK THE PART OF MR. MARTIN STOKES IN THE ORIGINAL PERFORMANCE, THE TITLE INSCRIBED BY THE AUTHOR IN HIS EARLY HAND: "J. P. Harley Esqre. From The *Author*".

   A copy described as the dedication copy was in the Jerome Kern sale in New York, 7th Jan., etc., 1929, lot 376. It was bound in polished calf gilt and was formerly in the Robert Hoe library.

17   The Village Coquettes: a Comic Opera. In Two Acts. By Charles Dickens. The Music by John Hullah, *libretto,* FIRST EDITION, *red morocco gilt, panelled back, other edges uncut, by Riviere*   8vo   R. *Bentley,* 1836

18   Songs, Choruses, and Concerted Pieces, in the Operatic Burletta of the Village Coquettes . . . the Drama and Words of the Songs by "Boz". The Music by John Hullah, *libretto, the names of the singers written in the margins against their songs, somewhat spotted, sewed, as issued*   sm. 8vo   *Bradbury & Evans,* 1837

FIRST AND EARLY EDITIONS

19   THE POSTHUMOUS PAPERS OF THE PICKWICK CLUB, IN THE ORIGINAL 20
MONTHLY PARTS IN 19, FIRST EDITION, *engraved vignette title and plates by R. Seymour,
R. W. Buss and Phiz [Hablot K. Browne], part 7 lacks sheet R, sheet Q being in
duplicate, sheets Q and R from another copy are loosely inserted, margins of a few plates
rather discoloured,* ORIGINAL GREEN WRAPPERS, UNCUT, *names of different owners on
upper covers of parts 4, 11 and 13, the blank inner side of the upper cover to part 3 is
inscribed "With the Publishers Compliments", several backs slightly defective, in 2 red
morocco gilt pull-off cases*   *8vo   Chapman & Hall,* 1836-37

> **   This copy includes the following points:
>   (a)   All the wrappers are dated 1836. The inner sides of the upper and lower
> covers to parts 1-3 are blank. The upper covers to parts 1 and 2 bear
> the words "With four illustrations by Seymour" and that to part 3
> "With illustrations by R. W. Buss".
>   (b)   All the advertisements, slips and addresses as listed by Hatton & Cleaver
> are present, with the exception of the "Phrenology Made Easy" slip in
> part 7, the very rare "George Mann" leaflet in part 9 and "Pigot's
> Coloured Views" in part 13. Part 3 has "The Toilet" advertisement at
> end.
>   (c)   All the plates are before letters.
>   (d)   The four plates by Seymour in part 1 are in the early states illustrated by
> Miller & Strange, pp. 8-15.
>   (e)   The plate of "The Dying Clown" by Seymour in part 2 is in the second
> state, after the signature.
>   (f)   Page 34 (part 2) is without the parenthesis within brackets in lines 14
> and 15 from the bottom.
>   (g)   The 2 plates by Buss are present in part 3.
>   (h)   The 2 plates in part 6 are in the first state, with the page-numerals
> interchanged.
>   (i)   The signature on X2 recto (part 9) is correctly printed.
>   (j)   The 2 plates in part 10 are in the first state.
>   (k)   The 2 plates in part 11 are in the first state.
>   (l)   The 2 plates in part 12 are in the first state.
>   (m)   The 2 plates in part 14 are in the first state.
>   (n)   The 2 plates in part 15 are in the first state.
>   (o)   The 2 plates in part 16 are in the first state.
>   (p)   The 2 plates in part 17 are in the first state.
>   (q)   The 2 plates in part 18 are in the first state.
>   (r)   In the last part "Mary and the Fat Boy", "Mr. Weller and his friends
> drinking to Mr. Pell", the frontispiece and the vignette title are in the
> first state, the last-named having the reading "Veller".

Inserted in the last part is a folded sheet of paper, once used as a wrapper,
addressed to Mr. Serjeant Talfourd M.P. in Dickens' hand, with franking signature
and seal. Also inserted is a leaf printed on both sides announcing the publication "this
day" of the first number of "Pickwick Papers". It bears the imprint of Chapman &
Hall.

FIRST AND EARLY EDITIONS

20   THE POSTHUMOUS PAPERS OF THE PICKWICK CLUB, IN THE ORIGINAL 20
MONTHLY PARTS IN 19, FIRST EDITION, *engraved vignette title and plates by R. Seymour,
R. W. Buss and Phiz [Hablot K. Browne], the engraved title and plates in part 4 spotted,*
ORIGINAL GREEN WRAPPERS, UNCUT, *names of different owners on upper covers of parts 11
and 17, backs of parts 1 and 2 defective, in a dark-green morocco pull-off case*
                                                    8vo   Chapman & Hall, 1836-37

** This copy includes the following points:
*
   (a)   All the wrappers are dated 1836. The inner sides of the upper and lower
         covers to parts 1-3 are blank. The upper covers to parts 1 and 2 bear the
         words "With four illustrations by Seymour" and that to part 3 "With
         illustrations by Buss".
   (b)   All the advertisements, slips and addresses as listed by Hatton & Cleaver
         are present with the exception of the "Phrenology Made Easy" slip in
         part 7, the very rare "George Mann" leaflet in part 9 and "Pigot's
         Coloured Views" in part 13. Part 3 has both "The Toilet" and "The
         Autobiography of an Oil Bottle" advertisements at the end.
   (c)   All the plates are before letters.
   (d)   The 4 plates by Seymour in part 1 are in the early states illustrated by
         Miller & Strange, pp. 8-15.
   (e)   The plate of "The Dying Clown" by Seymour in part 2 is in the first
         state, before the signature.
   (f)   Page 34 (part 2) has the parenthesis within brackets in lines 14 and 15
         from the bottom.
   (g)   The 2 plates by Buss are present in part 3.
   (h)   The 2 plates in part 6 are in the second state, with the page numbers
         correct. Copies of the plates in the first state, with the page numbers
         interchanged, are loosely inserted.
   (i)   The signature on X2 recto (part 9) is correctly printed.
   (j)   The 2 plates in part 10 are in the second state.
   (k)   The 2 plates in part 11 are in the first state.
   (l)   The 2 plates in part 12 are in the first state.
   (m) The 2 plates in part 14 are in the first state.
   (n)   The 2 plates in part 15 are in the first state.
   (o)   In part 16 "The Red-nosed man discourseth" is in the second state,
         "Mrs. Bardell encounters Mr. Pickwick in the prison" in the first state.
   (p)   The 2 plates in part 17 are in the first state.
   (q)   The 2 plates in part 18 are in the first state.
   (r) (s) In the last part "Mary and the Fat Boy", "Mr. Weller and his friends
         drinking to Mr. Pell", the frontispiece and the vignette title are in the
         first state, the last-mentioned having the reading "Veller".

   A slip-case containing 31 duplicate plates in various states (all before letters) and
12 pages of advertisements, one announcing the publication of the first number of
"Pickwick Papers", from the April, 1836, number of "The Domestic Magazine", is
included with this lot.

FIRST AND EARLY EDITIONS

21 THE POSTHUMOUS PAPERS OF THE PICKWICK CLUB, IN THE ORIGINAL 20 MONTHLY PARTS IN 19, FIRST EDITION, *engraved vignette title and plates by R. Seymour, R. W. Buss and Phiz [Hablot K. Browne]*, ORIGINAL GREEN WRAPPERS, UNCUT, *part 6 mostly unopened, part 9 wholly so, signature of G. H. Bosanquet on upper covers of parts 1-3, 4 and 7, corners of upper cover of last part renewed slightly affecting the engraved surface and advertisement on verso, repairs to several other covers, back of part 15 a little defective, in a dark-green morocco-backed cloth slip-case*

8vo   *Chapman & Hall*, 1836-37

_**_* This copy includes the following points:

(a) All the wrappers are dated 1836. The inner sides of the upper and lower covers to parts 1-3 carry advertisements. The inner side of the lower cover to part 4 and the inner sides of the upper and lower covers to parts 5 and 6 are blank. All the upper covers bear the words "With illustrations".

(b) With advertisements in parts 13 ("Argyle Rooms" lacking), 14 (complete), 15 (complete), 16 (complete), 17 (complete), 18 (Advertiser lacks 4 leaves, advertisements at end complete) and 19/20 (lacking Advertiser, Simpson's Herbal Pills and Mechi's Catalogue). All the other advertisements lacking. With the addresses in parts 10, 15, 17, 18 and 19/20, but lacking those in parts 2 and 3.

(c) All the plates are before letters.

(d) The 4 plates by Seymour in part 1 are in the early states illustrated by Miller & Strange, pp. 8-15.

(e) The plate of "The Dying Clown" by Seymour in part 2 is in the first state, before the signature.

(f) Page 34 (part 2) is without the parenthesis within brackets in lines 14 and 15 from the bottom.

(g) The 2 plates by Buss are present in part 3.

(h) The 2 plates in part 6 are in the first state, with the page-numerals interchanged.

(i) The signature on X2 recto (part 9) is correctly printed.

(j) The 2 plates in part 10 are in the first state.

(k) The 2 plates in part 11 are in the first state.

(l) The 2 plates in part 12 are in the first state.

(m) The 2 plates in part 14 are in the first state.

(n) The 2 plates in part 15 are in the second state.

(o) The 2 plates in part 16 are in the first state.

(p) The 2 plates in part 17 are in the first state.

(q) The 2 plates in part 18 are in the first state.

(r) In the last part "Mary and the Fat Boy", "Mr. Weller and his friends drinking to Mr. Pell", the frontispiece and the vignette title are in the first state, the last-named having the reading "Veller".

FIRST AND EARLY EDITIONS

22   The Posthumous Papers of the Pickwick Club, FIRST EDITION, EARLY ISSUE, *engraved vignette title and plates by R. Seymour, R. W. Buss and Phiz [Hablot K. Browne], with half-title, green morocco gilt, panelled back, t.e.g., by Riviere, bookplate of Thomas Hatton*   *8vo   Chapman & Hall,* 1837

***   This copy includes the following points:
(a)   The vignette title has the reading "Veller".
(b)   All the plates are before letters.
(c)   The first 4 Seymour plates are in the early states illustrated by Miller & Strange, pp. 8-15.
(d)   Page 34 has the parenthesis within brackets in lines 14 and 15 from the bottom.
(e)   The 2 plates by Buss are present.
(f)   The plates at pp. 154 and 169 are in the first state with the page-numerals interchanged. Copies of the second states with the correct numbering are bound in.
(g)   X2 is signed N2 in error.

23   The Posthumous Papers of the Pickwick Club, FIRST EDITION, *engraved vignette title ("Weller") and plates before letters by R. Seymour, Buss (2) and Phiz [H. K. Browne], with half-title, off-sets of text and spots on several plates, contemporary green half morocco gilt, one joint cracking, bookplate of George Cowen*
8vo   Chapman & Hall, 1837

24   The Posthumous Papers of the Pickwick Club, FIRST EDITION, *late issue, engraved vignette title ("Weller") and plates after letters by R. Seymour and Phiz, off-sets of frontispiece on engraved title, off-sets of text on some plates, original brown cloth, blocked in blind, uncut*   *8vo   Chapman & Hall,* 1837

25   The Posthumous Papers of the Pickwick Club, FIRST EDITION, *late issue, engraved vignette title ("Weller") and plates after letters by R. Seymour and Phiz [H. K. Browne], with half-title, plates spotted in the margins and faintly stained by the off-sets of the text, contemporary maroon morocco, g.e.*   *8vo   Chapman & Hall,* 1837

***   The fly-leaf is inscribed: "Eliza Moxon from Phiz".

26   THE POSTHUMOUS PAPERS OF THE PICKWICK CLUB . . . edited by "Boz", *5 vol., FIRST AMERICAN EDITION, FIRST ISSUE OF VOL. 1 (without volume number on title or label), 12 pages of advertisements at end of vol. 1, 4 pages of advertisements at beginning and end of vol. 3, 4 pages of advertisements at beginning of vol. 4, 4 pages of advertisements at beginning of vol. 5 and 2 pages at end, vol. 1 apparently lacks 2 preliminary leaves, vol. 1 stained at beginning and end, original boards, linen backs, upper cover of vol. 5 detached, 3 labels rubbed, in a brown morocco-backed cloth slip-case, bookplate of Frank Fletcher [Edgar & Vail, p. 16]*
12mo   Philadelphia, Carey, Lea & Blanchard, 1836-37

FIRST AND EARLY EDITIONS

27   The Posthumous Papers of the Pickwick Club, FIRST EDITION PRINTED IN INDIA, *lithographic vignette title ("Veller"), dated 1837, and lithographic plates before letters after R. Seymour, R. W. Buss (2) and Phiz [H. K. Browne], modern calf gilt, panelled back, red morocco labels, t.e.g.*   *8vo   Calcutta, W. Rushton, 1838*

28   The Posthumous Papers of the Pickwick Club, 2 vol., FIRST EDITION PRINTED IN FRANCE, *with half-titles, spotted, contemporary half sheep gilt, 8vo, Paris, Baudry's European Library, 1839, with the first Tauchnitz editions of "A Christmas Carol" and "The Cricket on the Hearth", the former with coloured frontispiece after Leech, cloth and boards, sm. 8vo, Leipzig, 1843-46*   (4)

29   The Posthumous Papers of the Pickwick Club, *in the original 8 monthly parts, Cheap Edition of the Works of Mr. Charles Dickens, 2 columns, frontispiece engraved on wood by J. Thompson after C. R. Leslie, with advertisements in all except parts 4 and 7, original green wrappers, uncut, with 6 full-page wood-engravings by W. T. Green, in a folder, and prospectus, all in a cloth case*   *8vo   Chapman & Hall, 1847*

30   The Posthumous Papers of the Pickwick Club, edited by Charles Dickens the Younger, 2 vol., *Jubilee Edition, vol. 1 inscribed by Walter Dexter to the Comte de Suzannet, illustrations, original cloth, 8vo, 1886, with the Topical Edition, 2 vol., plates, original cloth, large 8vo, 1909, and the Lombard Street Edition, 2 vol., plates, original cloth, 8vo, 1932;* The Mystery of Edwin Drood. Complete, *original cloth, 8vo, Brattleboro, Vt., 1873;* The Complete Mystery of Edwin Drood . . . the History, Continuations, and Solutions (1870-1912) by J. Cuming Walters, *portrait and plates, original cloth, 8vo, 1912;* The Life of Our Lord, FIRST EDITION, *portrait and plates, original lambskin, t.e.g., large 8vo, 1934;* Mrs. Gamp and the Strolling Players, FIRST EDITION, LIMITED TO 85 COPIES, *vignette title and plate by F. W. Pailthorpe, the original pen-and-ink and wash sketch for the former loosely inserted, portrait, original parchment, uncut, 8vo, New York, Privately Printed, 1899;* and six others   (16)

31   Die Pickwickier . . . aus dem Englischen von H. Roberts, 5 vol. in 3, FIRST EDITION OF PICKWICK PAPERS IN GERMAN, *lithographic plates after R. Seymour and Phiz [H. K. Browne], (wrongly described as after Cruikshank on titles to vol. 1-3), 2 folding, with half-titles in vol. 2-5, 2 or 3 plates slightly cropped, boards, roan gilt backs*   *12mo   Leipzig, J. J. Weber, 1837-38*

32   Die nachgelassenen Papiere des Pickwick-Clubbs . . . aus den Englischen übersetzt von O. v. Czarnowsky, 6 vol. in 3, FIRST EDITION OF THIS TRANSLATION, *6 frontispieces, 5 after R. Seymour and H. K. Browne, contemporary black half calf gilt, sm. 8vo, Brunswick, F. Vieweg und Sohn, 1839;* Die hinterlassenen Papiere des Pickwick-Club . . . übersetzt von Bauernfeld, 5 vol., FIRST EDITION OF THIS TRANSLATION, *5 frontispieces, advertisement leaf at end of vol. 2, original black cloth, gilt backs, covers of vol. 3 and 4 stained, sm. 8vo, Vienna, A. Mausberger, 1844;* and four others *(odd)* (12)

FIRST AND EARLY EDITIONS

33   Le Club des Pickwistes . . . traduit librement de l'anglais par Madame Eugénie Niboyet, 2 vol., FIRST EDITION IN FRENCH, *with half-titles, contemporary marbled boards, red morocco gilt backs, bookplate of Eugène Scribe*
8vo   Paris, Charpentier, 1838

34   [Thomas (William Thomas)], *W. T. Moncrieff.* Sam Weller, or, the Pickwickians. A Drama, in Three Acts, FIRST EDITION, *modern boards, uncut*
8vo   Published for the Author, and sold by all respectable Booksellers, 1837

35   Rede (William Leman) Peregrinations of Pickwick; a Drama, in Three Acts, *frontispiece, half parchment, t.e.g., original wrapper preserved*
12mo   Duncombe's Acting Edition of the British Drama, 1837

36   Beauties of Pickwick (The), collected and arranged by Sam Weller, *16 pages (including title), 2 columns, library stamp on title, cloth, uncut, padded with blanks*
8vo   W. Morgan, 1838

37   The Strange Gentleman; a Comic Burletta, in Two Acts. By "Boz", FIRST EDITION, *frontispiece by Phiz [H. K. Browne], modern red morocco gilt, t.e.g.*
sm. 8vo   Chapman & Hall, 1837

37A   The Strange Gentleman, a Comic Burletta in Two Acts . . . now first illustrated with reproductions from original drawings by John Leech, John Orlando Parry, etc. Also a reprint of the scarce original frontispiece by "Phiz", *original half parchment, sm. 4to, Privately Printed,* 1928; and another   (2)

38   Memoirs of Joseph Grimaldi. Edited by "Boz", 2 vol., FIRST EDITION, FIRST ISSUE (*"The last Song" before the border*), *engraved portrait of Grimaldi by W. Greatbatch after S. Raven, plates by George Cruikshank, no advertisements at end of vol. 2, original pink embossed cloth, gilt design on backs, uncut, bookplate of Kenneth H. M. Connal*
12mo   R. Bentley, 1838

⁎⁎   Loosely inserted in vol. 1 is a brief A.L.s. from Joseph Grimaldi.

39   Oliver Twist; or, the Parish Boy's Progress. By "Boz", 3 vol., FIRST EDITION, FIRST ISSUE (*with the "Fireside" plate, title-page reading as above, no list of illustrations and no publisher's imprint at the bottom of the backs*), *plates by George Cruikshank, 4 pages of advertisements at end of vol. 1 and 2 pages at beginning of vol. 3, original brown cloth, blocked in blind, uncut, stains on covers of vol. 1 and 3*
8vo   R. Bentley, 1838

FIRST AND EARLY EDITIONS

40   OLIVER TWIST, 3 vol., *third edition, containing the* FIRST PRINTING OF "THE AUTHOR'S INTRODUCTION TO THE THIRD EDITION", *plates by George Cruikshank, original brown cloth, blocked in blind, uncut, in a dark-green morocco-backed cloth slip-case*   *8vo   Chapman & Hall, 1841*

_**   PRESENTATION COPY TO WILLIAM CHARLES MACREADY, THE TITLE TO VOL. 1 INSCRIBED BY THE AUTHOR: "W. C. Macready From his affectionate friend Charles Dickens Christmas 1841."

41   Oliver Twist . . . von Boz . . . aus dem Englischen von Dr. A. Diezmann, 3 vol. in one, FIRST EDITION IN GERMAN, *plates after G. Cruikshank, with half-titles, original dark-green cloth, the sides blocked in blind*   *12mo   Brunswick, G. Westermann, 1838-39*

42   Almar (George) Oliver Twist. A Serio-Comic Burletta, in Three Acts, *engraved frontispiece by Pierce Egan the younger (spotted), half parchment, t.e.g., original wrapper preserved*   *12mo   Webster's Acting National Drama* [1839]

43   Sketches of Young Gentlemen, FIRST EDITION, *plates by Phiz* [*H. K. Browne*], *lacking the advertisements, Chapman & Hall*, 1838; Sketches of Young Couples, FIRST EDITION, *plates by Phiz* [*H. K. Browne*], *with half-title but lacking the advertisements, sm. 8vo, id.,* 1840—[Caswall (Edward)] Sketches of Young Ladies . . . by Quiz, FIRST EDITION, *plates by Phiz* [*H. K. Browne*], *id.,* 1837; *together* 3 vol., *uniform maroon morocco gilt, panelled backs, t.e.g., by Zaehnsdorf, original wrappers preserved, bookplate of Edward Huth*   *sm. 8vo* (3)

44   THE LIFE AND ADVENTURES OF NICHOLAS NICKLEBY, IN THE ORIGINAL 20 MONTHLY PARTS IN 19, FIRST EDITION, FIRST ISSUE (*with the misprints "visiter" and "latter" in line 17, p. 123, and line 6 from bottom, p. 160, respectively, plates 1-4 have the publishers' imprint, the caption on the first plate in part 8 omits the word "in" and the third plate in part 15 has the long caption), engraved portrait of Dickens by Finden after Maclise, plates by Phiz* [*H. K. Browne*], *with all the advertisements and slips as listed by Hatton & Cleaver, with the exception of* "*Heads of the People*" *at end of part 8,* ORIGINAL GREEN WRAPPERS, UNCUT, PARTS 8 AND 11 UNOPENED, *names on upper covers of parts 3, 4 and 7, booksellers' tickets on upper covers of parts 7, 12 and 17, in a dark-green morocco gilt pull-off case*   *8vo   Chapman & Hall, 1838-39*

_**   Included with this lot are 4 cloth slip-cases containing 2-5 copies of each part showing various states of the plates.

FIRST AND EARLY EDITIONS

45   THE LIFE AND ADVENTURES OF NICHOLAS NICKLEBY, FIRST EDITION, *second issue (with the correct readings "sister" and "letter" in line 17, p. 123, and line 6 from bottom, p. 160, respectively), engraved portrait of Dickens by Finden after Maclise, plates by Phiz [H. K. Browne], the caption on that at p. 248 includes the word "in", that at p. 457 has the long caption, with half-title, off-sets of text on most plates, some plates spotted, contemporary dark-green morocco gilt and blind, g.e., re-backed, in a dark-green morocco-backed cloth slip-case*   8vo   *Chapman & Hall*, 1839

⁎⁎⁎ PRESENTATION COPY TO SIR DAVID WILKIE, THE DEDICATION LEAF INSCRIBED BY THE AUTHOR: "Sir David Wilkie From his faithfully Charles Dickens".

Loosely inserted is an A.L.s. from Sir David Wilkie to Mrs. Ricketts, *3 pages, 4to, Kensington, London, 14th Oct*., 1839, giving an account of the dinner given by Dickens to celebrate the completion of *Nicholas Nickleby*.

". . . From Lowther Castle I had to hurry on to town to be present at a scene, which to some of the gentle readers in your house would have possessed some claim it was to be present at a fiesta given by Mr. Dickens to the publishers, printers and artist, with various of his friends about 20 in all on the completion of *Nicholas Nickleby*. It was at the Albion, Aldersgate St. Mr. Dickens our host was in the chair, and Mr. Macready to whom the work was dedicated, was on his right hand, and had to propose his health. Though a master of elocution, the occasion seemed to deprive him of the advantage this might be expected to give to a speaker but one passage for the advantage of Miss Taylor and Miss Anna I will venture to repeat, in remarking on the peculiar style of Mr. Dickens, he admired that faculty, of supplying to the reader, not merely the bold adventure, and the startling incident, but was equally happy in all the little details and minute feelings, of the every day intercourse of life, so finely as he said characterised in the lines of Wordsworth

'Those nameless and unremembered acts,
'That make the best part of a good mans life.'

"This led Mr. Dickens to speak to me of Mr. Wordsworth who he knew I had lately seen, and to express a very great admiration for his Genius, of which he thought the little poem of '*We are seven*' was one of the most striking examples. What he seemed to like in this was divesting death of its horror, by treating it as a separation and not an extinction, He deprecated what in families occurred, of never alluding to a near relation deceased, said he lately met a severe loss, but took every pains to recall, the person deceased to his family about him.

"My talented friend rose much in my mind by this reflection on the work of our great poet, and I repeat it, supposing that to yourself and the readers of his writings around you it will have the same effect . . ."

46   The Life and Adventures of Nicholas Nickleby, FIRST EDITION, *second issue (with the correct readings "sister" and "letter" in line 17, p. 123, and line 6 from bottom, p. 160, respectively), engraved portrait of Dickens by Finden after Maclise, plates by Phiz [H. K. Browne], faint off-sets of text on most plates, some plates spotted, half-title missing, contemporary maroon half morocco, t.e.g.*   8vo   *Chapman & Hall*, 1839

⁎⁎⁎ THE UPPER END-PAPER IS INSCRIBED: "Eliza Moxon from Phiz" IN THE ARTIST'S HANDWRITING.

47   The Life and Adventures of Nicholas Nickleby, FIRST AMERICAN EDITION IN BOOK FORM, *2 columns, plates by J. Yeager after Phiz [H. K. Browne], 12-page sm. 8vo catalogue of Lea & Blanchard's publications at end, original cloth, gilt design on back, lower cover badly stained [Edgar & Vail, p. 18]*
large 8vo   Philadelphia, Lea & Blanchard, 1839

FIRST AND EARLY EDITIONS

48   Leben und Abenteuer des Nicolaus Nickleby. Herausgegeben von Boz . . .
Aus dem Englischen von Karl Heinrich Hermes. Fortgesetzt von Dr. A. Diezmann,
7 vol., IN THE ORIGINAL 20 PARTS IN 18, FIRST EDITION IN GERMAN, *engraved portrait of
Dickens after Maclise and plates after Phiz [H. K. Browne], advertisements at end of
parts 9, 12, 15 and 19/20, slip (notice to the binder) at end of part 3, original green
pictorial wrappers, in a slip-case of marbled boards, red cloth back*
                              12mo   Brunswick, G. Westermann, 1838-39

49   Nicolas Nickleby . . . traduit de l'anglais par E. de la Bedollierre, 4 vol.,
Brussels, etc., Meline Cans et Cie, 1840; Olivier Twist . . . traduit de l'anglais par
Ludovic Benard, 3 vol., *id.,* 1841; Martin Chuzzlewitt . . . traduit par Madame
L. Sw.-Belloc, 6 vol., *id.,* 1846-47; Une Nuit de Noël . . . traduit de l'anglais par
SW. Belloc, *id.,* 1846; Le Cricri du Foyer, *id.,* 1846; Dombey Père et Fils . . . traduit
de l'anglais par Paul Hennequin, 4 vol., *id.,* 1847-50; Les Contes de Noël, 2 vol.,
plates, Paris, etc., À la Librairie des Livres Liturgiques Illustrés [1846]-48; *together
21 vol., early editions in French, uniform dark-green half morocco, t.e.g., original
wrappers preserved*   *12mo and sm. 8vo*   (21)

50   Stirling (Edward) Nicholas Nickleby. A Farce, in Two Acts, *engraved
frontispiece by Pierce Egan the younger, half parchment, t.e.g., original wrapper
preserved, Webster's Acting National Drama* [1839]; The Fortunes of Smike, or a
Sequel to Nicholas Nickleby. A Drama, in Two Acts, *engraved frontispiece by Pierce
Egan the younger (discoloured), half parchment, t.e.g., original wrapper preserved, id.*
[1840]   *12mo*   (2)

51   The Loving Ballad of Lord Bateman [by Charles Dickens], FIRST EDITION,
FIRST ISSUE (*with the reading "wine" in line 2 of stanza V*), *plates by George Cruikshank,
plate of music, 8 pages of advertisements at end, original limp cloth gilt, in a red morocco-
backed cloth pull-off case*   *sm. 8vo   C. Tilt, 1839*

52   Sketches of Young Couples, FIRST EDITION, *plates by Phiz [H. K. Browne],
4 pages of advertisements at end, plates slightly spotted, frontispiece waterstained,
name on half-title and initials on title, original light-blue pictorial boards, in a red
morocco-backed cloth slip-case*   *sm. 8vo   Chapman & Hall, 1840*

FIRST AND EARLY EDITIONS

53   The Pic Nic Papers. By various Hands. Edited by Charles Dickens, Esq., 3 vol., FIRST EDITION, FIRST ISSUE (*with the transposed words "publisher young" in line 3 of the Introduction and the imprint of Cox & Son on verso of title and on last page of vol. 1), plates by George Cruikshank, Phiz [H. K. Browne] and R. J. Hamerton, 2 pages of advertisements at beginning of vol. 1 and 8 pages at end, 2 pages of advertisements at end of vol. 3, frontispiece to vol. 1 spotted, original green cloth, blocked in blind, uncut and partly unopened*   *8vo   H. Colburn*, 1841

    **   Dickens contributed the *Introduction* and *The Lamplighter's Story* to this collection, which was issued for the benefit of the widow and children of John Macrone, publisher of *Sketches by Boz*.

54   Pic-Nic-Blätter. Herausgegeben von Boz (Charles Dickens) . . . Aus dem Englischen von Amalie Winter, 3 vol. in one, FIRST EDITION IN GERMAN, *3 engraved frontispieces, 2 after H. K. Browne and one after R. J. Hamerton (erroneously described as after George Cruikshank on titles), vol. 2 and 3 each with 2 general titles reading "Bibliothek der neuesten und besten Romane der Englischen Literatur", etc., and "Boz's (Charles Dickens) sämmtliche Werke", etc., off-sets on frontispieces, modern half vellum, t.e.g., other edges uncut, original wrapper preserved*
         sm. 8vo   Brunswick, F. Vieweg und Sohn, 1841

55   MASTER HUMPHREY'S CLOCK, 3 vol., IN THE ORIGINAL 88 WEEKLY PARTS, FIRST EDITION, *wood-engraved frontispieces and wood-engravings in the text by George Cattermole and Hablot Browne*, ORIGINAL WHITE WRAPPERS, UNCUT, *in a brown morocco gilt case*   *large 8vo   Chapman & Hall*, 1840-41

    **   Included with this lot are:
      (1)   "Four Plates engraved under the superintendence of Hablot K. Browne and Robert Young, to illustrate the cheap edition of The Old Curiosity Shop", *original green wrapper, 8vo, Chapman & Hall*, 1848.
      (2)   "The Old Curiosity Shop. Three Portraits of Little Nell. From a Painting by W. Maddox. Barbara, Ditto by Kenny Meadows. Mrs. Quilp. Ditto by H. Warren. Engraved by Edward Finden", *original green wrapper, 8vo*, 1848.
      (3)   The printed announcement of "Master Humphrey's Clock" from "The Examiner" of 29th March, 1840, 4 *pages, 8vo*.

56   MASTER HUMPHREY'S CLOCK, 3 vol., IN THE ORIGINAL 20 MONTHLY PARTS, FIRST EDITION, *wood-engraved frontispieces and wood-engravings in the text by George Cattermole and Hablot Browne, with all the advertisements as listed by Hatton & Cleaver with the exception of "Tyas's Popular Illustrated Publications" in part 1, "Great National Undertaking" in part 8 slightly defective, original green wrappers, uncut, the correct lower cover of part 20 missing and another supplied in its place, in a dark-green morocco pull-off case*   *large 8vo   Chapman & Hall*, 1840-41

FIRST AND EARLY EDITIONS

57   Master Humphrey's Clock, 3 vol., FIRST EDITION, *wood-engraved frontispieces and wood-engravings in the text by George Cattermole and Hablot Browne, original cloth, blocked in gilt and blind, marbled endpapers, m.e., stains on covers, large 8vo, Chapman & Hall,* 1840-41; The Haunted Man, FIRST EDITION, *wood-engraved pictorial title and frontispiece and wood-engravings in the text by Martin & Corbould and others after J. Tenniel, C. Stanfield, F. Stone and J. Leech, advertisement leaf at beginning, original red cloth gilt, borders in blind, g.e., covers stained, sm. 8vo, Bradbury & Evans,* 1848; Hunted Down, FIRST ENGLISH EDITION IN BOOK-FORM, *dark-red half calf gilt, t.e.g., bookplate of A. Edward Newton, sm. 8vo, J. C. Hotten, n.d.* [1870]; Bentley's Miscellany. Extraordinary Gazette. Speech of His Mightiness on Opening the Second Number of Bentley's Miscellany, edited by Boz [followed by advertisements and press notices], 8 *pages, woodcut by Phiz* [H. K. Browne], *half vellum, t.e.g., sm. 8vo, n.d.* [1837], *this brochure was inserted in various publications of the day*—Overs (John) Evenings of a Working Man . . . with a Preface relative to the Author, by Charles Dickens, FIRST EDITION, *title in red and blue, original green cloth, borders in blind, bookplates of John Ashton and C. E. Stewart, sm. 8vo, T. C. Newby,* 1844—The Keepsake, edited by Miss Power [*containing the first printing of Dickens' story "To be Read at Dusk"*], *plates, original red cloth gilt, g.e., large 8vo, D. Bogue, n.d.* [1852]   (8)

58   Master Humphrey's Wanduhr . . . von Boz. Aus dem Englischen von E. A. Moriarty, 9 vol., FIRST EDITION IN GERMAN OF THE FIRST PART OF MASTER HUMPHREY'S CLOCK, *containing The Old Curiosity Shop, 8 lithographic frontispieces after G. Cattermole and H. K. Browne, each vol. has a general title reading "Boz' Sämmtliche Werke. Aus dem Englischen von H. Roberts und E. A. Moriarty", etc., contemporary red morocco gilt*   *sm. 8vo   Leipzig, J. J. Weber,* 1841

59   THE OLD CURIOSITY SHOP, and other Tales, *second American edition in book form, 2 columns, engraved title (dated 1841), plates and woodcuts after Cattermole, Browne and Sibson, the plates engraved by J. Yeager, off-sets on engraved title and plates, original cloth, blocked in blind, title and vignette in gilt on back, in a dark-green morocco-backed cloth slip-case* [*this edition is not in Edgar & Vail*]
                              8vo   Philadelphia, Lea & Blanchard, 1842

** PRESENTATION COPY TO GEORGE MORRIS, THE PRINTED TITLE INSCRIBED BY THE AUTHOR: "George Morris From Charles Dickens New York. First June 1842."

60   Le Marchand d'Antiquités . . . traduit de l'anglais par A.-J.-B. Defauconpret, 2 vol., FIRST EDITION IN FRENCH (*Unauthorized*), *original wrappers, uncut, frayed, in a cloth case, from the Library of the Empress Elizabeth of Austria*
                              8vo   Paris, G. Barba, 1842

FIRST AND EARLY EDITIONS

61 Le Magasin d'Antiquités . . . traduit [par Alfred des Essarts], 2 vol., FIRST AUTHORIZED EDITION IN FRENCH (*with preface by Dickens in English and French*), *contemporary red half morocco gilt, worn, joints cracking*
         12mo   Paris, L. Hachette et Cie [1857]

 ⁎⁎ THE AUTHOR'S COPY, WITH HIS BOOKPLATE IN VOL. 1—see *Catalogue of the Library of Charles Dickens from Gadshill* [*etc.*], edited by J. H. Stonehouse, 1935, p. 35.

62 BARNABY RUDGE, FIRST AMERICAN EDITION IN BOOK FORM, *2 columns, engraved vignette title, plates and woodcuts after Cattermole, Browne and Sibson, the plates engraved by J. Yeager, off-sets on engraved title and frontispiece, original cloth, blocked in blind, title and vignette in gilt on back, in a dark-green morocco-backed cloth, cloth slip-case* [*Edgar & Vail, p.* 20]   *8vo, Philadelphia, Lea & Blanchard,* 1842

 ⁎⁎ PRESENTATION COPY TO GEORGE MORRIS, THE ENGRAVED TITLE INSCRIBED BY THE AUTHOR: "George Morris From Charles Dickens New York. First June 1842".

63 Barnaby Rudge. Von Boz. Aus dem Englischen von E. A. Moriarty, 8 vol. in 2, FIRST EDITION IN GERMAN, *8 frontispieces after G. Cattermole and H. K. Browne, contemporary half tree calf, gilt backs*   *sm. 8vo   Leipzig, J. J. Weber,* 1841

64 AMERICAN NOTES FOR GENERAL CIRCULATION, 2 vol., FIRST EDITION, FIRST ISSUE (*the first page-numeral in vol. 1 is XVI*), *one leaf of advertisements at beginning of vol. 1 and three at end of vol. 2, original brown cloth, blocked in blind, uncut, in a dark-green morocco-backed cloth slip-case, bookplate removed from the inside of the upper cover of each vol. and slight ink-stains on back and lower cover of vol. 1, but otherwise a clean copy*   *8vo   Chapman & Hall,* 1842

 ⁎⁎ PRESENTATION COPY TO W. H. PRESCOTT, THE HALF-TITLE TO VOL. 1 INSCRIBED BY THE AUTHOR: "W. H. Prescott From his friend Charles Dickens October Nineteenth 1842".

65 American Notes for General Circulation, 2 vol., FIRST EDITION, FIRST ISSUE (*the first page-numeral in vol. 1 is XVI*), *one leaf of advertisements at beginning of vol. 1 and 3 at end of vol. 2, original brown cloth, blocked in blind, uncut, upper cover of vol. 2 stained at top, but otherwise a clean copy, bookplate of Ellis Cancellor*
         8vo   Chapman & Hall, 1842

FIRST AND EARLY EDITIONS

66   American Notes for General Circulation [forming extra series, nos. 32 and 33, of The New World, Park Benjamin, Editor, J. Winchester, Publisher], *third American edition, 2 columns, spotted, original wrapper, the upper cover reading "Five Points Literature. 'Boz' raising the 'Dickens' with America, or How To Use Up the Yankees. A Novel in One Volume", uncut, in a cloth slip-case [Edgar & Vail, p. 21]*
folio   New York, Nov., 1842

67   Amerika . . . aus dem Englischen von Otto von Czarnowsky, *the original 3 parts in 2,* FIRST EDITION IN GERMAN OF AMERICAN NOTES, *each part with 2 general titles reading "Bibliothek der neuesten und besten Romane der englischen Literatur", etc., and "Boz's (Charles Dickens) sämmtliche Werke", original yellow wrappers, uncut, in a dark-red morocco-backed cloth slip-case*
sm. 8vo   Brunswick, F. Vieweg und Sohn, 1842

68   [Printed circular letter on the subject of international copyright], *1, Devonshire Terrace, York Gate, Regent's Park, Seventh July, 1842, 2 conjunct leaves, 4to, the first bearing the text of the letter on both sides,* THE WORD "SIR" AT THE BEGINNING AND THE NAME OF THE ADDRESSEE, "C. COWDEN CLARKE ESQUIRE", IN THE HANDWRITING OF DICKENS, *the second leaf blank except for the address: "C. Cowden Clarke Esquire* [AUTOGRAPH] *69 Dean Street Soho [in another hand]",* FRANKED BY DICKENS, *in a blue morocco plush-lined case*

69   THE LIFE AND ADVENTURES OF MARTIN CHUZZLEWIT, IN THE ORIGINAL 20 MONTHLY PARTS IN 19, FIRST EDITION, FIRST ISSUE *(with the transposed "£" on the engraved title), engraved vignette title and plates by Phiz [Hablot K. Browne], with all the advertisements and slips as listed by Hatton & Cleaver, with the exception of the rare "Scenes and Incidents of Foreign Travel" slip in part 7, a few plates spotted and stained,* ORIGINAL GREEN WRAPPERS *(that to the last part in the second state),* UNCUT, *in a dark-green morocco pull-off case*   *8vo   Chapman & Hall,* 1843-44

70   The Life and Adventures of Martin Chuzzlewit, FIRST EDITION, FIRST ISSUE *(with the transposed "£" on the engraved title), engraved vignette title and plates by Phiz [H. K. Browne], faint off-sets of text on several plates, off-set of frontispiece on engraved title, original blue cloth, blocked in blind, uncut, bookplate of the Hon. C. F. Stuart*
8vo   Chapman & Hall, 1844

71   The Life and Adventures of Martin Chuzzlewit, FIRST EDITION, *second issue (with the "£" correctly placed on the engraved title), engraved vignette title and plates by Phiz [H. K. Browne], engraved title and some plates spotted or stained in the margins, original blue cloth, blocked in blind, uncut, in a brown cloth case*
8vo   Chapman & Hall, 1844

FIRST AND EARLY EDITIONS

72   MRS. GAMP. BY CHARLES DICKENS. AS CONDENSFD BY HIMSELF, FOR HIS READINGS, *18 pages (including title), wood-engraved frontispiece by S. Eytinge junior (cut down and mounted), red half morocco gilt, m.e., in a cloth slip-case, red morocco gilt back*   *8vo   Boston, Ticknor & Fields*, 1868

** THE ACTUAL COPY USED BY DICKENS AT HIS LAST READINGS IN BOSTON, WITH AUTOGRAPH CORRECTIONS, ADDITIONS AND UNDERLININGS ON EACH PAGE OF THE TEXT EXCEPT THE LAST.

PRESENTATION COPY, THE TITLE INSCRIBED BY THE AUTHOR: "Charles Dickens His Reading Book To H. M. Ticknor, 20th: April, 1868". The upper endpaper bears the following inscriptions by members of the Ticknor family

"B. H. Ticknor, with the love of his brother, H.M.T. Nov. 12. 1868. T. B. Ticknor, with the love of his brother, B.H.T. Aug. 3. 1897".

Loosely inserted is a typewritten note signed by Thos. B. Ticknor & dated 27th Sept., 1917, which reads:

"This copy of 'Mrs. Gamp' was used by Charles Dickens at his last readings in Boston . . . As my eldest brother, Howard M. Ticknor, of the firm of Ticknor & Fields, Mr. Dickens's American publishers, assisted in the management of Dickens's last tour, Mr. Dickens presented him with this copy, as a memento. Before his death, my brother Howard gave it to my second brother, Benjamin H. Ticknor, duly inscribed, and in turn, he gave it to me. Its history and authenticity is thus established."

[*See* ILLUSTRATION]

73   Leben und Abenteuer Martin Chuzzlewit's. Von Boz (Dickens). Aus dem Englischen von E. A. Moriarty, 10 vol. in 5, FIRST EDITION IN GERMAN, *engraved vignette title and plates after Phiz* [*H. K. Browne*], *each vol. with a general title reading "Boz' Sämmtliche Werke", etc., wanting divisional titles in vol. 7-10, cloth, Leipzig, J. J. Weber*, 1843-44, *with another copy*, 10 vol. in 5, *wanting the engraved title, frontispiece to vol. 1 and all the general titles, contemporary half tree calf gilt, id.*, 1843-44; Bleak Haus . . . aus dem Englischen von J. Seybt, 10 vol. in 5, FIRST EDITION IN GERMAN, *vignette title and plates after Hablot K. Browne, lacking the plate "Tom All-Alone's", contemporary half calf, 5 original paper upper covers preserved, id.*, 1852-53   *sm. 8vo*   (15)

74   Stirling (Edward) Martin Chuzzlewit. A Drama in Three Acts, *Cumberland's British Theatre* [1844]; Mrs. Harris. A Farce in One Act, *engraved frontispiece by T. H. Jones, id.* [1844]—Webster (B.) Mrs. Sarah Gamp's Tea and Turn Out; a Bozzian Sketch, in One Act, *engraved frontispiece by Brewer, Webster's Acting National Drama* [1846], *uniform half parchment, t.e.g., original wrappers preserved*   12mo   (3)

75   A Christmas Carol, FIRST EDITION, FIRST ISSUE (*title in red and blue, "Stave I", green endpapers*), *4 coloured plates and 4 woodcuts by Leech, advertisement leaf at end, original brown cloth gilt, borders in blind, g.e., slight stains on lower cover and endpapers rubbed, but otherwise a clean copy*   *sm. 8vo*   *Chapman & Hall*, 1843

FIRST AND EARLY EDITIONS

76   A Christmas Carol, FIRST EDITION, *second issue (title in red and blue, "Stave I",*
yellow endpapers), 4 coloured plates and 4 woodcuts by Leech, advertisement leaf at end,
original brown cloth gilt, borders in blind, g.e., a clean copy
sm. 8vo   Chapman & Hall, 1843

77   A CHRISTMAS CAROL, FIRST EDITION, *second issue (title in red and blue,*
"Stave I", yellow endpapers), 4 coloured plates and 4 woodcuts by Leech, advertisement
leaf at end, original brown cloth gilt, borders in blind, g.e., in a dark-green morocco-backed
cloth slip-case   *sm. 8vo   Chapman & Hall, 1843*

**   PRESENTATION COPY TO MRS. TOUCHET, THE HALF-TITLE INSCRIBED BY THE
AUTHOR: "M^{rs}: Touchet From Charles Dickens Seventeenth December 1843".

Mrs. Eliza Touchet was Harrison Ainsworth's cousin who acted as his hostess
after he had separated from his wife. She was a brilliant talker with a sharp tongue.

78   A Christmas Carol, *second edition, title in red and blue, 4 coloured plates and*
4 woodcuts by Leech, advertisement leaf at end, Chapman & Hall, 1843; The Chimes,
FIRST EDITION, *second issue (the publishers' names beneath the cloud on the engraved*
title), engraved title and frontispiece by F. P. Becker after D. Maclise and wood-
engravings in the text by Linton and others after R. Doyle, J. Leech and C. Stanfield,
advertisement leaf at beginning, 1845; The Cricket on the Hearth, FIRST EDITION,
wood-engraved pictorial title and frontispiece and wood-engravings in the text by
G. Dalziel and others after D. Maclise, R. Doyle, C. Stanfield, J. Leech and E. Landseer,
advertisement leaf at end, Bradbury & Evans, 1846; The Battle of Life, FIRST EDITION,
fourth issue (no imprint or date on pictorial title), wood-engraved pictorial title and
frontispiece and wood-engravings in the text by Dalziel and others after D. Maclise,
R. Doyle, C. Stanfield and J. Leech, advertisement leaf at end, half of upper endpaper
missing, id., 1846; The Haunted Man, FIRST EDITION, *wood-engraved pictorial title and*
frontispiece and wood-engravings in the text by Martin and Corbould and others after
J. Tenniel, C. Stanfield, F. Stone and J. Leech, advertisement leaf at beginning, id., 1848;
original cloth gilt (A Christmas Carol brown, the rest red), borders in blind, g.e.
sm. 8vo   (5)

79   A Christmas Carol, FIRST AMERICAN EDITION, *title printed in red and black,*
4 coloured lithographic plates and 4 uncoloured illustrations after Leech, stains, original
brown cloth, the sides blocked in blind, with gilt design on back in imitation of that on the
bindings of the English editions, in a red morocco pull-off case [Edgar & Vail, p. 21]
12mo   Philadelphia, Carey & Hart, 1844

**   Pasted on to the upper endpaper is an AUTOGRAPH NOTE (third person)
written on a piece of *All the Year Round* notepaper:

"Mr. Charles Dickens presents his compliments to Mr. Buchheim, and begs to give him free
permission to make the extract he desires to introduce into his book on German prose composition,"
2nd Nov., 1867.

FIRST AND EARLY EDITIONS

80   A CHRISTMAS CAROL, *eleventh edition, title in red and blue, 4 coloured plates and 4 woodcuts by Leech, advertisement leaf at end, original red cloth gilt, borders in blind, g.e., in a dark-green morocco-backed cloth slip-case, a very clean copy*
sm. 8vo   *Bradbury & Evans*, 1846

**   PRESENTATION COPY, THE HALF-TITLE INSCRIBED BY THE AUTHOR: "Joseph Valckenberg From his friend Charles Dickens Twenty First January 1847".

Josef Valckenberg was a German wine merchant whom Dickens met on a Rhine trip.

81   The Chimes, FIRST FDITION, FIRST ISSUE (*the publishers' names within the cloud on the engraved title*), *engraved title and frontispiece by F. P. Becker after D. Maclise and wood-engravings in the text by Linton and others after R. Doyle, J. Leech and C. Stanfield, advertisement leaf at beginning, original red cloth gilt, borders in blind, g.e., bookplate of John F. Patrick, slight stain on upper cover, but otherwise a clean copy*
sm. 8vo   *Chapman & Hall*, 1845

**   Loosely inserted is a printed form filled up by hand in which Charles Dickens, Wm. Bradbury and Frederick Mullett Evans certify that they are the proprietors of the copyright of *The Chimes* and require [the officer of Stationers' Hall] to make entry in the Register Book of the Stationers' Company of their proprietorship of such copyright, dated 16th Dec., 1844.

82   The Chimes, FIRST AMERICAN EDITION, *2 columns, somewhat stained, modern half vellum, original wrapper preserved, t.e.g.* [*Edgar & Vail, p. 22*]
8vo   *New York, Harper & Brothers*, 1845

83   The Chimes, *second (or* FIRST ILLUSTRATED) *American edition, lithographic title and plates after D. Maclise, R. Doyle, J. Leech and C. Stanfield, original blue cloth, blocked in blind, with gilt designs on upper cover and back in imitation of those on the bindings of the English editions, in a blue morocco-backed cloth slip-case* [*Edgar & Vail, p. 22*]   12mo   *Philadelphia, Lea & Blanchard*, 1845

84   Lemon (Mark) and Gilbert A. à Beckett. The Chimes . . . a Drama, in Four Quarters, *engraved frontispiece by Clayton (discoloured), half parchment, t.e.g., original wrapper preserved*   12mo   *Webster's Acting National Drama* [1846]

FIRST AND EARLY EDITIONS

85   THE CRICKET ON THE HEARTH, FIRST EDITION, *wood-engraved pictorial title and frontispiece and wood-engravings in the text by G. Dalziel and others after D. Maclise, R. Doyle, C. Stanfield, J. Leech and E. Landseer, original red cloth gilt, borders in blind, g.e., in a red morocco slip-case, bookplate of Count D'Orsay*
sm. 8vo   Bradbury & Evans, 1846

**   PRESENTATION COPY TO COUNT D'ORSAY, THE PRINTED TITLE INSCRIBED BY THE AUTHOR: "Count D'Orsay From his Friend Charles Dickens Christmas 1845".

86   Smith (Albert) The Cricket on the Hearth . . . dramatized by Albert Smith . . . from early proofs of the work, by the express permission of the author, *original wrapper, in a dark-green morocco-backed cloth slip-case,* A CLEAN COPY
sm. 8vo   W. S. Johnson, 1845

87   PICTURES FROM ITALY, FIRST EDITION, *wood-engravings by Samuel Palmer, advertisement leaf at beginning and end, original blue cloth, blocked in blind, in a dark-green morocco-backed cloth slip-case*   sm. 8vo   Bradbury & Evans, 1846

**   PRESENTATION COPY TO THOMAS BEARD, THE HALF-TITLE INSCRIBED BY THE AUTHOR: "Thomas Beard Esquire From his old friend Charles Dickens Devonshire Terrace Nineteenth May 1846".

88   Pictures from Italy, FIRST EDITION, *wood-engravings by Samuel Palmer, leaf of advertisements at beginning and end, original cloth, blocked in blind, uncut, name on upper end-paper*   sm. 8vo   Bradbury & Evans, 1846

89   Dealings with the Firm of Dombey and Son, Wholesale, Retail, and for Exportation, IN THE ORIGINAL 20 MONTHLY PARTS IN 19, FIRST EDITION, *with the misprint "Capatin" in the last line of p. 324 (part 11), the word "if" in line 9 on p. 426 (part 14) is omitted, but the page-numeral on p. 431 in the same part is present, engraved vignette title and plates by H. K. Browne, with most of the advertisements and slips listed by Hatton and Cleaver, plates in part 1 spotted,* ORIGINAL GREEN WRAPPERS, UNCUT, *name on upper cover of part 13, several backs and a few covers repaired, in a cloth case*
8vo   Bradbury & Evans, 1846-48

**   Included with this lot is an oblong slip of paper inscribed by Dickens "With Charles Dickens' compliments Devonshire Terrace Twentieth June 1848".

FIRST AND EARLY EDITIONS

90 DEALINGS WITH THE FIRM OF DOMBEY AND SON, Wholesale, Retail, and for Exportation, FIRST EDITION, *"Captain" in the last line on p. 324 is correctly printed, the first word "if" in line 9 on p. 426 and the page-numeral on p. 431 are present, engraved vignette title and plates by Phiz, errata leaf at end, engraved title and frontispiece badly spotted and some other plates slightly so, contemporary dark-green half morocco gilt, m.e., in a dark-green morocco-backed cloth slip-case* 8vo *Bradbury & Evans*, 1848

** PRESENTATION COPY TO MADAME DE CERJAT, THE HALF TITLE INSCRIBED BY THE AUTHOR: Charles Dickens to M^rs: Cerjat. Twenty ninth March, 1849.

Mrs. Cerjat was the English wife of William de Cerjat, a Swiss friend of Dickens.

91 Dealings with the Firm of Dombey and Son, Wholesale, Retail and for Exportation, IN THE ORIGINAL 20 MONTHLY PARTS IN 19, FIRST AMERICAN EDITION, *full-page wood-engravings after H. K. Browne*, ORIGINAL WRAPPERS, UNCUT, *in a cloth case* 8vo *New York, Wiley & Putnam*, 1846-48

91A The Story of Little Dombey, *one page of advertisements at end, original green wrapper, back slightly defective* sm. 8vo *Bradbury & Evans*, 1858

92 Dombey und Sohn von Boz (Dickens). Aus dem Englischen von Julius Seybt, 10 vol. in 5, FIRST EDITION IN GERMAN, *plates after Hablot K. Browne, each vol. with a general title reading "Boz' Sämmtliche Werke", etc., vol. 2, 5, 6 and 10 with 4, 2, 2 and 8 pages of advertisements at end respectively, contemporary mottled boards, sheep backs* sm. 8vo *Leipzig, C. B. Lorck*, 1847-48

93 The Battle of Life, FIRST EDITION, *second issue (with "A Love Story" in a banderole and printed imprint and date on the pictorial title), wood-engraved pictorial title and frontispiece and wood-engravings in the text by Dalziel and others after D. Maclise, R. Doyle, C. Stanfield and J. Leech, advertisement leaf at end, original red cloth gilt, borders in blind, g.e., a clean copy* sm. 8vo *Bradbury & Evans*, 1846

94 The Battle of Life, FIRST EDITION, *third issue (with "A Love Story" in a banderole supported by a putto and printed imprint, but no date, on the pictorial title), wood-engraved pictorial title and frontispiece and wood-engravings in the text by Dalziel and others after D. Maclise, R. Doyle, C. Stanfield and J. Leech, advertisement leaf at end, inscription dated 25th Dec., 1847, on upper endpaper, original red cloth gilt, borders in blind, g.e., slight stain on upper cover, but otherwise a clean copy, bookplate of Albert M. Cohn* sm. 8vo *Bradbury & Evans*, 1846

FIRST AND EARLY EDITIONS

95   THE BATTLE OF LIFE, FIRST EDITION, *fourth issue* (*without imprint or date on the pictorial title*), *wood-engraved pictorial title and frontispiece and wood-engravings in the text by Dalziel and others after D. Maclise, R. Doyle, C. Stanfield and J. Leech, with half-title, but lacking the advertisement leaf at end,* PRESENTATION BINDING OF RED MOROCCO, *the sides stamped and tooled in gilt and blind, gilt tooled and panelled back, g.e., in a dark-green morocco-backed cloth slip-case   sm. 8vo   Bradbury & Evans, 1846*

** PRESENTATION COPY TO MRS. CERJAT, THE DEDICATION LEAF INSCRIBED BY THE AUTHOR (following the printed words "This Christmas Book is cordially inscribed to my English friends in Switzerland"): "and to M^{rs}: Cerjat this copy is sent with the true regard of Charles Dickens London. Christmas 1846."

Loosely inserted is an autograph certificate signed by Mademoiselle Jeanne de Cerjat and addressed to the Vicomte de Suzannet stating that this book was given by Charles Dickens to Madame de Cerjat and that since then it had not left her family till this day Monday, 25th October, 1925.

96   Smith (Albert) The Battle of Life, dramatized by Albert Smith . . . from early proofs of the work, with the express permission of the author, Charles Dickens, *6 pages of advertisements at end, W. S. Johnson* [1847]—Stirling (Edward) The Battle of Life; a Drama, in Three Acts, *engraved frontispiece by T. H. Jones, The New British Theatre* (*late Duncombe's*), [1847], *uniform half parchment, t.e.g., original wrappers preserved*   12mo   (2)

97   THE HAUNTED MAN, FIRST EDITION, *wood-engraved pictorial title and frontispiece and wood-engravings in the text by Martin and Corbould and others after J. Tenniel, C. Stanfield, F. Stone and J. Leech, advertisement leaf at beginning, original red cloth gilt, borders in blind, g.e., slight stains on covers, in a dark-green morocco-backed cloth slip-case, bookplate of W. K. Bixby*   sm. 8vo   Bradbury & Evans, 1848

** PRESENTATION COPY TO SIR THOMAS NOON TALFOURD, THE HALF-TITLE INSCRIBED BY THE AUTHOR: "T. N. Talfourd From his friend Charles Dickens Fourteenth December 1848."

98   THE PERSONAL HISTORY OF DAVID COPPERFIELD, IN THE ORIGINAL 20 MONTHLY PARTS IN 19, FIRST EDITION, *engraved vignette title and plates by H. K. Browne, with most of the advertisements and slips as listed by Hatton and Cleaver, plates in parts 6-19/20 spotted,* ORIGINAL GREEN WRAPPERS, UNCUT, *back of part 1 repaired, in a cloth case*
8vo   Bradbury & Evans, 1849-50

FIRST AND EARLY EDITIONS

99 THE PERSONAL HISTORY OF DAVID COPPERFIELD, FIRST EDITION, *engraved vignette title and plates by H. K. Browne, with half-title and errata leaf, vignette title and plates slightly discoloured, contemporary green morocco, gilt and panelled back, g.e., loose, in a green morocco-backed cloth slip-case*　　8vo　*Bradbury & Evans*, 1850

*** PRESENTATION COPY TO THOMAS BEARD, THE PRINTED TITLE INSCRIBED BY THE AUTHOR: "Thomas Beard. From his old friend Charles Dickens Sixth December 1850".

100 The Personal History of David Copperfield, FIRST EDITION, *engraved vignette title and plates by H. K. Browne, with half-title, brown calf gilt, panelled back, red and green morocco labels, t.e.g., other edges uncut, by Morrell, the original 19/20 green wrappers and some of the advertisements preserved*　　8vo　*Bradbury & Evans*, 1850

101 Lebensgeschichte und Erfahrungen David Copperfield's des Jüngern von Boz (Dickens). Aus dem Englischen von Julius Seybt, 10 vol. in 3, FIRST EDITION IN GERMAN, *plates after Hablot K. Browne, some leaves of text spotted, contemporary half cloth*　　sm. 8vo　*Leipzig, J. J. Weber*, 1849-50

102 Souvenirs de David Copperfield, 6 vol. in 2, *red cloth, morocco gilt backs* sm. 8vo, *Brussels, Rue des douze Apôtres, 13, no publisher, n.d.*; Le Neveu de ma Tante Histoire Personelle de David Copperfield . . . traduite . . . par A. Pichot, 2 vol., *modern black half morocco, original wrappers preserved*, 8vo, *Paris, M. Lévy Frères*, 1859; Vie et Aventures de Martin Chuzzlewit . . . traduit [par A. Des Essarts], 2 vol., FIRST AUTHORIZED EDITION IN FRENCH, *marbled boards, calf backs*, 12mo, *Paris, Hachette*, 1858; Aventures de Monsieur Pickwick . . . traduit . . . par P. Grolier, 2 vol., FIRST AUTHORIZED EDITION IN FRENCH, *marbled boards, brown morocco gilt backs*, 12mo, *id.*, 1859; Le Magazin d'Antiquités . . . traduit [par A. Des Essarts], 2 vol. in one, FIRST AUTHORIZED EDITION IN FRENCH, *marbled boards, red morocco gilt back, id.*, 1865; Les Temps Difficiles . . . traduit [par W. L. Hughes], *modern blue half morocco, original wrapper preserved*, 12mo, *id., n.d.*; Les Chefs-d'Oeuvre de Ch. Dickens traduits . . . par Amédée Pichot. La Cloche du Tocsin [Barnaby Rudge], etc., *modern blue half morocco, original wrapper preserved*, 12mo, *Paris, Amyot*, 1847; Les Contes de Ch. Dickens traduits . . . par A. Pichot [Christmas Books, Barnaby Rudge, etc.], 3 vol., *marbled boards, green morocco gilt backs*, 12mo, *id.*, 1847-53—La Pléiade. Ballades, Fabliaux, Nouvelles et Légendes [*including Le Baron de Grogzwig, a tale from Nicholas Nickleby*], *illustrations, red morocco gilt, panelled back, g.e., by Petit*, 12mo, *Paris, L. Curmer*, 1842　　　　　　　　　　　　　　　　　　　　　　　　　　　(15)

103 Household Words. A Weekly Journal. Conducted by Charles Dickens, 19 vol., *original cloth; sold as a magazine, not subject to return*　　8vo　1850-59

FIRST AND EARLY EDITIONS

104   The Christmas Numbers of "Household Words" and "All The Year Round", *the 9 numbers of the former, sewed, as issued, numbers 1-4 of the latter sewed, as issued, and numbers 5-9 original wrappers, as issued, in a dark-green half morocco slip-case*
8vo   1850-67

105   A Child's History of England, 3 vol., FIRST EDITION, *3 frontispieces by F. W. Topham, advertisement leaf at end of each vol., original brown cloth, blocked in gilt and blind, m.e.*   *sm. 8vo   Bradbury & Evans, 1852-53-54*

106   To Be Read At Dusk, WISE FORGERY, *unbound and uncut, in a green morocco gilt pull-off case* [*Carter & Pollard, pp.* 185-187]   *8vo   1852*

107   Bleak House, IN THE ORIGINAL 20 MONTHLY PARTS IN 19, FIRST EDITION, *engraved vignette title and plates by H. K. Browne, with most of the advertisements and slips as listed by Hatton and Cleaver, including the slip relating to the accident to one of the plates in part 9, engraved title and frontispiece rather spotted,* ORIGINAL BLUE WRAPPERS, UNCUT, *some backs repaired, in a cloth case*
8vo   Bradbury & Evans, 1852-53

108   BLEAK HOUSE, FIRST EDITION, *engraved vignette title and plates by H. K. Browne, with half-title, margins of engraved title and plates somewhat discoloured and in some cases spotted as well, off-sets of text, mostly faint, on many plates, contemporary red half morocco gilt, g.e., rather worn, in a green morocco-backed cloth slip-case*
8vo   Bradbury & Evans, 1853

*** PRESENTATION COPY TO CHARLES KNIGHT, THE DEDICATION LEAF INSCRIBED BY THE AUTHOR: "Charles Knight From Charles Dickens Third October 1853".

109   BLEAK HOUSE, FIRST EDITION, *engraved vignette title and plates by H. K. Browne, with half-title, the vignette title and plates somewhat discoloured, contemporary red half morocco gilt, g.e., upper cover detached, in a dark-green morocco-backed slip-case*   *8vo   Bradbury & Evans, 1853*

*** PRESENTATION COPY TO THOMAS BEARD, THE PRINTED TITLE INSCRIBED BY THE AUTHOR: "Thomas Beard From his old friend Charles Dickens December, 1853."

110   Bleak House, FIRST EDITION, *engraved vignette title and plates by H. K. Browne, with half-title, yellow calf gilt, panelled back, red and dark-green morocco labels, t.e.g., other edges uncut, by Zaehnsdorf, the original 19/20 blue wrappers and many of the advertisements preserved, the upper cover of part I missing*
8vo   Bradbury & Evans, 1853

FIRST AND EARLY EDITIONS

111   BLEAK HOUSE, *2 columns, frontispiece by H. K. Browne, original green cloth, the sides blocked in blind, with circular centrepiece enclosing the words "The Works of Charles Dickens Cheap Edition" on each cover, gilt back, in a cloth slip-case*
8vo   Chapman & Hall, 1866

**   WITH AN APPROPRIATE HEADLINE IN THE AUTHOR'S HANDWRITING ON THE RECTO OF EACH LEAF OF TEXT except B1 and KK6, the printed headline "Bleak House" having been struck out by him, apparently with a view to a new edition. We give some characteristic examples:

"Lady Dedlock bored to death" (p. 9)
"Ill weeds don't always grow apace" (p. 171)
"Put not your trust in chancery" (p. 191)
"Mr. Chadband enquires concerning Terewth" (p. 213)
"The right Ironmaster in the wrong place" (p. 233)
"The young man of the name of Guppy" (p. 237)
"The soot is falling, surely" (p. 265)
"Mrs. Smallweed as a Pig-headed Jackdaw" (p. 273)
"Discipline must be maintained" (p. 281)
"Warped by chancery" (p. 289)
"Not a pretty lady now" (p. 297)
"Mr. Vholes's hands are clean" (p. 325)
"The Lawyer not a man of gallantry" (p. 347)
"Sir Leicester Dedlock has been pained" (p. 353)
"Jo moving on—at last" (p. 373)
"Mr. Bucket and the second-hand Violincello" (p. 397)
"Bleak House thins fast" (p. 411)
"Mr. Bucket is a perfect Blue Chamber" (p. 423)
"Mr. Bucket wishes to know 'what's up' " (p. 429)
"Mr. Bucket appropriates the foreign female" (p. 437)
"Mr. Guppy puts my lady on her guard" (p. 445)
"Mr. Snagsby has no idea of anything" (p. 473)
"Miss Flite reverts to the baleful attraction" (p. 481)
"Magpie Property" (p. 493)
"More conversation Kenge than ever" (p. 495)
"Nothing left but costs" (p. 509)

Some of the headlines have been revised or completely changed *currente calamo*.

112   THE LATE MR. JUSTICE TALFOURD, *a pre-publication off-print of an article which appeared in Household Words, one page, 4to, with black border, 2 columns, with conjunct blank leaf, in a maroon morocco-backed cloth slip-case*

**   INSCRIBED BY THE AUTHOR: "Household Words, Saturday 25:th March 1854. Not yet published".

113   Hard Times, FIRST EDITION, *original green cloth, blocked in blind, uncut, bookplate of Kenneth H. M. Connal*
8vo   Bradbury & Evans, 1854

**   Included with this lot is a copy of Our Miscellany, edited by E. H. Yates and R. B. Brough, *olive morocco gilt, t.e.g., sm. 8vo, Routledge*, 1856. It contains a parody of Hard Times by "Charles Diggins".

FIRST AND EARLY EDITIONS

114   Speech of Charles Dickens, Esqr., delivered at the Meeting of the Administrative Reform Association, at Drury Lane Theatre, on Wednesday, June 27, 1855, FIRST EDITION, *second issue ("hundred" in line 6 on p. 1 correctly spelt), small hole through last leaf affecting 2 or 3 letters, title slightly soiled, sewed, as issued, in a cloth case*   8vo   *M. S. Rickerby*, 1855

***   There is another issue with the imprint of Effingham Wilson on the title and "Price Twopence" beneath.

115   Little Dorrit, IN THE ORIGINAL 20 PARTS MONTHLY IN 19, FIRST EDITION, FIRST ISSUE *(the name "Rigaud" is used instead of "Blandois" on pp. 469, 470, 472 and 473; the printed slip pointing this out appears in part 16), engraved vignette title and plates by H. K. Browne, with most of the advertisements and slips as listed by Hatton and Cleaver, ORIGINAL BLUE WRAPPERS, UNCUT, bookseller's embossed stamp on upper covers of all except parts 2, 6, 9 and 13, in a dark-green morocco gilt pull-off case*   8vo   *Bradbury & Evans*, 1855-57

116   Klein Dorrit . . . Aus dem Englischen von Moritz Busch, 10 vol. in 5, FIRST EDITION IN GERMAN, *plates after Hablot K. Browne, with general title reading "Boz (Dickens) Sämmtliche Werke", etc., in each vol. except 3, advertisement leaf at end of vol. 5, 7 and 8, contemporary half sheep*   sm. 8vo   *Leipzig, J. J. Weber*, 1856-57

117   The Two Apprentices [i.e. The Lazy Tour of Two Idle Apprentices, by Charles Dickens and Wilkie Collins], FIRST EDITION IN BOOK FORM, *2 columns, 24 pages of advertisements at end, green morocco gilt, t.e.g., original wrapper preserved [not in Edgar & Vail]*   8vo   *Philadelphia, T. B. Peterson, n.d.* [1857]

***   This story first appeared in the October number of *Household Words*, 1857. The volume also contains *A Wife's Story* [anonymous].

118   A TALE OF TWO CITIES, IN THE ORIGINAL 8 MONTHLY PARTS IN 7, FIRST EDITION, FIRST ISSUE *(p. 213 misnumbered 113 in part 7/8), engraved vignette title and plates by H. K. Browne, with most of the advertisements as listed by Hatton and Cleaver, ORIGINAL BLUE WRAPPERS, UNCUT, in a green morocco gilt case*   8vo   *Chapman & Hall*, 1859

***   Included with this lot is a leaf printed on one side only headed " 'Lucie Manette', a Dramatic Overture on Charles Dickens' 'Tale of Two Cities', composed by James Waterson". At the foot of the page is printed "This description of Mr. Waterson's Overture was written expressly for him by the late Charles Dickens". On the verso is a signed note in the composer's hand addressed to Mr. Sowerby asking him to "print as usual this description. Written for me by Charles Dickens".

FIRST AND EARLY EDITIONS

119   A TALE OF TWO CITIES, FIRST EDITION, FIRST ISSUE (*p. 213 misnumbered 113*), *engraved vignette title and plates by H. K. Browne, original red cloth, the sides blocked in blind, gilt back, uncut, dull, in a green morocco-backed cloth slip-case*
8*vo   Chapman & Hall*, 1859

** PRESENTATION COPY TO THOMAS BEARD, THE PRINTED TITLE INSCRIBED BY THE AUTHOR: "Charles Dickens To Thomas Beard December, 1859".

120   Zwei Städte . . . aus dem Englischen von Julius Seybt, 4 parts in one vol., FIRST EDITION IN GERMAN *of "A Tale of Two Cities", vignette title and plates after Hablot K. Browne, some plates and leaves of text spotted, contemporary brown half morocco gilt*   sm. 8*vo   Leipzig, J. J. Weber*, 1859

121   ALL THE YEAR ROUND. A Weekly Journal. Conducted by Charles Dickens [*First Series*], 20 vol., *red half morocco gilt, m.e.,* with the BOOKPLATE OF CHARLES DICKENS IN EACH VOL. [*see Catalogue of the Library of Charles Dickens from Gadshill, etc., edited by J. H. Stonehouse, 1935, p. 38*]; *sold as a magazine, not subject to return*
8*vo* 1859-68

**   Included with this lot are vol. 1-4 of the New Series, *red half calf gilt*, 1868-70.

122   All the Year Round, conducted by Charles Dickens, a set of the 9 Christmas numbers, in one vol., *red morocco gilt, panelled back, t.e.g., other edges uncut, by Riviere, the original blue wrappers of numbers 5-9 preserved (numbers 1-4 were issued without wrappers*   8*vo   Chapman & Hall*, 1859-67

123   A Curious Dance round a Curious Tree, FIRST EDITION, FIRST ISSUE (*purple wrapper with period after "Tree" on upper cover and the last paragraph in the same type as the rest of the pamphlet), in a dark-red morocco-backed cloth slip-case*
sm. 8*vo*   [1860]

**   This piece originally appeared in *Household Words* for Jan., 1852, and was issued in pamphlet form in aid of St. Luke's Hospital with the author's consent.

124   THE UNCOMMERCIAL TRAVELLER, FIRST EDITION, *32 pages of advertisements dated Dec., 1860, at end, original lilac cloth, the sides blocked in blind, gilt design on back, uncut, dull, in a dark-green morocco-backed cloth slip-case*
8*vo   Chapman & Hall*, 1861

**   PRESENTATION COPY TO FRANK BEARD, THE TITLE INSCRIBED BY THE AUTHOR: "Frank Beard with kind regards From Charles Dickens Christmas, 1860".

Dr. Francis Carr Beard was the brother of Thomas Beard.

FIRST AND EARLY EDITIONS

125   The Uncommercial Traveller, FIRST EDITION, *32 pages of advertisements dated Dec., 1860, at end, original lilac cloth, the sides blocked in blind, gilt design on back, uncut*   8vo   *Chapman & Hall*, 1861

⁂   The half-title bears the following MS. note: "Messrs. Finch Hill & Paraire Architects to the Brittania [*sic*] Theatre respectfully call your attention to Page 42." On pp. 42-44 the passages relating to the Britannia Theatre, Hoxton, are marked by vertical lines in ink in the margins and there is a MS. note at the foot of p. 44.

126   THE UNCOMMERCIAL TRAVELLER, *second edition, original lilac cloth, the sides blocked in blind, gilt design on back, uncut, dull, in a red morocco-backed cloth slip-case, bookplate of Edmund Yates*   8vo   *Chapman & Hall*, 1861

⁂   PRESENTATION COPY TO EDMUND YATES, THE TITLE INSCRIBED BY THE AUTHOR: "Charles Dickens to Edmund Yates June, 1861".

Edmund Yates was a novelist and founder of "The World".

127   The Uncommercial Traveller, *first cheap edition (containing 11 additional papers which appeared here for the first time), 2 columns, frontispiece, green half morocco gilt, t.e.g., 8vo, Chapman & Hall,* 1866; Christmas Books, FIRST COLLECTED EDITION, *2 columns, frontispiece, original cloth, gilt back, 8vo, id.,* 1852; and two others   (4)

128   GREAT EXPECTATIONS, 3 vol., FIRST EDITION, *32 pages of advertisements dated May, 1861, on pp. 1, 2 and 5, original purple cloth, blocked in blind, gilt backs, uncut, in a dark-green morocco-backed cloth slip-case*   8vo   *Chapman & Hall*, 1861

⁂   PRESENTATION COPY TO THOMAS BEARD, INSCRIBED BY THE AUTHOR: "Thursday Fourth July 1861. Thomas Beard From Charles Dickens" on a piece of headed Gad's Hill Place notepaper which has been stuck into vol. 1 following the title.

129   Our Mutual Friend, 2 vol., IN THE ORIGINAL 20 MONTHLY PARTS IN 19, FIRST EDITION, *full-page wood-engravings after Marcus Stone, with all the advertisements and slips as listed by Hatton and Cleaver,* ORIGINAL GREEN WRAPPERS, UNCUT, PARTS 1-3, 5-8, 11, 12, 15, 16 AND 18 UNOPENED, *in a dark-green morocco gilt pull-off case*
8vo   *Chapman & Hall*, 1864-65

130   OUR MUTUAL FRIEND, 2 vol., FIRST EDITION, *full-page wood-engravings after Marcus Stone, with half-titles but lacking the slip at the beginning of vol. 1 relating to the title of the novel, contemporary red half morocco gilt, g.e., slightly worn, in a red morocco-backed cloth slip-case, bookplate of Roderick Terry*
8vo   *Chapman & Hall*, 1865

⁂   PRESENTATION COPY TO CHARLES KENT, THE DEDICATION LEAF INSCRIBED BY THE AUTHOR: "Charles Dickens To Charles Kent. Seventeenth November, 1865".

Charles Kent was perhaps the most devoted of Dickens' friends. His attachment to the novelist bordered on hero-worship.

FIRST AND EARLY EDITIONS

131   Our Mutual Friend, 2 vol. in one, FIRST EDITION, *wood-engraved title and full-page wood-engravings by Marcus Stone, advertisement leaf at end of vol. 2, lacking half-titles and the slip at the beginning of vol. 1 relating to the title of the novel, some plates waterstained or spotted, original green cloth, blocked in blind, uncut, upper cover badly stained*   *8vo   Chapman & Hall,* 1865

132   Collins (Wilkie) The Frozen Deep. A Drama, in Three Acts, ?FIRST EDITION, *46 pages, modern half vellum, t.e.g., original wrapper preserved*
                              sm. 4to   Not Published, imprint on verso of title:
                                    Watford, S. A. Bradley, n.d.

**   The British Museum copy and that described by Eckel, ed. 1932, pp. 166-167, are dated 1866 and the sizes are given as 8*vo* and 16*mo* respectively. They have the same number of pages as the present copy.
   "The changes [made by Dickens at the rehearsals] were so numerous that the drama almost may be ascribed to Dickens"—Eckel, *loc. cit.*

133   Procter (Adelaide Anne) Legends and Lyrics . . . with an Introduction by Charles Dickens, *new edition, with additions, portrait, full-page wood-engravings after Samuel Palmer, J. Tenniel, G. Du Maurier and others, original green cloth, the upper cover and back gilt, the lower cover blocked in blind, g.e., slightly loose, but otherwise a clean copy*   *sm. 4to   Bell & Daldy,* 1866

**   The introduction by Dickens appeared for the first time in this edition.

134   No Thoroughfare. A Drama. In Five Acts [by Charles Dickens and Wilkie Collins], FIRST EDITION, *original wrapper, in a red morocco gilt pull-off case*
                    sm. 8vo   Published at the Office of All the Year Round, 1867

135   The Mystery of Edwin Drood, IN THE ORIGINAL 6 MONTHLY PARTS, FIRST EDITION, *engraved portrait of the author, engraved title with oval view, full-page wood-engravings after S. L. Fildes, with all the advertisements and slips as listed by Hatton and Cleaver,* ORIGINAL GREEN WRAPPERS, UNCUT, 8vo, *Chapman & Hall,* 1870— [Morford (Henry) and others] John Jasper's Secret: being a Narrative of certain Events following and explaining "The Mystery of Edwin Drood", IN THE ORIGINAL 8 MONTHLY PARTS, FIRST ENGLISH EDITION [*originally published in Philadelphia in* 1871], *full-page wood-engravings, advertisements in parts 1-3,* ORIGINAL GREEN WRAPPERS, UNCUT, 8vo, *Publishing Offices, No. 342, Strand* [*printed by Wyman & Sons*], 1871-72, *the 2 works in a cloth case*

136   The Mystery of Edwin Drood, IN THE ORIGINAL 6 MONTHLY PARTS, FIRST EDITION, *engraved portrait of the author, engraved title with oval view, full-page wood-engravings after S. L. Fildes, with most of the advertisements and slips as listed by Hatton and Cleaver,* ORIGINAL GREEN WRAPPERS, UNCUT, *all backs except one slightly defective, in a cloth case*   *8vo   Chapman & Hall,* 1870

FIRST AND EARLY EDITIONS

137   The Lamplighter, a Farce . . . (1838). Now first printed from a Manuscript in the Forster Collection at the South Kensington Museum, FIRST EDITION, LIMITED TO 250 COPIES, *red morocco gilt, t.e.g., original wrapper preserved*   *sm.* 8*vo*   1879

138   The Mudfog Papers, etc., FIRST COLLECTED EDITION, *original red cloth,*
A CLEAN COPY   8*vo*   *R. Bentley & Son,* 1880

139   The Letters of Charles Dickens, edited by his sister-in-law and his eldest daughter, 3 vol., FIRST COLLECTED EDITION, *original cloth,* 8*vo,* 1880-82; Letters to Wilkie Collins, 1851-1870, selected by Miss Georgina Hogarth, edited by Laurence Hutton, *original cloth,* 8*vo,* 1892; Charles Dickens and Maria Beadnell. Private Correspondence, edited by G. P. Baker, *limited to 493 copies, portraits (2 coloured), plates and facsimiles, original half parchment, in slip-case, large* 8*vo, Boston, The Bibliophile Society,* 1908; The Dickens-Kolle Letters, edited by Harry B. Smith, *limited to 483 copies, portraits and facsimiles, original half parchment, in slip-case, large* 8*vo, id.,* 1910; Charles Dickens as Editor, being Letters written by him to William Henry Wills his Sub-Editor, selected and edited by R. C. Lehmann, *portraits, original cloth,* 8*vo,* 1912; The Unpublished Letters of Charles Dickens to Mark Lemon, edited by Walter Dexter, *with presentation inscription in the editor's hand, facsimiles, original half vellum, t.e.g., bookplate of Walter Dexter,* 4*to,* 1927; A Dickens Friendship told in his own Letters, with Notes by W[ilfrid] M[eynell], LIMITED TO 75 COPIES, *the title signed by the editor, 5 A.Ls.s. from him loosely inserted, dark-green half morocco, t.e.g., original wrapper preserved, large* 8*vo, Privately Printed,* 1931; Dickens to his oldest Friend: some Unpublished Letters to Thomas Beard in the Collection of Count de Suzannet, ONE OF 50 COPIES PRINTED BY WALTER DEXTER FOR HIS FRIENDS, *with presentation inscription in the editor's hand, facsimile, dark-green half morocco, t.e.g., original stiff wrapper preserved, bookplate of Walter Dexter, large* 8*vo,* 1931; Letters of Charles Dickens to the Baroness Burdett-Coutts, edited by Charles C. Osborne, *portraits, plates and facsimiles, original cloth, buckram back, t.e.g.,* 8*vo,* 1931; Dickens to his first Publisher, John Macrone: some hitherto Unpublished Letters, ONE OF 50 COPIES PRINTED BY WALTER DEXTER FOR HIS FRIENDS, *facsimile, with presentation inscription in the editor's hand, dark-green half morocco, t.e.g., original stiff wrapper preserved, large* 8*vo,* 1931; Dickens to his oldest Friend: the Letters of a Lifetime from Charles Dickens to Thomas Beard, edited by Walter Dexter, *limited to 500 copies, with presentation inscription in the editor's hand, facsimiles, original buckram, t.e.g.,* 8*vo,* 1932; Charles Dickens's Letters to Charles Lever, edited by Flora V. Livingston, *original cloth,* 8*vo, Cambridge,* 1933; Dickens's Correspondence with John Hullah, hitherto Unpublished. From the Collection of Count de Suzannet, ONE OF 30 COPIES PRINTED BY WALTER DEXTER FOR HIS FRIENDS, *with presentation inscription in the editor's hand, facsimile, dark-green half morocco, t.e.g., large* 8*vo,* 1933; Dickens's First Publisher: Correspondence with John Macrone, ONE OF 50 COPIES PRIVATFLY PRINTED BY WALTER DEXTER, *with presentation inscription in the editor's hand, facsimile, dark-green half morocco, t.e.g., original stiff wrapper preserved, large* 8*vo,* 1934—Mr. and Mrs. Dickens, His Letters to Her, with a Foreword by their daughter Kate Perugini and Notes, Appendices, etc., by Walter Dexter, *2 portraits, original cloth,* 8*vo,* 1935; Charles Dickens to John Leech: Correspondence now first published, ONE OF 20 COPIES PRIVATELY PRINTED BY WALTER DEXTER, *with presentation inscription in the editor's hand, illustrations, half parchment, t.e.g., original wrapper preserved,* 8*vo,* 1938; and three others; *sold as a collection, not subject to return*   (21)

COLLECTED EDITIONS

140   DICKENS (CHARLES) WORKS, vol. 1-14 and 18-22, *Library Edition, engraved vignette titles, original cloth*   *8vo   Chapman & Hall*, 1858-59

** PRESENTATION COPY, INSCRIBED BY THE AUTHOR on a sheet of Tavistock House headed notepaper inserted in vol. 1 of Pickwick Papers: "Tenth November, 1859 To Peter Cunningham This set of my Library Edition, in remembrance of an old engagement between us. Charles Dickens."

141   Dickens (Charles) Works, 42 vol., *Household Edition, engraved portrait of Dickens, engraved frontispieces after F. O. C. Darley and John Gilbert, original cloth gilt*   *8vo   New York, Sheldon & Co.*, 1864-66

142   DICKENS (CHARLES) [WORKS], 23 vol., NONESUCH PRESS EDITION, *plates and other illustrations after R. Seymour, Hablot K. Browne, George Cruikshank and others, original buckram of various colours, t.e.g., with the original steel plate by Hablot K. Browne, chromium-plated, for "Before the Prison Tribunal" from "A Tale of Two. Cities", in a uniform buckram case, also* Retrospectus and Prospectus, the Nonesuch Dickens, *illustrations, original cloth,* and [Meynell (Francis)] A Note on the Format, the Nonesuch Dickens, *original wrapper*   *8vo* 1937-38

DICKENSIANA, BIOGRAPHY AND CRITICISM

143   Carlyle (Thomas) Chartism, *second edition, original cloth, bookplate of Charles Dickens, original cloth, 8vo, 1840*—Menken (Adah Isaacs) Infelicia [dedicated to Dickens], FIRST EDITION, *portrait of the authoress and facsimile of a letter from Dickens to her, head and tailpieces, olive morocco gilt, t.e.g., original cloth, upper cover and back preserved, sm. 8vo, 1869*—Townshend (Chauncy Hare) Religious Opinions . . . published as directed in his Will, by his Literary Executor [Charles Dickens], *olive morocco gilt, t.e.g., 8vo, 1869*—Andersen (Hans Christian) Bilderbuch ohne Bilder. Ein Besuch bei Dickens. Ragaz. Skagen. Silkeborg [In Spanien], 2 vol. in one, *half calf gilt, worn, sm. 8vo, Leipzig, L. Wiedemann, n.d.*   (4)

144   Catalogue of the beautiful Collection of Modern Pictures, Water-Colour Drawings, and Objects of Art, of Charles Dickens deceased . . . which will be sold by Auction, by Messrs. Christie, Manson & Woods . . . on Saturday, July 9, 1870, *priced, modern half vellum*   *8vo* 1870

DICKENSIANA, BIOGRAPHY AND CRITICISM

145   Forster (John) The Life of Charles Dickens, 3 vol., FIRST EDITION, *3 portraits, original cloth,* 8*vo,* 1872-74, with another edition, edited and annotated by J. W. Ț. Ley, *portrait and other illustrations, original cloth, large* 8*vo,* 1928—Stanley (Arthur Penrhyn, *Dean of Westminster*) Sermon preached . . . in Westminster Abbey, June 19, 1870 . . . being the Sunday following the Funeral of Charles Dickens, *half parchment, original wrapper preserved,* 8*vo,* 1870—Mackenzie (R. Shelton) Life of Charles Dickens, *portrait and facsimile, original cloth,* 8*vo, Philadelphia,* 1870—Kent (Charles) Charles Dickens as a Reader, *original cloth,* 8*vo,* 1872—Edmund Yates: his Recollections and Experiences, 2 vol., *2 portraits, original cloth,* 8*vo,* 1884—Pemberton (T. Edgar) Charles Dickens and the Stage, *3 plates, original cloth,* 8*vo,* 1888—Kitton (Fred G.) Dickensiana, *portrait, original cloth,* 8*vo,* 1886; Charles Dickens, his Life, Writings, and Personality, *plates, original cloth,* 8*vo,* 1902—Gissing (George) Charles Dickens, a Critical Study, FIRST EDITION, *original cloth,* 8*vo,* 1898—Fitzgerald (Percy) The Life of Charles Dickens as revealed in his Writings, 2 vol., *2 portraits and 2 facsimiles, original cloth,* 8*vo,* 1905; Memories of Charles Dickens, *plates, original cloth, large* 8*vo,* 1913—Chesterton (G. K.) Charles Dickens, FIRST EDITION, *2 portraits, original cloth,* 8*vo,* 1906—Swinburne (Algernon Charles) Charles Dickens, FIRST EDITION, *original cloth,* 8*vo,* 1913—Matz (B. W.) Dickensian Inns and Taverns, *illustrations, original cloth,* 8*vo,* 1922; The Inns and Taverns of "Pickwick", *illustrations, original cloth,* 8*vo,* [1922]—Dexter (Walter) The Kent of Dickens, *frontispiece, Presentation Copy, inscribed by the author, original cloth,* 8*vo,* 1924; The England of Dickens, *plates, Presentation Copy, inscribed by the author, original cloth,* 8*vo,* 1925; Days in Dickensland, *plates, Presentation Copy, inscribed by the author, original cloth,* 8*vo,* 1933—Dickens to his Oldest Friend: the Letters of a Lifetime from Charles Dickens to Thomas Beard, edited by Walter Dexter, *limited to 500 copies, original buckram, t.e.g.,* 8*vo,* 1932—Maurois (André) Un Essai sur Dickens, ONE OF 19 COPIES ON OR TURNER, *original wrapper, uncut, in slip-case,* 8*vo, Paris,* 1927—Delattre (Floris) Dickens et la France, *half vellum, t.e.g., original wrapper preserved,* 8*vo, Paris,* 1927—Quiller-Couch (*Sir* Arthur) Charles Dickens and other Victorians, *original cloth,* 8*vo, Cambridge,* 1925—Straus (Ralph) Dickens: a Portrait in Pencil, *plates, original cloth,* 8*vo,* 1928—Philip (Alex J.) A Dickens Dictionary, *portrait, original cloth, 4to, Gravesend,* 1928—Dickens (*Sir* Henry F.) Memories of my Father, *plates, original cloth, loosely inserted are 2 A.Ls.s. from Sir Henry Dickens to Walter Dexter and 3 A.Ls.s. from Lady Dickens to the Comte de Suzannet, original cloth,* 8*vo,* 1928; The Recollections of Sir Henry Dickens, K.C., *plates, original cloth,* 8*vo,* 1934—Sitwell (*Sir* Osbert) Dickens, SPECIAL EDITION, LIMITED TO 110 COPIES, SIGNED BY THE AUTHOR, *original decorated boards, buckram back,* 8*vo,* 1932—Leacock (Stephen) Charles Dickens, his Life and Work, *original cloth,* 8*vo,* 1933—Storey (Gladys) Dickens and Daughter, *plates, original cloth,* 8*vo,* 1939—Lemonnier (Léon) Dickens, *plates, half vellum, t.e.g., original wrapper preserved,* 8*vo, Paris,* 1946—Pope-Hennessy (*Dame* Una) Charles Dickens, 1812-1870, *plates, original cloth, with dust-wrapper,* 8*vo,* 1945—Pearson (Hesketh) Dickens, his Character, Comedy, and Career, *plates, original cloth, with dust-wrapper,* 8*vo,* 1949—Johnson (Edgar) Charles Dickens, his Tragedy and Triumph, 2 vol., *plates, original cloth, with dust-wrappers,* 8*vo,* 1953; and others; *the lot sold not subject to return*   (*about* 110)

DICKENSIANA, BIOGRAPHY AND CRITICISM

146   Forster (John) The Life of Charles Dickens, *with 500 portraits, facsimiles and other illustrations collected, arranged and annotated by B. W. Matz, 2 vol., Memorial Edition, green half morocco gilt, t.e.g., large 8vo, 1911*—[Hotten (John Camden)] Charles Dickens, the Story of his Life, *illustrations, brown morocco gilt, t.e.g., 8vo, J. C. Hotten, n.d.* [1870]—Marzials (Frank T.) Life of Charles Dickens, EXTRA-ILLUSTRATED *by the insertion of plates from the novels by H. K. Browne and G. Cruikshank, upper covers of the monthly parts, etc., brown morocco gilt, t.e.g., 8vo, 1887*—Sala (George Augustus) Charles Dickens, *brown morocco gilt, t.e.g., original wrapper and advertisements preserved, sm. 8vo, Routledge, n.d.*—Fitzgerald (Percy) The History of Pickwick, *brown morocco gilt, t.e.g., original cloth upper cover and back preserved, 8vo, 1891*—The Best of all Good Company. Edited by Blanchard Gerald. A Day with Charles Dickens, *brown morocco gilt, original wrapper preserved, large 8vo, 1871*; and five others   (12)

147   GAD'S HILL GAZETTE (THE), edited by H. F. Dickens, for January 6th, 1866, and February 3rd, 1866, *3 pages and 4 pages respectively, 8vo, 2 columns, each with the Dickens crest in blue at the head of the first page, unbound, as issued, loosely inserted in a specially prepared cardboard folder lettered on upper cover*   (2)

**   This little weekly newspaper was written, edited and printed by Charles Dickens' sixth son, Henry Fielding Dickens (1849-1933) when a boy. Each number contained reports of the preceding week's happenings at Gad's Hill and in the surrounding neighbourhood. For a full account of its inception and progress see *The Recollections of Sir Henry Dickens, K.C.*, 1934, pp. 21-24.

VERY RARE. A few odd numbers have appeared in the sale room during the present century, the last being in 1925.

147A   GAD'S HILL GAZETTE (THE), edited by H. F. Dickens, PROOF COPY OF THE NUMBER FOR 30 DECEMBER 1865, CORRECTED IN THE HAND OF H. F. DICKENS, 4 pages, *8vo, outer margins frayed and repaired, slightly worn and neatly strengthened in folds, unbound, loosely inserted in a specially prepared cardboard folder lettered on upper cover*

**   This issue describes the serious railway accident at Staplehurst on 9 June 1865 in which Dickens was involved when returning (with Ellen Ternan) from a short holiday in Paris.

148   Gadshill Place. Higham, near Rochester, Kent. A Very Valuable and Beautiful Freehold Property known as "Gadshill Place", for many years the favorite Abode of Charles Dickens . . . which will be sold by Auction, by Messrs. Norton, Trist, Watney & Co., at the Mart, Tokenhouse Yard, near the Bank of England, on Friday, 5th August, 1870, *sale catalogue, 2 coloured lithographic views, 2 folding coloured lithographic plans, modern half vellum, original pictorial wrapper preserved   folio   1870*

DICKENSIANA, BIOGRAPHY AND CRITICISM

149   Goldsmith (Oliver) The Vicar of Wakefield, *illustrations by William Mulready, original green morocco gilt, g.e., rebacked, the original back laid down, bookplate of Sir John Martin-Harvey; sold as an association copy, not subject to return*

sm. 4to   J. van Voorst, 1843

⁎⁎ PRESENTED BY JOHN FORSTER TO GEORGINA HOGARTH, the title inscribed by him "Georgina Hogarth 22ᵈ January 1843."

150   Kitton (Frederic G.) Charles Dickens by Pen and Pencil and a Supplement to Charles Dickens by Pen and Pencil, 2 vol., *portraits, plates and facsimiles, mostly on India Paper, a few coloured, illustrations in the text, maroon morocco gilt, panelled sides and backs, t.e.g., the paper upper covers of the original parts preserved folio* 1890

⁎⁎ Loosely inserted is the wash drawing by Leonardo Cattermole for the vignette at the head of p. 177, vol. 2, "Charles Dickens in one of Lord Byron's chairs."

151   [Mogridge (George)] Sergeant Bell, and his Raree-Show, FIRST EDITION, *woodcut frontispiece and woodcuts in the text by George Cruikshank and others, original brown cloth, borders in blind, gilt designs on upper cover and back* [Cohn, 569]

sm. 8vo   T. Tegg, etc., 1839

⁎⁎ In August, 1836, Dickens agreed to write a children's book for Tegg to be called *Sergeant Bell and his Raree Show* for the sum of £100, but the project fell through and the work was undertaken by Mogridge instead—see *The Letters of Charles Dickens, Nonesuch Press edition,* vol. 1, pp. 77-78.

151A   [Newton (*Mrs.* Richard)] *Gillan Vase.* A Great Mystery Solved: being a Sequel to "The Mystery of Edwin Drood", 3 vol., *original slate-grey cloth, blocked in blind*

8vo Remington & Co., 1878

152   [Penn (Richard, *F.R.S.*)] Maxims and Hints for an Angler, and Miseries of Fishing . . . to which are added Maxims and Hints for a Chess Player, FIRST EDITION, *lithographic plates on India Paper and vignettes by Robert Seymour, calf gilt, t.e.g., by Riviere, bookplate of Edward Thomas McGowan* [*Westwood & Satchell, p.* 168]

sm. 8vo J. Murray, 1833

⁎⁎ In Seymour's illustrations to this book, *The Heiress,* 1830, and *The Book of Christmas,* 1835-36, "a portly, elderly gentleman appears, with a marked resemblance to Mr. Pickwick"—see *The Letters of Charles Dickens, The Pilgrim Edition,* vol. 1, p. 136, note 1.

DICKENSIANA, BIOGRAPHY AND CRITICISM

153   Playbill. Private Theatricals. Stage Manager, Mr. Charles Dickens. On Saturday Evening, April 27, 1833, At Seven o'clock precisely
J. & G. Nichols, Printers, Earl's Court, Cranbourn Street, Soho

** The programme consisted of an Introductory Prologue, the Opera of Clari, the favourite Interlude of the Married Bachelor and the farce of Amateurs and Actors, in all of which Dickens took a part. The performance took place at the home of Dickens' parents, 18 Bentinck Street. This playbill was reproduced in facsimile in *Charles Dickens and Maria Beadnell*, Boston, The Bibliophile Society, 1908.

154   Reynolds (George W. M.) Pickwick Abroad, FIRST EDITION, *engraved vignette title and plates by Alfred Crowquill [A. H. Forrester], and John Phillips, woodcuts by Bonner, 8 pages of advertisements dated 1843 at beginning, original blind-stamped cloth, uncut*   *8vo   For T. Tegg, etc.,* 1839

154A   Yates (Edmund) Mr. Thackeray, Mr. Yates, and the Garrick Club. The Correspondence and Facts. Stated by Edmund Yates, FIRST ISSUE, *with the misprint "Dickes" for "Dickens" in line* 15 *from the bottom on p.* 14, *green morocco gilt, g.e. by F. Bedford*   *8vo   Printed for Private Circulation,* 1859

BIBLIOGRAPHY

155   British Museum. Charles Dickens: an Excerpt from the General Catalogue of Printed Books in the British Museum, *half vellum, t.e.g.   folio   W. Clowes,* 1926

155A   Brussel (I. R.) Anglo-American First Editions, 1826-1900, 2 vol., *limited to 500 copies, plates, original marbled boards, vellum backs*
8vo   Bibliographia, Nos. IX and X, 1935-36

156   Carter (John) Binding Variants in English Publishing, 1820-1900, *limited to 500 copies, plates, original marbled boards, vellum back, Bibliographia No. VI,* 1932; More Binding Variants, *original cloth,* 1938   *8vo   (2)*

157   Carter (John) and Graham Pollard. An Enquiry into the Nature of certain Nineteenth Century Pamphlets, *4 plates, original cloth*   *8vo   1934*

BIBLIOGRAPHY

158   Chapman (R. W.) Cancels, *limited to 500 copies, facsimiles, folding plate of diagrams, original marbled boards, vellum back*   8vo   *Bibliographia No. III*, 1930

159   Cohn (Albert M.) George Cruikshank, a Catalogue Raisonné of the Work executed during the Years 1806-1877, LIMITED TO 500 COPIES, *plates, one coloured, original buckram, t.e.g.*   4to   1924

*** Loosely inserted is a brief A.L.s. from George Cruikshank to Routledge, Warne & Routledge requesting them to give the bearer 4 volumes of the "Fairy Library", *263 Hampstead Road, 5th Jan.*, [18]65.

160   De Ricci (Seymour) The Book Collector's Guide, *original cloth*
8vo   *Philadelphia, etc.*, 1921

161   Eckel (John C.) The First Editions of the Writings of Charles Dickens, LARGE PAPER, LIMITED TO 250 COPIES, *signed by the author and publishers, portrait and facsimiles, original cloth, vellum back, t.e.g.*   4to   *Chapman & Hall*, 1913

162   Eckel (John C.) The First Editions of the Writings of Charles Dickens, *second edition, facsimiles, original leather*   8vo   *New York*, 1932

163   Eckel (John C.) The First Editions of the Writings of Charles Dickens, *portrait and facsimiles, original buckram, t.e.g.*, 1913—Miller (W.) and E. H. Strange. A Centenary Bibliography of the Pickwick Papers, *illustrations, original cloth*, 8vo, 1936—Cavanagh (Cortes W.) Charles Dickens, his Life as traced by his Works. Early American Editions of the Works of Charles Dickens, by Herman Leroy Edgar and R. W. G. Vail, *portrait and facsimiles, half vellum gilt, red morocco label, t.e.g., original wrapper preserved*, 4to, *New York*, 1929—Miller (William) The Dickens Student and Collector, *Presentation Copy, inscribed by the author to the Comte de Suzannet, 2 A.Ls.s. from the former loosely inserted, original cloth*, 8vo, *Cambridge* [*Mass.*], 1946— Catalogue of an Exhibition of the Works of Charles Dickens, *blue quarter morocco, t.e.g., original wrapper preserved*, 12mo, *New York, The Grolier Club*, 1913; and five others   (10)

164   Goelet (Ogden) The Library of the late Ogden Goelet [*sale catalogue*], 2 vol., *facsimiles, priced, half vellum gilt, red morocco labels, t.e.g., original wrappers preserved*   8vo   *New York, American Art Association*, 1935

BIBLIOGRAPHY

165　Hatton (Thomas) and Arthur H. Cleaver. A Bibliography of the Periodical Works of Charles Dickens, LARGE PAPER, LIMITED TO 250 COPIES, SIGNED BY THE AUTHORS, *facsimiles, original buckram, t.e.g., with dust-wrapper*　　4to　1933

*** PRESENTATION COPY, inscribed by Thomas Hatton to the Comte de Suzannet.

166　Kern (Jerome) The Library of Jerome Kern [*sale catalogue*], 2 parts in one vol., *facsimiles, priced, half vellum gilt, brown morocco label, t.e.g., original limp boards preserved*　　4to　*New York, The Anderson Galleries, 1929*

167　Kitton (Frederic G.) Dickens and his Illustrators, *portraits and plates, original buckram, t.e.g.,* 4to, 1899—Browne (Edgar) Phiz and Dickens, *portraits, plates after H. K. Browne, several coloured, original cloth gilt, t.e.g.,* 4to, 1913—Grego (Joseph, *Editor*) Pictorial Pickwickiana: Charles Dickens and his Illustrators, 2 vol., *illustrations, original cloth gilt, t.e.g.,* 8vo, 1899　　　(4)

168　Lehmann (Frederick W.) A Charles Dickens Collection of superlative merit and equally fine First Editions of American and English Authors, the Library of the Honorable Frederick W. Lehmann, *plates and facsimiles, priced, half vellum gilt, olive morocco label, t.e.g., original wrapper preserved*
4to　*New York, American Art Association, 1930*

169　Miller (W.) and E. H. Strange. A Centenary Bibliography of the Pickwick Papers, *illustrations, Presentation Copy, inscribed by the authors to the Comte de Suzannet, green half morocco gilt, t.e.g.,* 8vo, 1936—Eckel (John C.) Prime Pickwicks in Parts . . . with a Foreword by A. Edward Newton, *limited to 440 copies, signed by the author and A. Edward Newton, illustrations, original cloth,* 8vo, New York, 1928–Osborne (E. Allen) The Facts about *A Christmas Carol,* ONE OF 55 COPIES ON HAND-MADE PAPER, *original buckram, A.L.s. from the author to the Comte de Suzannet loosely inserted,* 8vo, 1937—A Dickens Library, Exhibition Catalogue of the Sawyer Collection of the Works of Charles Dickens, *Presentation Copy, inscribed by J. E. S. Sawyer to the Comte de Suzannet, portrait and facsimiles, original boards,* 4to, *Privately Printed,* 1936—The Dickens Exhibition held at the Memorial Hall, London . . . Catalogue of Exhibits, compiled and edited by F. G. Kitton, *half vellum gilt, blue morocco label, t.e.g., original wrapper preserved, sm.* 4to, 1903—Catalogue of a Pickwick Exhibition held at the Dickens House, 48, Doughty Street, London . . . arranged by William Miller, *Presentation Copy, inscribed by William Miller to the Comte de Suzannet, facsimiles, half vellum gilt, t.e.g., original wrapper preserved,* 8vo, 1936—Victoria and Albert Museum Guides. Dickens Exhibition, *half vellum gilt, t.e.g., original wrapper preserved,* 8vo, 1912—Catalogue of the Library of Charles Dickens from Gadshill . . . Catalogue of his Pictures and Objects of Art . . . Catalogue of the Library of W. M. Thackeray . . . edited by J. H. Stonehouse, *limited to 275 copies, signed by the editor, plates, original cloth,* 8vo, 1935—Darton (F. J. Harvey) Dickens: Positively the First Appearance, *plates, original boards, parchment back,* 8vo, *Argonaut Press,* 1933; and another　(10)

BIBLIOGRAPHY

170   Muir (Percy H.) Points, 1874-1930; Points, *Second Series*, 1866-1934, 2 vol., *limited to 500 and 750 copies respectively, plates and facsimiles, original marbled boards, vellum backs*   8vo   Bibliographia, Nos. V and VIII, 1931-34

171   Parrish (M. L.) Victorian Lady Novelists: George Eliot, Mrs. Gaskell, the Brontë Sisters, LIMITED TO 150 COPIES, *plates and facsimiles, original cloth, t.e.g.*
4to   1933

172   Parrish (M. L.) Wilkie Collins and Charles Reade, LIMITED TO 150 COPIES, *plates and facsimiles, original cloth, t.e.g., with dust-wrapper*   4to   1940

173   Partington (Wilfred) Thomas J. Wise in the Original Cloth . . . with an Appendix by George Bernard Shaw, *plates, original cloth, with dust-wrapper*
8vo   1946

174   Rosenbach (A. S. W.) A Catalogue of the Writings of Charles Dickens in the Library of Harry Elkins Widener, *original cloth, t.e.g., bookplate of Beverly Chew*
4to   Philadelphia, Privately Printed, 1918

175   Rosenbach (A. S. W.) A Book Hunter's Holiday, LIMITED EDITION, SIGNED BY THE AUTHOR, PRESENTATION COPY, INSCRIBED BY THE AUTHOR TO THE COMTE DE SUZANNET, *plates and facsimiles, original cloth*   8vo   Boston, 1936

176   Rosenbach (A. S. W.) The Unpublishable Memoirs, *frontispiece, original cloth*, 1924; Books and Bidders, *plates, original cloth, Boston*, 1927—To Doctor R. Essays here collected and published in honor of the Seventieth Birthday of Dr. A. S. W. Rosenbach, July 22, 1946, *plates, original cloth, Philadelphia*, 1946   8vo   (3)

177   Sadleir (Michael) Trollope, a Bibliography, LIMITED TO 500 COPIES, *plates and facsimiles, original cloth, t.e.g.*   8vo   1928

178   Sadleir (Michael) The Evolution of Publishers' Binding Styles, 1770-1900, *limited to 500 copies, plates, original marbled boards, vellum backs*
8vo   Bibliographia, No. I, 1930

BIBLIOGRAPHY

179   Sale Catalogues. The Renowned Collection of the Works of Charles Dickens formed by Thomas Hatton, *facsimiles, priced, New York, The American Art Galleries,* 1927, *bound with* First Editions, Letters and MSS. of Barrie, Dickens, Galsworthy, Shaw, Trollope and others from the Library of Thomas Hatton, *facsimiles, not priced, New York, American Art Association, 1929, half vellum gilt, red morocco label, t.e.g., original wrappers preserved, 8vo*—Catalogue of the Important Collections mainly of the Writings of Charles Dickens . . . forming part of the Library of Thomas Hatton, *plates, partly priced, half vellum, t.e.g., original wrapper preserved, 8vo, Sotheby,* 1931— The Library of George B. Ulizio, part I (First Editions of English Authors), *facsimiles, not priced, half vellum gilt, brown morocco label, t.e.g., original wrapper preserved, 4to, New York, American Art Association,* 1931—The Works of Charles Dickens . . . Collection formed by Mr. and Mrs. Edward C. Daoust, *illustrations, not priced, half vellum gilt, red morocco label, t.e.g., original wrapper preserved, 8vo, id.,* 1929—The Renowned Collection of First Editions of Charles Dickens and William Makepeace Thackeray formed by George Barr McCutcheon, *facsimiles, priced, half vellum gilt, red morocco label, t.e.g., original wrapper preserved, 8vo, id.,* 1926—Rare Books, Original Drawings, Autograph Letters and Manuscripts collected by the late A. Edward Newton, part I (A-D), *plates, one coloured, priced, original boards, with dust-wrapper, 4to, New York, Park-Bernet,* 1941   (6)

180   Sawyer (Charles) and F. J. Harvey Darton. English Books, 1475-1900, a Signpost for Collectors, 2 vol., *facsimiles, original buckram, t.e.g.*   *8vo*   1927

181   Spencer (Walter T.) Forty Years in my Bookshop, *coloured and plain plates, original cloth,* 1923—Arnold (William Harris) Ventures in Book Collecting, *portraits and facsimiles, original boards, cloth back, New York,* 1923—Storm (Colton) and Howard Peckham. Invitation to Book Collecting, *plates, original cloth, with dust-wrapper, id.,* 1947—Ellis (S. M.) William Harrison Ainsworth and his Friends, 2 vol., *plates, original cloth, t.e.g.,* 1911; and four others   *8vo*   (9)

182   Suzannet (*Le Comte* Alain de) Catalogue des Manuscrits, Livres Imprimés et Lettres Autographes composant la Bibliothèque de la Petite Chardière. Oeuvres de Charles Dickens, LIMITED TO 15 COPIES, *dark-green half morocco, t.e.g.*
8vo   Lausanne, 1934

183   Thomson (David Croal) Life and Labours of Hablôt Knight Browne, "Phiz", LIMITED TO 200 COPIES, INITIALLED BY THE AUTHOR, *portrait, plates, illustrations in the text on India Paper, green half morocco gilt, panelled back, t.e.g.*
large 4to   Chapman & Hall, 1884

ORIGINAL DRAWINGS

184   BROWNE (HABLOT K., *Phiz*) THE ORIGINAL PENCIL AND WASH DRAWING, "DISCOVERY OF JINGLE IN THE FLEET", FOR THE PLATE AT P. 453 OF THE FIRST EDITION OF "PICKWICK PAPERS", *unsigned* (6⅝*in. by* 5$\frac{1}{16}$*in.*), *mounted*   [1837]

**   The plate is in reverse and is approximately the same size as the drawing.

[*See* ILLUSTRATION]

Lot 184

ORIGINAL DRAWINGS

185   BROWNE (HABLOT K., *Phiz*) FIVE ORIGINAL PENCIL AND WASH DRAWINGS
FOR THE FIRST EDITION OF "MARTIN CHUZZLEWIT", *unsigned, with a copy of the*
published plate after each drawing, in reverse and approximately the same size, mounted
in an oblong folio vol., brown morocco gilt, gilt inside borders, brown watered silk
linings, t.e.g.   [1843-44]

$*_*^*$ The drawings comprise:
    (1)   Mr. Jonas exhibits his presence of mind (*p.* 485; $7\frac{7}{16}$*in. by* $4\frac{7}{8}$*in.*)
    (2)   Truth prevails and Virtue is triumphant (*p.* 120; 7*in. by* $4\frac{5}{8}$*in.*)
    (3)   Mr. Moddle is both particular and peculiar in his attentions (*p.* 384;
        $6\frac{7}{8}$*in. by* $4\frac{9}{16}$*in.*)
    (4)   Balm for the wounded orphan (*p.* 296; $6\frac{7}{8}$*in. by* $4\frac{9}{16}$*in.*)
    (5)   Mr. Jefferson Brick proposes an appropriate sentiment (*p.* 199;
        $7\frac{1}{8}$*in. by* $4\frac{15}{16}$*in.*)

[*See* ILLUSTRATION]

Lot 185

Lot 186 (See page 214)

after the 1st Verse of "How beautiful
at Eventide"—

The gay morning breaks,
The mists roll away,
all nature awakes
To the glorious day.
In my heart alone
Dark shadows remain,
The peace it has known,
It can never regain.

My fair home is no longer mine
From its roof-tree I'm driven away,
alas! who will tend the old Vine
Which I planted in infancy's day!
The garden, the beautiful flowers,
The oak with its branches on high,
Dear friends of my happiest hours
among thee, I once hoped to die.
The brier, the moss, and the bramble,
Upon the green paths will run wild;
The paths where I once used to ramble
an innocent, light hearted child!

Lot 195 (See page 225)

ORIGINAL DRAWINGS

186 BROWNE (HABLOT K., *Phiz*) A COMPLETE SET OF FORTY-TWO DRAWINGS FOR "LITTLE DORRIT", *mostly for the first edition, and including an* ALTERNATIVE VERSION OF ONE WHICH WAS APPARENTLY NEVER USED, SOME DIFFERING IN DETAILS FROM THE PUBLISHED PLATES, *all in reverse of the published plates except where otherwise stated and approximately the same size, mounted in four folio vol., black straight-grained morocco gilt, g.e., by Riviere*   [1855-57]

** The drawings comprise:

(1) The design for the upper cover of the wrapper, *pencil and pen-and-ink, signed Phiz and differing in a number of details from the published version* (8*in.* by 5$\frac{5}{16}$*in.*)

(2) The frontispiece, *pencil and wash, unsigned* (6$\frac{7}{16}$*in.* by 4$\frac{1}{2}$*in.*)

(3) The vignette title, *pencil and wash, unsigned* (6$\frac{11}{16}$*in.* by 4$\frac{1}{4}$*in.*)

(4) The Birds in the Cage (*p.* 2), *charcoal, unsigned* (4$\frac{7}{8}$*in.* by 3$\frac{9}{16}$*in.*)

(5) Under the Microscope (*p.* 20), *pencil and wash, unsigned* (5$\frac{1}{2}$*in.* by 4$\frac{1}{8}$*in.*)

(6) Mr. Flintwinch mediates as a friend of the Family (*p.* 37), *pencil and wash, unsigned* (4$\frac{7}{8}$*in.* by 4$\frac{1}{16}$*in.*)

(7) The Room with the Portrait (*p.* 40), *charcoal, unsigned* (4$\frac{15}{16}$*in.* by 3$\frac{3}{4}$*in.*)

(8) Little Mother (*p.* 73), *pencil and wash, unsigned* (6$\frac{13}{16}$*in.* by 4$\frac{3}{8}$*in.*)

(9) Making off (*p.* 96), *charcoal, unsigned* (6$\frac{3}{16}$*in.* by 3$\frac{13}{16}$*in.*)

(10) Mr. F.'s Aunt is conducted into retirement (*p.* 114), *pencil and wash, unsigned, differing in several details from the published plate* (5$\frac{7}{16}$*in.* by 4$\frac{7}{16}$*in.*)

(11) Little Dorrit's Party (*p.* 128), *charcoal, unsigned, facing the same way as the plate from which it differs in minor details* (7*in.* by 4*in.*)

(12) Mr. and Mrs. Flintwinch (*p.* 134), *pencil and wash, unsigned, differing considerably from the published plate* (5*in.* by 4$\frac{5}{16}$*in.*)

(13) The Ferry (*p.* 146), *pencil and wash, unsigned* (6$\frac{7}{16}$*in.* by 4$\frac{1}{16}$*in.*)

(14) The Brothers (*p.* 161), *pencil and wash, signed Phiz, facing the same way as the published plate, with pencil note on the mount reading "Not the original drawing but a copy made by H.K.B. from his etching"* (6$\frac{1}{8}$*in.* by 4$\frac{1}{2}$ *in.*)

(15) Miss Dorrit and Little Dorrit (*p.* 172), *pencil, unsigned, differing considerably from the published plate* (7$\frac{1}{4}$*in.* by 4$\frac{3}{4}$*in.*)

(16) Visitors at the Works (*p.* 195), *charcoal, unsigned, differing in a few minor details from the published plate* (6$\frac{3}{8}$*in.* by 3$\frac{13}{16}$*in.*)

(17) The Story of the Princess (*p.* 215), *pencil and wash, unsigned, differing in several details from the published plate* (5$\frac{5}{16}$*in.* by 4$\frac{5}{16}$*in.*)

(18) Five and Twenty (*p.* 243), *pencil and wash, signed Phiz, facing the same way as the published plate, with pencil note on the mount reading "not the original drawing but copied from his etching by H.K.B."* (6$\frac{15}{16}$*in.* by 4$\frac{5}{16}$*in.*)

(19) Floating away (*p.* 250), *charcoal, unsigned* (6$\frac{7}{8}$*in.* by 3$\frac{11}{16}$*in.*)

ORIGINAL DRAWINGS

(20) Mr. Flintwinch has a mild attack of irritability (*p.* 257), *charcoal and wash unsigned* (6$\frac{13}{16}$*in. by* 5$\frac{1}{16}$*in.*)

(21) Another version of the preceding, APPARENTLY NEVER USED, *charcoal, unsigned* (5$\frac{5}{8}$*in. by* 3$\frac{3}{4}$*in.*)

(22) The Pensioner—Entertainment (*p.* 277), *pencil wash, unsigned* (6$\frac{11}{16}$*in. by* 4$\frac{15}{16}$*in.*)

(23) Society expresses its views on a question of Marriage (*p.* 290), *pencil and wash, unsigned* (5$\frac{5}{8}$*in. by* 4$\frac{5}{8}$*in.*)

(24) The Marshalsea becomes an Orphan (*p.* 318), *pencil and wash, unsigned, differing in one or two details from the published plate* (8$\frac{1}{8}$*in. by* 4$\frac{7}{16}$*in.*)

(25) The Travellers (*p.* 325), *pencil and wash, unsigned* (6$\frac{15}{16}$*in. by* 4$\frac{3}{8}$*in.*)

(26) The family dignity is affronted (*p.* 344), *pencil and wash, signed Phiz, facing the same way as the published plate, with pencil note on the mount reading "Not the original drawing but copied from his etching by H.K.B."* (7$\frac{1}{16}$*in. by* 4$\frac{1}{2}$*in.*)

(27) Instinct stronger than training (*p.* 369), *pencil and wash, unsigned* (6$\frac{15}{16}$*in. by* 4$\frac{7}{16}$*in.*)

(28) Mr. Sparkler under a reverse of circumstances (*p.* 373), *pencil and wash, unsigned* (6$\frac{15}{16}$*in. by* 4$\frac{7}{16}$*in.*)

(29) Rigour of Mr. F.'s Aunt (*p.* 402), *pencil and wash, unsigned* (6$\frac{5}{8}$*in. by* 4$\frac{5}{16}$*in.*)

(30) Mr. Flintwinch receives the embrace of friendship (*p.* 410), *pencil and wash, unsigned* (6$\frac{1}{16}$*in. by* 4$\frac{7}{16}$*in.*)

(31) The Patriotic Conference (*p.* 419), *pencil and wash, unsigned, differing in one or two details from the published plate* (6$\frac{9}{16}$*in. by* 4$\frac{5}{16}$*in.*)

(32) Mr. Baptist is supposed to have seen something (*p.* 432), *pencil and wash, unsigned* (5$\frac{15}{16}$*in. by* 4$\frac{3}{16}$*in.*)

(33) Missing and Dreaming (*p.* 474), *pencil and wash, unsigned* (6$\frac{13}{16}$*in. by* 4$\frac{5}{16}$*in.*)

(34) Reception of an old friend (*p.* 476), *pencil and wash, unsigned, differing in several minor details from the published plate* (6$\frac{7}{16}$*in. by* 4$\frac{1}{4}$*in.*)

(35) An unexpected After Dinner Speech (*p.* 489), *pencil and wash, unsigned* (7$\frac{1}{16}$*in. by* 4$\frac{1}{4}$*in.*)

(36) The Night (*p.* 492), *pencil and wash, unsigned* (6$\frac{7}{16}$*in. by* 4$\frac{1}{8}$*in.*)

(37) Flora's tour of inspection (*p.* 519), *pencil and wash, unsigned, differing in several details from the published plate* (6$\frac{3}{16}$*in. by* 4$\frac{1}{2}$*in.*)

(38) Mr. Merdle a borrower (*p.* 530), *pencil and wash, signed Phiz, facing the same way as the published plate from which it differs in several details, with pencil note on the mount reading "not the original drawing but a copy made by H.K.B. from his etching"* (6$\frac{7}{8}$*in. by* 4$\frac{5}{8}$*in.*)

(39) At Mr. John Chivery's tea-table (*p.* 548), *pencil and wash, signed Phiz, facing the same way as the published plate, from which it differs in several details, with pencil note on the mount reading* (5$\frac{1}{2}$*in. by* 4$\frac{5}{16}$*in.*)

ORIGINAL DRAWINGS

(40) In the old room (*p*. 562), *pencil, wash and charcoal, unsigned, differing in two or three details from the published plate* (6⅝*in. by* 4 7/16*in.*)

(41) Damocles (*p*. 595), *charcoal and wash, unsigned, differing in two or three details from the published plate* (6½*in. by* 4*in.*)

(42) The Third Volume of the Registers (*p*. 624), *pencil and wash, unsigned, differing in several minor details from the published plate* (6 11/16 *in. by* 4 3/16 *in.*)

Loosely inserted in vol. 1 is a brief A.L.s. from Hablot K. Browne to an unnamed correspondent

99 Ladbroke Grove Road
May 15. [18]78

Dear Sir,
    The Sketches which you have are the originals from which I executed my etchings for "Little Dorritt" [*sic*]

Yrs. faithfully
H. K. Browne

[*See* ILLUSTRATION]

ORIGINAL DRAWINGS

187   BROWNE (HABLOT K., *Phiz*) FOUR CIRCULAR PENCIL AND WATER-COLOUR DRAWINGS BY HIM OF HIS ILLUSTRATIONS TO "PICKWICK PAPERS", namely, the title-page vignette (Mr. Weller senior immersing Mr. Stiggins' head in the horse trough), "The red-nosed man discourseth", "Mary and the fat boy" and "Mr. Weller and his friends drinking to Mr. Pell", *all facing the same way as the published plates and signed Phiz* (*approximately 5in. in diameter*)

⁂   F. W. Cosens, a patron of the Arts, commissioned Phiz, who was in financial difficulties at the time, to make a series of coloured illustrations to Dickens' works and these were commenced early in 1866. They were copied from the published plates and each set was accompanied by a written guarantee by the artist stating that they were THE ONLY COLOURED ILLUSTRATIONS IN EXISTENCE—see David Croal Thomson, *The Life and Labours of Hablot Knight Browne*, 1884, p. 78.

187A   [*Clarke (J. Clayton)*] *Kyd.* TWO ORIGINAL PEN-&-INK AND WATER-COLOUR DRAWINGS: "The first meeting of Dick Swiveller with the Marchioness" (11¼ by 8¹⁵⁄₁₆ ins.) and "Betsy Prig declares she believes there is no such person as Mrs. 'Arris" (11¾ by 8¾ ins.), *both signed Kyd*

188   LEECH (JOHN) ORIGINAL PEN-AND-INK DRAWING for one of the series of 12 humorous coloured lithographs entitled "The Rising Generation", published by Punch Office, *c.* 1848, depicting a small boy standing with his back to the fire while his father looks down at him indignantly, *unsigned, mounted* (5⅞in. by 4¹¹⁄₁₆in.), *with a copy of the coloured lithograph*

⁂   The caption beneath the drawing reads: "Juvenile. I tell you what it is governor, the sooner we come to some understanding the better. You cant expect me to be always at home and if you dont like the way I go on why I must have chambers and so much a week".

This series of lithographs was praised by Dickens—see Forster's *Life*, original edition, 1872-74, vol. 2, pp. 384-388.

189   PALMER (SAMUEL) AN ORIGINAL PENCIL DRAWING OF THE ROMAN CAMPAGNA FOR THE FIRST EDITION OF "PICTURES FROM ITALY", which was evidently engraved on wood but did not appear in the book, *unsigned* (4⁹⁄₁₆in. by 3⅛in.), *mounted*   [1846]

⁂   With Palmer's autograph instructions to the engraver in pencil beneath:

"With respect to their darkness & gradation the tender clouds have exactly the appearance desired.

"This drawing differs from the block in several of its details: but is lent for reference as giving the general gradations of depth from foreground to distance. It is requested that great care be taken of it & that it be returned with the proof."

END OF FIRST DAY'S SALE

SECOND DAY'S SALE:

Tuesday, 23rd November, 1971

AT ELEVEN O'CLOCK PRECISELY

AUTOGRAPH LETTERS OF CHARLES DICKENS

190   A.L.s. to "his oldest friend", Thomas Beard, *1 page, 8vo, 70 Margaret Street Cavendish Square, Saturday February 4th:* [1832], inviting him to "join in a friendly quadrille" in celebration of his (Dickens's) birthday on 8 (should be 7) February, *conjugate leaf, endorsed*

** THIS IS THE THIRD EARLIEST LETTER OF DICKENS KNOWN TO THE EDITORS OF THE PILGRIM EDITION OF THE LETTERS. It is also the only one from this address, "perhaps one of the many temporary lodgings John Dickens took in his efforts to escape his creditors".

Thomas Beard (1807-91) recommended Dickens to his own employers on the *Morning Chronicle*, was Dickens's best man, godfather to his eldest son, life-long friend, adviser and guest.

191   A.L.s. to H. G. Hartland, *4 pages, 8vo, 15 Fitzroy Street, Sunday, December 9th* [*1832*], about the employment (including as poll clerk at Charles Tennyson's election) he could have given Hartland on *The Mirror of Parliament* had he known his address, and promising him a post on the staff of the journal after the commencement of the new session, *some stains*

** This letter shows that Dickens's duties at *The Mirror* already involved more than just reporting parliamentary debates.

192   A.L.s. to Richard Earle, private secretary to Edward Stanley, Secretary of State for Ireland, *4 pages, 8vo, 18 Bentinck Street, Cavendish Square, Thursday June 6th* [*1833*], soliciting a position as a shorthand writer in his periods of un-employment as a parliamentary reporter during the recess, *endorsed "Not likely to have opportunity, but shd. one occur, shd. not hesitate to recommend June 7" and "Dickens June 6. 1833 Shorthandwriting"*

Addenda

During a recent examination of some of the autograph letters of Charles Dickens, the following misreadings were noticed in the Sale Catalogue.

lot 195 (3) *For* Thursday Afternoon
             read Monday Afternoon

lot 222   *For* one could send a warm pressure of the hand
             read we could send a warm pressure of the hand

lot 224   *For* a christening ring for the Chapman's expected child (or two rings, if twins)
             read a christening mug for the Chapmans' expected child (or two mugs, if twins)

lot 245   *For* but the Frenchman can speak a very little English.
             read but the Frenchman can speak a very little English with which he helps the Englishman out of abysses and ravines of difficulty.

lot 248   The 'picture' referred to by the cataloguer is actually a mental image of Lausanne which, Dickens writes, 'rises up in my mind very often'

 ,,   *For* the reality of a stirring life
             read the reality of a striving life

lot 263   *For* in a Russian jacket
             read in a Prussian jacket

lot 272 (4) *For* the effect of seeing the ship before him
             read the effect of seeing his sons Charley and Walter going aboard the ship before him

 ,,   *For* Time has fluffed his wings
             read Time has flapped his wings

lot 272 (6) *For* Mrs. Harris's
             read Mr. Harris's

 ,,   ,,   *For* Who is owling!
             read Who is a owling!

 ,,   ,,   *For* Howls my dear Madame? No, no, no. What are you thinking, of.
             read Howls my dear Madam? No, no, no. What are we thinking of.

lot 272 (8) *For* I have derived great gratification from what I read of yours today
             read I have derived great gratification of heart from what I have read of yours today

lot 272 (12)	*For*	my heart is so jagged and rent out of shape	
	read	my heart is so jagged and rent and out of shape	
,, (14)	*For*	Twenty Sixth July, 1858	
	read	Tuesday Sixth July, 1858	
,, (15)	*For*	that daughter of honest good –	
	read	that daughter of poor honest good – !	
,, (18)	*For*	ravin' mad with consciousness o' villany	
	read	ravin' mad with the consciousness o' willany	
,, (19)	*For*	Tuesday Twentieth April, 1859	
	read	Tuesday Nineteenth April, 1859	
,, (22)	*For*	in the Cock in Fleet Street	
	read	at the Cock in Fleet Street	
,, (26)	*For*	when I dwell in my mind over the many times	
	read	when I dwell in my mind on the many times	
,, (28)	*For*	Wednesday Thirtieth September, 1865	
	read	Wednesday Thirteenth September, 1865	
lot 282	*For*	a little record imputing that we loved one another	
	read	a little record importing that we loved one another	
lot 291	*For*	through a bright and picturesque imagination	
	read	through the aid of a bright and picturesque imagination	
lot 301	*For*	I went to the new Theatre in Long Acre	
	read	I went into the new Theatre in Long Acre	
,,	*For*	and, captivating the Count, allows a coquettishness	
	read	and, in captivating the Count, allows a coquettishness	

70 Margaret Street Cavendish Square
Saturday February 4.th

Dear Beard,

Intend keeping the anni=
versary of my Birth Day, which
occurs on Wednesday next the eighth
instant, by asking a chosen few to
join in a friendly quadrille.

If you will make one of
our family circle by seven o'Clock,
or as early as the house will allow
you, it will give us the greatest
pleasure to see you.

Believe me
Yours truly
Charles Dickens

Thomas Beard Esqre.

Lot 190

219

AUTOGRAPH LETTERS OF CHARLES DICKENS

193 ALBUM CONTAINING 21 EARLY A.LS.S. BY DICKENS TO HIS FRIEND, HENRY
WILLIAM KOLLE (? 1808-1881), bank clerk, who acted as go-between for Dickens and
his first love, Maria Beadnell, during their unhappy friendship, while Kolle successfully
courted Maria's sister, Anne; comprising all but three of Dickens's early letters to
Kolle and some of the earliest he ever wrote—BEGINNING WITH THE FOURTH LETTER
TO HAVE SURVIVED IN THE ORIGINAL—the collection contains some of Dickens's first
references to his writings and important information about his early life, his first
love affair, his career as parliamentary reporter and the beginning of his work as a
creative writer, *together with 2 A.Ls.s. by Kolle's wife giving the provenance of the
collection and a description of the letters written in the 1890s, mostly in fine condition,
neatly mounted or inlaid, two engravings, bookplates of Harry Bache Smith and
Comte Alain de Suzannet, red morocco*

THIS IS THE MOST EXTENSIVE SERIES OF EARLY LETTERS FROM DICKENS TO ANY SINGLE
CORRESPONDENT; between the date of his earliest surviving written communication
(an invitation tentatively dated 1820-1) and the last letter in the present lot (? January
1835), his other most constant correspondents were Thomas Beard (10), Thomas
Mitton (7) and Maria Beadnell (6).

(1) A.L.s. *4 pages, 8vo, North End Friday Evening* [*?April-May* 1832], about horses for their ride
on the following Sunday, one of which was possibly the model for the "immense brown horse displaying great symmetry of bone" which annoyed Mr. Pickwick and Mr. Winkle during their journey to
Dingle Dell); Kolle's "pilgrimage" to the Beadnell household (". . . I trust when the Shrine at which
you pay your devotion is once more removed you will shew yourself a little more frequently . . .");
and about his temporary lodgings (". . . The people at Cecil Street put too much water in the hashes,
lost the nutmeg grater, attended on me most miserably, dirtied the Table cloths &c &c—. . ."); he
subscribes himself "Envying you your devotions notwithstanding the pilgrimage attendant thereon
and wishing you every success and happiness . . ."
    ". . . In reply to your enquiry respecting a *sizeable poney* I have also great satisfaction in being
enabled to say that I can procure you a "oss" which I have had once or twice since I have been here.
I am a poor judge of distance but I should certainly say that your legs would be off the ground when
you are on his back. To look at the animal in question you would think (with the exception of Dog's
Meat) there was no earthly purpose to which he would be applied . . . we can mount, dismount &
ride eight or ten miles without seeing a Soul the *Peasantry* excepted . . ."
    ₊ THE SUBSCRIPTION TO THIS LETTER CONTAINS (IN DICKENS'S ENVY) THE FIRST HINT OF HIS
AFFECTION FOR MARIA BEADNELL IN HIS CORRESPONDENCE.

(2) A.L.s. *4 pages, 8vo* [*?July 1832*], apologising for failing to keep an appointment and for
mis-spelling Kolle's name ("Kollie"), MAKING WHAT IS PROBABLY HIS FIRST ACTUAL REFERENCE TO
MARIA BEADNELL IN HIS CORRESPONDENCE (". . . With my best remembrances to (?) . . .") and
mentioning his intention of terminating his employment with the *True Sun* which was failing in its
attempt to rival the *Sun* (". . . The Sun is so obscured that I intend living under the planet no longer
than Saturday Week next . . ."), *about five words slightly obscured where inlaid, partly torn up vertical
fold*
    ₊ Forster, who was for a time the paper's theatrical and literary critic, notes that Dickens
gave his "first parliamentary service" to the *True Sun*, not the *Sun*; the editors of the Pilgrim Edition
of the *Letters* assume that the pun explains Dickens's apparent mistake.

(3) A.L.s. *3 pages, 8vo, Fitzroy Street Monday Morning,* [*30 July 1832*] inviting him to join
himself and "one or two young men together for the purpose of knocking up a song or two . . .",
watermark date 1830.
    ₊ One of the other "young men" was Mr. Longhurst, possibly George Longhurst, translator
and shorthand writer or Thomas Longhurst, solicitor.

AUTOGRAPH LETTERS OF CHARLES DICKENS

(4) A.L.s. *1 page, oblong 8vo, Fitzroy Street, Tuesday Morning* [*Summer* 1832], asking him to deliver another note to Maria Beadnell (". . . I was requested in a note I received this morning to forward my answer by the same means as my first note . . .") when Kolle practised his "customary duet" (with Anne Beadnell) that afternoon, and fondly hoping that he would soon be able to return the favour, *laid down, foxed*

** THIS LETTER CONTAINS THE EARLIEST REFERENCES IN DICKENS'S SURVIVING CORRESPONDENCE TO HIS WRITTEN COMMUNICATION WITH HIS FIRST LOVE, MARIA BEADNELL, AND TO KOLLE'S PART AS GO-BETWEEN.

(5) A.L.s. *2 pages, 4to, Fitzroy Street* [*Summer 1832*], asking him the "*very great* favor" of delivering a further note to Maria Beadnell, giving his reasons for not feeling any "delicacy" in doing so (". . . I should not have written it [for I should have communicated its contents verbally] were it not that I lost the opportunity by keeping the old gentleman [*viz.* Maria's father, George Beadnell] out of the way as long as possible last night [? for Kolle's benefit] . . .") and requesting that he entreat Maria to read it only when "*quite* ALONE (of course in this sense I consider you as nobody) . . .", *integral address leaf, watermark date* 1831.

** THIS LETTER CONTAINS THE FIRST MENTION OF MARIA BEADNELL BY NAME IN DICKENS'S SURVIVING CORRESPONDENCE.

(6) A.L.s. *3 pages, 8vo, Fitzroy Street. Wednesday* [? *August 1832*], inviting him to visit him while the Dickens family was in Highgate for a fortnight (". . . The Spot we have chosen is in a very pleasant Neighbourhood, and I have discovered a green lane which looks as if nature had intended it for a Smoking place . . .") and apologising in advance for not being able to offer him a bed (". . . we are so pressed for room that I myself hang out at "*The Red Lion*" . . .")

(7) A.L.s. *3 pages, 8vo, Fitzroy Street, Thursday Morning* [20 *December* 1832], regretting that he had missed "a chat and Cigar" with him the previous evening which he had unfortunately selected for his "*annual* visit to Drury Lane", inviting Kolle to spend Christmas with him and his family, apologising for failing to return two books (". . . Our man [?himself] shall bring them this week without fail . . .") and expressing a desire to give his opinion about one Miss Evans (". . . I long to give you my opinion of that Miss Evans and to communicate some monstrously strong circumstantial Evidence to prove that she must tell the most confounded ——— As yours are "ears polite"—I shall leave your imagination and observation to supply the blank . . ."), *watermark date* 1830, *split across fold in second leaf.*

(8) A.L.s. *2 pages, 8vo, Fitzroy Street. Thursday Morning* [? *1832*], returning eighteen pence he owed, rueing his bad luck in getting "a BAD five shilling piece" in change from a cab driver, describing his cold as "about as bad as a Cold can be", but adding "I feel tolerably happy and comfortable to day, the state of the weather being so admirably adapted to dispel any gloomy ideas of which I always have a so plentiful stock . . ."

(9) A.L.s. ("this elegant Epistle") *3 pages, 8vo* (*Fitzroy Street*) *Saturday January 5th,* 1833, postponing a visit by Kolle and one of his brothers on account of the Dickens family's disorganized removal to 18 Benedict Street, *watermark date* 1830

". . . the Piano will be in one place and we in another. In addition to this, we shall be all in a bustle, and I fear should impress your Brother with a very uncomfortable idea of our domestic arrangements. Will you therefore let me hope to see you on Sunday Week when perhaps we shall be enabled to get *a friend* [presumably Anne Beadnell] of yours to meet you? . . ."

(10) A.L.s. *1 page, 4to, Bentinck Street Saturday Morning* [*2 February 1833*], enclosing an invitation (no longer present) to Kolle and both his brothers (John Henry and Charles Edward) for the 11th and making what is probably an allusion to Kolle having drunk too much (". . . I was sorry to hear you were *disLiver'd* the other night . . .), *address panel*

(11) A.L.s. *4 pages, 8vo, Bentinck Street. Monday Morning* [?15 *April* 1833] contrasting his own unhappy relations with Maria Beadnell with Kolle's success in becoming engaged to her sister Anne (". . . and although unfortunately and unhappily for myself I have no *fellow feeling* with you—no cause to sympathise with your past causes of annoyance, or your present prospects of happiness— I am not the less disposed to offer my heartfelt congratulations to you because you are, or at all events will be what I never can—happy and contented; taking present grievances as happiness

AUTOGRAPH LETTERS OF CHARLES DICKENS

compared with former difficulties and looking cheerfully and steadily forward to a bright perspective of many happy years . . .") and touching on various matters relating to their production of *Clari* (". . . The family are busy, the *Corps dramatique* are all anxiety, the scenery is all completing rapidly, the machinery is finished, the Curtain hemmed, the Orchestra complete—and the manager *grimy* . . ."), *some letters on the fourth page are slightly obscured where inlaid*

₊   Dickens's private production of J. H. Payne's opera, *Clari: or, The Maid of Milan* was performed on 27 April 1833. Dickens played Rolamo; Kolle The Nobleman.

(12) A.L.s. ("CD.") *2 pages, 8vo [?19 or 20 April 1833]*, asking him to give the enclosed fourteen shillings (no longer present)—payment for cigars—to Henry Frith Bramwell, Duke Vivaldi in *Clari* and Mr. O. P. Bustle in *Amateurs and Actors*, mentioning a rehearsal and the scenery for *Clari* and questioning Kolle about his marriage plans; he ends: "I am busy and therefore will not give you the trouble of deciphering any more of my iligant writing . . ."

(13) A.L.s. *4 pages, 8vo, Bentinck Street Tuesday Morning* [23 *April* 1833], philosophically expressing his understanding of Kolle's silence and failure to visit, and asking him if he intends to take his part in *Clari* and when he might collect the scenery Kolle was making

". . . I will not say that I have been surprised at our not hearing from or seeing you on the day you mentioned in your note or at any other time since its receipt, because of course we know from practical experience in other cases that a little flow of prosperity is an excellent cooler of former friendships, and that when other and more pleasant engagements can be formed visits—if not visits of convenience—become excessively irksome. This is everybody's way and of course therefore I attach no blame to you that it is yours also. I do not say this with any ill natured feeling or in any unkind spirit . . ."

(14) A.L.s. ("CD") *1 page, oblong 8vo, Tuesday Evg. [14 May 1833]*, requesting him to deliver a letter to Maria Beadnell *"immediately"* (See Pilgrim Edition of the *Letters*, pp. 22-23) requiring her consent to his sending a note (also formerly enclosed) to her friend Mary Anne Leigh in which he berated the latter for her "duplicity and disgusting falsehood" in pretending to be the confidante of both himself and Maria Beadnell.

(15) A.L.s. (boldly signed) *1 page, oblong small folio, Bentinck Street Thursday [16 May 1833]*, beginning "Least said soonest mended", he thanks Kolle for performing his "commission in the midst of your multifarious concerns so kindly and punctually" and asking to be allowed to trouble him with another, *laid down with integral address panel inlaid, postmarks*

(16) A.L.s. *1 page, oblong 8vo, Sunday [19 May 1833]*, enclosing a note for Maria Beadnell (". . . a very conciliatory note sans pride, sans reserve sans anything but an evident wish to be reconciled . . ."), remarking that Kolle's marriage would relieve him of the burden of similar troublesome commissions and describing the after-effects of the wedding reception (". . . if I had many friends in the habit of marrying which said friends had brothers who possessed an extensive assortment of choice hock I should be dead in no time. Yesterday I felt like a Maniac—to day my interior resembled a Lime Basket . . .") *laid down with integral address panel inlaid*

₊   Dickens was Kolle's best man.

(17) A.L.s. *3 pages, 8vo, Bentinck Street Tuesday Morning [3 December 1833]*, CONTAINING THE EARLIEST REFERENCE IN HIS SURVIVING CORRESPONDENCE TO THE FIRST OF HIS SKETCHES BY BOZ (as they were later entitled), "A Dinner at Poplar Walk", and including a statement by Dickens of his nervous anticipation at its publication, *watermark date 1832, small tear in second leaf*

". . . I . . . write . . . to beg Mrs. K's criticism of a little paper of mine (the first of a Series) in *the Monthly* (not the New Monthly) Magazine of this month I haven't a Copy to send but if the Number falls in your way, look for the Article. It is the same that you saw lying on my table but the name is transmogrified from "A Sunday out of town" to "A dinner at Poplar Walk" . . . I am so dreadfully nervous, that my hand shakes to such an extent as to prevent my writing a word legibly."

₊   The sketch appeared as "A Dinner at Poplar Walk" in the *Monthly Magazine* for December 1833; the title was later changed to "Mr. Minns and His Cousin".

Dickens published in the preface to the first cheap edition of *Pickwick* an account of dropping the manuscript of this sketch "with fear and trembling, into a dark letter-box, in a dark office, up a dark court in Fleet Street" and of buying the Number of the *Monthly Magazine* and finding his sketch "in all the glory of print".

222

AUTOGRAPH LETTERS OF CHARLES DICKENS

(18) A.L.s. *4 pages, 8vo, Bentinck Street. Tuesday Morng.* [*?10 December 1833*], explaining why he had not answered Kolle's invitation; mentioning the pirating of "A Dinner at Poplar Walk" in the weekly journal, *The Thief*; giving details of papers and series he was preparing for the *Monthly Magazine* or the *Metropolitan*; MAKING WHAT IS PROBABLY THE FIRST MENTION OF OLIVER TWIST IN HIS CORRESPONDENCE (". . . I shall cut my proposed Novel up into little Magazine Sketches . . ."); and, while describing his hectic life, alluding to a new girl friend, possibly Lucina Pocock (". . . . Business in the shape of masses of papers, plans, and prospectusses;—and pleasure in the shape of a very nice pair of black eyes,—call me to Norwood.—Of course the call is imperative and must be obeyed . . ."), *some foxing, some letters slightly obscured where inlaid*

In the last paragraph Dickens makes a delightful request to be considered as godfather to Kolle's first born: ". . . When there *is* a vacancy for a Godfathership either to a young lady or young gentleman—for I am not particular,—who can afford to have one poor Godfather will you bear me in mind? —Hint this delicately to your *Missus* . . ."

The letter ends with a reference to his nervousness as an author ("More *nervous* than ever") and with the one-word postscript "Grimy" (cf. No. II of this series).

Dickens was godfather to Kolle's first child, a son, Henry, born on 20 April 1834.

(19) A.L.s. *3 pages, 8vo, Bentinck Street. Monday Evening.* [*April* 1834], promising to let him see his sketch "The Boarding House" (". . . the Boarding House of which I am the Proprietor . . ."), mentioning his unpublished operatic burlesque "O'Thello" and writing amusingly about a lottery, *some brown spots*

". . . I think if we win we had better sacrifice the discount and take ready money—unless indeed you prefer gold bars. I see by the announcement in the different Lottery Office Windows that the lucky purchaser of a ticket may have the value "in money or freehold houses". Suppose we have £10 worth of freehold houses. Of course this will afford a small street. I'll have one side of the way, and you shall have the other. I shall improve my property by the erection of brass knockers, and patent Water Closets . . ."

(20) A.L.s. *1 page, Bentinck St. Friday Evening.* [*?Summer 1834*], promising to "be at the Balls Pond Chapel [Islington] please God on Sunday next at ½ past two precisely" and sending his "duty" to Mrs. Kolle

*** The occasion was almost certainly the christening of Kolle's son to whom Dickens became godfather.

(21) A.L.s. *3 pages, 8vo, Furnivals Inn Wednesday Morning* [*? January 1835*], explaining that work (at *The Mirror of Parliament*) prevents him from keeping to his engagement with Kolle and his wife (". . . As you know of old my excellent good-luck in small matters, I think it hardly necessary to say that *of course* I have received a summons from the office . . .") and asking that another arrangement be made (". . . If you don't do so at once *I'll* be offended . . ."), *watermark date 1832, torn up vertical fold*

AUTOGRAPH LETTERS OF CHARLES DICKENS

194   Series of 4 A.Ls.s. and 1 A.L. to his first illustrator, George Cruikshank, INCLUDING HIS THREE EARLIEST SURVIVING LETTERS TO HIM, about *Sketches by Boz* and Cruikshank's illustrations for them as described below:

(1) A.L. (in the third person) *1 page, 8vo, 13 Furnivals Inn Monday Morning* [*23 November 1835*], sending a volume of the *Monthly Magazine* containing four of his stories, promising to obtain two further volumes and suggesting that he and Macrone call on Cruikshank to conclude "the arrangement"
₊   The three volumes contained eight of Dickens's nine tales, all published in the first series of the *Sketches by Boz.*

(2) A.L.s. *2 pages, 4to, 13 Furnivals Inn Monday Afternoon* [*30 November 1835*] sending his "small secretary" [presumably his brother Fred] for an answer concerning the return of his books and Cruikshank's list of intended illustrations and frontispieces, needed so that the contents of each volume could be arranged and some copy dispatched to the printer, *three small drawings by Cruikshank of human faces and a devil*

(3) A.L.s. *2 pages, 4to, 13 Furnivals Inn. Tuesday Morning* [*8 December 1835*], asking for a note of introduction to George Chesterton, governor of Coldbath Fields Prison, because he wished to go over the prison again to remind himself of some particulars for his sketch, "A Visit to Newgate"

(4) A.L.s. *2 pages, 8vo, Furnivals Inn Monday Morning* [*?1 February 1836*] returning his portfolio, praising his illustrations for the *Sketches*, asking for time to talk over an idea relating to a now untraceable satire, and mentioning *The Village Coquettes* (". . . The opera I was busy on, when I saw you, has been accepted by [John] Braham with most flattering encomicums; and an assurance that it must succeed"), *integral address leaf*

(5) A.L.s. *2 pages, 8vo, Furnivals Inn. Monday Morning* [*28 November 1836*], about the publication of the second series of the *Sketches* and his involvement with *The Village Coquettes*

ALSO IN THIS LOT are an A.L.s. and a fragment of an A.L. by Cruikshank to Macrone about the wrapper for the *Sketches, 1½ pages, 8vo, 6 December 1836 and 15 June 1837, integral address leaves, postmarked, together with a note of their purchase in 1916*

AUTOGRAPH LETTERS OF CHARLES DICKENS

195   Series of 15 A.Ls.s. to John Pyke Hullah (1812-1884), composer, teacher of choral singing and writer on music, comprising the greater part (all but five) of Dickens's surviving letters to him about the sentimental comic opera, *The Village Coquettes*, on which they collaborated, and all but eight (including the five already mentioned) of all Dickens's letters to Hullah (for another of them see lot 298)

(1) A.L.s. *3 pages, 4to, 13 Furnivals Inn Tuesday Evening.* [*?29 December 1835*], discussing the relative merits of setting their projected opera in Venice or England (". . . . I will frankly confess that while I am at home in England, I am in Venice abroad indeed . . ."), suggesting that they have "a very grave discussion" about it, and alluding to "a little story" written but unpublished that would dramatize well, *integral address leaf, signed, tears and fraying*
 ***   Hullah had suggested that he and Dickens should collaborate in the production of an opera entitled "The Gondolier; or a Night in Venice". In the present letter Dickens argues for "the expediency of dropping the Venetian idea altogether, and making the Drama an English one"; he had his way; the result was *The Village Coquettes*.

(2) A.L.s. *3 pages, 8vo, Furnivals Inn Tuesday Evening* [*12 January 1836*], telling him that "the first scene (a long one) (of *The Village Coquettes*) is nearly complete" and that it will be finished tomorrow; on the back Dickens has written the Round and Chorus from *The Village Coquettes*, I.i., "Hail to the merry Autumn Days when yellow corn Fields shine . . .", prefaced by "[The] following is the opening affair" (*scored through*) and ending with "(The last few lines are repeated in another part of the scene)", *original tear at seal affecting one word*
 ***   In the present copy of the Round and Chorus there are three literary revisions.

(3) A.L.s. *1 page, 4to, Furnivals Inn. Thursday Afternoon. 7 oClock* [*?May 1836*], telling him of the interest shown by the singer, John Braham in *The Village Coquettes* and of the "low comedy" part [*viz*. Martin Stokes] Braham wished to have introduced into it (for John Pritt Harley), *three small tears*
 ". . . Braham . . . was *far more full* of the opera, than he ever was; speaking highly of my Works and "fame" (!) and expressing an earnest desire to be the first to introduce me to the Public as a dramatic Writer . . ."
 ***   Dickens's "fame" was probably a consequence of the better reviews of the second Number of *Pickwick*.
 John Pritt Harley, actor and singer, stage-manager and leading comedian at St. James's Theatre, played parts in Dickens's *The Village Coquettes*, *The Strange Gentleman* and *Is She His Wife?*; *The Village Coquettes* was dedicated to him.

(4) A.L.s. *3 pages, 4to, Furnivals Inn. Tuesday afternoon* [*?19 July 1836*], reporting his progress with, and concerning alterations to *The Village Coquettes* and giving as a postscript twenty lines (verse) from the songs of Lucy (Act I, Sc. i.) and of Rose ("Fair Home", Act I. Sc. ii.), *offsetting, especially at heavy, bold signature*
 ***   For the differences between the text of the verse given here and both the manuscript copy submitted to the Lord Chamberlain and the published version see the footnotes in the Pilgrim Edition of the *Letters* p. 155.

(5) A.L.s. *3 pages, 4to, 15 Furnivals Inn Tuesday Morning* [*26 July 1836*], fixing the date for the return of *The Village Coquettes*, mentioning difficulties in having it copied and incorporating an autograph transcript of a letter (signed with initials) to John Braham, in which he reports the near-completion of the piece and some early reactions to it while promising to forward it on Saturday [*viz*. 30 July]; in a postscript he indicates that Robert Hogarth was to have a part in the copying, *integral address leaf, some slight offsetting, original hole at fragment of seal, one tear*
 ". . . You will perhaps not be displeased to hear that we read the piece & tried the Music, on Saturday Evening, before a few confidential friends, literary and musical, some of whom will be called upon to express their opinion of it on its first appearance. These are not people who usually express any very strong opinion of a composition submitted to their private judgement, but they are enthusiastic in praise of the whole affair, from beginning to end. Macrone the Bookseller, purchased the copyright of the first Edition of the Piece at the termination of the first act . . ."
 ***   THE LETTER TO BRAHAM IS KNOWN ONLY FROM THIS AUTOGRAPH COPY.

(6) A.L.s. *2 pages, 8vo, Furnivals Inn Wednesday Evening* [*?10 August 1836*], imploring Hullah to let him know when the music for *The Village Coquettes* would be ready and relating that Cramer & Co, having been promised first refusal of the piece by Dickens's father-in-law ("who had acted Godfather for us"), *"should be very sorry to let it slip through their hands"*, *integral address leaf, part of one word torn away, but adhering to seal*

AUTOGRAPH LETTERS OF CHARLES DICKENS

". . . When, oh *when*, will this Music be ready. I really begin to grow alarmed lest Braham think we are playing him some nonsense . . . A day's loss now, may be a month's after the Season has commenced. It is very disheartening . . ."

(7) A.L.s. *1 page, 8vo, Wedy Morng* [*?17 August 1836*], arranging to consult about Braham's enquiry concerning "their views with regard to pecuniary compensation" for *The Village Coquettes, integral address leaf, fragments of wafer seal*

(8) A.L.s. *4 pages, 4to, Petersham Monday Evening*[*? 22August 1836*], giving accounts of the enthusiastic reactions of John Braham and John Pritt Harley to *The Village Coquettes*, mentioning some necessary changes and additions (including Braham's suggestion of another song for Elizabeth Rainforth), alluding to his farce, *The Strange Gentleman*, and describing Petersham (" . . . Beautiful place—meadow for exercise—horse for your riding—boat for your rowing—room for your studying —anything you like"), *small tears at horizontal folds*

". . . Harley wrote, when he had read the whole of the opera, saying "Its'a sure card—nothing wrong *there*. Bet you ten pound it runs fifty nights. Come; dont be afraid. You'll be the gainer by it, and you needn't mind betting; its' a capital custom."—They tell the story with infinite relish . . ."

(9) A.L.s. *2 pages, 8vo, Edwards Street Sunday afternoon.* [*?4 September 1836*], about suggestions for the opening and reading of his farce (*The Strange Gentleman*) and an arrangement to meet at the theatre after seeing Cramer & Co about *The Village Coquettes, integral address leaf, one ink smudge, small tears in margins*

". . . Immediately after I left you the other day, I fell into the arms of Bentley; and immediately after that, into the ditto's of Harley who dragged me home with him, and forced me into town, again to-day . . . He has copied out his part in the Village Coquettes, himself, for the convenience of learning, and looks over it daily. They want to open, if they possibly can, *tomorrow fortnight* . . ."

(10) A.L.s. *2 pages, 8vo, Edwards Street, Saturday Night.* [*?10 September 1836*], giving his impressions of Kitty and Julia Smith, nieces of the actress and singer, Catherine Stephens, alluding to *The Village Coquettes*, informing him of the rehearsal of his farce, *The Strange Gentleman*, and of an arrangement he had made for both of them to meet John Orlando Parry, the musician, comedian and entertainer, *integral address leaf, seal tear, margins a little frayed, central fold torn down*

". . . the Miss Smiths' are very nice-looking, well dressed, agreeable-mannered, lady-like girls. I should say that Rose [*viz.* Julia] especially, is a very knowing little person—*rather* fat, but not a bit too much so, with a very nice smiling pretty face. The father is all bows and politeness; and they all readiness and satisfaction. I don't think you could have picked out a nicer looking girl for the part, if you had picked all London through . . ."

⁎ Kitty and Julia Smith played Fanny and Mary Wilson in *The Strange Gentleman* and Julia played Rose in *The Village Coquettes*. Parry played Young Benson in *The Coquettes* and acted in several of the dramatizations of Dickens's novels.

(11) A.L.s. *2 pages, 8vo, Petersham Tuesday* ("*Morning*" *scored through*) *Night* [*20 September 1836*], about objections that had been raised to Squire Norton's song, "There's a charm in Spring", in *The Village Coquettes* (". . . I . . . cannot consent to give up (what I consider) the best verse of the best song in the whole piece. If the young ladies are especially horrified at the bare notion of anybody's going to bed, I have no objection to substitute for the objectionable line "around, old stories go." But you may respectively signify to Cramer's that I will see them d——d before I make any further alteration . . . we ought not to emasculate the very spirit of a song to suit boarding-schools . . ."), *integral address leaf, postmarked, original seal tear in blank margin*

⁎ In both the manuscript sent to the Lord Chamberlain and the published version the "objectionable line"—"well warmed to bed we go"—was retained.

(12) A.L.s. *1 page, oblong 4to, Furnivals Inn. Sunday Afternoon* [*?25 September 1836*], sending "both the Duett and song" and explaining their part in *The Village Coquettes, integral address leaf, signed, original tear at intact wafer seal*

⁎ The duet and song were added by Dickens to the manuscript sent to the Lord Chamberlain.

(13) A.L.s., *2 pages, 8vo, Brompton Saturday Evening* [*?19 November 1836*], reporting Braham's "entire and perfect satisfaction" with *The Village Coquettes* and outlining the factors affecting the date of its production, *integral address leaf, signed*

⁎ In the Pilgrim Edition of the *Letters* the title of the opera is spelled normally where Dickens refers to it in parenthesis; in the original he almost certainly left off the final 's' of "Coquettes".

(14) A.L.s. *2 pages, 8vo, Furnivals Inn. Sunday Morning* [*11 December 1836*], light-heartedly going over the reviews of *The Village Coquettes, integral address leaf, original tear at seal, seal obscuring one word*

AUTOGRAPH LETTERS OF CHARLES DICKENS

". . . Have you seen the *Examiner?* It is *rather* depreciatory of the Opera, but like all their inveterate critiques against Braham, so well done that I cannot help laughing at it, for the life and soul of me.

I have seen the *Sunday Times,* the *Dispatch,* and the *Satirist,* all of which blow their little trumpets against unhappy me, most lustily . . ."

₊ The editors of the Pilgrim Edition of the *Letters* comment: "The *Examiner* notice, presumably by Forster, found fault with both the production (an "inefficient" orchestra and "absolutely disfiguring" costumes) and the opera, with its "utterly insignificant" music and a libretto "totally unworthy of Boz." The audience, however, "screamed for Boz" at the end, although when CD appeared they "were left in perfect consternation that he neither resembled the portraits of Pickwick, Snodgrass, Winkle, nor Tupman. Some critics in the gallery were said to have expected Samuel Weller."

(15) A.L.s. *4 pages, 8vo, Furnivals Inn. Thursday Evening* [*?12 January 1837*], sending for his acceptance both a copy of *The Village Coquettes* and one of the new series of the *Sketches by Boz,* and expressing his dissatisfaction with Cramer & Co, *some offsetting*

". . . For myself I have no hesitation in saying that I have suffered the most severe and unlooked for inconveniences from their (*viz.* Cramer & Co's) negligence and delay. Depending upon them, with the same certainty with which I am accustomed to depend on booksellers and other people with whom I am engaged in business. I have accepted payment in bills where I should otherwise have required ready money, and have put money to uses to which I should never have put it at all, had it not been for a reasonable calculation of the Profits of the Opera; and this at a time when of all others, my expenses are the most heavy, and my engagements the most pressing. As yet, it has proved in every way, nothing but a source of loss, and annoyance to me . . ."

₊ In the Pilgrim Edition of the *Letters* the word "feeling" in the third paragraph is transcribed in the plural.

[*See* ILLUSTRATION]

AUTOGRAPH LETTERS OF CHARLES DICKENS

196   A.L.s. to Edward George Geoffrey Smith Stanley, later fourteenth Earl of Derby, three times Prime Minister, translator of the *Iliad*, at the time Secretary of State for Ireland, DICKENS'S ONLY KNOWN LETTER TO HIM, *3 pages, 4to, 15 Furnivals Inn. Monday February 8*th *1836,* reminding his correspondent that he had been pleased with his (Dickens's) report of his famous speech on the first reading of the Suppression of Disturbances (Ireland) Bill, made when Dickens was a reporter on *The Mirror of Parliament,* and sending him, with suitable expressions of esteem, a presentation copy of *Sketches by Boz* (". . . the accompanying Volumes—the first I ever published . . ."), *second leaf mounted*

> . . . The wish of Authors to place their works in the hands of those, the eminence of whose public stations, is only to be exceeded by the lustre of their individual talents, is, and always has been, so generally felt, even by the greatest Men who have ever adorned the Literature of this country, that I hope it may be pardoned when it displays itself in so humble a candidate for public favor, as My Lord Your Lordship's most obedient Humble Servant . . .

***   The advance copy inscribed for Stanley was probably the one (the only one) which Dickens actually sent; he had to return to John Macrone two of the three copies he had inscribed (see his letter to Macrone (9 February 1836) in the Pilgrim Edition of the *Letters*).

AUTOGRAPH LETTERS OF CHARLES DICKENS

197   Album containing correspondence between Dickens and Sir John Easthope, proprietor of the *Morning Chronicle*, comprising six A.Ls.s. by Dickens, BEING ALL HIS SURVIVING LETTERS TO EASTHOPE, one A.L.s. and an autograph draft of a letter by Easthope, prefaced by an introduction by F. J. Harvey Darton in typescript, *calligraphic title-page in red and black, each letter neatly inserted and accompanied by a typed transcript, red morocco, gilt, in the centre of each cover a facsimile of Dickens's signature surmounted by his crest in gilt, cream water-silk linings, bookplate of the Comte de Suzannet, cloth case, 4to*

(1) A.L.s. to Easthope, *2 pages, 4to, 15 Furnivals Inn, Thursday Morning* [*? April 1836*], hoping that there was nothing in an earlier letter about his *Sketches* [*by Boz*] displeasing to Easthope and promising to concur with any arrangement for the insertion of his new series of sketches in the *Morning Chronicle, integral address leaf, endorsed, fragment of seal, two brown stains.*

(2) EASTHOPE (JOHN) A.L.s. *1 page, 4to, M*[*orning*] *C*[*hronicle*] *Office, Thursday* [*? April 1836*], replying to the previous letter with assurances that Dickens's earlier letter had not aroused "the slightest annoyance or discontent".

(3) A.Ls. to Easthope, *1 page, 4to, Furnivals Inn, Tuesday Evening* [*1 November 1836*], complaining that his sketches were being pirated in *Bell's Life* and the *Carlton Chronicle*, asking (in vain as it proved) that a remonstrance be printed in the *Morning Chronicle* and explaining that ill-health had prevented the production of Sketch No. 5, *integral address leaf, endorsed, slight stains.*

(4) A.L.s. to John Easthope, *2 pages, 4to, 15 Furnivals Inn, Saturday, November 5th* [*1836*], resigning his post as parliamentary reporter on the *Morning Chronicle* and promising further *Sketches* until the expiry of his notice, *integral address leaf, endorsed.*

(5) A.L.s. to John Easthope, *4 pages, 4to, 15 Furnivals Inn, Friday Morning* [*18 November 1836*], written soon after he had announced his resignation, rebuking his ex-employer for a meaness of spirit in reprimanding him for not appearing at the office (the reasons for which he explains here since illness has prevented him from doing so personally) and (giving incidentally a fine picture of his life as a reporter) for suggesting that in two years' employment he had been over-paid by six guineas; he ends with sound advice on the treatment of employees, *one endorsement, slight stains*

". . . I should have been well content to have left; and to have considered the constrained and abrupt terms of your former letter, as one of those matters of course which so often pass between master and servant, when the servant gives his month's warning, and takes his services elsewhere. But I will say now, in the same frankness and honesty with which you express your feelings to me, that I *did* expect on leaving, to receive some slight written acknowledgement from the Proprietors of the *Morning Chronicle* of the sense they entertained of the services I had performed. I may say now that on many occasions at a sacrifice of health, rest and personal comfort, I have again and again, on important expresses in my zeal for the interests of the paper, done what was always before considered impossible, and what in all probability will never be accomplished again . . . I am happy to say that I can afford to part with the thanks of the Proprietors, although I feel much hurt, and much surprised at the conduct they think proper to pursue towards me . . ."

(6) EASTHOPE (JOHN) Draft A. L. partly crossed out, *2 pages, 8vo, M*[*orning*] *C*[*hronicle*], *Friday, 19 November* [*1836*], in reply to the previous letter at once regretting that Dickens should have written it and that he should have been ill (". . . I cannot help thinking that it is to that cause I may attribute your Irritation . . .")

(7) A.L.s. to Sir John Easthope, *2 pages, 8vo, 1 Devonshire Terrace, Fifteenth February 1844*, apologising for not replying by means of Easthope's servant (". . . I was much engaged with visitors two deep; and lived in hopes of their business being brief—which it was not . . .") and agreeing to the arrangements for meeting that Easthope had suggested, *recipient's endorsement*

(8) A.L.s. to Sir John Easthope, *2 pages, 8vo, Devonshire Terrace, Thursday afternoon*, [*15 February 1844*], altering the arrangements agreed to in the previous letter, *recipient's endorsement*

AUTOGRAPH LETTERS OF CHARLES DICKENS

198 A.L.s. to John Braham, the celebrated tenor singer, *1 page, 4to, Furnivals Inn. Saturday Morning* [*30 July 1836*], sending him the completed and entirely rewritten comic opera *The Village Coquettes* ("Drama of the Village Coquettes"), with the names of the performers inserted in pencil against the *dramatis personae*, and promising to forward the music when he received it, *with part of the integral address leaf, repaired, slightly brown and frayed*

_* *The Village Coquettes* was first performed on 6 December 1836 and ran for sixteen nights; Hullah conducted and John Braham played Squire Norton. On ? 10 August 1836 Dickens wrote to Hullah: "When, oh *when* will this Music be ready. I really begin to grow alarmed lest Braham think we are playing him some nonsense; and there is every reason to fear that he will have left town, *long* before it reaches his hands." On ? 22 August, however, Dickens was able to report to Hullah: "Depend upon it Sir"—said Braham to Hogarth yesterday, . . . "Depend upon it Sir, that there had been no such music since the days of Sheil, and no such piece since the Duenna . . ."

This letter was discovered in Mauritius by J. A. Lloyd Hyde in the possession of "one of the old French families" (*letter giving the provenance enclosed*).

199 Two A.Ls. (one signed, the other in the third person) to Thomas Tegg, the bookseller and publisher, *2 pages, 4to, 15 Furnivals Inn, Tuesday Morning* (? *9 August 1836*) *and Thursday August 11th 1836*, in the first asking for information about, and in the second accepting, his proposal for a children's book to be called "*Soloman Bell the raree Showman*" which was to be of about the same length as "Peter Parley's tales", *one integral address leaf, recipient's endorsements*

_* Possibly because of his agreement with Bentley on 22 August, Dickens never wrote "Soloman Bell the raree Showman"; the book entitled "Sergeant Bell and his Raree-show", published by Tegg in 1839, was probably written by George Mogridge, one of the users of the pseudonym "Peter Parley". For the third letter in this series see the Pilgrim Edition of the *Letters*, vol. i, p. 162 (THE ONLY LETTER APART FROM THE PRESENT ONES TO TEGG)

200 A.L. (in the third person) to William Ayrton, music writer and critic, "A" in Hazlitt's *Essays, 1 page, 8vo, 15 Furnivals Inn. Saturday Evening.* [*3 December 1836*], sending a book of the songs in *The Village Coquettes* and offering him a few admissions for the first night on the following Tuesday [6 December], *conjugate blank*

_* THIS IS DICKENS'S ONLY KNOWN LETTER TO AYRTON.

AUTOGRAPH LETTERS OF CHARLES DICKENS

201   A.L.s. to Charles Hicks, foreman-printer of Bradbury & Evans, who printed for Chapman & Hall, *2 pages, 8vo, Furnivals Inn. Friday Evening [? 23 December 1836]*, sending the manuscript of the end of a number of *Pickwick*, asking him to send a messenger for the proof and telling him that a short address which was to face the plates would be ready in the morning, *integral address leaf partly in another hand, formerly mounted down one edge, spindle hole*

⁎⁎ The editors of the Pilgrim Edition of the *Letters* note that Dickens must have been sending the end of the number ("The Story of the Goblins who stole a Sexton") when the earlier part was already in print, a circumstance that may account for the fact that the second and third chapters of *Pickwick* No. X are both numbered 28. In the short address mentioned in the letter Dickens announced the conclusion of "half his task" and his determination not to extend the book beyond the twenty numbers originally promised.

202   L.s. (the text in the hand of the "Great Unpaid", John Dickens) to [George William] Lovell, the playwright, DICKENS'S ONLY SURVIVING LETTER TO HIM, *2 pages, 4to, 48 Doughty Street 12 February 1838*, asking him to contribute, as Ainsworth, Cruikshank and he were, to a book [*viz. Pic-Nic Papers*] which would be sold for the benefit of the widow of John Macrone, the publisher, "left, after several meetings of her deceased husband's creditors, in a state of utter destitution . . .", *conjugate blank*

⁎⁎ Although he was in the midst of *Master Humphrey's Clock* Dickens undertook the management of the *Pic-Nic Papers;* he contributed the Introduction, rewrote his un-acted farce "The Lamplighter" for it (renamed "The Lamplighter's Story"), edited the remainder of the work, except the third volume, and was thus able to raise £300 for Mrs. Macrone. George Lovell's contribution was a long narrative poem, "The Spanish Maid".

203   A.L.s. to George Cruikshank, *2 pages, 8vo, Elm Cottage Petersham, Friday Night [? May 1839]*, returning "the song" (*viz.* the *Loving Ballad of Lord Bateman*) with some alterations (". . . a line or a word here and there, and . . . a new last verse for the old one . . ."), suggesting that Cruikshank write to Mrs. Burnett (Fanny Dickens) to arrange when he can call on her and hum the tune for her to write down (". . . *Tell her to be sure to mark the shakes and the expression . . .*") and recommending that he send the proofs to him, *on the conjugate leaf Cruikshank has written in pencil a line from the ballad with the variant spelling "Darter" for "daughter"*

⁎⁎ Cruikshank's pencil notes are not printed with the letter in the Pilgrim Edition of the *Letters*.

Henry Burnett claimed that he, not his wife, took down the music and that Cruikshank stopped him making the fair copy he had intended. "The clef was one-sided, the notes leaning this way and that—and just so it appeared from Cruikshank's hand".

AUTOGRAPH LETTERS OF CHARLES DICKENS

204   A.L.s. ("CD.") to George Cruikshank, *1 page, 8vo, Petersham, Wednesday Morning* [*3 July 1839*], noting that the *Morning Post* had mentioned him (Boz) as author of the Introduction and Notes to the *Loving Ballad of Lord Bateman*, begging Cruikshank for "weighty reasons" not to publicise his connexion with the work and praising the eleven illustrations Cruikshank had done for it (". . . You never did anything like those etchings—never . . ."), *annotated at the head by Cruikshank ("Mem get the MS. from Printer"), integral address leaf with Dickens's signature, wafer seal*

** Cruikshank's memorandum, which perhaps suggests that the manuscript that went to the printer bore Dickens's autograph corrections, is not printed with the text of this letter in the Pilgrim Edition of the *Letters*.

This letter (like the previous lot) is important for establishing Dickens's part in the production of *Lord Bateman*.

205   A.L.s. to George Cattermole, the illustrator, *1 page, 8vo, Devonshire Terrace, Wednesday Morning* [*? 12 February 1840*], sending him the greater portion of No. 2 of *Master Humphrey's Clock* and promising another story (probably "Mr Pickwick's Tale") in the course of the week (". . . I am writing such things as occur to me without much regarding, for the present order in which they will appear . . ."), *conjugate blank*

** Cattermole did two illustrations for the second number of Master Humphrey which appeared on 11 April 1840.

206   A.L.s. to Thomas Beard, *3 pages, 8vo, Devonshire Terrace Sunday Morning March 22nd* [*1840*], explaining that, since he was finding that he had to write all the material for *Master Humphrey's Clock* himself, there was not, at present, the opening in connection with it that he had suggested to Beard, making an arrangement to meet and mentioning the "misty notion" he had of "some queer old farm house distant about 20 miles from town, and of the goings down and comings up all through the Summer! ! ! ! ! ! ! ! ! ! ! ! ! ! . . .", *with the autograph envelope, signed, postmarked*

207   A.L.s. to Thomas Beard, *3 pages, 8vo, 37 Albion Street Broadstairs, Monday Night June 1st: 1840*, describing in a light-hearted manner how they had settled in (". . . We have been in the house two hours, and the dining-parlor closet already displays a good array of bottles, duly arranged by the writer hereof—the Spirits labelled "Gin", "Brandy". "Hollands" in autograph character—and the wine tasted and approved . . . the writing table is set forth with a neatness peculiar to your estimable friend . . ."), mentioning that they intend to stay a month and telling him the times of the steamer so that he could join them, *with the autograph envelope, stamped and postmarked, slight stains*

. . . For occasional manly sports in July and August, I shall endeavour to find some queer cabin at Cobham in Kent . . .

the when to ask your friend Mr Blackburn to dinner, who has
been kind enough to send me a very interesting Calcutta newspaper
and also about a certain misty notion I have upon the form
of some queer old farm house distant about 20 miles from
town, and of goings down and comings up all through the
Summer ! ! ! ! ! ! ! ! ! ! ! ! !

Faithfully Yours always

Charles Dickens

Thomas Beard Esquire

LOT 206

208 A.L.s. to the poet Samuel Rogers, *2 pages, 8vo, Devonshire Terrace
13th August 1840*, asking if he may dedicate to him the first volume of collected
Numbers from *Master Humphrey's Clock, small tear at fold*

. . . Have you any objection to my dedicating the book to you, and so having one page in it which
will afford me earnest and lasting gratification? I will not tell you how many strong and cordial feelings
move me to this enquiry; for I am unwilling to parade, even before you, the sincere and affectionate
regard which I seek to gratify . . .

* For the two dedications that Dickens wrote, one of which he discarded,
see his letters to Forster of 6 September and to Rogers ? 8 or 9 September in the
Pilgrim Edition of the *Letters*.

209 A.L.s. ("CD.") to his solicitor Thomas Mitton, *2 pages, 8vo, Devonshire
Terrace. Monday 9th Nov. [1840]*, telling him that he would not be going to the
Adelphi that evening to see the adaptation, *The Old Curiosity Shop; or, One Hour
from Humphrey's Clock*, and mentioning some improvements he had made to it on
Saturday, *inlaid, with the autograph envelope, stamped*

* Despite Dickens's scepticism about it (". . . The thing may be better than
I expect, but I have no faith in it at all . . ."), the piece found favour with the reviewers.
Thomas Mitton was one of Dickens's earliest close friends; they were clerks
together for a time during 1828-1829 in Charles Molloy's office. He was Dickens's
solicitor for twenty years.

AUTOGRAPH LETTERS OF CHARLES DICKENS

210   A.L.s. to the publishers Chapman & Hall, *1 page, 8vo, Devonshire Terrace November twenty four 1840.*, enclosing what was probably a draft of the announcement that *Barnaby Rudge* would be published in *Master Humphrey* ("... I have not shown it to anybody ...") and commenting of the correspondence he had received about the fate of "Little Nell", *mounted by blank conjugate leaf, partly missing*

> ... I am inundated with imploring letters recommending poor little Nell to mercy.—Six yesterday, and four today (it's not 12 o'Clock yet) already! ...

211   A.L.s. ("on greasy paper ... This is like butter") to George Cattermole, *2 pages, 8vo, Devonshire Terrace. Thursday Night January 28. 1841.*, about the illustrations for *Barnaby Rudge*, particularly offering him the subject of Grip, the raven, *contemporary endorsement*

> ... I want to know whether you *feel* Ravens in general, and would fancy Burnaby's raven in particular. Barnaby being an idiot my notion is to have him always in company with a pet raven who is immeasurably more knowing than himself. To this end, I have been studying my bird, and think I could make a very queer character of him ...

*** Cattermole clearly declined the offer since Browne ('Phiz') did all the illustrations containing Grip.

212   A.L.s. to Basil Hall, captain in the navy and author, *2 pages, 8vo, Devonshire Terrace, Twenty Eighth January 1841*, explaining his reasons for declining an invitation to meet Maria Edgeworth ("... The plain Truth is that in the beginning of a new story—with all my thoughts and interest hanging about the old one—and the difficulty of settling down into the track I must pursue ... I cannot break in upon my mornings work ... If the Queen were to send for me at such times, I wouldn't go to her ...")

*** The letter begins: "I am not, I confess, a good hand at roaring, and do indeed shrink from it with most invincible repugnance ..." This was occasioned by Hall's letter of 27 January "... I shrewdly suspect, my friend, that you have a great fancy for wagging your tail, & that this is the explanation of your inability to go out roaring in the woods! ... A mere accident prevented me from seeing Lord Byron & possibly you may regret some day that you have cut old Maria Edgeworth ..."

The editors of the Pilgrim Edition of the *Letters* note that the invitation was certainly an honour and that Maria Edgeworth had chosen to visit London at this quiet time of the year particularly to avoid "the bustle and dissipation and lionising"; for though she was "such a minnikin lion now, and so old, literally without teeth or claws," there were people who might "rattle at the grate" to make her "stand up to play tricks for them" and this she was "not able or inclined to do".

AUTOGRAPH LETTERS OF CHARLES DICKENS

213 A.L.s. to John Scott, THE FIRST OF THE ONLY TWO KNOWN LETTERS FROM DICKENS TO HIM, *4 pages, 8vo, 1 Devonshire Terrace. York Gate Regents Park. March The Twenty Second 1841.*, defending himself against the charge evidently reported by Scott that he forgets old friends and associates and asking Scott to believe that he is responsible for anything he has recently written "in extremely good spirits" in *Master Humphrey's Clock*

. . . There is no character I so detest and abhor as a man who presumes on his prosperity . . . Happily, although I have made many friends, I have never since my schooltime lost *one*. The pleasantest and proudest part of my correspondence is that in which I have stored the congratulations of some from whom I had been separated by distance or accident for several years . . . I have never in my life—and expecially in my later life—no, not once, treated any single human being with coldness or hauteur . . .

** John Scott was probably a friend of Dickens's from his days as a reporter; he was apparently also a friend of W. F. Lemaitre of the *Morning Chronicle*.

214 A.L.s. to the actor and singer, John Pritt Harley, *1 page, 8vo, Devonshire Terrace, April The Third 1841*, inviting him to join him and the staff of *Master Humphrey's Clock* at dinner "in honor of our next volume" during Passion Week when the two patent theatres, Covent Garden and Drury Lane, were closed

** Harley's reply is printed in the Pilgrim Edition of the *Letters*.

215 A.L.s. to Charles Ollier, publisher and author, friend of Leigh Hunt, DICKENS'S ONLY KNOWN LETTER TO HIM, *1 page, 8vo, Devonshire Terrace Thursday June The Third 1841.*, relative to *Barnaby Rudge;* he declines the offer of "the trials" (Dickens owned Cobbett and Howell, *Complete Collection of State Trials*), states that he has obtained a portrait of Lord George Gordon from Upcott and declares ". . . As to the Riot, I am going to try if I can't make a better one than he [*viz.* Gordon] did . . ."

216 A.L.s. to Frederick Salmon, the surgeon who had operated on Dickens for fistula on 8 October, *3 pages, 8vo, White Hart Hotel Windsor. Sunday Seventh November 1841.*, describing in a light-hearted manner the symptoms of his ill-health (although *"immeasurably better"* today) and his domestic remedy for it, and asking Salmon if he recommends any further action, *pin holes at head and foot*

. . . yesterday and the evening before, all manner of queer pains were floating about my illustrious person: now twitching at the calves of my legs—now sticking shadowy pins into the soles of my feet—now entertaining themselves with my knees—now (but not often) shooting through that region which you have made as tender as my heart—and now settling in the small of my back; but particularly favoring the back; and the calves before mentioned. I had an odd sort of nervousness about me besides . . . I parboiled my feet last night in hot water with plenty of salt in it, and rubbed my back with camphor liniment . . .

** Dickens attributes his illness partly to "having stood too long finishing Barnaby". He had completed *Barnaby Rudge* on 5 November, but probably went on to compose the Preface.

AUTOGRAPH LETTERS OF CHARLES DICKENS

217   A.L.s. to the painter Francis Alexander, *1 page, 4to, 1 Devonshire Terrace York Gate, Regents Park London Friday Second [should be 3rd] December 1841,* agreeing to sit for a portrait by him when he arrived in Boston and expressing his sense of gratification on receiving Alexander's letter and similar ones from other Americans, *formerly mounted*

***   This letter disposes of the story told by H. W. French (*Art and Artists in Connecticut*) that Alexander met the boat in Boston and immediately asked Dickens to sit for him, and that Dickens, although he then agreed, later remarked: "The impertinence of the thing was without limit; but the enterprise was most astonishing and deserved any kind of reward demanded.". Among the letters received by Dickens was one from the "Young Men of Boston" inviting him to "a public dinner or more private entertainment to take place in honor of your arrival, at such a time and in such a manner as may be most agreeable to yourself."

218   A.L.s. ("Boz.") [to the painter Francis Alexander] *1 page, 8vo, Tremont House [Boston U.S.A.], "Wednesday Night", n.d. [but 26 January 1842],* asking him to "bespeak" his pupil and friend George W. Putnam to act as his secretary during his stay in Boston, and, if he proves satisfactory, to travel with him while he is in the States; he suggests Putnam calls on him early the next morning and ends "Yours and Mrs Alexander's Affectionately (and pro: tem: knockedup) . . .", *small tears where formerly mounted [in Francesca Alexander's scrapbook]*

***   This letter is printed without that part of the subscription in brackets by Edward Payne, *Dickens Days in Boston* (The Riverside Press, Cambridge, 1927) but not in the Nonesuch Edition of the *Letters*.

Inundated with correspondence, Dickens crossed the street in the morning of 26 January 1842 from Tremont House to 12, West Cedar Street, the home of his friend Francis Alexander, at the time engaged on a portrait of the novelist, and appealed to him to find him a secretary. Alexander suggested Putnam and Dickens hurried back to the hotel to meet distinguished visitors, among them Longfellow, Richard Dana and Charles Sumner. As these three were leaving they met Mr. and Mrs. Alexander on the stairs. It was after the Alexanders left on this occasion that Dickens hurriedly penned the present letter which reached them at the studio just as they met George Putnam. The latter records in his reminiscences:

"While we were talking a note came from Mr. Dickens requesting that Mr. Alexander would bring me to the Tremont House. So I went with him and was received with great cordiality and kindness by Mr. Dickens and his wife and made an appointment to commence my duties on the following morning."

Tremont House.

Wednesday night

My dear Sir.

Will you (I ought to ask you
didn't now) speak to Mr Putnam for
me, and bespeak his assistance
during the time I am in Boston? If I
find him very useful, then I can propose
where to travel with me, in such a
manner as will not displease him.

I need hardly say that if he can
call upon me early tomorrow morning, he
will relieve me very much.

Yours and Mrs Alexander's
affectionately
(and temporarily pro tem - knidely)

D̄D̄ δε.

LOT 218

237

AUTOGRAPH LETTERS OF CHARLES DICKENS

219   A.L.s. to Jonathan Chapman, Mayor of Boston, *4 pages, 8vo, Carlton House, New York. Twenty Second February 1842.*, describing his feelings about his life in New York (". . . I am sick to death of the life I have been leading here—worn out in mind and body—and quite weary and distressed . . . I am a splendid illustration of the wisdom of the old man and his ass. Half the population take it ill if I *do* go where I am asked; and the other half take it ill if I don't . . .") and pouring out his heart over the treatment he had received from the American press over the International Copyright question, *one corner a little creased, light staining down one edge.*

. . . I have never in my life been so shocked and disgusted, or made so sick and sore at heart, as I have been by the treatment I have received here (in America I mean) in reference to the International Copyright question . . . attacking me in such terms of vagabond scurrility as they would denounce no murderer with. I vow to Heaven that the scorn and indignation I have felt under this unmanly and ungenerous treatment has been to me an amount of agony such as I never experienced since my birth. But it has had the one good effect of making me iron upon this theme . . .

** Among the errors of transcription in the text printed in the Nonsuch Edition of the *Letters* are the misreading of "loser" as "cock" and "motives" as "notices".

220   L.s. (autograph subscription and corrections, text in the hand of his secretary in America, George Putnam) POSSIBLY THE MOST IMPORTANT DICKENS LETTER RELATING TO AMERICA, to the Editor of an American newspaper, *5 pages 4to, Niagara Falls Thirtieth (altered by Dickens from Twenty seventh) April 1842* incorporating copies by Putnam of: (1) an address "To the American People" from Edward Lytton Bulwer, Thomas Campbell, Alfred Tennyson, T. N. Talfourd, Thomas Hood, Leigh Hunt, Henry Hallam, Sydney Smith, H. H. Milman, Samuel Rogers, John Forster and Barry Campbell; (2) a letter from the same writers to Dickens; and (3) a letter to Dickens from Thomas Carlyle, constituting AN APPEAL TO THE AMERICAN PEOPLE FOR AN INTERNATIONAL COPYRIGHT LAW and showing that not only American and British authors would benefit but also the public at large and American literature in general through the encouragement that would thus be given to authors, *traces of former guarding*, ANNOTATED AT HEAD AND ENDORSED BY THE EDITOR OR ONE OF HIS STAFF "MONDAY'S [*viz.* 9 May 1842] PAPER INSIDE" AND "INSIDE OF THE PAPER" *one corner torn away affecting three words, neatly repaired*

** THIS LETTER IS THE CLIMAX OF DICKENS'S YEARS OF WORK TO PREVENT THE PIRATING OF THE WORKS OF ENGLISH AUTHORS BY AMERICAN PUBLISHERS. Throughout his American tour Dickens had spoken in no measured terms of this practice and had aroused the public to violent discussion for and against an international copyright law. In its favour he secured the cooperation of American authors and himself presented their petition to Congress to Henry Clay, but the American publishers united the press against him. Despite all this agitation and the present appeal it was not until 1891 that an International Copyright was effected between America and Britain.

The present letter is almost certainly one of the four copies sent by Dickens to his Boston friend, C. C. Felton, for distribution to leading American papers. Dickens himself suggested that one be sent for simultaneous publication in each of the *New York Evening Post*, the *National Intelligencer*, a Boston paper and either the *Knickerbocker* or the *North American Review*. It appeared in the *New York Evening Post* on Monday 9 May 1842 and probably in the other papers Dickens mentioned.

There are a number of minor differences from the present text, including some verbal ones (e.g. "course" for "cause" and "individual" for "indivisible"), in that reprinted by W. Glyde Wilkins, *Charles Dickens in America*, from the *New York Evening Post* for 9 May 1842.

AUTOGRAPH LETTERS OF CHARLES DICKENS

221   Fine long A.L.s. to Thomas Beard, *3 closely written pages, 4to, plus postscript, Niagara Falls* (*Upon the English Side*) *First of May—Sunday—1842, with postscript from Montreal, Canada. May Twelfth 1842,* GIVING AMUSING DESCRIPTIONS OF HIS CROSSING THE ATLANTIC AND OF HIS TOUR OF AMERICA, and also giving some account of his time at the Falls, *integral address leaf, signed, postmarked, wafer seal, endorsement, one letter affected by original seal cut, small tear at horizontal fold*

. . . I have a horrible fear that I shall return "a bore"—not to anticipate which dire consummation, I will only add, on this head, that we sail from New York, per George Washington Packet-*ship* (none of your steamers) on Tuesday the Seventh of June. Hoo-ray-ay-ay-ay-ay-ay-ay!!!!!

You will naturally enquire about the medicine chest—oh! Shade of Sir Humphrey Davy!—If you could only have seen me, Beard, endeavouring (with that impossible pair of scales, and those weights, invisible to the naked eye) to make up pills in heavy weather, on the rolling Atlantic! . . . Anne struck at last . . . She made distant allusions too, to having her wages "ris", and to physic not being in her articles of engagement . . . . . . One day—it's impossible to say how I got there—I found myself on deck—the ship, now on the top of a mountain; now in the bottom of a deep valley. It was blowing hard; and I was holding on to something—I don't know what. I think it was a pump—or a man—or the cow. I can't say for certain which. My stomach, with its contents, appeared to be in my forehead. I couldn't understand which was the sea and which the sky; and was endeavouring to form an opinion, or a thought, or to get some distant glimmering of anything approaching to an idea, when I beheld, standing before me, a small figure with a speaking trumpet . . . It waved its trumpet, moved its jaws, and evidently spoke very loud . . . I *felt* it remonstrated with me for standing up to my knees in water.—I was in fact doing so . . . I tried to speak—to jest—at all events to explain. But I could only get out two words. They bore reference to the kind of boots I wore, and were these—"cork soles".—I repeated in the feeblest of voices, and with my body all limp and helpless.—"cork soles".—perhaps a hundred times (for I couldn't stop; it was part of the disease)—The captain, seeing that I was quite childish, and for the time a maniac, had me taken below to my berth. And when consciousness returned I was still saying to myself, in a voice that might have melted a heart of sheer steel—"cork soles, cork soles!"— . . .

* There are several errors in the transcription of capital letters and punctuation in the text printed in the Nonesuch Edition of the *Letters;* also, one of Dickens's paragraph breaks is ignored.

222   A.L.s. to Jonathan Chapman, the Mayor of Boston, *2 pages, 4to, Carlton House, New York. Second June 1842.,* a warm friendly letter, explaining his failure to write, bidding him farewell and telling Chapman that he will remember him "earnestly, heartily, and affectionately . . . " *slightly brown and brittle, outer edges stained by celophane which is still adhering to them, some tears, with integral address leaf, signed, postmarks*

. . . The ocean can no more divide you and me, than darkness can shut out Heaven from a blind man. Were it twenty times as broad as it is, one could send a warm pressure of the hand, across it, and I feel, besides, an inexpressible confidence that, on one side of it, or the other, we shall meet again . . . I write God bless you, once more, as if that were a satisfaction. Who that has ever reflected on the enormous and vast amount of leave-taking there is in this Life, can ever have doubted the existence of another!

I have more than half a mind to write those three words of farewell, again . . .

* In the text printed in the Nonesuch Edition of the *Letters* one word of this letter is omitted and "Sixth" is printed "6th".

239

AUTOGRAPH LETTERS OF CHARLES DICKENS

223 A.L.s. to [G. L.] Chesterton, governor of the Middlesex house of correction, *one page, 8vo, "Private", Broadstairs, Kent. Sunday Eleventh September 1842*, concerning a note he wished to include in his *American Notes, with the autograph envelope, signed, stamp affixed*

※ In his *Catalogue* the Comte Alain de Suzannet records that the note referred to in this letter was included in the first edition of the *American Notes*.

224 A.L.s. to Edward Chapman, the senior partner of Chapman & Hall, *2 pages, 8vo, Broadstairs Sixteenth September 1842.*, thanking him for an extract [from the American press] which he wanted for a chapter on slavery [Chapter XVII in *American Notes*] (". . . Mr Forster seems to have got it into his head (and the quantity of hair he wears, probably prevents its coming out again) that I mean to use them for a separate chapter . . .") and mentioning Prescott, the firm of Chapman & Hall, summer-time and a christening ring for the Chapman's expected child (or two rings, if twins)

225 A.L.s. to Philip Hone, DICKENS'S ONLY KNOWN LETTER TO HIM, *one page, 4to, Broadstairs, Kent, England, Sixteenth September 1842*, thanking him for his letter and vehemently denying the authenticity of a letter attributed to him in America, *integral address leaf, signed, postmarks, fragments of seal*

. . . The letter to which you refer, is, from beginning to end, in every word and syllable, the cross of every t, and the dot of every i, a most wicked and nefarious Forgery. I have never published one word or line in reference to America, in any quarter whatever, except the Copyright Circular. And the unhung scoundrel who invented that astounding lie knew this as well as I do.

It has caused me more pain, and more of a vague desire to take somebody by the throat, than such an act should, perhaps, have awakened in an honourable man . . .

※ Philip Hone (1781-1851), New York merchant and mayor of the city in 1825, was one of the founders of the Mercantile Library Association; he kept a diary of Dickens's visit to New York. For the background to this letter see Chapter XIII "International Copyright" in William Wilkins, *Charles Dickens in America*.

The text printed in the Nonesuch Edition of the *Letters* is imperfect in the following respects: four words, three commas, one set of inverted commas and a hyphen are omitted; four commas not in the original are inserted; two of Dickens's paragraph breaks are ignored; two capital letters are suppressed and one colon is printed as a comma.

AUTOGRAPH LETTERS OF CHARLES DICKENS

226   A.L.s. to Jonathan Chapman, Mayor of Boston, *3 pages, 4to, 1 Devonshire Terrace York Gate Regents Park. Fifteenth October 1842.*, justifying at length the writing of his forthcoming *American Notes*, Chapman's copy of which would be delivered by Longfellow, *with integral address leaf, signed, postmarked, torn up central fold, slight stain down one blank edge of the address leaf*

. . . I dispassionately believe that in the slow fulness of time, what I have written, will have some effect in purging your community of evils which threaten its very existence. And I know that it is written kindly and good-humouredly; and that I have never, for an instant, suffered myself to be betrayed into a hasty or unfair expression, or one I shall, at any time, regret . . .

. . . Our darlings are all well, and send all manner of messages in broken English, to yours . . . and I am always—stay; not always—conditionally—conditionally on your not, at anytime, talking about the length of your letters, or committing any such monstrous absurdity—Your faithful friend . . .

**   In the text of this letter printed in the Nonesuch Edition of the *Letters* three words are mistranscribed ("like" as "take", "promotion" as "approbation" and "is" as "was"), one word ("stay") is omitted, and four paragraph breaks, four question-marks and one "etc" are inserted.

227   Two A.Ls.s. to his friend, the artist John Leech, *5 pages, 8vo, 1 Devonshire Terrace, Saturday Evening Fifth November 1842. and Monday Seventh November [1842]*, in the first congratulating him on his success (and himself ". . . on having my eye upon the means by which you have attained it . . .") and hoping to avail himself of Leech's "genius" in his own forthcoming monthly work (*viz. Martin Chuzzlewit*) if consistent with his arrangements with Browne ('Phiz'), and in the second, telling Leech that the project mentioned in his other letter was unfortunately impracticable, but, wishing "to lay a small quantity of salt on your private and personal coat", extending an invitation to dinner, *with the autograph envelopes, signed, wafer seals*

228   A.L.s. to the American historian William Hickling Prescott, ONE OF THE ONLY TWO KNOWN LETTERS FROM DICKENS TO HIM, *2 pages, 4to, London. 1 Devonshire Terrace York Gate Regents Park Second March 1843*, explaining how he considered Prescott to be "playing at blindmans buff with International copyrights," giving his views about piratical publishing and quoting Leigh Hunt, *integral address leaf, postmarks, contemporary endorsement, tears down vertical folds*

". . . As to the Pirates, let them wave their black flag, and rob under it, and stab into the bargain, until the crack of doom. I should hardly be comfortable if I knew they *bought* the right of black-guarding me in the Model Republic; but while they steal it, I am happy. So hurrah for the Spring; which, I hope, by the time you get this, will be dawning upon us in England; and may we all enjoy what Leigh Hunt calls "the leafy greenery" as much as Heaven meant us to, in sending it!

**   There are some minor errors of transcription in the text printed in the Nonesuch Edition of the *Letters*.

AUTOGRAPH LETTERS OF CHARLES DICKENS

229   A.L.s. to Douglas Jerrold, *4 pages, 8vo, Devonshire Terrace, Third May 1843*, thanking him for some books, praising his opening paper ("Elizabeth and Victoria") in the *Illuminated Magazine* ("... written with the finest end of that iron pen of yours ... I vow to God that I think the Parrots of Society are more intolerable and mischievous than its Birds of Prey. If ever I destroy myself, it will be in the bitterness of hearing those infernal and damnably good times, extolled ..."), mentioning that he is writing "a little history of England" (*viz. A Child's History of England*) for his son, giving a fine description of a hospital dinner, imagining a "colony of common Sense" made up of fifty families such as theirs' and pointing out "a great mistake" in the *Arabian Nights*

... Oh Heaven, if you could have been with me at a Hospital Dinner last Monday! There were men there—your city aristocracy—who made such speeches, and expressed such sentiments, as any moderately intelligent dustman would have blushed through his cindery bloom to have thought of. Sleek, slobbering, bow-paunched, over-fed, apoplectic, snorting cattle—and the auditory leaping up in their delight! ...

  ⁎   In the Nonesuch Edition of the *Letters* the word "mask" has been included in the inverted commas in Dickens's phrase "or named at least, like a "classical" mask (oh damn that word!)". A number of the capital letters and commas in the original have been suppressed in the same edition.

230   Autograph notice, *one page, 4to, Saturday, Tenth June 1843*, written on behalf of the committee for the testimonial to William Macready, giving the arrangements for a presentation that was to be made to Macready on 19 June by the Duke of Cambridge on the former's retirement as manager of Drury Lane Theatre, *traces of wax in the four corners of the verso, note at foot by T. S. Serle, actor and dramatist*

  ⁎   The text of this notice is apparently UNPUBLISHED; only a catalogue description is printed in the Nonesuch Edition of the *Letters*.

231   A.L.s. to William Harness, author of a *Life of Shakespeare, one page, 8vo, Devonshire Terrace Friday Decʳ 22ⁿᵈ 1843*, sending a copy of *The Christmas Carol* (delayed by the shortage of copies) and asking Harness for his niece's name and the return of the book so that he can inscribe it for her, *inlaid*

  ⁎   "The Rev. William Harness ... was almost an idolator where Dickens was concerned". (J. W. T. Ley, *The Dickens Circle*)

232   A.L.s. to F. O. Ward, *2 pages, 8vo, Devonshire Terrace. Tuesday Twenty Sixth March 1844.*, expressing his great regard for Hood and promising to write something short for *Hood's Magazine, formerly mounted*

  ⁎   Ward, sub-editor of *Hood's Magazine and Comic Miscellany*, gave much gratuitous help in getting the early numbers of the *Magazine* to the press during Hood's illness. Faithful to his promise, Dickens wrote an article entitled *Threatening Letter to Thomas Hood, from an Ancient Gentlemen*, a satire on the current craze for the midget, Tom Thumb.

AUTOGRAPH LETTERS OF CHARLES DICKENS

233   Two A.Ls.s. to John Leech, *one page, 4to, and 2 pages, 12mo, Piazza Coffee House Covent Garden Sunday December First 1844 and Tuesday Morning [3 December 1844]*, about Leech's illustrations for *The Chimes, one integral address leaf, penny-red stamp affixed, postmarks, original tear at seal, fragment of the autograph envelope for the other letter*

234   A.L.s. to Thomas Beard, *2 pages, 4to, Palazzo Peschiere, Genoa, Twentieth May 1845.*, addressing Beard as "My Dear Bardolph" and writing at first in mock 'legalese', Dickens invites him to dinner on his own return to England (". . . Said Writer purporting to leave the sunny clime of Italy (respecting which clime, much Gammon is afloat among the subjects of her Britannic Majesty) very early in June next . . ."); gives an amusing general picture of his life during the last half year; describes the Palazzo Peschiere (". . . It stands in the midst of Terrace Gardens—overlooks the towers and steeples of the town, and comprehends, beyond them, the whole blue range of the Mediterranean . . . Moreover there is a marble bath below stairs, from which in all weathers, cold or warm, wet or dry, the heels of the Inimitable B may be beheld protruding, as the Clock strikes 8 every morning . . ."); and mentions the success of *The Chimes, integral address leaf with postmarks and endorsement, original tears at seal, on thin blue paper, some light brown marks and small tears*

. . . I take it for granted my dear Beard that you have occasionally declaimed, with mingled vehemence and misgivings, against the apparently oblivious memory of the humble Individual who has the honor to &c. But the life I have led, roaming from place to place, and scene to scene—the objects I have crammed and crowded into my inimitable mind—the gentlemanly vagabond I have been, for the last six or eight months—the extraordinary beds I have slept in—and bewildering amount of fleas, mosquitoes, bugs, and other Insects I have unwillingly bepastured—these things have hardly left me any leisure in my holiday, until within the last four or five weeks. During the whole of which time, I have been employed, chiefly, in lying on my back on sofas, and leaning out of windows and over balconies, in a sort of mild intoxication . . .

235   Series of 4 A.Ls.s. to John Leech (three with initials, one letter being written on the second leaf of an L.s., the text of which is in the hand of Georgina Hogarth), *7 pages, 8vo, 1 Devonshire Terrace, October 1st 1845, Second October 1845, Tuesday Evening Eighteenth November 1845, Wednesday Night [19 and Saturday Evening End of November 1845]*, concerning illustrations by Leech and Edwin Landseer for *The Cricket on the Hearth* and charges for amateur theatricals, *with two autograph envelopes, signed, and two integral address leaves, one signed*

***   In the Nonesuch Edition of the *Letters* the business letter in the hand of Georgina Hogarth (1 October 1845) is separated from Dickens's letter of 2 October 1845 without any indication that they are written on conjugate leaves of the same sheet of paper.

AUTOGRAPH LETTERS OF CHARLES DICKENS

236   A.L.s. ("CD") to Thomas Beard, *2 pages, 8vo, Devonshire Terrace, Tuesday Fourth November 1845.*, saying that the collapse of "a Great Broker in the city" would render impossible the establishment of *The Daily News, with the autograph envelope, signed, postmarked*

 ⁎   The paper was in fact saved from failure at the eleventh hour.

Two paragraph breaks and hyphens in the phrase "four and twenty hours" not in the original are inserted in the text published in the Nonesuch Edition of the *Letters*.

237   Two A.Ls.s. to Bradbury & Evans, the publishers, *15 pages, 8vo, Devonshire Terrace Thursday November Sixth 1845. and Friday Morning November Seventh 1845.*, about the near-failure of *The Daily News* before it had been launched because of the collapse of a brokerage house and Dickens's conclusion that "the heart of the enterprise is broken and dead" and his decision to extricate himself from the venture.

 ⁎   There are several errors of transcription in the text printed in the Nonesuch Edition of the *Letters* including the omission of words and letters and the re-arrangement of Dickens's paragraphs.

238   A.L.s. to Rev. Edward Tagart, Unitarian divine, *3 pages, 8vo, Devonshire Terrace Tuesday Second December 1845*, about the writing of *Cricket on the Hearth*, the performance of it, Fletcher's *Elder Brother* and Peake's *Comfortable Lodgings*, and giving some personal news (". . . I walk to Harrow still—was nearly blown away yesterday on Hampstead Heath—went to Finchley the other day in the pouring rain—take a cold shower Bath every morning—and oil the machinery of the Daily News, till the afternoon . . ."), *modern cloth case with the Comte de Suzannet's bookplate*

. . . I had great satisfaction in the writing of it, and have an uncommonly strong belief in it.

I hadn't the courage to go to the English Opera House on Saturday, but they tell me it is very well played there. I took great pains with the "getting up" of the little piece: to the end that I might be slaughtered as gently as possible, and from what I saw of the Rehearsals, I really believe it is better done than anything of the kind has yet been . . .

 ⁎   Dickens was a member of Tagart's congregation at Little Portland Street, Regent Street; in 1844 a service of plate was given to the minister with an inscription by Dickens.

239   A.L.s. to the publishers Bradbury and Evans, *4 pages, 8vo, Devonshire Terrace Friday Morning Thirtieth January 1846.*, firmly expressing his lack of confidence in their advisers, his disagreement with the policy of *The Daily News* on railway matters and his objection to their criticism of one of the sub-editors, his nominee, and announcing his probable resignation as editor of the paper

. . . When I tell you, distinctly, that I shall leave the Paper immediately, if you do not give me this information [the authority for the sub-editor's unfitness], I think it but fair to add that it is extremely probable I shall leave it when you have done so . . .

 ⁎   Dickens ended his connexion with the paper on 9 February.

Two paragraph breaks in this original are ignored in the text printed in the Nonesuch Edition of the *Letters*.

AUTOGRAPH LETTERS OF CHARLES DICKENS

240   A.L.s. TO A NEW DICKENS CORRESPONDENT, Monsieur Amédée Pichot, poet and critic, authority on Byron, director of the *Revue Britannique* and translator of *David Copperfield, one page, 4to, London. 1 Devonshire Terrace Sixteenth February 1846.*, concerning Pichot's offer to help the foreign staff of *The Daily News*, Dickens's own connexion with the paper (". . . I have a very strong interest in its well-doing, and was active in projecting and establishing it . . .") Pichot's version of *The Cricket on the Hearth*, and a reference in *The Chimes, integral address leaf, postmarks, fragment of seal*

✱✱   No letters from Dickens to Pichot are printed in the Nonesuch or Pilgrim Editions of the *Letters.*

241   Substantial fragment (the complete first sheet) of a long A.L. to Madame Emile De la Rue, *4 pages, 8vo, closely written, Devonshire Terrace. Friday Seventeenth April 1846.*, discussing: his break with the *Daily News* (". . . In the course of a little more time, I saw so much reason to believe that they (*viz.* the managers) would be the Ruin of what might otherwise have been a very fine property—and that their proceedings would so commit and involve me, who had no power either of getting rid of them or controlling them—that I straightway stopped my letters, and walked bodily, out of the concern . . ."); his desire to go abroad, preferably to Genoa, to write "a new story in twenty monthly parts" (*viz. Dombey and Son*); his training for the law; his literary reputation (". . . the good people of England seem to be fonder of their favourite (your humble servant and physician) now, than ever . . ."); a patient suitable for mesmerism; the publication of *Pictures from Italy* (". . . I like them very much, and I think the Holy Week will make you laugh and remind you of the reality . . . I talk to all the Italian Boys who go about the streets with organs and white mice, and give them mints of money per l'amore della Bell'Italia . . ."); and the painter Maclise

. . . Maclise has been painting a large picture for the Royal Academy Exhibition which opens in May. The subject is the Superstition of the Ordeal by Touch . . . It is very fine indeed, and buyers are fighting for it. He can have a Thousand Pounds for it, easily; but he says he "don't know"—and says nothing. His last invention has been the abolition of straps to his trousers . . .

✱✱   Mme. De la Rue, the wife of a Swiss banker, who lived at Genoa, received mesmeric treatment from Dickens and aroused the jealousy of the novelist's wife, Catherine. In the present letter Dickens states that while he would prefer to go to Genoa, his wife, "who was never very well there, cannot be got to contemplate the Peschiere—though I have beset her in all kinds of ways".

The text printed in the Nonesuch Edition of the *Letters* contains several errors in transcription including the omission of the last four words of the letter, of a set of inverted commas, six commas and one double-underlining, the insertion of commas and one colon, and such misreadings as "believe" for "belief", commas as colons or semi-colons, dashes as commas, *etc.*

AUTOGRAPH LETTERS OF CHARLES DICKENS

242　A.L.s. to Joseph Valckenberg, ONE OF THE ONLY TWO KNOWN LETTERS FROM DICKENS TO HIM, *2 pages, 4to, Rosemont, Lausanne, Switzerland Twenty Fifth June 1846.*, promising to call on him when in Worms and to "drink . . . the health of everybody, great and small, in that large family-house at Worms" when a consignment of Liebfraumilch arrives, and also giving his intended itinerary and describing the arrival of his children (". . . they look as if they were in one perpetual Sunset . . ."), *integral address leaf, signed, postmarks, small tear in lower margin*

　** Joseph Valckenberg, a well-known wine merchant at Worms, had accosted Mrs Dickens on the boat soon after they had left Mayence.

　One of the errors in the text printed in the Nonesuch Edition of the *Letters* is the mistranscription of "6th" as "5th".

243　A.L.s. to his friend and biographer John Forster, Editor of the *Examiner*, *2 pages, 4to, Rosemont, Lausanne. Twenty Fifth June 1846.*, concerning, partly with reference to the *Daily News* and *Pictures from Italy*, his "besetting anxiety" about Bradbury and Evans and his wish that Forster would arrange for Chapman and Hall to be the publishers of his new book [*viz. Dombey and Son*] in monthly parts, *slightly stained, integral address panel, signed, postmarks, traces of seal*

　** The letter contains a long account of Dickens's relations with Bradbury and Evans.

　One paragraph break in this original is ignored in the text printed in the Nonesuch Edition of the *Letters*.

244　A.L.s. to Thomas Chapman, *3 pages, 4to, Rosemont, Lausanne. Friday Third July 1846*, expressing his horror and disbelief at Thomas Powell's defrauding of Chapman & Hall; giving his opinion of the recently deceased painter, Benjamin Haydon (". . . he most unquestionably was a very bad painter . . ."); commenting on politics and the *Daily News;* outlining his progress with *Dombey and Son* and *The Battle of Life;* and inviting Chapman to stay with him in Switzerland, *integral address leaf, signed, postmarks*

　. . . I little thought once upon a time, that I should ever live to praise Peel. But D'Israeli and that Dunghill Lord have so disgusted me, that I feel disposed to champion him—and should have done so, even if he hadn't shown a striving artist, such deliberate attention and compassion as he shewed to Haydon. I suppose he is out of office by this time . . .

　** In the text printed in the Nonesuch Edition of the *Letters* five words are omitted, "usually" is given as "invariably" and "of" as "for".

AUTOGRAPH LETTERS OF CHARLES DICKENS

245   A.L.s. to Thomas Beard, *2 pages, 4to, Geneva. October Twenty First 1846.*, outlining his plans and inviting Beard to stay with him in Paris ("... come and unbend that bow which is kept strung in Shoe Lane ..."); mentioning the completion of *The Battle of Life* and the success of *Dombey and Son* ("... Dombey is a prodigious success. Enthusiastic bulletins reach me daily ..."); describing with much amusement the antics, particularly on the boat near Chillon, of a Frenchman and an Englishman ("really good specimens") who were travelling companions; noting the subjects he had intended to write about and telling him how hearty he is ("... my main object after all ..."), *integral address panel, signed, postmarks, traces of seal, endorsement*

... An immense Frenchman, with a face like a bright velvet pincushion—and a very little Englishman, whose head comes up to about the middle of the Frenchman's waistcoat ... The Englishman can't speak a word of French, but the Frenchman can speak a very little English. The Englishman instead of being obliged by this, condescends, good humouredly, to correct the Frenchman's pronunciation—patronizes him—would pat him on the head, if he could reach so high—and screeches at his mistakes. There he is now, staggering over the stones in his little boots, and falling up against a watchmaker's window, in perfect convulsions of joy, because the beaming Giant, without whom he couldn't get a single necessary of life, has made some mistake in the English language! I never saw such a fellow ...

⁎⁎ In the Nonesuch Edition of the *Letters* a paragraph break is made which is not in this original and two colons are printed as commas.

246   A.L.s. ("CD.") to Douglas Jerrold, *1½ pages, 4to, closely written, Geneva. Saturday October Twenty Four 1846*, about the completion of the *Battle of Life* ("... my little Christmas Book ..."); a review of *Dombey and Son* in *Douglas Jerrold's Weekly Newspaper;* friendship ("... The pain of unjust malice is lost in an hour. The pleasure of a generous friendship is the steadiest joy in the world ..."); Jerrold's work and opinions; the delivery of newspapers and journals ("... The number that ought to have come with the letter I am acknowledging, is brilliantly replaced by The Spectator ! ! ! There is a printed slip inside from the Post Office, saying that the envelopes of a great many newspapers, being badly put on, have come off that evening: and they hope the Paper they forwarded me, may prove to be the right one ..."); his own opinion of the *Comic History of England* ("... Such joking is like the sorrow of an undertaker's mute, reversed—And is applied to serious things with the like propriety and force ..."); Jerrold's domestic troubles; his own plans for going to Paris and his hopes that Jerrold can join him there; Switzerland and the Swiss, his life at Lausanne and the revolution there; his magnetic powers, *etc.,* *integral address panel, signed, postmarks, fragment of seal*

... The revolution here just now (which has my cordial sympathy) was conducted with the most gallant, true, and Christian spirit; the conquering party, moderate in the first transports of triumph, forbearing, and forgiving. I swear to you that some of the appeals to the Citizens of both parties posted by the new Government (the people's) on the walls, and sticking there now almost drew the tears into my eyes as I read them; they are so truly generous, and so exalted in their tone— so far above the miserable strife of politics, and so devoted to the general Happiness and Welfare ...

⁎⁎ There are several errors of transcription in the text printed in the Nonesuch Edition of the *Letters*, including the omission of fifteen commas, of one word in the subscription and the triple underlining of the words "The Spectator". Also the phrase printed as "What B. and E. call the "adds" " should read "What B and He call ..."

AUTOGRAPH LETTERS OF CHARLES DICKENS

247   A.L.s. to Charles Sheridan, *2 pages, 8vo, at the Paris Phenomonon (Rue de Courcelles) Thursday Night, Seventh January 1847.*, about the completion of No. 5 of *Dombey and Son*, the issue in which Paul Dombey dies (". . . I am slaughtering a young and innocent victim—and it takes a deal of time . . .") and describing the use made of his wall by the French, *conjugate blank*

> . . . I think of demanding my passport in consequence of the immense extent to which the French nation makes a water-closet of my wall. If the British Lion were (?) bred [Nonesuch *Letters* "here"] for *this*, he had better have been born a jackall or hyaena, and then he might at least have got an honest livlihood out of it . . .

248   A.L.s. to the Hon. Mrs. Richard Watson, *3 pages, 8vo, Paris, 48 Rue de Courcelles. Twenty Fifth January 1847*, describing a picture and how it revives memories of the times he had spent in Lausanne (". . . in the quiet pleasure of its aspect rather daunts me as compared with the reality of a stirring life . . ."), expressing pleasure at the illustration she had sent him for his Christmas Book [*viz. The Battle of Life*] (". . . Except Stanfield's, they [the illustrations] all shocked me, more or less. I was delighted with yours . . . it hangs up over my chair in the drawing room . . ."), and relating how well her husband looks (". . . he took an extraordinary bath, in which he was rubbed all over with chemical compounds, and had everything done to him that could be invented for seven francs . . ."), *with the autograph envelope, signed*

*** There are several minor inaccuracies in the text printed in the Nonesuch Edition of the *Letters*.

249   A.L.s. to Francis Sylvester Mahony ("Father Prout"), humorist, *4 pages, 8vo, 148 King's Road, Brighton Twenty Sixth May 1847*, declining to edit the letters Mahony had written as correspondent in Rome of the *Daily News* (*viz. Facts and Figures from Italy, by Don Jeremy Savonarola, Benedictine Monk, addressed to Charles Dickens, Esq., being an Appendix to his Pictures*, i.e. to Dickens's *Pictures from Italy*) partly on the grounds of his own breach with the *Daily News* in the previous year

> . . . I made a false step in ever connecting myself with the Daily News. I retraced it, at some cost of money, mental uneasiness and personal inconvenience. I succeeded in detaching myself from it, very early in its existence, by a great wrench and anything, arising now, that would connect me with its columns, would undo all I did with so much pain. The very thought puts me in a perspiration . . .

*** Dickens in fact wrote a preface of twenty-five words for *Facts and Figures*, dated 1 July 1847. Dickens's punctuation in this letter is not reproduced with complete accuracy in the Nonesuch Edition of the *Letters*.

AUTOGRAPH LETTERS OF CHARLES DICKENS

250   A.L.s. to Thomas Beard, *3 pages, 8vo, Athenaeum. Sunday Twenty Seventh June 1847.*, about their holiday plans at Broadstairs, the opening of the Margate Theatre, Leigh Hunt's pension (". . . Having shamed the Government into doing something handsome for Leigh Hunt . . .") and theatrical performances, *last page endorsed, with the autograph envelope, postmarks, penny-red stamp affixed*

. . . I have taken the house next Barnes's, mainly because it is the most cheerful, and partly because (I don't know how many years ago) I started the old man and the child on their Curiosity-Shop wanderings, from that mansion . . .

∗∗   In the text printed in the Nonesuch Edition of the *Letters* "Barnes's" in the passage quoted above is given as "Ballard's", an error perhaps the result of research in other sources for the footnote: "No. 37 Albion Street. Ballard was the landlord of the Albion . . .".

251   A.L.s. ("CD.") to Mark Lemon, editor of *Punch*, one of the leading members of Dickens's company of amateur actors, *1 page, 8vo, Broadstairs. Wednesday Eleventh August 1847*, mentioning that he had begun *Dombey and Son* (*viz.* a monthly number of it) that morning and sending substitute titles for "The New Pilgrim's Progress" (inverted commas omitted in the Nonesuch Edition of the *Letters*), *with the autographed envelope, signed*

∗∗   Dickens intended to write "The New Pilgrim's Progress" in an effort to raise "the much longed-for hundred pounds" towards the benefit-fund for Leigh Hunt. "It was to be, in the phraseology of that notorious woman [*viz.* Mrs. Gamp (*Martin Chuzzlewit*)], a new "Piljians Projiss"; and was to bear upon the title page its description as an Account of a late Expedition into the North, for an Amateur Theatrical Benefit, written by Mrs. Gamp (who was an eye-witness), Inscribed to Mrs. Harris, Edited by Charles Dickens, and published, with illustrations on wood by so and so, in aid of the Benefit-Fund." (Ley's edition of Forster, *Life of Dickens*, p. 458 and ff.).

252   A.L.s. to Thomas Beard, *1 page, 8vo, Devonshire Terrace Thirtieth March 1848.*, inviting him to attend "a solemn "Dombey Dinner" " and "for a half a pint or so of the rosy", *conjugate leaf, endorsed, with the autograph envelope, signed, postmarks*

∗∗   The dinner was in celebration of the completion of *Dombey and Son*.

253   A.L.s. to David Macbeth Moir, physician and author, *8 pages, 8vo, London, 1 Devonshire Terrace York Gate Regents Park Seventeenth June 1848*, apologising for not answering Moir's letter before (". . . I have been, ever since its receipt, so occupied in one way or other that although I have been thinking of it almost every day, I have never laid violent hands upon a pen to answer it . . ."), reviewing his dealings with publishers, his financial position, the status of Literature in England and the public's recognition of him (giving particular illustrations of the last), outlining his plans for visiting Edinburgh, expressing the hope that Moir would come to London (". . . When will there be no patients in Musselburgh and thereabouts? And then we will smoke a cigar together, on the top of Saint Pauls . . .") and sending news of his family, *etc., with the autograph envelope, signed*

. . . Dombey has been the greatest success I ever achieved. Although Literature as a profession has no distinct status in England, I am bound to say that what I experience of its recognition, all through Society, in my own person, is honorable, ample, and independent . . .

of them. This is the last thing I can
say ... in the way of thanks. DXX.

The Household Words has sold
at this minute I being published
this morning

18, OOO

! ! !

I am proud of its rising a trifle
ahead of those created with Klein.
In this present number I shall
call upon you to certify Mr Bailey

Please write me ورسیون of the E. S. as explain
with my friend Foy!

Yrs affectionately

Charles Dickens

AUTOGRAPH LETTERS OF CHARLES DICKENS

254 Series of 3 A.Ls.s. (two signed with initials) to John Leech, *8 pages, 8vo, Devonshire Terrace (2) and Bedford Hotel Brighton, Monday Night Thirtieth October 1848., Twenty Second November 1848., and First December 1848.*, about the Christmas Book for 1848, *The Haunted Man* and the illustrations for it; the letter contains the first mention of Tenniel in his correspondence, *on black-edged paper, with the three autograph envelopes, signed*

255 A.L.s. to William Bradbury, partner in the publishing firm, Bradbury & Evans, *4 pages, 8vo, Bedford Hotel Brighton Friday First December 1848.*, announcing the completion of *The Haunted Man*, and making arrangements about the proofs and illustrations, *on black-edged paper*

   . . . I finished last night, having been crying my eyes out over it—not painfully but pleasantly as I hope the readers will—these last three days . . .

256 A.L.s. ("CD.") to Mark Lemon, *4 pages, 8vo, Devonshire Terrace Wednesday Thirteenth Decr 1848*, discussing alterations to Lemon's dramatisation of *The Haunted Man* and giving a rendez-vous for later in the day, *black-edged paper, formerly mounted*

   ** The last word of the letter, described in the Nonesuch Edition of the *Letters* as torn away, although in fact previously obscured only by mounting tape, is "quo".

257 A.L.s. to Thomas Beard, *3 pages, 8vo, Devonshire Terrace Tuesday Night Nineteenth December 1848.*, thanking him for his letter and interest in the "inimitable B[oz]" (". . . I feel such things more than most men, I am sure—and am, so far, worthy of them . . ."), telling him about the sales of *The Haunted Man* and inviting him to the dinner which he was "gravely devising" for "those concerned with him" i.e. *The Haunted Man* (". . . I shall call upon you to occupy your Dombey place on the occasion, my buck. So, as Captain Cuttle [in *Dombey and Son*] says, Stand by! . . ."), *on black-edged paper, last page endorsed, with the autograph envelope, signed, postmarks, penny-red stamp affixed*

   ** The dinner was held on 3 January 1849.

AUTOGRAPH LETTERS OF CHARLES DICKENS

258   A.L.s. to his friend the Hon. Richard Watson, *4 pages, 8vo, Devonshire Terrace. Twenty First July 1849.*, declining, on account of his involvement in the writing of *David Copperfield*, his offer of a holiday in Switzerland and inviting them instead to visit Mrs. Dickens and himself in the Isle of Wight (". . . our cottage (I believe it is the identical "humble shed" that Young Love lived in, in the song) is in a charming situation . . ."); he also mentions his thoughts on the Franco-Italian question, Talfourd's state over a vacant judgeship, the House of Commons, Lord Lansdowne and Disraeli (". . . Everybody else wants everything and gets nothing—which seems to me to be an expressive summary of the House of Commons. There has been a kind of grim imbecility and gouty Chesterfieldianity about Ld Lansdowne this year, remarkable to behold. It delights me that D'Israeli has done such justice to his conscience—less self, in regard of the Jews . . ."), *with the autograph envelope, signed, postmarks*

> . . . after considering the feasibility of this delightful journey (only postponed, I sincerely hope) I became afraid, in this stage of my story [*viz. David Copperfield*] of so entirely departing from my inventive habits for a fortnight or more . . . And with so much before me, and the necessity always present to me of doing my best and sustaining my reputation at its highest point, I feel it better and wiser to keep near my oar . . .

**   David Copperfield is dedicated to Watson and his wife.

There are some errors of transcription in the text printed in the Nonesuch Edition of the *Letters* including the transposition of words in the phrase "more opportunities to Mrs. Watson for sketching".

259   A.L.s. ("CD.") to John Leech, written "with a sickly mask of mirth", *2 pages, 8vo, Broadstairs Friday Fifth October 1849*, giving personal news and describing Broadstairs, *with the autograph envelope, signed, penny-red stamp affixed, postmarked, wafer seal*

> . . . I went over to Canterbury yesterday—alone—and refreshed myself with a day's rain there. I returned at night, not wholly free from snases Bloomfieldian . . .

> . . . the air so brisk and bracing as it is nowhere but at Broadstairs—the Channel so busy and alive with shipping as it is nowhere but off Broadstairs, the hotel so cosy and like a private house as it is nowhere but in Broadstairs—everything as nothing is out of Broadstairs. Veeve la Broadstairs! . . .

260   A.L.s. to Thomas Chapman, the chairman of Lloyd's, a "much-valued friend", *2 pages, 8vo, Devonshire Terrace Twentieth October 1849*, telling him of his intention of inserting in a new preface for the reprint of his *American Notes* a denunciation of "that execrable rascal" Thomas Powell and of Powell's "easy connexion with an American newspaper, as a striking proof of the justice of the estimation in which I hold that Press . . .", *with the autograph envelope, signed, penny-red stamp affixed, postmarks, wafer seal*

**   Thomas Powell, a former employee of Chapman and Hall, fled to America after robbing the firm and there published his *Living Authors of England* which contained an abusive chapter on Dickens.

In the Nonesuch Edition of the *Letters* one word from this letter is omitted.

AUTOGRAPH LETTERS OF CHARLES DICKENS

261   A.L.s. to John T. Lawrence, *2 pages, 8vo, Devonshire Terrace, London Monday Tenth December 1849*, regretfully declining an invitation (". . . But at this time of the month, and for about ten days onward, every month, I am the Slave of the Lamp called Copperfield. It would hardly light you on the 1ˢᵗ of January, if I were to make the holiday you propose; and I am assured by what you say of it, that you would rather miss me than it . . .")

***   *David Copperfield* was published in parts between May 1849 and November 1850.

262   A.L.s. to the solicitor Robert Rogers, DICKENS'S ONLY KNOWN LETTER TO HIM, *2 pages, 8vo, Devonshire Terrace Twenty First December 1849.*, promising to modify Miss Mowcher in *David Copperfield* following the complaint of Mrs. Seymour Hill, a chiropodist in the neighbourhood of Devonshire Terrace, that Dickens was caricaturing her in that character, *with the autograph envelope, penny-red stamp affixed, postmarked*—TOGETHER WITH contemporary copies of the above letter, of Mrs. Hill's letter to Dickens and of Dickens's reply (*both dated 18 December 1849*) as well as of Rogers's letter which evoked the present A.L.s. from Dickens and a contemporary extract from Forster's *Life* referring to this correspondence

. . . I have been for years in the habit of meeting in the Streets some one unknown to me by name or pursuit, whom it resembles almost if not quite as much as it resembles you—If I had had the least thought of presenting you personally in my book I could have had your portrait drawn any morning in the week and put there . . .

***   THE LETTER FROM DICKENS TO MRS. SEYMOUR HILL DATED 18 DECEMBER 1849 IS NOT PRINTED IN THE NONESUCH EDITION OF THE LETTERS, IS APPARENTLY UNPUBLISHED AND THE ORIGINAL IS NOT KNOWN TO HAVE SURVIVED. The letters from Mrs. Hill and Rogers to Dickens are not known to have been published.

263   A.L.s. to Louis D'Elboux, *4 pages, 8vo, 1 Devonshire Terrace York Gate Regents Park Twenty Fourth December 1849*, thanking him for his letter and account of his life after twenty-five years, giving in return a brief account of his own family (". . . Fanny my eldest sister, died (poor girl!) last September twelvemonth . . .") and promising to call on him if one of his "flying expeditions about the country" should bring him to Southampton (". . . I shall present myself before you (but not, as of yore, in a Russian jacket, and a soldierly young cap), and try if you know me . . ."), *with the autograph envelope, postmarks*

***   The editors of the Nonesuch Edition of the *Letters* omitted to print the amusing five-line postscript in this original and transcribed the word "ten" as "two" in the sentence: ". . . when I came ["come" in printed version] to your mention of ten children I was quite as much amazed as if, instead of having eight of my own, I hadn't one . . .".

D'Elboux's letter may, like others, have been evoked by autobiographical scenes in *David Copperfield* which had been appearing in monthly parts since May 1849.

AUTOGRAPH LETTERS OF CHARLES DICKENS

264   A.L.s. to Augustus [Dickens], *1 page, 8vo, Brighton, Tenth March 1850,* regretting that he cannot help Mr. Chapman (presumably to become a member) because he himself had retired from the Parthenon Club about five years before and asking Augustus to thank John Barrow for "his valuable assistance in the matter of the slandered Powell", *a little worn, small tears at folds*

** This letter is not printed in the Nonesuch Edition of the *Letters* and is apparently UNPUBLISHED.

The "slandered Powell" was Thomas Powell, formerly an employee of Chapman & Co., who after robbing the firm, fled to America and published his *Living Authors of England* which contained an abusive chapter on Dickens. For Dickens's extended opinion of Powell see the Nonesuch Edition of the *Letters*, ii. 182.

265   A.L.s. to William J. Thomas, founder of *Notes and Queries*, A NEW DICKENS CORRESPONDENT, *2 pages, 8vo, 1 Devonshire Terrace Thirtieth May, 1850,* sending a subscription "towards the repair of brave old Chaucer's Tomb" and expressing his great pleasure at seeing "my good friend Captain Cuttle's name (and sentiment) appended to your very curious and interesting publication . . .", *with the autograph envelope, signed, wafer seal, and enclosing a receipt for five shillings from Dickens, dated 30 May 1850 made out and signed by Thomas as Treasurer to the Committee for Chaucer's Monument*

** Thomas had used Captain Cuttle's sentiment [*Dombey and Son*]—"When found make a note of"—as the epigraph to *Notes and Queries*. Except for a description of the present letter and one other in the private *Catalogue* of the Comte de Suzannet, Dickens's correspondence with Thomas is unknown. The present letter is apparently UNPUBLISHED IN FULL; NOT PRINTED IN THE NONESUCH EDITION OF THE LETTERS.

266   A.L.s. to the actor William Charles Macready *5 pages, 8vo, Devonshire Terrace Twenty Seventh February 1851,* reasoning that the sonnet written by Tennyson on Macready's retirement should not be read after the proposing of his health at the actor's Farewell Dinner on 1 March, touching on other arrangements for that occasion and, while describing the effect on him of Macready's last appearance on the stage at Drury Lane Theatre the previous night (26 February), giving a short account of his early devotion to Macready and of the importance of Macready's example to his own career, *mounted down one edge, endorsed at head*

. . . I cannot forbear a word about last night. I think I have told you sometimes, my much-loved friend, how, when I was a mere boy, I was one of your faithful and devoted adherents in the Pit—I believe as true a member of that true host of followers as it has ever boasted. As I improved myself and was improved by favouring circumstances in mind and fortune, I only became the more earnest (if it were possible) in my study of you. No light portion of my life arose before me when the great vision to which I am beholden, in I don't know how great a degree, or for how much—who does?— faded so nobly from my bodily eyes last night . . .

** The text printed in the Nonesuch Edition of the *Letters* is imperfect in the following respects: a nine-word postscript about the style of his signature in this particular letter and one word in the last paragraph are omitted; eight words underlined by Dickens are not printed in italic type; inverted commas not in the original are inserted round the words Auld Lang Syne; one paragraph break is ignored; some punctuation is suppressed or altered; and the word "great" in the phrase "when the great vision to which I am beholden" quoted above is printed as "quiet".

At the Farewell Dinner, chaired by Bulwer, Forster read the sonnet by Tennyson and Dickens, Thackeray and Bunsen made speeches (*DNB sub* Macready).

AUTOGRAPH LETTERS OF CHARLES DICKENS

267   A.L.s. ("Wilmot") to "Middlesex" *viz.* Frank Stone, the artist, *4 pages, 8vo, Broadstairs, Kent. Wednesday Sixteenth July, 1851.*, incorporating a copy of a letter he had sent to [? George] Robins relating to his purchase of Tavistock House (". . . It is very well suited to my purpose, but would require considerable decoration and improvement . . ."), *black-edged paper*

*** THIS LETTER IS NOT PRINTED IN THE NONESUCH EDITION OF THE LETTERS AND IS APPARENTLY UNPUBLISHED; THE LETTER TO ROBINS IS ALSO UNPUBLISHED AND IS NOT KNOWN TO SURVIVE IN THE ORIGINAL.

The form of address ("Middlesex") and the signature ("Wilmot") are explained by the parts played by Stone (Duke of Middlesex) and Dickens (Lord Wilmot) in Bulwer Lytton's comedy, *Not So Bad as We Seem.* Frank Stone occupied a portion of Tavistock House until Dickens bought it and thereafter lived in a smaller house in the same square.

268   A.L.s. to Sir Cusack Patrick Roney, Secretary to the Royal Literary Fund and author of books on travel, particularly on Ireland, THE ONLY KNOWN LETTER FROM DICKENS TO HIM, *2 pages, 8vo, Tavistock House, London. Second May 1853.*, explaining how impossible a journey to Ireland would be (". . . not . . . much more easy to me than a journey to the Moon . . .") and asking him to let "James" know that he is curious to know "whether any remembrances of old times were revived in him by any parts of David Copperfield"

*** Only part of this letter is printed (from a sale catalogue) in the Nonesuch Edition of the *Letters.*

AUTOGRAPH LETTERS OF CHARLES DICKENS

269   A.L.s. ("CD.") to William Henry Wills, assistant editor of *Household Words*, *4 pages*, *8vo*, *Chateau des Molineaux Boulogne Saturday Night*, *Eighteenth June 1853*, arranged under the headings: "H(OUSEHOLD) W(ORDS) (discussing the number for 9 July); "BLEAK HOUSE" (concerning his progress with No. 17); "MONEY" (sending a cheque) and "GENERAL MOVEMENTS OF INIMITABLE", i.e. himself (describing the chateau, stating his intention of staying there until after the completion of no. 18 of *Bleak House*, inviting Wills to visit, mentioning the improvement in his own health, Wills's parcel, *etc.*), *modern cloth case with the Comte de Suzannet's bookplate*

. . . It [the chateau] is in the country, though not more than ten minute's walk from the Post Office, and is the best doll's house of many rooms in the prettiest French grounds and the most charming situation I have ever seen—the best place I have ever lived in, abroad, except at Genoa. You can scarcely imagine the beauty of the air on this richly wooded hill side. As to comforts in the house, there are all sorts of things, beginning with no end of the coldest water and running through the most beautiful flowers down to English footbaths and a Parisian liquer-stand . . .

270   A.L.s. to [Peter] Cunningham, *3 pages*, *8vo*, *Tavistock House*, *Saturday Eleventh March 1854*, mildly rebuking him for making mis-statements about his new book (*viz.* *Hard Times*) in the *Illustrated London News* and offering to verify any facts for him in future

. . . The mischief of such a statement is twofold. First, it encourages the public to believe in the impossibility that books are produced in that very sudden and cavalier manner (as poor Newton used to feign that he produced the elaborate drawings he made in his madness, by winking at his table) . . .

* The text printed in the Nonesuch Edition of the *Letters* is incorrect in two particulars: it introduces a paragraph break not in the original and the word "pernicious" is omitted from Dickens's elaboration of the second "mischief".

271   A.L.s. ("CD.") to his sister-in-law Georgina Hogarth, *4 pages*, *8vo*, *Office of Household Words*, *Saturday Twenty Second July 1854*, discussing family affairs and intended journeys, praising Wilkie Collins's new book [*viz.* Hide and Seek], giving personal news, mentioning the proofs of *Hard Times* and relating that his wife, Catherine, is described in Harriet Beecher Stowe's book, presumably *A Key to Uncle Tom's Cabin, lightly guarded*

. . . Neither you nor Catherine did justice to Collins's book. I think it far away the cleverest Novel I have ever seen written by a new hand. It is much beyond Mrs. Gaskell, and is in some respects masterly . . . In short, I call it a very remarkable book, and have been very much surprised by its great merit . . .

. . . Oh!—Something else for Catherine!—She is described in Mrs. Stowe's book; which Forster, in a languid state of rhematico—colchico—hiccoughy—frousy—aperient—medical mystery, informed me yesterday he had "been obliged to assault dreadfully." Mrs Stowe is of opinion that she is "large", I believe.

* Among the errors in the text printed in the Nonesuch Edition of the *Letters* are the misreading of "very" (half-way down the second page) as "my" and the insertion of a paragraph break not in the original.

AUTOGRAPH LETTERS OF CHARLES DICKENS

272 Album containing 34 original letters by Dickens, comprising 30 A.Ls.s. and 1 A.L. to Edmund Yates, 1 A.L.s. to Frederick Yates, Edmund's father, 1 A.L.s. to Mrs. Elizabeth Yates, Edmund's mother, and 1 A.L.s. to the publishers, Fields, Osgood & Co., *together with* a copy by Yates of a letter sent to him by Dickens, the original of which is not known to exist, and an original printed playbill for performances of works by Dickens and Wilkie Collins, *mostly mounted by conjugate blank leaves*, FINE ILLUMINATED TITLE-PAGE EXECUTED FOR YATES BY MARCUS WARD & Co., *contemporary russia, slightly rubbed, decorated border in green and citron, sunken black-rimmed panel edged in gilt, re-backed, 4to*

⁎⁎ THIS COLLECTION CONTAINS ALL BUT THREE OF THE KNOWN LETTERS FROM DICKENS TO EDMUND YATES, ONE OF WHICH IS ONLY PARTLY PUBLISHED, ADDS ONE AUTOGRAPH LETTER PREVIOUSLY UNKNOWN AND INCLUDES DICKENS'S FIRST AND LAST LETTERS TO YATES.

"Greatest favourite of all the band of 'Dickens's young men'." Edmund Hodgson Yates (1831-94) novelist, journalist, lecturer and founder of *The World*, contributed to *Household Words* and *All the Year Round* and was the cause of the famous estrangement of Dickens from Thackeray (referred to in these letters).

Unless otherwise stated the letters in this album are addressed to Edmund Yates.

(1) A.L.s. to Frederick Yates, Edmund Yates's father, *2 pages, 8vo, 48 Doughty Street. Friday Morning* [? December *1837*], requesting the use of his private box [at the Adelphi] for Mrs. Dickens, "his better half to behold Valsha there from" and apologising for thus adding to his "numerous managerial nuisances", *black-edged paper*

⁎⁎ An initialled note by Edmund Yates at the head of the first page (not mentioned by the editors of the Pilgrim Edition of the *Letters*) reads: "To my Father. I assume this to have been written about 1837, when he was mourning for Mary Hogarth."
Frederick Yates, 1797-1842, theatre proprietor and actor, produced dramatic adaptations of *Oliver Twist* and *Nicholas Nickleby* and acted Pickwick in the *Peregrinations of Pickwick*, Fagin in *Oliver Twist* and Mr. Chester and Miss Miggs in *Barnaby Rudge*. Yates also played Mr. Mantillini in the adaptation of Nickleby.
(2) A.L.s. "HIS FIRST LETTER TO ME EY.", *2 pages, 8vo, Boulogne. Thirtieth July 1854*, thanking Yates for the gift of his book [presumably his series of sketches, *My Haunts and their Frequenters*] which he had brought with him "to read under a Haystack here," sending a "small parcel of thanks" in return, and hoping to see him under his "London Haystack (metaphorical for ceiling)" when back in England.
⁎⁎ In the text printed in the Nonesuch Edition of the *Letters* two capital letters are suppressed, two commas and one semi-colon inserted and one comma omitted.
(3) Original printed playbill for performances of Wilkie Collins's *The Lighthouse* and *Mr Nightingale's Diary* by Mr Crummles [*viz*. Dickens] and Mark Lemon on 18 June 1855 at "The Smallest Theatre in the World! Tavistock House", *1 page, folio, silked, printed in red and black*
(4) A.L. (subscription and signature torn away) *Tavistock House* (but, as Dickens explains in the letter, in fact from Southampton) *Sunday Nineteenth July. 1857*, explaining, with a charming reflection on growing old, his purpose in being at Southampton (". . . I am here to send Walter away over what they call in Green Bush melodramas, "The Big Drink" and I don't at all know this day how he comes to be mine, or I, his . . ."), telling Yates the effect of seeing the ship before him (". . . I suddenly came into possession of a photograph of my own back at 16 and 20, and also into a suspicion that I had doubled the last age . . ."), inviting him to stay at Gad's Hill, and thanking him "heartily" for an account of the play in the *Daily News*
". . . I have come here on an errand which will grow familiar to you before you know that Time has fluffed his wings over your head. Like me, you will find those babies grow to be young men, before you are quite sure they are born. Like me, you will have great teeth drawn with a wrench, and will only then know that you ever cut them . . ."
⁎⁎ Dickens's second son, Walter Landor Dickens, was going to India as a cadet in the service of the East India Company.

AUTOGRAPH LETTERS OF CHARLES DICKENS

In the first paragraph of the text printed in the Nonesuch Edition of the *Letters* fifteen words in parenthesis have been omitted and the words "as above" appear as "ashore", while in the last paragraph the word "Play" has been mistranscribed as "reading".

(5) A.L.s. *2 pages, 8vo, Tavistock House, Monday Night Sixteenth November, 1857*, giving insights into his own views on composition while commenting on a story by Yates
". . . The opening is excellent. But it passes too completely into the Irishman's narrative—does not light it up with the life about it, or the circumstances under which it is delivered—and does not carry through it, as I think it should with a certain indefinable subtlety, the thread with which you begin your weaving. I will tell [Henry] Wills to send me the Proof, and will try to shew you what I mean when I shall have gone over it carefully . . ."

*** In the Nonesuch Edition of the *Letters* the word subtlety is mistranscribed as "subtleness", four dashes are printed as commas and two commas are omitted.

(6) A.L.s. ("CD.") *2 pages, 8vo, Tavistock House Tuesday Second February 1858*, showing in detail that a quotation (?) from *Martin Chuzzlewit* (about Mrs. Harris's—the husband of Mrs. Gamp's imaginary friend—fit when his wife was having her first child) as used by Yates was "all wrong"
". . . "What owls are those! Who is owling! Not my ugebond! "Upon which, the Doctor, looking round one of the bottom posts of the bed, and taking Mrs Harris's pulse in a re-assuring manner, says, with admirable presence of mind, "Howls my dear Madame? No, no, no. What are you thinking, of. Howls, my dear Mrs Harris? Ha ha ha! Organs Maam, organs. Organs in the streets Mrs Harris. No howls" — . . ."

*** The text printed in the Nonesuch Edition of the Letters is inaccurate in the following particulars: three apostrophes, one hyphen, one dash, one question mark and one comma are inserted; the final 's' of "Harris's", one set of inverted commas and one exclamation mark are omitted; the double-underlining of "NOT" is printed in italics; four capital letters are suppressed; two dashes are given as commas, one colon as a comma, one comma as a colon and another as a semi-colon.

(7) A.L.s. ("CD.") *3 pages, 8vo, Tavistock House, Tavistock Square, London. W.C. Wednesday Twenty Eighth April, 1858*, sending "an orthopaedic shield to defend your manly bosom from the pens of the enemy" and giving a fine account of his persecution by charitable societies which includes a phonetic report of his servants complaint at the Burton Arms
". . . Benevolent men get behind the piers of the gates, lying in wait for my going out; and when I peep shrinkingly from my study-windows, I see their pot-bellied shadows projected on the gravel. Benevolent bullies drive up in Hansom cabs (with engraved portraits of their benevolent Institutions hanging over the aprons, like banners on their outward walls), and stay so long at the door, that their horses deposit beehives of excellent manure all over the front court. Benevolent area-sneaks get lost in the kitchens, and are found to impede the circulation of the knife-cleaning Machine . . ."

*** The thirteen-word clause describing the generous defecations of 'benevolent' horses (quoted above) is omitted (without indication) from the text printed in the Nonesuch Edition of the *Letters*; there are also a number of minor errors of transcription there.

(8) A.L.s. *1 page, 8vo, Tavistock House, Tavistock Square, London. W.C. Friday Thirtieth April, 1858*,—"I have derived great gratification from what I read of yours today, and I cordially thank you;—not alone because you have written it, but because I am sure you have earnestly felt it . . ."

*** The letter possibly refers to a newspaper report by Yates of the first public Reading Dickens gave for his own benefit on 29 April 1858, or possibly to a preview Dickens may have had of Yates's adulatory notice of him in the first number (May 1858) of the new paper, *Town Talk*, of which Yates was the editor.

(9) A.L.s. to the former actress, Mrs Elizabeth Yates, Edmund's mother, *2 pages, 8vo, Tavistock House, Tavistock Square, London. W.C. Saturday Evening Fifteenth May 1858*, saying how sorry he was at her absence the previous Thursday, possibly from one of his Readings, and paying a moving tribute to her effect on him as a youth
". . . No one alive can have more delightful associations with the lightest sound of your voice than I have; and to give you a minutes interest and pleasure, in acknowledgement of the uncountable hours of happiness you gave me when you were a mysterious Angel to me, would honestly gratify my heart . . ."

*** The first page is inscribed by Edmund Yates: "To my mother. EY."
Elizabeth Yates had been one of the important figures on the theatrical scene during Dickens's youth and had clearly had a profound effect upon him.

AUTOGRAPH LETTERS OF CHARLES DICKENS

(10) A.L.s. *2 pages, 8vo, Tavistock House, Tavistock Square, London. W.C. Monday Evening Thirty First May, 1858*, sending (on the second page), primarily for his mother Mrs Yates's benefit, a copy of the declaration (dated 29 May 1858) by his own mother-in-law Mrs Hogarth and her daughter, Helen, of their disbelief in "certain statements" to the effect that the difference between Dickens and his wife, which had resulted in their recent separation, ". . . were occasioned by circumstances deeply affecting the moral character of Mr Dickens and compromising the reputation and good name of others . . ."

(11) A.L.s. ("CD") *1 page, 8vo, Tavistock House, Tavistock Square, London. W.C. Tuesday Fifteenth June, 1858,* inviting Yates to dinner and emphasizing that Yates could count on him in all things, *some offsetting where folded before ink was dry, conjugate blank*

*** The following note in pencil is written in a modern hand on the album leaf next to the letter: "First consultation on the subject of Yates's quarrel with Thackeray".

In the second number of his paper (12 June), *Town Talk*, Yates had written an impertinent and unfriendly sketch of Thackeray. The ensuing famous quarrel resulted in Yates's name being struck off the list of members of the Garrick Club (20 July 1858) and some bitter exchanges and allusions in print. Dickens acted as chief adviser to Yates throughout the affair, a role which led to his own estrangement from Thackeray.

(12) A.L.s. ("CD.") *1 page, 8vo, Tavistock House, Tavistock Square, London. W.C. Tuesday Eighth June 1858*, expressing his feelings about his present situation, i.e. his separation from his wife and the circumstances surrounding it, *conjugate blank*

". . . If you could know how much I have felt within this last month, and what a sense of wrong has been upon me, and what a strain and struggle I have lived under, you would see that my heart is so jagged and rent out of shape, that it does not this day leave me hand enough to shape these words . . ."

*** The letter consists of one paragraph, not two as in the text printed in the Nonesuch Edition of the *Letters.*

(13) A.L.s. ("CD.") *1 page, 8vo, Gad's Hill Place, Higham by Rochester, Kent. Wednesday Seventh July, 1858*, agreeing to dine at the Albion the next day and reassuring Yates of his interest in his letters "be they ever so numerous", *conjugate blank, some offsetting where folded before ink was dry.*

(14) A.L.s. *3 pages, 8vo, Gad's Hill Place, Higham by Rochester, Kent. Twenty Sixth July, 1858*, giving Yates reasoned advice (because of his quarrel with Thackeray) not to attend in person the general meeting [of the Garrick Club]

*** At the general meeting Dickens, Wilkie Collins and Samuel Lover were among those who spoke in Yates's defence.

(15) A.L.s. ("CD.") *2 pages, Swan Hotel, Worcester* (*should be Wolverhampton, according to the editors of the Nonesuch Edition of the Letters*) *Wednesday Eleventh August 1858.*, ascribing a cutting to Cole, describing the preparation of Arthur [Smith, his manager 'friend and secretary'] for the Reading that evening, and discussing dinner engagements

". . . To night's room has to be transformed (after 4 o'Clock, if you please) from a Corn Exchange into a St. Martin's Hall. He [*viz.* Arthur Smith] has consequently, in some strange way, covered himself with dust and ashes, as a preparation for work. In which costume he is going to dine with me at 3 to the end that he may drag the forms about without a moments loss of time . . ."

*** The letter ends with the following paragraph in which two words have been erased: "What a bitch —, that daughter of honest good — "

Two words underlined by Dickens in this original are not italicised in the Nonesuch Edition of the *Letters.*

(16) A.L.s. ("CD.") *2 pages, 8vo, Adelphi Hotel, Liverpool Saturday Twenty First August 1858.*, advising Yates on a legal matter (doubtless in relation to the quarrel with Thackeray), giving an account of the great success of his Reading that evening, and describing an encounter with Thackeray and Fladgate on the steps of the Reform Club (". . . Fladgate's eyebrows went up into the crown of his hat, and he twisted himself into extraordinary forms . . .")

". . . A wonderful house here last night. The largest in numbers, and the largest in money we have ever had, including St. Martin's Hall. There were 2,300 people, and 200 guineas. The very books were all sold out, early in the evening, and Arthur [Smith] bathed in checks—took headers into tickets —floated on billows of passes—dived under weirs of shillings—staggered home, faint with gold and silver . . ."

AUTOGRAPH LETTERS OF CHARLES DICKENS

(17) A.L.s. ("CD.") *1 page, 8vo, Tavistock House, Tavistock Square, London. W.C. Saturday Nineteenth February 1859*, arranging to fix a time for finishing" the Pamphlet";—the letter begins: "Like a besotted Blockhead I have forgotten that I must be out tomorrow morning . . .", *some off-setting where folded before ink was dry, conjugate blank*

*** The pamphlet referred to in this letter was Yates's version of his quarrel with Thackeray, *Mr Thackeray, Mr Yates, and the Garrick Club*, privately printed in 1859.

(18) A.L.s. ("CD.") *3 pages, 8vo, Tavistock House, Tavistock Square, London. W.C. Tuesday Twenty Ninth March 1859*, advancing the advantages of Gad's Hill as "the place for the [local] letter box"; stating the reasons for the production of *The Pic Nic Papers* (for the benefit of the widow and children of his first publisher, John Macrone) and for the addition of a third volume by Colburn; describing his own part in it (editing, and *The Lamplighter*); and referring to an advertisement in *The Times* (". . . as Mr Samuel Weller expresses it somewhere in Pickwick "ravin' mad with con-sciousness o' villany" . . .")

*** The paragraph about the letter box is probably explained by the fact that Yates (like Trollope) was in the employ of the Post Office.

(19) A.L.s. ("CD.") *1 page, 8vo, Office of All the Year Round, Tuesday Twentieth April 1859*, discussing contributions by Yates presumably to *All the Year Round* (". . . The Lord John bit is very droll but I do not like to use it . . .") *conjugate blank*

(20) A.L.s. *2 pages, 8vo, Gad's Hill Place, Higham by Rochester, Kent. Thursday Nineteenth May 1859*, asking Yates to make his excuses to [W.R.] Sculthorpe for not being able to dine with him "in that wonderful little Bower" on the following Monday (". . . I am at work on my own story [*viz. The Tale of Two Cities* then appearing in parts in *All the Year Round*], and am completely its slave, and must do it in its own time and way . . .")

". . . I would have written to Mr Sculthorpe myself, but that I doubt whether "Honeysuckle Cottage"—or "Bachelor Flower Bed"—or "Ingenuity Cabin, Telegraph Hill"—or the like would find him . . ."

*** This letter is not printed in the Nonesuch Edition of the Letters and is not known to be published elsewhere. It is loosely inserted in the album together with an A.L.s. by Yates, *2 pages, 8vo*, to Sculthorpe, in which he enclosed the letter from Dickens.

(21) A.L.s. *2 pages, 8vo, Cambridge Tuesday Eighteenth October 1859.*, providing Yates with reasons that he could use to put off an unnamed writer who wished to be introduced to Dickens

(22) A.L.s. ("CD.") *1 page, 8vo, Tavistock House, Tavistock Square, London. W.C. Wednesday Evening Twenty Fifth January 1860*, arranging to meet Yates at the Britannia [Theatre] on Saturday, when Wilkie [Collins] would probably join them, and to have "a British steak in the Cock in Fleet Street at ½ past 4", *conjugate blank*

(23) A.L.s. ("CD.") *1 page, 8vo, Gad's Hill Place, Higham by Rochester, Kent. Tuesday Seventeenth April, 1860.*, alluding to a postal problem and Yates's "Kentish Town trial", and making a moving remark about Yates's mother

". . . I think of your mother, as of a beautiful part of my own youth, and this dream that we are all dreaming seems to darken . . ."

*** Elizabeth Yates died at Kentish Town on 30 August 1860 after a long and painful illness.

(24) A.L.s. ("CD.") *2 pages, 8vo, Gad's Hill Place, Higham by Rochester, Kent. Sunday Twenty Third September 1860*, explaining why he had not written to Yates when his mother died, making his tribute to her, and discussing a contribution by Yates, presumably to *All the Year Round*, entitled "Holding up the Mirror"

". . . *You* know what a loving and faithful remembrance I always had of your mother, as a part of my youth no more capable of restoration than my youth itself. All the womanly goodness, grace, and beauty of *my* Drama went out with her. To the last I never could hear her voice without emotion . . ."

*** In the Nonesuch Edition of the *Letters* the following sentence, partly a misquotation from no. 23 in this album, has been interpolated into this letter immediately after the passage quoted above: "I think of her as a beautiful part of my own youth, and this dream that we are all dreaming seems to darken". This error may have arisen from the editors reliance on the National Edition (as is suggested by their marginal abbreviation "SC") although they did have direct access to the original. There are also a number of minor errors of transcription in the Nonesuch text.

AUTOGRAPH LETTERS OF CHARLES DICKENS

(25) A.L.s. ("CD.") *3 Hanover Terrace, Regents Park Sunday Twenty Fourth February 1861.*, reassuring Yates of his continued friendship (". . . not in the least alienated by any cause whatever, real or imaginary . . ."), and giving details of his own involvements

". . . Before Christmas, my story and what I had to do for Christmas kept me in actual bondage for weeks together. After Christmas . . . I was unwell, at the office to be near my Doctor, and did not once get to Gad's Hill where all the household were. Chronically, when I have a book to write I give myself up to it. Waywardly, my small private rubs make me uncertain in my humour sometimes, and unwilling to tie myself to the slightest engagement . . ."

** ONLY THREE SENTENCES OF THIS LETTER ARE QUOTED (FROM A SALE CATALOGUE) IN THE NONESUCH EDITION OF THE LETTERS; the remainder of the letter is not known to have been published elsewhere.

(26) A.L.s. ("CD.") *2 pages, 8vo, Gad's Hill Place, Higham by Rochester, Kent. Sunday Sixth October 1861.*, about the funeral of his manager, Arthur Smith ("our poor dear fellow") and Smith's earlier concurrence in the appointment of Thomas Headlands as his own successor

". . . I was so very much distressed last night in thinking of it all, and I find it so very difficult to preserve my composure when I dwell in my mind over the many times fast approaching when I shall sorely miss the familiar face, that I am hardly steady enough yet, to refer to the Readings like a man . . ."

** THE FIRST AND LAST PARAGRAPHS OF THIS LETTER (ELEVEN LINES) ARE NOT PRINTED IN THE NONESUCH EDITION OF THE LETTERS (text there apparently from the National Edition) AND THEY ARE NOT KNOWN TO HAVE BEEN PUBLISHED ELSEWHERE.

(27) A.L.s. ("CD.") *2 pages, 8vo, Kensington, Thursday Evening Third April 1862*, announcing his London Reading of Copperfield, making an arrangement to meet, suggesting caution to the actor Fechter before employing Walter Montgomery (". . . when he was last at Birmingham (just now) he was getting dissipated . . ."), and recommending Maria Ternan as suitable for Fechter to "take among his young ladies . . ."

". . . I have acted with her [*viz.* Maria Ternan], and believe her to have more aptitude in a minute than all the other people of her standing on the stage in a month. A lady besides, and pretty, and of a good figure, and always pains-taking and perfect to the letter. Also . . . a wonderful mimic . . . When I first knew her, I looked her in the eyes one morning at Manchester, and she took the whole Frozen Deep out of the look and six words . . ."

** Maria Ternan was the daughter of the celebrated actress, Frances Eleanor Ternan, who had, in 1855, taken part with Dickens and other celebrities in the production of Wilkie Collins's *Frozen Deep* at Manchester.

(28) A.L.s. ("CD.") *2 pages, 8vo, Hotel du Helder, Paris Wednesday Thirtieth September 1865*, severely criticising a new story by Yates (". . . I have been completely baffled. At first, I thought I must be out of sorts—and tried again. But I was worse the second time. And remain still worse at this present writing . . ."), informing him of his plans to return home, and sending amusing anecdotes as the latest news from the French capital, *slight staining*

". . . Three paving blouses came to work at the corner of this street last Monday—pulled up a bit of the road—sat down to look at it—and fell asleep. On Tuesday, one of the Blouses spat on his hands, and seemed to be going to begin, but didn't. The other two have shewn no sign of life whatever. This morning the industrious one ate a loaf. You may rely upon this, as the latest news from the French Capital . . ."

** There are some minor errors of transcription, including the words "set" and "put" as "get", in the Nonesuch Edition of the *Letters*.

(29) A.L.s. ("CD.") *1 page, 8vo, 6 Southwick Place Hyde Park Wednesday Seventh March, 1866*, discussing Yates's book *Land at Last, on Gad's Hill headed note-paper*

". . . Perhaps I cannot better express what I think of its execution than by saying honestly, that all the things in the book the most difficult to do, are the best done . . ."

(30) A.L.s. ("CD.") *1 page, 8vo, Carrick's Royal Hotel, Glasgow Tuesday Seventeenth April 1866*, sending a letter for Yates to use "in *any* serviceable way", giving his own intended itinerary, and reporting the success of his Readings (". . . Far ahead of all my previous experience . . ."), *on Gad's Hill headed note-paper, conjugate blank*

(31) A.L.s. *1 page, 8vo, Gad's Hill Place, Higham by Rochester, Kent. Sunday Tenth June 1866*, warmly praising the third volume of one of Yates's books (*? Broken to Harness*)

AUTOGRAPH LETTERS OF CHARLES DICKENS

". . . I have read your book with great surprise, and have been profoundly affected by it. It has touched me deeply, and moved me to many tears. Hold fast, I adjure you, to the deeper emotional faculty that you unquestionably possess, and do justice to the tenderness that is most beautifully and pathetically wrought out in the last of these three volumes . . ."

(32) Copy in the hand of Edmund Yates of a letter to himself from Dickens, *1 page*, *8vo* [*March 1867*], expressing his willingness to support Yates in his application to the committee of the S.P.C.K. for the editorship of a new journal (". . . You cannot overstate my recommⁿ. of you . . .")

₊ THE ORIGINAL OF THIS LETTER IS NOT KNOWN TO HAVE SURVIVED. The initials "S.P.C.K." are omitted from the text (possibly taken from that given in Yates's own *Recollections*) printed in the Nonesuch Edition of the *Letters*.

(33) A.L.s. ("CD.") *1 page*, *8vo*, *Gad's Hill Place*, *Higham by Rochester*, *Kent*. *Tuesday Twelfth May 1868.*, assuring Yates that he had not doubted him "for a moment", expressing his "great pleasure" with Yates's book, *The Black Sheep*, outlining the complexity of his own affairs, and spurring Yates on to fulfil himself (". . . I earnestly hope that you will now get right and clear. You are quite young enough, and have a sufficiently free stage before you, to play the play out yet to everybody's satisfaction . . ."), *conjugate blank*

(34) A.L.s. ("CD.") "LAST NOTE BUT ONE, RECEIVED FROM HIM. EY." *1 page*, *8vo*, *5 Hyde Park Place W. Monday Sixteenth May 1870*, arranging to meet in June (". . . after I have struck this tent . . .") and stating that he had lost the use of one foot

(35) A.L.s. ("CD.") "HIS LAST LETTER TO ME; WRITTEN FOUR DAYS BEFORE HIS DEATH EY." *2 pages*, *8vo*, *Gad's Hill Place*, *Higham by Rochester*, *Kent*. *Sunday Fifth June 1870*, asking him to forward a letter (see next item) to the publishers Fields, Osgood & Co, and outlining a difficulty in relation to the serialisation of *Edwin Drood* in America

₊ DICKENS IS NOT KNOWN TO HAVE WRITTEN MORE THAN FOUR LETTERS AFTER THIS ONE BEFORE HIS DEATH.

(36) A.L.s. to the publishers, Fields, Osgood & Co., *1 page*, *8vo*, *Gad's Hill Place*, *Higham by Rochester*, *Kent*. *Sunday Fifth June 1870*, introducing his "particular friend," Edmund Yates, and recommending "a new Serial Novel he is writing, called *Nobody's Fortune* . . .", *inscribed at head by Yates*, "*Enclosure in the foregoing*"

₊ DICKENS APPARENTLY WROTE ONLY THREE OTHER LETTERS AFTER THIS ONE.

AUTOGRAPH LETTERS OF CHARLES DICKENS

273   A.L.s. to Mrs. Winter (formerly Maria Beadnell) *1 page, 8vo, Tavistock House Twenty Ninth March 1855*, sending a pass for a box at the Adelphi (". . . Here is a box . . .") and expressing the hope that he would "fill up an empty corner thereof" if not "waylaid by Household Words", *conjugate blank*

***   Dickens subscribed himself "always very faithfully yours".

274   A.L.s. ("CD.") to Mark Lemon, *3 pages, 8vo, Tavistock House Saturday Twenty First April, 1855*, concerning quarrels in the Fielding (a club founded by Thackeray and several of his friends) particularly with Andrew Arcedeckne (whom Thackeray used as the model for Foker in *Pendennis* and described here by Dickens as "A lunatic . . . whom I suppose to be the terrible Dragon of that Symposium") and also concerning Dickens's efforts to reform the Royal Literary Fund and his attitude to the Queen's request that he and his company put on a performance for the benefit of the Fund

. . . if I am asked (as I am, in a note from the bothering albert who is in written communication with Phipps perpetually) to help them "as a compliment which the queen will appreciate", and unconditionally refuse, I am afraid I may not only do a surly thing personally towards the Court (and an ungracious one, after the Guild business), but may by the simplest means in the world damage a great cause . . .

275   A.L.s. to Whitwell Elwin, *4 pages, 8vo, Tavistock House Tuesday Night First May 1855*, concerning his attendance at the Literary Fund dinner

. . . I have not been in the habit of attending that dinner—have only done so twice, in about twenty years. Consequently my non-attendance is no new or marked thing. Then, observe. If I were there, I could hardly be there without speaking. The Bishop of Oxford is not wholly free from that kind of land-seamanship which is expert in weaving and tacking; and he *might* (I do not say would), execute a manoeuvre or so which I might feel it necessary to reduce to the level of an ordinary straightforward comprehension. Supposing this not to be the case, I have still a rather strong misgiving that the authorities would be scared if Mr Blewitt reported that I had informed him of my intention to come, and that they would very much rather on the whole that I stayed away. Lastly I must confess for myself, that I could not possibly say anything without referring to my hopes of a change . . .

***   This letter is only partly published (from a sale catalogue) in the Nonesuch Edition of the *Letters;* much of the passage quoted above is not reproduced there, nor is there any indication of its omission.

Dickens's correspondent, Whitwell Elwin (1816-1900), friend and executor of Forster, was editor of the *Quarterly Review* and rector of Booton, Norfolk. He edited five volumes of the standard edition of Pope.

Dickens did attend the Literary Fund dinner in 1855 and "indicted the extravagance and nepotism with which its affairs were administered" (E. Johnson, *Charles Dickens*).

AUTOGRAPH LETTERS OF CHARLES DICKENS

276   A.L.s. to Leigh Hunt, *3 pages, 8vo, Tavistock House Friday Fourth May 1855*, thanking him for his book, apologising for not calling on him (". . . I have never (as you know) got to your teapot, though I have very often (as you don't know) paved the road to Hammersmith with good intentions . . .") and giving a fine description of his "disjointed state", his "unlaid ghost-like plight" of beginning a new book [presumably *Little Dorrit*], *with the autograph envelope, signed, postmarked and with penny-red stamp*

   . . . I am now, to boot, in the wandering-unsettled-restless-uncontrollable state of being about to begin a new book. At such a time I am as infirm of purpose as Macbeth, as errant as Mad Tom, and as ragged as Timon. I sit down to work, do nothing, get up and walk a dozen miles, come back and sit down again next day, again do nothing and get up, go down a Railroad, find a place where I resolve to stay for a month, come home again next morning, go strolling about for hours and hours, reject all engagements to have my time to myself, get tired of myself and yet can't come out of myself to be pleasant to anybody else, and go on turning upon the same wheel round and round and over and over again until it may begin to roll me towards my end . . .

277   A.L.s. to the actor William Charles Macready, *4 pages, 8vo, Folkestone Fourth October 1855. Thursday*, concerning the writing of *Little Dorrit;* his feelings about the British Constitution, the apathy of the English and social inequalities, on the last of which themes he was "blowing off a little of indignant steam [in No. III of *Little Dorrit*] which would otherwise blow me up"; a Reading he was to do at Folkestone "in a long carpenter's shop"; and personal and family matters, *hinged in a sunk panel, bound in red morocco by Sangorski & Sutcliffe, calligraphic title-page in red and black, typescript of text with four hand-painted red letters, g.e., 8vo*

". . . I have been hammering away in that strenuous manner at my book . . . having a horrible temptation when I lay down my book-pen to run out on the breezy Downs here, tear up the hills, slide down the same, and conduct myself in a frenzied manner for the relief that only exercise gives me . . .

   . . . As to the suffrage, I have lost hope even in the Ballot, we appear to me to have proved the failure of Representative Institutions, without an educated and advanced people to support them. What with teaching people to "keep in their stations"—what with bringing up The Soul and Body of the land to be a good child, or to go to the Beershop to go a-poaching and go to the Devil—what with having no such thing as a Middle Class (for, though we are perpetually bragging of it as our safety, it is nothing but a poor fringe on the mantle of the upper)—what with flunkeyism, toadyism, letting the most contemptible Lords come in for all manner of places, making asses of ourselves for Prince Albert to saddle—reading the Court Circular for the New Testament . . . I do reluctantly believe that the English people are, habitually, consenting parties to the miserable imbecility into which we have fallen, *and never will help themselves out of it* . . . at present we are on the down-hill road to being conquered . . .

   ** Fifty words of this letter are omitted from the text printed (from the National Edition) in the Nonesuch Edition of the *Letters*.

AUTOGRAPH LETTERS OF CHARLES DICKENS

278   A.L.s. to Mrs. Winter (formerly Maria Beadnell), *2 pages, 8vo, 49 Champs Elysees, Paris Fifth February 1856*, thanking her for acknowledging the receipt of his books

> . . . My own writing so absorbs my time and attention, and my business correspondence is so very large, that the letters I write for pleasure are miraculously few. That they are also laudably short, let this sheet of paper witness . . .

279   A.L.s. ("CD.") to William Henry Wills, assistant editor of *Household Words, 4 pages, 8vo, Tavistock House, printed address head Tavistock Square, London. W.C. "That is to say: Dundee" Saturday Second October 1856*, giving instructions and answering queries relating to *Household Words* (". . . Pray, pray, *pray*, dont have Poems unless they are good. We are immeasurably better without them. "Beyond", is really Beyond anything I ever saw, in utter badness . . ."), alluding to the Christmas Number, *A House to Let*, DESCRIBING THE SUCCESS OF HIS READINGS and reporting an amusing remark by Harriet Martineau, *modern cloth case with the Comte de Suzannet's bookplate*

> . . . There was certainly in Edinburgh, a coldness beforehand, about the Readings. I mention it, to let you know that I consider the triumph there, by far the greatest I have made. The city was taken by storm, and carried. The Chimes shook it; Little Dombey blew it up. On the two last nights, the crowd was immense, and the turn-away enormous. Everywhere, nothing was heard but praises— nowhere more than at Blackwood's shop, where there certainly was no predisposition to praise. It was a brilliant victory, and could have been represented in no mere money whatever . . .

> The letter ends: ". . . With which large button of arrogant conceit from the head and front of a strait waistcoat, I beg to subscribe myself,—Ever Anti Politico-Economically,—Anti De Morganic-ally,—and the like . . .

***   In the Nonesuch Edition of the *Letters* the inverted commas are omitted from the word Beyond.

280   A.L.s. to William Woodley Frederick de Cerjat, Dickens's friend in Lausanne and "Christmas correspondent", *2 pages, 8vo, Tavistock House, London Sixteenth February 1857*, thanking him for pointing out an error in *Little Dorrit* and wishing that he had seen the play (". . . Though I say it as shouldn't, I am pretty sure nothing so complete was ever seen before, or will ever be seen again . . ."), *with the autograph envelope, signed, stamp cut away, postmarks, small tears at folds and in upper blank margin of second leaf of letter*

AUTOGRAPH LETTERS OF CHARLES DICKENS

281　A.L.s. ("CD.") to Hablot Knight Browne (*"Phiz"*), *1 page, 8vo, Tavistock House Friday Sixth March 1857*, sending the captions for two of Browne's illustrations for *Little Dorrit* and asking a question about one of them

⁎ On the verso of the above letter is an A.L.s. in pencil by Browne (signed both "Phiz" and "HKB") to "Bob" [? Robert Buss] explaining that he cannot come tomorrow (". . . some blocks having come in wanted, as usual, in a violent hurry . . .")

282　A.L.s. to his best-loved friend, the artist Clarkson Stanfield ("Stanny"), *2 pages, 8vo, Tavistock House Wednesday Evening Twentieth May, 1857*, explaining that since the copy of *Little Dorrit* which he is arranging to have put in "a cheerful dress" for him will be some time at the binder's he is sending now the proofs of the closing numbers so that Stanfield would "know the end of the book before the rest of its readers can", *small pencil sketch of a galleon on verso of one page*

". . . I say nothing of the pleasure it has been to me to put your name on the opening page [*viz.* of THE DEDICATION COPY], or to leave behind us both (as I hope its being there, may), a little record importing that we loved one another . . ."

⁎ THIS LETTER IS NOT PRINTED IN THE NONESUCH EDITION OF THE LETTERS AND IS APPARENTLY UNPUBLISHED.

283　A.L.s. to Georgina Hogarth, *4 pages, 8vo, closely written, Allonby, Cumberland Wednesday Night, Ninth September 1857*, giving a fine account of the mountaineering expedition undertaken by Wilkie Collins and himself the previous day and the injury sustained by Collins (". . . We went up a Cumberland mountain yesterday—a huge black hill, 1,500 feet high. We took for a Guide, a capital Innkeeper hard by. It rained in torrents—as it only does rain in a hill country—the whole time. At the top, there were black mists and the darkness of night. It then came out that the Innkeeper had not been up for 20 years—and he lost his head and himself altogether, and we couldn't get down . . .") and describing (with a splendid phonetic rendering of a conversation with a local) Allonby and Wigton, Cumberland, *second leaf inlaid*

. . . This [Allonby] is a little place with 50 houses, 5 bathing-machines, 5 girls in straw hats, 5 men in straw hats, and no other company. The little houses are all in mourning—yellow stone on white stone, and black—and it reminds me of what Broadstairs might have been, if it had not inherited a cliff, and had it been born an Irishman . . .

. . . Wigton—also in half mourning—with the wonderful peculiarity that it had no population, no business, no streets to speak of, but 5 Linen-draper's within range of our small window, 1 Linen Draper's next door, and 5 more linen draper's round the corner . . .

⁎ Among the inaccuracies in the text printed in the Nonesuch Edition of the *Letters* is the following transposition of words in one of the phrases quoted above: "he lost himself and his head".

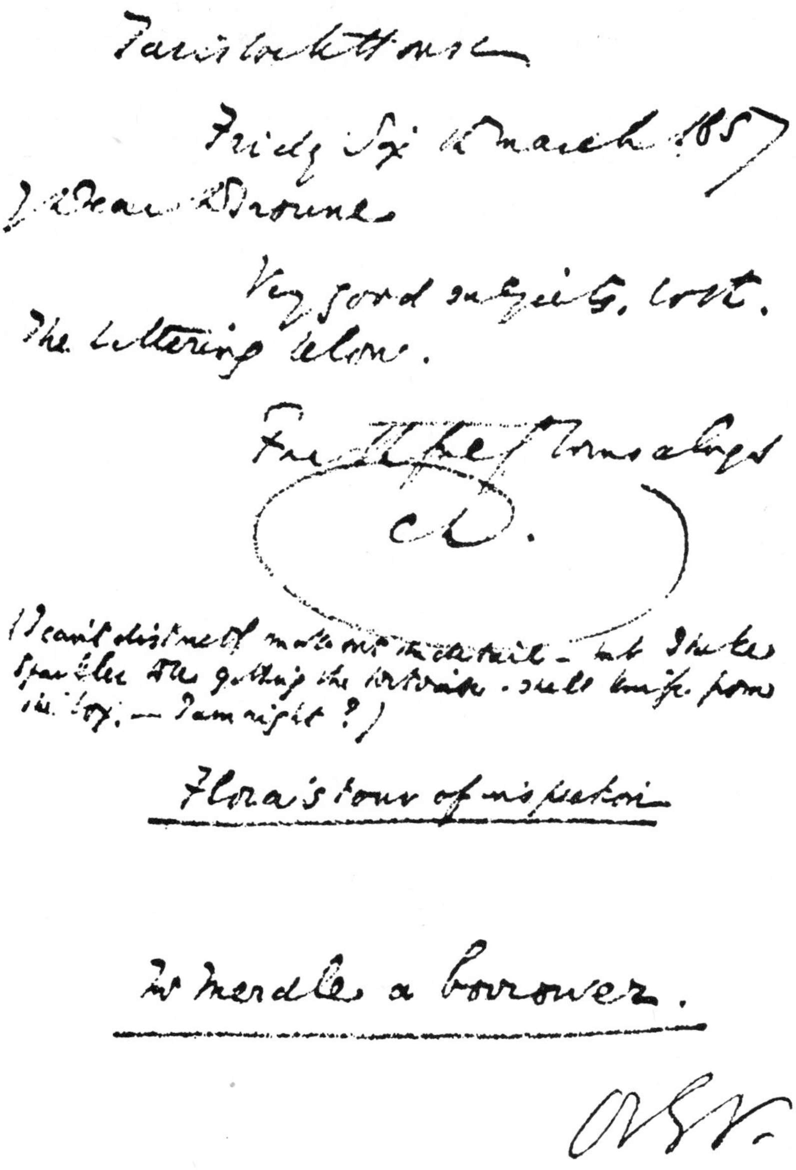

Tavistock House

    Friday Sixth March 1857

My Dear Browne

    Very good subject. Lost.
The Lettering alone.

    Fire the Arms always
       CD.

(I can't distinctly make out the detail — but I take
Sparkler to be getting the wristband. a [illegible] knife from
the boy. — am I right?)

Flora's tour of inspection

is Merdle a borrower.

          CD.

LOT 281

267

AUTOGRAPH LETTERS OF CHARLES DICKENS

284   A.L.s. to Henry Morley, author and populariser of literature, contributor to *Household Words* and *All the Year Round*, *2 pages, 8vo, Gad's Hill Place, Higham, by Rochester, Kent. Sunday Eighteenth October 1857*, asking him to consider the feasibility of a situation (outlined here) for a story to be included in *Household Words*, or to suggest ". . . any more probable set of circumstances, in which a few English people—gentlemen, ladies, and children—and a few English soldiers, would find themselves in a strange wild place and liable to hostile attack? . . ."

** The situation referred to in this letter was to be used in *The Perils of Certain English Prisoners*, the Christmas story written in collaboration with Wilkie Collins and printed in *Household Words* (Christmas 1857).

There are some minor errors of transcription in the text printed in the Nonesuch Edition of the *Letters*.

285   A.L.s. to [Peter] Cunningham, *2 pages, 8vo, Gad's Hill Place, Thursday Night Twenty Ninth October 1857*, asking him on behalf of a lady if every public department has a housekeeper, noting the date of their audit day (? at the *Household Words* Office) and informing him of his return to London

** THIS LETTER IS NOT PRINTED IN THE NONESUCH EDITION OF THE LETTERS AND IS APPARENTLY UNPUBLISHED.

286   A.L.s. to Lady [Laura] Olliffe, *1 page, 8vo, Tavistock House Monday Thirtieth November 1857*, sending her an advance copy of his latest work (*viz. The Perils of Certain English Prisoners*, the Christmas story in *Household Words* for 1857) and noting that "Chapter 2 is by Wilkie Collins; all the rest by me . . .", *some offsetting where closed before ink dry, conjugate blank, a photographic portrait of Dickens is included in this lot*

** Lady Olliffe was the wife of Dickens's great friend Sir Joseph Olliffe, physician to the British Embassy in Paris.

287   A.L.s. ("CD.") to Mark Lemon, *1 page, 8vo, Tavistock House, Monday Night Eighth March 1858*, noting his absence over the last two days and claiming payment for an article in a periodical (presumably *Punch*) he encloses (no longer present) since it had been taken from *Master Humphrey's Clock*, *formerly mounted, black-edged paper*

AUTOGRAPH LETTERS OF CHARLES DICKENS

288   A.L.s. to Mrs. [Frances] Dickinson, *2 pages, 8vo, Tavistock House, Tavistock Square, London. W.C. Monday Nineteenth April, 1858*:—

. . . If I burn your letter, may I be D— I mean B-u-r-n-t myself! It is much too earnest and cordial for any such fate. I shall put it by, until I get another as good; and then I must get you to write me a better.

I am charmed by your having been so pleased. If you don't come again, I shall have the Drapery dyed black.

O yes (as to your party) O yes! It is all very well to break your Manager's heart by not asking him, and then when you know he is going somewhere else, to shew him (as if he were Scrooge), the shadows of the things that might have been! But he feels it, and encloses a tear.

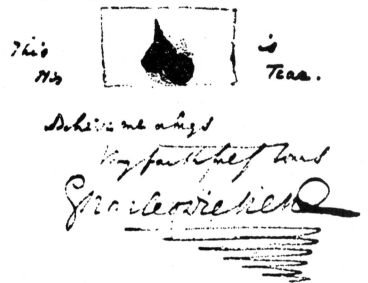

*** Mrs. Dickinson, a friend of Wilkie Collins, played with Dickens in *The Frozen Deep* at the Gallery of Illustration on 18 July 1857; she later married Gilbert Elliot, Dean of Bristol.

AUTOGRAPH LETTERS OF CHARLES DICKENS

289 Album containing 20 original letters by Dickens, comprising 17 A.Ls.s.,
1 A.L. and an autograph certificate, signed, to his friend in Ireland Francis Danzell
Finlay (1832-1917), proprietor and editor of the Belfast *Northern Whig*, and 1 A.L.s.
to Georgina Hogarth, his sister-in-law, *together with* various other pieces, briefly
described at the end below, and notations by Finlay relating to the majority of items,
mostly laid down, nineteenth-century brown half-morocco, 8vo

** The volume, CONTAINING ALL DICKENS'S KNOWN LETTERS TO FINLAY, was
presented to Janet Finlay on 20 April 1872 by her husband, the recipient of most of
the letters, on the occasion of the seventh anniversary of their marriage.

Unless otherwise stated the letters in this album are addressed to Finlay.

(1) A.L. (subscription and signature cut away "begged by an autograph-hunter" according to
a note by Finlay) *2 pages, 8vo, with an autograph postscript on the page facing the recto of the second
leaf, Tavistock House, Tavistock Square, London. W.C. "(which means, Limerick)" Thursday Second
September 1858.*, asking Finlay to order Irish jaunting-cars for himself and Arthur Smith, his manager
(". . . we will astonish the counties of Kent and Sussex . . ."), reflecting on his Readings at Cork and
Limerick, telling him of his own return to London and thanking Finlay for his "friendly aid", *small
tear in blank margin, a few brown spots, notation by Finlay*
". . . Cork was an immense success. We found upwards of a thousand Stalls let, for the three
readings. A great many people were turned away too, on the last night. I did not think them, when
I read the Carol, nearly as good an audience as Dublin or Belfast, in respect of demonstrative
satisfaction. But they were excellent as to Dombey and the Boots too. Perhaps, on the occasion of
the first reading, the fault was in myself. For I was not in very good spirits that evening . . ."

(2) A.L.s. *1 page, 8vo, Gad's Hill Place, Higham by Rochester, Kent. Twenty Eighth June 1859*,
inviting Finlay to stay at Gad's Hill and promising to fetch him from the station in his jaunting-car
("THE car")

(3) A.L.s. *2 pages, 8vo, Gad's Hill Place, Higham by Rochester. Thursday First July, 1859*, telling
Finlay the time of the train to Higham (". . . a very good train (considering that it runs on the worst
Railway in England) . . ."), promising to meet him in the Irish jaunting-car Finlay had obtained for
him (". . . You will observe the great national vehicle at the Higham platform, opening its arms to
receive you . . .") and mentioning that Edmund Yates may be down on the same train, *loosely inserted*

(4) A.L.s. *1 page, 8vo, Gad's Hill Place, Higham by Rochester, Kent. Wednesday Thirteenth
June 1860.*, accepting an offer made by Finlay to send a parcel to his son Walter (". . . my Indian
interest . . .") by Finlay's brother Henry who was leaving for India

(5) A.L.s. *2 pages, 8vo, 3 Hanover Terrace, Regents Park. Monday Sixth May, 1861.*, about the
Reading copies of his works, his itinerary (". . . my daughter has scant prospect at present of the
parental escort to the first gem of the sea . . ."), and the weather
". . . There are no printed abridgements of the Carol, Dombey, &c as I read them, or nearly as
I read them. Nor is there any such abridgement in existence, save in my own copies; and there it is
made, in part physically, and in part mentally, and no human being but myself could hope to follow
it . . ."

(6) A.L.s. *1 page, 8vo, London, Twenty Seventh March 1862*, describing as "sheer invention of
the wildest kind" the claim made by Mr Lucas, the original of Mr Mopes, the hermit in *Tom Tiddler's
Ground*, in a newspaper report that Dickens had visited him (". . . I have never seen the person in
question but once in my life . . .")

(7) A.L.s. *1 page, 8vo, Office of All the Year Round, Monday Thirty First March 1862*, referring
to his letter of 27 March, hoping to persuade him to visit Gad's Hill and mentioning *Copperfield*
". . . Make what use you like of my note. The custom of astonishingly audacious assertion that
is gradually expanding in print, cannot be too decisively "put down" . . ."
** In the Nonesuch Edition of the *Letters* "put down" is printed in italics.

(8) A.L.s. *1 page, small 8vo, Monday Tenth October, 1864*, congratulating Finlay on his engagement to Janet, daughter of Alexander Russel, editor of the *Scotsman*
. . . I hope you will make as good a report of me as you can, beforehand. For it is but fair that
she should be prepared to like me, when I am in such an admirable state of preparation to like her . . .

AUTOGRAPH LETTERS OF CHARLES DICKENS

(9) A.L.s. *2 pages, 8vo, Adelphi Hotel, Liverpool Monday Twenty First Jany 1867*, enquiring of Finlay, just before his return to Ireland, how and where the tickets for his Readings there had been sold previously, *on Gad's Hill headed note-paper, part of blank area of second page cut away*

(10) A.L.s. *3 pages, 8vo, Leicester, Friday Night Twenty Fifth January 1867*, about the sale of tickets and other arrangements for Readings in Ireland, a dinner arrangement, and his opinion of Russel (". . . I have (though I have never yet seen him), a great regard for your wife's father, as an independent upright and rare man who is an honor to his calling and country . . ."), *on Gad's Hill headed notepaper*

(11) A.L.s. *2 pages, 8vo, Shelbourne Hotel Dublin Monday Eighteenth March 1867.*, expressing sorrow at Finlay's ill-health, inviting him and his wife to Gad's Hill, recommending the use of cane chairs, complaining of noise from the next room and mentioning that his Readings are "making a great noise in Dublin", *on Gad's Hill headed note-paper*
". . . You know by this time, I may assume, the importance of always using an open-work cane chair? I can testify that there is nothing like it. Even in this episodical hotel-life, I invariably have my cane chair brought from a bedroom, and give the gorgeous stuffed abominations to the winds.
A horrible fellow-creature (female as I judge) is practising the scales on a bad piano in the next room where the sound is worse than it would be here . . ."
₊ One word is omitted from the text of this letter in the Nonesuch Edition of the *Letters*.

(12) A.L.s. ("CD.") to his sister-in-law Georgina Hogarth, *2 pages, 8vo, Dublin, Friday Twenty Second March 1867*, reporting the success of his Readings in Ireland (". . . never made a more brilliant success . . ."), mentioning the bad weather, giving a favourable account of Finlay's wife but a dismal one of Finlay's health and describing how he declined an offer of dinner from the Lord Lieutenant and his wife, *on Gad's Hill headed note-paper*
". . . Finlay's wife is a very prepossessing little Scotch girl. Something remarkably pleasant both in her face and speech. A very natural manner. I was greatly pleased with her . . ."
₊ The last sentence of this letter—"This rather to the astonishment of [*viz.* Percy] Fitz Gerald"—(which is scored through in blue crayon) is omitted from the text printed in the Nonesuch Edition of the *Letters*; at another point the word "He" is interpolated by the editors.

(13) A.L.s. *1 page, 8vo, Gad's Hill Place, Higham by Rochester, Kent. Wednesday Seventeenth April 1867*, rejoicing at the improvement in Finlay's health and once more advocating the use of cane chairs
₊ A third of this letter—that part relating to cane chairs—is omitted from the text printed in the Nonesuch Edition of the *Letters* and is apparently unpublished.

(14) Autograph certificate, signed, *1 page, 8vo, Gad's Hill Place, Higham by Rochester, Kent. Tuesday Third September 1867*, amusingly contradicting a newspaper report that he is in a critical state of health and had been recommended to proceed to the United States "for the cessation of literary labour"
₊ In the Nonesuch Edition of the *Letters* words underlined once in this letter are printed in majuscules and words in inverted commas, in italics.
A reference to Finlay's paper *The Northern Whig* makes it clear that this certificate was addressed to Finlay.

(15) A.L.s. *2 pages, 8vo, Gad's Hill Place, Higham by Rochester, Kent. Monday Second* (*should be 3rd, according to the editors of the Nonesuch Edition of the* Letters) *August, 1868*, thanking Finlay and his wife for their invitation to stay with them when he is next in Belfast (". . . If I ever did such a thing, under Reading circumstances as stay at a friend's house, believe me I would come to yours . . ."), and making a compact to come to dinner with them on his night off in Belfast (". . . I beg to send Mrs Finlay something as near my love as is lawful . . .")

(16) A.L.s. *2 pages, 8vo, Gad's Hill Place, Higham by Rochester, Kent, Sunday Fourth October, 1868*, declining a proposal made through Alexander Russel, editor of the *Scotsman*, that he should allow himself to be put forward as a parliamentary candidate for Edinburgh (". . . I reconsidered it [his conviction not to stand] some weeks ago, when I had a stirring proposal from the Birmingham people, and I then set it up on a rock for ever and a day . . .")

(17) A.L.s. *1 page, 8vo, Kennedy's Hotel, Edinburgh, Saturday Twelfth December, 1868*, appointing a day to dine with Finlay in Belfast and sending the message to Mrs. Finlay (". . . with as much love as I may venture to send her . . .") that he had dined with her father (Dickens spells his name "Russell"), Peter Fraser, "Ballantine" and John Blackwood (". . . the extreme rigor of the Spartan law being relaxed for this special occasion . . ."), *on Gad's Hill headed note-paper*

AUTOGRAPH LETTERS OF CHARLES DICKENS

(18) A.L.s. *3 pages, 8vo, The Atheneum (blind-stamped note-paper), New Year's Day, 1868 (i.e. 1869)*, sending seasonal greetings, declining (with his reasons) the Mayor of Belfast's proposal of a public banquet in Dickens's honour, giving the itinerary of his Readings, and mentioning Georgina Hogarth's ill-health.

". . . My time in Ireland is all anticipated, and I could not possibly prolong my stay . . . And the work is so hard and my voice is so precious, that I fear to add an ounce to the fatigues or I might be over-weighted. The avoidance of gas and crowds when I am not in the act of being cooked before those lights of mine, is an essential part of the training to which . . . I strictly adhere . . ."

** The most serious errors of transcription in the text of this letter printed in the Nonesuch Edition of the *Letters* are the omission of twenty-nine words.

(19) A.L.s. *1 page, 8vo, Office of All the Year Round, Wednesday Sixth January 1869*, re-arranging the day of a dinner party

** Finlay has noted on the album leaf that "The party came off on Thursday the 14th: himself, Georgina Hogarth, Lord Dufferin, Mr. Russel & Mary, my wife & myself."

Three words underlined twice in the original are printed in italics in the Nonesuch Edition of the *Letters*.

(20) A.L.s. *1 page, 8vo, Office of All the Year Round, Thursday Fourteenth October 1869*, accepting Finlay's contribution ["A Deadly Mist"] for *All the Year Round* ("I . . . am heartily glad it was no worse:— I don't mean the paper, but the adventure . . .")

** A copy of Finlay's article is pasted into the present album, following this letter.

The other pieces in this album are as follows:—

(1) Photograph of Dickens and his dog, Turk, taken by Mason and presented to Finlay by Dickens in the library at Gad's Hill on 23 November 1863, together with the dated signature formerly on the back of the portrait;

(2) off-print of an article by Finlay printed in the *Northern Whig* on 16 November 1861 countering the charge that *Pickwick* was immoral;

(3) Extract from *All the Year Round* of Finlay's article "A Deadly Mist";

(4) A.L.s. by Finlay to an unnamed friend written on Gad's Hill headed notepaper, GIVING AN ACCOUNT OF HIS VISIT TO DICKENS IN JUNE 1862;

(5) A.L.s. by Georgina Hogarth dated 12 March 1866;

(6) A.L.s. by Mary Dickens, the novelist's eldest daughter, dated 22 June, relating to Dickens's letter to Finlay of 13 June 1860;

(7) A.L.s. by Charles Collins, Dickens's son-in-law, n.d.;

(8) autograph envelope signed by Dickens;

(9) 3 cards, one with an autograph blazon of Dickens's crest, another with an autograph address;

(10) fragment of A.L.s. by Charles Dickens Junior;

(11) 2 A.Ls.s. from Henry Fielding Dickens, the novelist's sixth son, dated 3 June 1880 and 11 February 1892;

(12) 2 A.Ls.s. by Kate Perugini, Dickens's second daughter.

AUTOGRAPH LETTERS OF CHARLES DICKENS

290   A.L.s. ("CD.") to Georgina Hogarth, *2 pages, 8vo, Office of All the Year Round, Monday Sixteenth May 1859*, about his purchase of *Household Words, two small tears repaired, lightly guarded*

. . . Joyce was the bidder for the Whitefriars Gang; and all the witnesses agree that Arthur [*viz.* Arthur Smith, Dickens's manager] covered himself with Glory. He affected to relate anecdotes to the said Joyce and to Shirley Brooks, and to F. Evans, and then bid—as it were, accidentally—to the great terror and confusion of all the room.

We had also arranged, at a previous consultation, that Fred^k Chapman should bid against him up to a certain point; the consequence of which feint, was, that Nobody could make out what Arthur was bidding for at all, or why he was there . . .

291   Two A.Ls.s. to the friend of his youth Henry William Kolle, *5 pages, 8vo, Gad's Hill Place, Higham by Rochester, Saturday Eighteenth June 1859 and Tuesday Twenty Sixth December, 1865*, commenting frankly on the poetical aspirations of Kolle's daughter, Anne, TOGETHER WITH three A.Ls.s. by Anne Kolle written in 1890 when negotiating the sale of the letters by Dickens in this lot, *second leaves inlaid*

(1859) . . . A facility of versification is certainly to be observed in it, though it has many very weak and lame lines. But it seems to me to stop at turning prose into rhyme—and I don't see much good in that. When I say this, I mean that I do not find the writer to *see* the story poetically, or to place any scene in it, vividly, through a bright and picturesque imagination, before the reader. After laying the piece down, I do not remember any thought in it, any fancy, any image, any little touch of description, that gives me the least notion connected with the story of which I was not already possessed . . . my advice to her, is to leave it [composition] alone . . . pray assure your daughter that I am *not* a Dragon, but that I tell her the truth, as her father's old friend should . . .

(1865) . . . They are very musical, very creditable, very good. As editor of a periodical, I read many much worse, and many much better . . . I find her on a level with hundreds—thousands—of unheard of amateurs . . .

*** These letters are not included in the Nonesuch Edition of the *Letters* but careless transcripts of them are published in *The Dickens-Kolle Letters*, privately printed for Harry B. Smith (1910).

292   A.L.s. ("CD.") to Georgina Hogarth, *2 pages, 12mo, Office of All the Year Round, Wednesday Ninth January 1861.*, telling her that " "We" are in full swing of stopping [theatre] managers from playing a Message from the Sea" [the story in the Christmas Number of *All the Year Round* in 1860, written in collaboration with Wilkie Collins], that he soon hoped to be out of the hands of the "Medico", and that he was to dine that day with Laura [*viz.* Lady Olliffe, daughter of William Cubitt, the Lord Mayor] at the Mansion House, *lightly guarded*

293   A.L.s. to the Hon. Mrs Richard Watson, *1 page, 8vo, Bedford Hotel Brighton Friday Eighth November, 1861.*, telling her of his efforts to find Lady Spencer and describing a Reading of *Copperfield, black-edged paper, conjugate leaf, with the autograph envelope, slightly torn, signed, postmark*

. . . It was a great disappointment to me not to have you again, to sit before my fire in that bleak withdrawing room. I doubt if you can ever hear Copperfield to greater advantage than you would have heard it last night. The audience understood the most delicate points and it "went" quite delightfully . . .

*** One of Dickens's paragraph breaks is ignored in the Nonesuch Edition of the *Letters*.

AUTOGRAPH LETTERS OF CHARLES DICKENS

294   A.L.s. to Thomas Beard, *2 pages, 8vo, Gad's Hill Place, Higham by Rochester, Kent. Wednesday Twenty Fourth December 1862,* sending seasonal greetings and discussing his holiday plans, readings at the Paris Embassy and the sales of "Somebody's Luggage", *with autograph envelope, signed, Dickens's monogram on flap, postmarks, penny-red stamp affixed*

. . . On Monday last, the small number of one hundred and eighty five thousand copies of Somebody's Luggage had been sold! I wonder how many people among those purchasers have an idea of the number of hours of steamboat, railway train, dusty French walk, and looking out of the window, boiled down in "His Boots"? . . .

***   "Somebody's Luggage" was the title of the Christmas number of *All the Year Round* in 1862, "His Boots" being one of the chapters Dickens contributed to it. In January 1863 Dickens gave four readings at the Embassy in Paris for the benefit of the British Charitable Fund. In the Nonesuch Edition of the *Letters* "His Boots" is printed without the inverted commas.

295   A.L.s. ("Wilmot") to Peter [Cunningham] *1 page, 8vo, Gad's Hill Place, Higham by Rochester, Kent Saturday Night Fifth December, 1863.,* thanking him for his letter (". . . I am delighted to get the hearty letter of my old Will's-Coffee-House friend, Le Trimmer; and again the shade of poor dear Middlesex crosses me, "Here's Peter—won't come on, you know!" Then, in a ghostly manner, raps gold snuff box, and fades into the other world . . ."), discussing "Mrs. Lirriper's Lodgings" and praying for some "Christmas thoughts" (presumably for the annual Christmas story); he subscribes himself: "Ever faithfully (albeit once managerially) Your noble friend Wilmot", *on black-edged paper, conjugate blank*

***   "Mrs. Lirriper's Lodgings" was the title of the extra Christmas number of *All the Year Round* in 1863.

296   A.L.s. to the painter David Roberts, *2 pages, 8vo, Gad's Hill Place, Higham by Rochester, Kent. Saturday Twenty Sixth December 1863,* confirming that Marcus Stone had been "much misrepresented and hardly treated in reference to his painful domestic affairs" and as the "old and intimate friend" of Frank Stone, Marcus's father, confiding his knowledge of Frank Stone's wishes for his family (". . . This knowledge of mine I confide to you. As you may suppose, I have never parted with it, to influence a family misery or widen a family break . . ."), *black-edged paper*

***   THIS LETTER IS NOT PRINTED IN THE NONESUCH EDITION OF THE LETTERS AND IS NOT KNOWN TO HAVE BEEN PUBLISHED ELSEWHERE.
Frank Stone (1800-1859), painter, was one of Dickens's most intimate friends: he went on a number of holidays with the novelist; was "one of the leading heavy men" in the amateur theatricals; did three illustrations for *The Haunted Man* and designed the frontispiece for the first Cheap Edition of *Martin Chuzzlewit*. Dickens made Sairey Gamp describe him as "a fine looking, portly gentleman, with a face like an amiable moon." He thought that after his own death his children and their mother should live apart.
Marcus Stone, the artist, "a sort of extra son" to Dickens, exhibited at the Royal Academy when only 17 years of age. He did the original illustrations for *Our Mutual Friend* and illustrations for later editions of other of Dickens's works, notably for *Great Expectations* when it appeared in book form.

AUTOGRAPH LETTERS OF CHARLES DICKENS

297 A.L.s. ("C D.") to his solicitor Frederic Ouvry, the antiquary, *1 page, 8vo, Gads Hill Place, Higham by Rochester, Kent, Thursday Twentieth July, 1865,* asking him to prevent the pirating of *Our Mutual Friend* which was at the time appearing in parts as he wrote it, *conjugate blank*

. . . Here is a New Zealand vagabond playing the old nefarious game with Our Mutual Friend (who now has me by the throat, and will hold me until the end of August.) Terrify him, terrify him, terrify him! . . . .

298 A.L.s. to his old collaborator John Pyke Hullah, *6 Southwick Place Hyde Park Tuesday Eighth May 1866,* giving his permission for the re-publication of the songs from *The Village Coquettes,* ". . . making no mention whatever of the ingenious author's name [*viz.* Dickens's], but leaving him to blush anonymously . . .", *on Gad's Hill headed note-paper*

". . . I am not proud of my share in The Village Coquettes, and would rather let the songs (the words of the songs, I mean) die quietly, than receive them with the name of their respected parent attached . . ."

299 A.L.s. (THE ONLY KNOWN LETTER TO THIS CORRESPONDENT) to Antonin Roche, French examiner in London University and director of the Educational Institute, *Gad's Hill Place, Higham by Rochester, Kent. Monday Eighth October 1866,* assuring him that his "charming negotiator" had not failed in her mission (". . . surely it was quite a novelty, and rather an inconsistent one, to ask me to be selected from, and also to select from myself . . ."), and giving permission, with particular mention of Joan of Arc's story from *A Child's History of England,* for Roche to make extracts from any of his books ". . . except the "Sketches by Boz". I would rather not have Mr Sparkins or any of his immediate family quoted, because they are juvenile and hasty productions . . ." *with the autograph envelope, penny-red stamp affixed, postmarks*

* THIS LETTER IS MOSTLY UNPUBLISHED; only a short extract from a sale catalogue is quoted in the Nonesuch Edition of the *Letters.*

A daughter of Antonin Roche, probably the present "charming negotiator", married Henry Fielding Dickens.

AUTOGRAPH LETTERS OF CHARLES DICKENS

300   A.L.s. to Thomas James Serle, actor and dramatist, *3 pages, 8vo, Gad's Hill Place, Higham by Rochester, Kent, Wednesday Twenty Ninth July, 1868*, discussing Serle's suggestion for an alteration in the English copyright law to try to prevent the piracy of literary material in America, *with the autograph envelope, signed, addressed to Serle at Novello Cottage (his wife's maiden name was Novello), postmarks, penny-red stamp affixed*

*** THE LAST PARAGRAPH, COMPRISING 14 LINES OF TEXT, IS NOT INCLUDED IN THE TRANSCRIPT OF THE LETTER PRINTED IN THE NONESUCH EDITION OF THE LETTERS AND IS APPARENTLY UNPUBLISHED. In it Dickens alludes to the railway accident in which he had been involved on 9 June 1865 near Staplehurst and—noting that Mary Cowden Clarke, Serle's sister-in-law and one of the 'Novello circle', was a passenger on the train—describes the long-term effects of his ordeal:

   . . . It is remarkable that my watch (a special chronometer) has never gone quite correctly, since. And to this day there sometimes comes over me—on a railway, in a Hansom cab—in any sort of conveyance—for a few seconds, a vague sense of dread that I have no power to check. It comes and passes, but I cannot prevent its coming . . .

301   A.L.s. ("CD") to Lady [Andalusia] Molesworth, a well-known member of London society, *2 pages, 8vo, Gad's Hill Place, Higham by Rochester, Kent. Christmas Day, 1868*, sending seasonal greetings, telling her of the illness in Paris of his friend, the music critic [Henry Fothergill] Chorley, giving an account of his many commitments, including the itinerary of his "Farewell Readings", and describing a recent evening at the theatre, *contemporary endorsement*

   ". . . The other night I went to the new Theatre in Long Acre, and saw the prettiest piece of acting I have seen for a long time. It is Burlesque acting (I am sorry to add) but quite original and singularly graceful and pleasant. Miss Hodson as Mrs Haller, in a burlesque on the Stranger. She is most charmingly dressed as a quakeress, dances with a modest piquancy that has a peculiar refinement in it, and, captivating the Count, allows a coquettishness to sparkle out of her quaint quiet dress that is quite captivating. Ever affectionately Yours (And ever faithfully your co-old-stager) CD"

*** "Lady Molesworth was one of the select few for whom the postilions were turned out at Gadshill. She was 'an old dear friend'. But we have no record of this friendship, and none of Dickens's letters to her are preserved." (J. W. T. Ley, *The Dickens Circle*). Georgina Hogarth, *The Letters of Charles Dickens*, recorded that Lady Molesworth had herself told her "that she had long ceased to preserve any letters addressed to her." There are some minor errors of transcription in the text of this letter printed in the Nonesuch Edition of the *Letters*.

302   A.L.s. to the essayist and dramatist Andrew Halliday, *2 pages, 12mo, Office of All the Year Round, No. 26, Wellington Street, Strand, London, W.C. Saturday, Second January 1869*, discussing Halliday's notes for the dramatization of *David Copperfield*, that is *Little Emily, slight stains*

*** Halliday adapted several of Dickens's books. *Little Emily* was produced at the Olympic Theatre on 9 October 1869.

LITERARY MANUSCRIPTS OF CHARLES DICKENS

303　THE PICKWICK PAPERS. THE FIRST TWELVE PAGES OF THE AUTOGRAPH MANUSCRIPT OF CHAPTER XXXVII (numbered XXXVI in the manuscript and in the original edition due to the error which had numbered two chapters XXVIII, but renumbered XXXVII in subsequent editions), WITH DELETIONS AND REVISIONS ON EVERY PAGE (SOMETIMES EXTENSIVE), *written on one side only of twelve leaves of quarto paper numbered from 69 to 80, four versos (fols. 70, 77, 79 and 80) contain abortive beginnings of text in Dickens's hand, one clean marginal tear in fol. 70 (where the ink of a vigorous deletion has corroded the paper), one small repair with transparent paper (applied on the verso) in the margin of fol. 74, the leaves generally in very good condition, traces of former guards (where the leaves have been removed from an album) surviving on the inner edges, unbound, contained in a red morocco slipcase, 4to*

⁎⁎ Of the original manuscript of *Pickwick* only 44 pages in all are known to survive, and of these the 12 consecutive pages contained in the present lot are the only ones that still remain in private possession. The extant leaves owe their preservation to the foresight of Charles Hicks, foreman-printer to the firm of Bradbury and Evans who printed for Chapman and Hall (cf. lot 201). The present leaves contain evidence of their use by the printer in the form of a compositor's name written at the top of page 74 and in the occasional (unobtrusive) trace of a compositor's thumb-print.

It is clear that Dickens numbered separately each successive instalment of manuscript delivered monthly to the printer for the original publication in parts, and his numbering on the present leaves refers to their position in the manuscript for part XIII (which contains chapter XXXIV to XXXVI according to the original—erroneous—numbering i.e. chapters XXXV-XXXVII). Page 81 of this part of the manuscript (i.e. the page immediately following the last of the present pages) was given to Dickens House by Suzannet in 1937 (a photograph of this page is included in the lot), and page 82 is now in the British Museum. The only other extant portions of the *Pickwick* manuscript are located as follows: five pages of chapter XIX in the British Museum; one page of chapter XXVIII, formerly in the collection of Owen D. Young and now in the Berg collection of the New York Public Library; nineteen pages of chapter XXXVI and five pages of chapter XXXIX in the Rosenbach Foundation, Philadelphia. In addition, a four-line fragment of chapter XXXVII cut from page "86" was inserted in a copy of *Pickwick* in parts formerly owned by George Ulizio.

The only consecutive portion of the *Pickwick* manuscript to exceed the present twelve leaves in length is the nineteen leaves of chapter XXXVI (beginning in the middle of the story of Bladud and numbered 50 to 68) now in the Rosenbach Foundation. The consecutive leaves contained in the present lot, however, have the advantage of starting with the beginning of a chapter—and that celebrated chapter which "Honorably accounts for Mr Weller's absence, by describing a soirée to which he was invited, and went . . ." The last complete paragraph in the manuscript is that beginning "The green-grocer and his wife then [put *deleted*] arranged upon the table" and it breaks off at the foot of page "80" with the words " 'Harris'—said Mr Tuckle in a [*deletion*]" (cf. page 396 of the first edition).

[*See* ILLUSTRATION]

69

Chapter XXXVI

Honorably accounts for Mr Weller's absence, by describing a soirée to which he was invited, and went. Also relates how he was entrusted by Mr Pickwick with a private mission of delicacy and importance.

"Mr Weller" — said Mrs Craddock upon the morning of this very eventful day. "Here's a letter for you."

"Werry odd, that" — said Sam "I'm afeerd there must be somethin' the matter, for I don't recollect any gen'lm'n in my circle of acquaintance as is capable o' writin' one."

"P'rhaps somethin' uncommon has taken place" — observed Mrs Craddock.

"It must be somethin' werry uncommon indeed as could perduce a letter out o' any friend o' mine" — replied Sam, shaking his head dubiously "nothin' less than a nat'ral convulsion, as the young gen'lm'n observed ven he was' took with fits. It can't be from the gov'ner" — said Sam, looking at the direction

~~the~~ outbreak with a violent blow upon the
table as if in the heat of the moment he had
mistaken it for the chest or ribs of Mr Wackford
Squeers; and having by this open ~~----~~ declaration
of his real feelings quite precluded himself from
offering Nicholas any cautious worldly advice (which
had been his first intention) Mr Noggs went
straight to the point.

"The day before yesterday "- said Newman "your
~~uncle~~ uncle received this letter. I took a hasty
copy of ~~it~~ it while he was out. Shall I read
it?"

"If you please "- replied Nicholas, and Newman
Noggs ~~----~~ read as follows

            · Dotheboys Hall.
            " Thursday Morning

"Sir
     "My pa requests me to write to you. The doctors
considering it doubtful whether he will ever recover
the use of his legs which prevents his holding a
pen.

     "We are in a state of mind beyond everything,
and my pa is one ~~of~~ mask of ~~----~~
bruises both blue and green likewise two forms
are steeped in his Goar. ~~----~~ We were Kimpelled
to have him carried down into the kitchen where
he now lays. ~~----~~

Lot 308 (See page 279)

LITERARY MANUSCRIPTS OF CHARLES DICKENS

304   THE ALBUM OF ELLEN BEARD, containing "A Fable (Not a *gay* one)" composed and written by Dickens in 1834 in a careful "copperplate" version of his early hand and signed "Boz," *other contributions in various other contemporary (mostly feminine) hands including several signed "Fanny" (?Dickens's sister), inscribed inside upper cover "20th September 1834/Ellen Beard", original decorated dark green cloth, 12mo; contained in a half morocco slipcase*

**   Dickens's *Fable* consists of 48 lines of rhymed verse amusingly parodying his feelings of despondency after the end of the Maria Beadnell affair: the verses occupy two pages of the album.

The owner of this album was a sister of Dickens's close and lifelong friend, the journalist Thomas Beard.

305   THE AUTOGRAPH MANUSCRIPT OF THE DEDICATION to J. P. Harley, dated December 1836, of Dickens's comic opera "The Village Coquettes", *1 page, 4to, somewhat worn and one clean tear at foot of vertical centre fold, lightly hinged in an album and bound with blanks, half morocco, from the library of A. Edward Newton*

**   Dickens must have revised the text of this Dedication in proof, for the printed version differs from the manuscript in the following respects: (1) the words "no matter how numerous they may be or how quickly they follow in succession" are omitted in the printed version from the end of the first paragraph; (2) the epistle is signed *Boz* in the manuscript and *Charles Dickens* in print; (3) the day of the month (viz. 15 December) is added to the date in the printed version.

306   THE PART OF BATESON IN "THE FROZEN DEEP", 7 pages, comprising 4 pages in Dickens's hand and 3 pages in the hand of Dickens's eldest daughter Mary, *stitched in the original wrappers inscribed on upper cover by Dickens "Bateson / In / The Frozen Deep", margins somewhat frayed, 8vo*

**   This manuscript booklet, which contains Bateson's complete part including cues and stage directions, was evidently used during the rehearsals for the original production, which was to take place at Tavistock House on 6 January 1857. The part of Bateson was performed by Edward Hogarth. Of the play itself in its ultimate form, "Dickens had suggested so many of the situations and written or revised so many of the lines that it was almost as much his work as it was [Wilkie] Collins's" (Edgar Johnson, *Charles Dickens*, 1953, II, p. 866).

307   MRS. LIRRIPER'S LODGINGS. Heavily-revised fragment of the Autograph Manuscript (c. 20 closely-written lines, comprising the upper portion of an octavo leaf written on one side only and numbered '22' at top), *inlaid and bound in a copy of the Christmas Number of "All the Year Round" for 1863 containing the first publication of the story, dark green morocco gilt by Sangorski and Sutcliffe, original wrappers bound in, 8vo: contained in a folding box*

**   The manuscript is bound facing page 9 of the printed text on which appears the passage it contains (beginning "which came out next day four and twenty hours after he was found" and ending "wrapped up in a cabbage [leaf]").

LITERARY MANUSCRIPTS OF CHARLES DICKENS

308 NICHOLAS NICKLEBY. The first twenty-two pages of the Auto-graph Manuscript of Chapter xv, with deletions and revisions throughout, *written on one side only of twenty-two leaves of quarto paper numbered from 1 to 22, three versos (nos. 9, 16 and 17) contain abortive beginnings of text in Dickens's hand, clean marginal tears neatly repaired in fols. 1, 8 and 9, the leaves generally in very good condition, traces of former guards (where the leaves have been removed from an album) surviving on the inner edges, unbound*

** This lot contains the only portion of the original manuscript of *Nicholas Nickleby* still in private hands. Of the approx. 150 pages that are all that is known to survive of the *Nickleby* manuscript, Chapter IX (39 pages) is now in Dickens House (presented by Suzannet in 1938) and there are single pages in he Pierpont Morgan Library and the Free Library, Philadelphia. The residue—comprising Chapter X complete and portions of Chapters XVI, XVII and XX—is now in the Rosenbach Foundation, Philadelphia. The total of surviving pages is completed by the 22 consecutive leaves in the present lot which contain the greater part of Chapter XV including the immortal letter from Fanny Squeers to Ralph Nickleby. The last paragraph in the manuscript is that which begins "This was nothing less than the sudden pouring forth" which breaks off at the foot of page 22 with the words "a strange cat had come in and sucked" (cf. page 136 of the first edition).

The surviving portions of the *Nickelby* manuscript owe their preservation to the foresight of Charles Hicks, foreman printer of Bradbury and Evans, who also preserved from destruction all that is known to survive of the *Pickwick* manuscript (cf lot 303).

The leaves of *Pickwick* and *Nickleby* contained in the present sale comprise the only original manuscript of any of Dickens's major novels still in private hands.

[*See* Illustration]

MANUSCRIPT DICKENSIANA

309   AINSWORTH (WILLIAM HARRISON) Important early series of four A.Ls.s. (three signed with initials) *19 pages, 4to and 8vo, one addressed from Kensal Lodge, 22 June, 28 July and 14 November 1836 and n.d.* (*but 1836*), to John Macrone, ABOUT DICKENS'S AGREEMENT WITH MACRONE, HIS FIRST PUBLISHER (". . . Master Dickens . . . for both the "Sketches" and the "Novel" . . ., *viz.* "Gabriel Vardon", later re-named *Barnaby Rudge*); Macrone's intention of republishing *Sketches by Boz* in monthly parts; Ainsworth's own books (*Rookwood, The Elms* and *Crichton*) and literary affairs; advice to Macrone on publishing (". . . . I feel confident that I can not only make you a successful but what in my opinion is of as much consequence a *récherché* and gentlemanlike publisher . . ."); AINSWORTH'S FIRST IMPRESSIONS OF MACRONE'S "NEW" POET, ROBERT BROWNING, AND ABOUT BROWNING'S ASSOCIATION WITH MACREADY (". . . he is a pile of genius . . . I am induced to form a very high opinion of him . . ."); the *Examiner;* his own mother's delight on reading *Sketches by Boz;* and mentioning Moore, Ollier, Maclise, Moran, Forster, Bentley, Hansard, Lady Blessington *etc., three integral address leaves, postmarks, seals, endorsements*

. . . I now write, in the strictest confidence, and I trust to your honour as a gent[n]. not to quote me, or to show this letter—I now write I say to advise you to place the matter between Mr Dickens and yourself *immediately* in legal hands . . . Mr Dickens clearly has no right to destroy his agreement: but this information will be much better convey'd to him by a Solicitor . . .

*** Dickens separated from Macrone because of a dispute over the agreement for *Barnaby Rudge* and his anger at the latter's intention of republishing his *Sketches* in monthly parts. Ainsworth, who had introduced Dickens to his first publisher (as he was to introduce him to his first illustrator and his first biographer) was clearly on Macrone's side over the agreement, but by 1837 had himself transferred to Bentley, perhaps because of Macrone's unbusiness-like attitude which is apparent from these letters. However, despite the breach between them, Dickens undertook in 1838 to edit the *Pic Nic Papers* (published 1841) to raise money for Macrone's widow and children.

MANUSCRIPT DICKENSIANA

310 AINSWORTH (WILLIAM HARRISON) A.L.s. ("a very rambling Egotistical letter"), *4 closely written pages, 8vo, Kensal Lodge, Harrow Road, London, 16 January 1838*, to an unnamed correspondent, possibly John Gibson Lockhart or William Barclay David Donald Turnbull, archivist and antiquary, founder of the Abbotsford Club and bookcollector, thanking him for (and commenting on) a copy of the "Abbotsford Miscellany" (". . . I have rarely met with so handsome a book . . ."); accepting the offer to make use of his correspondent's library; describing the "Tale" on which he was working *viz. Jack Sheppard;* expressing his pleasure at their friendship (". . . No circumstance connected with my literary career has given me so much pleasure as the gratifying acquaintance, which, in your case, it has procured me . . ."); and OUTLINING HIS PLAN FOR A NEW MONTHLY PUBLICATION IN CONJUNCTION WITH DICKENS (". . . with designs by Cruickshank, to be entitled "Ancient and Modern London". Mr. Dickens will illustrate the metropolis of the present day: I shall endeavour to revive its departed glories . . .")

> . . . It [*viz. Jack Sheppard*] is another attempt at the *novela picaresca*, in the old Rockwood style, (a class of fiction, which, I regret to say, obtains more favour at the hands of the booksellers, than romances of much higher pretension;) and is intended to introduce the escapades of Jack Sheppard, and the rogueries of Jonathan Wild . . . the book . . . *ought* to be completed by the end of February, though I have, as yet, written little more than the first chapter. I am getting rather tired of highwaymen and housebreakers, and long for a little better society . . .

*** Ainsworth had agreed to write the collection of stories about London mentioned in this letter under the title "The Lions of London; or Country Cousins in Town", for Macrone in 1836. After Macrone's death Ainsworth asked Dickens to collaborate in it, but, although the idea of collaboration was discussed, it came to nothing. Cruickshank's cover design for it, the only tangible relic, was later used for the monthly parts of *Old St. Paul's*.

311 BROWNE (HABLOT KNIGHT, 'Phiz') Two A.Ls.s. *1 page, 4to, and 3 pages, 8vo, Friday Evening "Jany. something—[18]41", and 99, Ladbrooke Grove Road, 6 December 1877*, to Edward Chapman and Frederick Cosens, asking the first for some money ("Tin"), and telling the second that he had some years before burned a quantity of his papers and sketches, many of them relating to Dickens, Ainsworth and others, but has nonetheless managed to find "a bit of Dickens," *formerly mounted*

312 BUSS (ROBERT WILLIAM, 1804-1875, *painter*) Long A.L.s. [to John Forster], *12 pages, 8vo, 15 Camden Street, Camden Town, 11 December 1871*, congratulating him on his *Life of Dickens* (of which Buss must have had an early copy); recalling reading Dickens's early contributions to the *Morning Chronicle;* outlining the extent of the novelist's appeal; GIVING IMPORTANT INFORMATION ABOUT PICKWICK including support for Seymour's claim to be originator of Pickwick, the interruption of the work by Seymour's suicide, Buss's succession to him as illustrator (". . . I am quite willing to admit that my alleged illustrations were not good . . .") and his replacement by Phiz (whose ". . . first designs were so *poor*, that they had to be *re-etched* . . ."), Phiz's methods of work, the quality and importance of his illustrations (". . . The outward bodily form of Dickens' characters is stamped upon the public mind by Phiz . . .") and the treatment of Browne by Dickens

MANUSCRIPT DICKENSIANA

313   CATTERMOLE (GEORGE, *illustrator*) A.L.s. *1 page*, 8*vo*, *Clapham Rise, 1 March n.d.* [*but? 1840-1*] to Edward Chapman, mentioning Dickens had requested some blocks, presumably for illustrations in *Master Humphrey, conjugate leaf mounted*

314   CHAPMAN & HALL, publishers. A.L.s. to Bradbury & Evans, *2 pages*, 8*vo*, *193, Piccadilly London, W. May 1st. 1867*, offering, after a discussion with the novelist, £3,000 for their fourth share of Dickens's copyright, stereotypes, stock, illustrations etc., *contemporary endorsement*

315   CRUIKSHANK (GEORGE) Draft A.L.s. (WITH TWENTY-SEVEN WORDS AND SOME CORRECTIONS IN DICKENS'S HAND) to Dr. G. K. Nagler, a German critic, *2 pages*, 4*to, no address or date*, stating that the ascription to himself of the phrase the "Real Simon Pure" (the use of which he explains) was done to distinguish him from other artists of the name of Cruikshank and was not intended to suggest, as Nayler had evidently assumed, that they were his given names, *conjugate blank endorsed*

. . . You will therefore please to understand that. I do not wish to be set down as a *simpleton*, or pass off as a very doubtful pattern of *purity*—

I beg there to subscribe myself neither Simon nor Pure . . .

316   DICKENS (CHARLES, 1837-1896, *compiler, eldest son of the novelist*) Two A.Ls.s. *4 pages*, 8*vo*, *Office of All the Year Round, 28 and 29 September 1886*, to Thomas Beard, concerning the dedication of the Jubilee Edition of *Pickwick* to him (". . . To Thomas Beard, my father's oldest friend and my godfather . . ."), *slight brown stains*

317   FORSTER (JOHN, *friend and biographer of Dickens*) Four A.Ls.s. (one with initials), *5 pages*, 8*vo*, *3 pages, 12mo, and 3 pages 16mo, 2 December 1844, 25 May and 14 December 1859, and 25 November 1873*, to William Johnson Fox, preacher, politician and man of letters, Bradbury and Evans, the publishers, and Frank Beard respectively, inviting Fox to a gathering at which Dickens was to read "his little story" [viz. *The Chimes*—see Dickens's letter to his wife of 2 December 1844]; referring, in his letters to Bradbury and Evans, to a note they had inserted in *Household Words* (7 May 1859) under the heading "Mr. Charles Dickens and his late Publishers", and alluding to Dickens's rupture with their firm and the part taken by Forster himself in the *Household Words* affair; and asking Beard if he wishes to say anything about Dickens's last illness for inclusion in his *Life, the letter to Fox inlaid, two autograph envelopes, one inlaid*

MANUSCRIPT DICKENSIANA

318 FORSTER'S LIFE OF DICKENS. A.Ls.s. to Forster from James T. Fields, Charles and Mary Cowden Clarke, John Morley, Baron Tauchnitz and Albany Fonblanque (the last annotated by Forster "Poss F's last letter . . ."), congratulating him on his achievement, *11 pages, 8vo, 1872-1874*

> . . . Nothing could be more tender, more judicious, more perfect in every possible way . . .

> . . . The finest biography I ever read . . .

> . . . it has given me a pleasure—hardly second to the pleasure one has in Dickens's own best books . . .

319 HUGHES (WILLIAM R., author of *A Week's Tramp in Dickens-Land*). Autograph "Notes of a Dickens Collector", signed and dated (1896) at the end, describing his passion for, and collection of Dickens's works, *15 pages, 4to, portrait of Hughes enclosed*

> . . . People, nowadays, who read Dickens in the complete book, have no conception of the intense expectation and excitement . . . which each Monthly Number evoked . . .

> . . . I have always felt that I should require the purse of a Milllionaire to obtain Manuscripts and Letters . . .

320 LEMON (MARK) The Autograph Manuscript, with revisions and deletions of his farce "Mr Nightingale's Diary", *c. 67 pages (several revised passages entered on inserted slips), modern half morocco, 4to*

** Mark Lemon's original version of this farce, preserved in this manuscript, has never been published or performed. Lemon offered it to Dickens in the spring of 1851 to be performed by the Company of Strolling Players which Dickens had formed to give performances in aid of the Guild of Literature and Art. Dickens accepted the play, but altered it so extensively in the course of rehearsals that the version eventually produced at Devonshire House on 27 May 1851 has been claimed to be as much Dickens's work as it was Lemon's. This final version, which remained constantly in the repertory of the Strolling Players, was privately printed in 1851.

321 LYTTON (EDWARD GEORGE EARLE LYTTON BULWER, *novelist*) A.L.s. to Charles Dickens, *5 pages, 8vo, Portland Club, 11 October 1867*, praising Charles Fechter's performance [as Claude Melnotte] in his own (i.e. Lytton's) play *The Lady of Lyons* (". . . there is that creative genius in his personation which takes the character not only out of histrionic convention, but even out of the author's hands . . ."), thanking Dickens for the pains he had taken over the performance and asking if he might consult him about his new play [*The Captives*], AUTOGRAPH ENDORSEMENT BY DICKENS

** For Dickens's replies and comments see his letters to Lytton dated 14 and 25 October 1867.

MANUSCRIPT DICKENSIANA

322 LYTTON (EDWARD ROBERT BULWER, *statesman and poet*) A.L.s. to Dickens, *4 pages, 8vo, Grove Mill, Watford Herts, 13 April 1867*, explaining that he had not written for free tickets but for good ones to Dickens's Reading [of *David Copperfield*] at St. James's Hall on Tuesday evening [9 April], praising Dickens's performance and thanking him for ". . . those two perfect hours of enjoyment wʰ have been a great event in our little lives . . .", *black-edged paper*

. . . You play with the heart, like the Japanese Juggler with his paper butterfly . . . Certainly Voice was never more felicitously "married to immortal words" than yours . . . on Tuesday night, when I had the delight of listening to its magical utterance in a luxury of tears and laughter. For the multitudinous creations of your surpassing genius stimulated every emotion, and I confess I was heartily *blubbering* all the time that Mr Pegotty was talking to us . . .

*** In his reply to this letter, dated 17 April 1867, Dickens said: ". . . Your appreciation has given me higher and purer gratification than your modesty can readily believe . . . what a delight it is to be delicately understood . . . your earnest words cannot fail to move me . . ."

323 OVERS (John A., 1808-1844, cabinet-maker and author), Autograph study of Thomas Carlyle's *Chartism*, a copy of which Dickens had loaned him, written in the form of an A.L.s. to Dickens, *16 pages, 4to, 2 Duke Street Little Britain, July 20th 1840*

. . . Subdued by a fit of spleen,—or rather, perhaps, I should say usurped by a snarling fiend of discontent and despondency which occasionally obtains the mastery I know not why or wherefore, I dare not venture to convey to you certain remarks or rhapsodies which have arisen in my mind partly from your conversation, and partly from the digestion of the book by Thomas Carlyle entitled "Chartism" which your kindness has enabled me to peruse. I have therefore waited till the murrain passed away, which I hope you will receive as an apology for the all unconscionable time that I have detained your book, and which I herewith return with many thanks . . . if there be any matter connected with, or concerning the working man on which I have too cursorily touched, the which you should like to have resolved, I shall have much pleasure in furnishing such information as you demand . . .

*** Dickens refers to the present manuscript in his letter to Overs of 27 October 1840: "I received, and read, your notes on the Chartist book, some of which I will show to Mr. Carlyle as I am sure he would be glad to see them."

Dickens helped Overs on several occasions with his writings, advised him on their publication, wrote on his behalf to several editors (e.g. see Sotheby catalogue for 6 & 7 July 1971, lot 773), and corrected the proofs and wrote the preface to his *Evenings of a Working Man.*

MANUSCRIPT DICKENSIANA

324   SHAW (WILLIAM, THE ORIGINAL OF SQUEERS IN NICHOLAS NICKLEBY) A.L.s. *2 pages, 4to, Bowes, 2 February 1826*, to Mr. Brooks, announcing the serious illness of his correspondent's son, George (who died the same night), and asking the boy's father to come down at once (". . . It is with feelings indescribable, I again inform you respecting your dear boy, who I am sorry to say continues gradually hastening away from us . . . this Morning he has begun with convulsion fits, and has not left us any hope . . . I must say, he always attracted my particular attention being so very peaceable and clean in his person . . .") *integral address leaf, postmarked, original tear at seal, light stains, some small tears, pencil annotation recording the time of the boy's death*, TOGETHER WITH: A.L.s. by GEORGE BROOKS (the boy referred to in the above letter), *3 pages, 4to, Bowes, 14 November 1825*, (viz. less than three months before his death) writing, DOUBTLESS FROM A COPY SET BY SQUEERS HIMSELF, in appreciation of his life at the school ("Dotheboy's Hall"), INTEGRAL ADDRESS LEAF WRITTEN IN THE HAND OF "SQUEERS", *postmark, signature affected where seal cut*

⁂   The following extracts are from George Brooks's letter to his parents:—
. . . on Saturday 5th of November we had a jovial and merry day and night in burning old Guy upon the hill . . . I am glad to say I have enjoyed the best of health since I last wrote to you . . . I feel very happy and comfortable and have been so ever since I came . . . we had roast Geese and giblet pies as usual last week . . . we will all write separately the next month by our Master, who the latter end of it intends going to London and remaining about 3 weeks, and will inform you when he returns, that any parcel may be brought us . . . Mr and Mrs Shaw's compliments who are very kind to me . . .

Brooks's name is included in the list, taken from the Burial Registers, of the 29 boys (aged between 7 and 12 with one aged 18) who were buried in Bowes churchyard in unrecorded graves between 1810 and 1834 (see *The Dickensian*, 1939 vol., pp. 107-8). It is not known whether Dickens actually inspected these Registers, but he does use the name Brooks for one of the pupils at Squeers's school.

325   YATES (EDMUND) A.L.s. to John Forster, *1 page, 8vo, 14a Upper Wimpole Street, 9 February 1872*, telling him: ". . . I thought of you as the one link left between me and my dear dead friend and master . . ." *conjugate blank*

END OF SALE

SOTHEBY & CO.

34/35, New Bond Street, London, W.1.

Sale of

AUTOGRAPH MANUSCRIPTS
AND LETTERS, ORIGINAL
DRAWINGS AND FIRST
EDITIONS OF
CHARLES DICKENS

Mon/Tues. 22nd/23rd Nov. 1971. **PRICE LIST**

Lot		£	Lot		£	Lot		£
1	Quaritch	260.00	53	House of El Dieff	80.00	104	Stone, H.	50.00
2	Fletcher, H.M.	30.00	54	Baile	70.00	105	House of El Dieff	75.00
3	Sims, G.F.	32.00	55	Dawson	220.00	106	Sawyer, C.J.	60.00
4	Edwards, F.	280.00	56	Spencer, W.T.	170.00	107	Dawson	160.00
5	Henderson, R.L.	48.00	57	Sims, G.F.	52.00	108	Flemming, J.	300.00
6	House of El Dieff	920.00	58	Baile	60.00	109	Flemming, J.	300.00
7	House of El Dieff	240.00	59	Quaritch	140.00	110	Thorp	40.00
8	House of El Dieff	60.00	60	Baile	60.00	111	Hoffmann & Freeman	800.00
9	Henderson, R.L.	35.00	61	Rota	55.00	112	House of El Dieff	150.00
10	Baile	40.00	62	Edwards, F.	120.00	113	House of El Dieff	42.00
11	Quaritch	160.00	63	Seven Gables Bk'sh	25.00	114	House of El Dieff	55.00
12	Hoffmann & Freeman	24.00	64	Spencer, W.T.	300.00	115	Thorp	90.00
13	Maggs	26.00	65	Henderson, R.L.	42.00	116	Quaritch	50.00
14	Sims, G.F.	35.00	66	Baldur Bookshop	6.00	117	House of El Dieff	70.00
15	Sims, G.F.	30.00	67	Baile	60.00	118	Teale, J.E.	800.00
16	Edwards, F.	300.00	68	Seven Gables Bk'sh	260.00	119	Flemming, J.	400.00
17	Portsmouth Library	75.00	69	Henderson, R.L.	220.00	120	Quaritch	55.00
18	Seven Gables Bk'sh	60.00	70	Seven Gables Bk'sh	32.00	121	Bentley, N.	70.00
19	House of El Dieff	1700.00	71	Dickens-Hawksley, E.	18.00	122	Oreck	22.00
20	Seven Gable Bk'sh	1700.00	72	House of El Dieff	3600.00	123	Henderson, R.L.	55.00
21	Self, W.	1100.00	73	Baldur Bookshop	2.00	124	House of El Dieff	260.00
22	House of El Dieff	600.00	74	House of El Dieff	50.00	125	House of El Dieff	70.00
23	Dickens Old Curiosity Shop	18.00	75	Henderson, R.L.	90.00	126	Flemming, J.	210.00
24	House of El Dieff	50.00	76	House of El Dieff	95.00	127	Staples, L.	28.00
25	D'Arch Smith	22.00	77	House of El Dieff	700.00	128	Hoffmann & Freeman	480.00
26	Fox, P.	50.00	78	Dickens Old Curiosity Shop	130.00	129	Thorp	95.00
27	Mortlake	12.00	79	House of El Dieff	80.00	130	Flemming, J.	350.00
28	Baile	10.00	80	House of El Dieff	400.00	131	Edwards, F.	10.00
29	Seven Gables Bk'sh	18.00	81	House of El Dieff	60.00	132	House of El Dieff	95.00
30	Sims, G.F.	55.00	82	Beecham	6.00	133	Staples, L.	16.00
31	Seven Gables Bk'sh	14.00	83	Mortlake	4.00	134	House of El Dieff	95.00
32	Baile	14.00	84	Portsmouth Library	35.00	135	House of El Dieff	110.00
33	Baker	110.00	85	House of El Dieff	520.00	136	Sharpe, H.	22.00
34	House of El Dieff	35.00	86	Portsmouth Library	20.00	137	Portsmouth Library	32.00
35	House of El Dieff	28.00	87	Teale, J.E.	260.00	138	House of El Dieff	16.00
36	House of El Dieff	26.00	88	Bentley, N.	14.00	139	Hoffmann & Freeman	170.00
37	Teale, J.E.	350.00	89	Dawson	80.00	140	Bentley, N.	35.00
37a	Edwards, F.	8.00	90	Flemming, J.	400.00	141	Lamb	12.00
38	Henderson, R.L.	70.00	91	Quaritch	45.00	142	Maggs	750.00
39	Thorp	85.00	91a	Dickens Old Curiosity Shop	9.00	143	Myers, Miss	35.00
40	House of El Dieff	480.00	92	Baile	50.00	144	Henderson, R.L.	26.00
41	Seven Gables Bk'sh	16.00	93	House of El Dieff	55.00	145	Baldur Bookshop	260.00
42	House of El Dieff	18.00	94	Beecham	220.00	146	Mortlake	48.00
43	House of El Dieff	75.00	95	Flemming, J.	400.00	147	Henderson, R.L.	240.00
44	Henderson, R.L.	520.00	96	Maggs	55.00	147a	House of El Dieff	150.00
45	Flemming, J.	650.00	97	Flemming, J.	190.00	148	Self, W.	26.00
46	Edwards, F.	22.00	98	Henderson, R.L.	240.00	149	Maggs	32.00
47	Edwards, F.	14.00	99	Flemming, J.	400.00	150	Mushlin	40.00
48	Baile	50.00	100	Seven Gables Bk'sh	30.00	151	House of El Dieff	40.00
49	Baile	90.00	101	Quaritch	55.00	151a	Mortlake	95.00
50	Portsmouth Library	20.00	102	Seven Gables Bk'sh	55.00	152	Self, W.	40.00
51	Maggs	75.00	103	Thorp	45.00	153	Fletcher, H.M.	58.00
52	House of El Dieff	22.00				154	Seven Gables Bk'sh	14.00
						154a	Hoffmann & Freeman	35.00

Lot		£	Lot		£	Lot		£
155	Edwards, F.	4.00	210	Maggs	70.00	274	Newlyn, Miss	50.00
155a	Teale, J.E.	35.00	211	Maggs	75.00	275	Quaritch	50.00
156	Berne, R.C.	40.00	212	Quaritch	120.00	276	Maggs	150.00
157	Self, W.	28.00	213	Edwards, F.	90.00	277	Maggs	190.00
158	Quaritch	20.00	214	Staples	40.00	278	Self, W.	80.00
159	Henderson, A.C.	32.00	215	Pickering & Chatto	100.00	279	Maggs	140.00
160	Edwards, F.	7.00	216	Edwards, F.	95.00	280	Wilson, J.	32.00
161	House of El Dieff	18.00	217	Quaritch	55.00	281	Caplan, F.	70.00
162	Teale, J.E.	35.00	218	Fletcher, H.M.	160.00	282	Tait, Capt.	85.00
163	Ohio University	36.00	219	Fletcher, H.M.	240.00	283	Edwards, F.	120.00
164	Edwards, F.	5.00	220	Quaritch	320.00	284	Seven Gables Bk'sh	50.00
165	House of El Dieff	38.00	221	Edwards, F.	220.00	285	Quaritch	38.00
166	Edwards, F.	16.00	222	Peabody, M.	30.00	286	Wilson, J.	38.00
167	Mushlin	35.00	223	Baldur Bookshop	30.00	287	Wilson, J.	25.00
168	Quaritch	28.00	224	Peabody, M.	30.00	288	Maggs	130.00
169	Edwards, F.	28.00	225	Maggs	70.00	289	Quaritch	850.00
170	Teale, J.E.	30.00	226	Maggs	150.00	290	Maggs	55.00
171	House of El Dieff	35.00	227	Newlyn, Miss	80.00	291	Tait, Capt.	75.00
172	Edwards, F.	35.00	228	Peabody, M.	120.00	292	Self, W.	40.00
173	Quaritch	8.00	229	Edwards, F.	80.00	293	Wilson, J.	45.00
174	Sims, G.F.	16.00	230	Quaritch	70.00	294	Edwards, F.	50.00
175	Teale, J.E.	20.00	231	Seven Gables Bk'sh	28.00	295	Self, W.	38.00
176	Edwards, F.	12.00	232	Quaritch	45.00	296	Maggs	70.00
177	Wolfson, Mrs. L.	20.00	233	Wilson, J.	60.00	297	D'Arch Smith	48.00
178	Golding, E.	22.00	234	Summersby, F.T	80.00	298	Wilson, J.	42.00
179	Baldur Bookshop	16.00	235	Queenswood, M.	150.00	299	Edwards, F.	60.00
180	Sawyer, C.J.	24.00	236	Mushlin	25.00	300	Wilson, J.	55.00
181	Quaritch	18.00	237	Newlyn, Miss	110.00	301	Peabody, M.	45.00
182	Owen, M.	130.00	238	Edwards, F.	50.00	302	Maggs	42.00
183	Henderson, A.K.	32.00	239	Queenswood, M.	80.00	303	Grace	9000.00
184	House of El Dieff	480.00	240	Quaritch	150.00	304	Reardon, J.	320.00
185	House of El Dieff	2200.00	241	Maggs	85.00	305	Mushlin	240.00
186	Harland, J.	4400.00	242	Sawyer	60.00	306	Maggs	320.00
187	Edwards, F.	320.00	243	Mushlin	100.00	307	Stone, H.	170.00
187a	Dickens Old Curiosity Shop	30.00	244	Seven Gables Bk'sh	75.00	308	Quaritch	12000.00
188	D'Arch Smith	26.00	245	Summersby, F.T.	85.00	309	Lansdowne	80.00
189	Seven Gables Bk'sh	300.00	246	Reardon, J.L.	70.00	310	Edwards, F.	45.00
1st day's Total		£37,385.00	247	Maggs	50.00	311	Mushlin	45.00
			248	Newlyn, Miss	30.00	312	Quaritch	140.00
2nd day's Sale			249	D'Arch Smith	40.00	313	Fletcher, H.M.	25.00
			250	Maggs	50.00	314	Wilson, J.	14.00
190	Maggs	140.00	251	Quaritch	50.00	315	Maggs	55.00
191	Edwards, F.	100.00	252	Wilson, J.	55.00	316	Myers, Miss	20.00
192	D'Arch Smith	120.00	253	Queenswood, M.	60.00	317	Baldur Bookshop	38.00
193	Newlyn, Miss	400.00	254	Wilson, J.	80.00	318	Tillotson	35.00
194	Pickering & Chatto	600.00	255	Quaritch	65.00	319	Myers, Miss	10.00
195	Reardon, J.L.	550.00	256	Newlyn, Miss	35.00	320	Hawkins, P.	150.00
196	Maggs	200.00	257	Baldur Bookshop	45.00	321	Maggs	60.00
197	Newlyn, Miss	380.00	258	Quaritch	60.00	322	D'Arch Smith	55.00
198	Mortlake	80.00	259	D'Arch Smith	55.00	323	Maggs	240.00
199	Edwards, F.	100.00	260	Newlyn, Miss	45.00	324	Quaritch	160.00
200	Baldur Books	30.00	261	Maggs	55.00	325	Baldur Bookshop	22.00
201	Edwards, F.	140.00	262	Quaritch	120.00			
202	Peabody, M.	55.00	263	Peabody, M.	65.00	2nd day's Total		£35,835.00
203	Pickering & Chatto	240.00	264	Quaritch	40.00	1st day's Total		£37,385.00
204	Pickering & Chatto	220.00	265	Quaritch	45.00			
205	Edwards, F.	70.00	266	Wilson, J.	90.00	Total		£73,220.00
206	Seven Gables Bk'sh	110.00	267	Stroudes, Mrs. P.	75.00			
207	Edwards, F.	80.00	268	D'Arch Smith	50.00			
208	Quaritch	95.00	269	Stone, H.	75.00			
209	Dickens Old Curiosity Shop	35.00	270	Maggs	50.00			
			271	Seven Gables Bk'sh	100.00			
			272	Stroudes, Mrs. P.	1000.00			
			273	Maggs	100.00			

Index

NOTE

No attempt has been made to provide a comprehensive entry for Dickens himself.
The published work of Dickens's illustrators has not been indexed and publishers
have been indexed only where letters are to or from them.